DETERMINED

to have life more abundantly

Lawrence Bowman

Go Soulwinning Ministries

DETERMINED
to have life more abundantly

All scripture quotations are taken from the King James Version (KJV) of the Holy Bible.

The words of the Lord Jesus Christ on the back cover are quoted from the scripture text of John 10:10 inside the Holy Bible.

ISBN-13: 9780692485033
ISBN-10: 0692485031

Printed in the United States of America

Copyright © 2015 by Go Soulwinning Ministries

CONTENTS

DEDICATION

MOST BOOKS WRITTEN SERVE SOME GOOD to an accomplished end, and no doubt we may in all sincerity be grateful for them; but the trouble with many books is that they are no more than rehashes of other works that have appeared before them. They carry no evidence that they are in any sense original. They were put together out of pieces borrowed from others rather than born out of the anguish and joy of personal experience.

With that said, I openly expose myself to the critics and admit that none of my material is original. I am not an original thinker nor an intellect. Surely, others before me have gone much farther into this important topic than I have done. Nothing here is new except in the sense that it is a discovery which my own heart has made of spiritual realities most delightful and wonderful to me.

The matters that I present to you have been birthed because of a heavy heart for people. My heart is greatly troubled, burdened, and weighed down by the woes of our existence in this busy, modernized, so-called "better world." So many people are seemingly living the *good life*, but secretly they are lonely, disconnected, desperate, and even miserable. They act in tune with the *good life*, but in reality are separated from the *best life*—having life, and life more abundantly.

Therefore, I have written this book to inspire you to forsake self-regard, and to escape religiosity, humanism, and the powerless methodologies of the mainstream church in our generation. I hope to do more than to persuade the intellect of your mind, but with Holy Ghost power I hope to get your conscience in trouble and to convince your heart to courageously make the appropriate adjustments that God seeks you to understand. It is my utmost desire that you have life more abundantly.

ACKNOWLEDGMENTS

DETERMINED owes its existence to the passion and generosity of the Lord Jesus Christ and to many friends who have been a great encouragement.

I am especially indebted to Jesus, who not only created this world out of nothingness but who also brought me out of darkness and gave me life more abundantly in this pilgrimage on earth with Him. I am appreciative to the friends that God has surrounded me with and my mother Penny Bowman. This book was birthed through many personal pains. If it were not for the faithfulness of Christ and His collective body of believers who encourage and inspire me to persevere through many shadows of death, I might have become a casualty under troubles, discouragements, and depression.

I am much appreciative of the old and tried ways, which are excellent and strong for life. I am grateful for the pure wheat of the Word of God, which nourishes our souls.

This book was improved by the discerning critiques of my friends Christine Glynis Winkle, Kenneth (Ken) Bradley and William (Bill) Pierce, and my editor Emily Sather; they are not responsible for any errors that remain.

In some cases during the reading of this book, you, the reader, might come across a saying which you have heard before. This is due to the overwhelming familiarity we have with the writings about the truths of God's Word, so much so that we find ourselves quoting them verbatim. Indulgence is begged, therefore, and if there has been any failure of proper acknowledgement I sincerely apologize, and I appreciate your warmest understanding and prayers.

To You

HE WHO WROTE THIS MESSAGE will be greatly disappointed if it does not guide many to the Lord Jesus. The writer will be similarly disappointed if it does not provoke many to walk in newness of life and experience the richness of Christ's abundant life. It is sent forth in childlike dependence upon the power of God the Holy Ghost, to use it in the conversion of millions, if so He pleases. No doubt many poor men and women will take up this little book, and the Lord will visit them with grace. To answer this end, the very plainest language has been chosen, and many homely expressions have been used. But if individuals of wealth and status should glance at this book, the Holy Ghost can impress them also; since that which can be understood by the unlettered is nonetheless attractive to the instructed. Oh, that some might read it who will become great winners of souls!

Who knows how many will find their way to joy and peace by what they read here? A more important question to you, dear reader, is this—*Will you be one of them?*

A certain man placed a fountain by the wayside, and he hung up a cup near it by a little chain. He was told some time after that a great art critic had found much fault with its design. "But," said he, "do many thirsty individuals drink at it?" Then they told him that thousands of poor people, men, women, and children, quench their thirst at this fountain. He smiled and said that he was little troubled by the critic's observation, only he hoped that on some hot summer's day the critic himself might fill the cup, and be refreshed, and praise the name of the Lord.

Here is my fountain, and here is my cup: find fault if you please; but *do drink of the water of life*. I only care for this. I would rather bless the soul of the poorest beggar, vagabond, or onlooker than please an heir of the achieved, and fail to convert him to God.

Reader, do you mean business in reading these pages? If so, we are agreed at the outset; but nothing short of your finding Christ and His promises is the business aimed at here. Oh that we may see this together! I do so by dedicating this little book with prayer. Will not you join me by looking up to God, and asking Him to bless you while you read? Providence has put these pages in your way. You have a little spare time in which to read them, and you feel willing to give your attention to them. These are good signs. Who knows but that the set time of blessing has come for you? At any rate, the Holy Ghost saith, "Today, if ye will hear his voice, harden not your hearts."

Chapter One

DO YOU HEAR GOD CALLING?

HAVE YOU EVER NOTICED that many people seem to have the answers to everything? At least, they sure sound as if they have the answers. For whatever reason, over this past year, I have come across so many individuals with such a view. Perhaps they genuinely have a concern for other people and therefore are resolved to study and seek remedies to the peculiarities of life, or perhaps they are just presumptuous and full of themselves. I do not know. Whichever the case, within our culture there is a growing trend of people aspiring to have the answers to everything.

I am afraid that we are in serious jeopardy. There is a great danger in having all the answers and not knowing the questions. I say this because if we do not periodically take breaks, examine matters, and *think*, then we may very well find ourselves so busy busying ourselves that we become sidetracked from what really matters and never get to the bottom line, the most important and best issues of life.

For example, a major theme written in the precious words of the Holy Bible is *others*. It is a simple word, but one of great importance: *others*. The essence of the word immediately causes a person to take his eyes off himself. This is significant and of grave importance, because life should not revolve around oneself as much as we would like to think it does. *Others* is plural. *Others* demands relationships, fellowship, communion, interaction, communication, and attention. And this is just what the Holy Bible talks about extensively.

The more I learn, the more I recognize how much there is that I do not know or understand. This is one reason I daily read my Bible and other books, for others. I try to saturate myself in God's Holy Bible so that I may learn of God and have the mind of Christ, and be a better servant to others. I read other books so that I may broaden my understanding of things and hope to consider matters through the perspectives of others.

For example, I recently read a fantastic book by David Platt that encouraged me greatly, entitled *Radical*. It bore witness to my zeal for the fulfillment of God's great purpose for our lives. His book stirred my desire even more to continue seeking to enrich my experience of Christ and the abundant life He promises to believers, which I shall expound on in this book.

Inside Mr. Platt's little book, the author exhorts Christians to break away from selfish habits and actually go get involved in others' lives, and make a godly difference. The author writes in appropriate language, reproving mainstream Christianity for its self-indulgence and busybody exploits. In addition, he challenges readers to evaluate their lives and, without delay, make fitting changes to priorities: Jesus first, then people, and lastly, ourselves.

I do not mean to sound negative, and I promise that I will soon get to the positives within this book; nonetheless, I must say that I am in complete agreement with the author. All too often many believers are focused on themselves and not on Christ or others. We need an overhaul and an adjustment to our Christianity. We need to stop being in awe of ourselves and enamored with this world. Our eyes are to be fastened on Christ, and then and only then can we correctly view people through the lens of God's heart. Jesus plainly said, *"But seek ye first the kingdom of God, and his righteousness"* (Matthew 6:33). *His*—meaning Christ. I like how David Platt put it—we need to live in a *radical way for Christ!* A Christian whose life is radical for Christ will whet others' appetite to desire Christ. Then others will be truly benefited and God will be exalted.

This desire of mine to know truth and experience the life that God wants for me began when I was twelve years old. At this age I was beginning to dislike religion, and was not interested in Christian traditions, customs, and rules. So I began to read the Holy Bible to discover what God had to offer instead of relying on what man has to say about God.

After three years of diligently reading the Bible and taking serious consideration of what I learned, I was astonished to learn of the provisions God had made for us to simply receive and enjoy.

I was 15 ½ when I completely understood my greatest need; it was at this time that I made the decision to place my trust in Jesus Christ as my personal

Savior. On the evening of February 18, 1995, in my family's dining room, I acknowledged my sinfulness to God and asked the Lord Jesus Christ to have mercy and save me.

Many months leading up to this date, my daily Bible reading had brought my mind to a thought that I had never carefully considered before—that I had broken God's law. Yes, I knew I had willfully made mistakes and wrong choices before; however, for the first time, I carefully thought about and took into account my actions.

A personal self-evaluation quickly revealed to me that I had indeed lied, cheated, lusted, and most certainly disobeyed my parents. I thought about other bad deeds that I had committed, such as using God's name in vain. These thoughts brought me to the realization that I was guilty before God.

Continuing to read my Bible, I then came to understand that because of my sinful choices I stood condemned before a holy God, and that my end would be an eternal death separated from Him. I did not desire to be isolated from God and eventually go to Hell, as the Bible explains. This brought about an earnest concern for me to get right with God. At first, I thought that my church attendance and "good works" would reconcile me to God. (*Works*—my efforts.) Therefore, I sought to do more works that I deemed were good. However, it soon became clear to me in my Bible reading that no man can redeem himself, nor give to God a ransom for sin. Salvation is not what we achieve but what we believe. I shortly afterward read in my Bible that if I would repent and believe on the Lord Jesus Christ then I could be saved and forgiven. Christ suffered once for sins that He might redeem us from all sin and give us eternal life (1 Peter 3:18; Titus 2:14).

Likewise, because of my newfound understanding, I was relieved to learn that salvation from my sins could be obtained and assured. I was even more relieved to find out that salvation had nothing to do with me, but was entirely accomplished by Jesus Christ. That evening in my family's dinning room, I believed the gospel of the Lord Jesus Christ, *"how that Christ died for our sins according to the scriptures; And that he was buried, and that he rose again the third day according to the scriptures"* (1 Corinthians 15:3-4). I put my trust in the Lord Jesus Christ as my Savior, and responded to Him by repenting of my sins. For the first time in my life, that I recall, I humbled myself and spoke to God from my heart.

To my excitement, God saved me and made me a child of His! No fireworks went off; no great emotional experience took place; I simply took Jesus at His word and put my trust in Him. He did the impossible, and He faithfully took all my guilt away. Christ made me into a new creature. The

3

Bible explains, *"Therefore if any man be in Christ, he is a new creature: old things are passed away; behold, all things are become new"* (2 Corinthians 5:17).

Even though I did not have any of the crying or shouts of joy that some people might experience, I do remember that for the first time in my life, when I laid my head on my pillow, I had a peace that I had never experienced before. It was on that evening I realized God actually was in my life and that I had indeed become His child (John 1:12). Let's just say I had a peaceful sleep in the wonderful hands of God.

God has a gift He desires to give to each individual. The gift of God is eternal life, and it is freely given to all those who believe on the Lord Jesus Christ. The scriptures say, *"Whosoever believeth on him shall not be ashamed. For there is no difference between the Jew and the Greek: for the same Lord over all is rich unto all that call upon him. For whosoever shall call upon the name of the Lord shall be saved"* (Romans 10:11-13). Romans 6:23 also tells us, *"The wages of sin is death; but the gift of God is eternal life through Jesus Christ our Lord."* God desires to not only save us from an eternal condemnation in the lake of fire (Revelation 20:15), but also to rescue us from sinful, stupid decisions during this lifetime.

The gift of salvation certainly is the escape route from Hell and a free ticket to Heaven, but it is much more than that. Salvation is God's ability to empower you to turn away from ungodly choices and to enable you to do God's desire and will. Salvation is the enjoyment of God in the here and now, experiencing a little bit of Heaven on Earth!

Because of God's great grace and faith in the Lord Jesus, you now have a future residency with Jesus Christ in the sinless state of Heaven; in addition, your salvation enables you to enjoy life *now* and to have it more abundantly *in* Christ Jesus. God has made the way for you to enjoy your salvation in this sinful world, but this enjoyment in this sinful world only comes about by lordship—and this is our sanctification (1 Thessalonians 4:3): giving God the liberty to be Lord of our lives.

Although I trusted Jesus Christ to be my Savior as a teenager, regrettably, it was not until my early twenties that I began to allow Jesus to be the Lord of my life. I was saved and on my way to an eternity with God, but for several years, I, as a Christian, still lived for my own ambitions. Lawrence Bowman was the main concern of my life, rather than Jesus Christ and others. Today, I am very grateful that God extended His longsuffering and patience toward me even while I lived as a self-centered child of God. I thank God He showed great mercy and grace toward me, and eventually got my attention to transform my life according to His plan.

During my early twenties God saw fit to frequently remind me that He was yearning to have a closer walk with me, just as He desires a dynamic love relationship with each person. God would regularly impress upon my heart that my personal decisions and the manner of my life were not according to His will or pleasure. God made known to me that my choices were not the best plans He envisioned.

I remember one afternoon reading a passage that greatly moved my heart, Jeremiah 29:11-13. The scripture says, *"For I know the thoughts that I think toward you, saith the LORD, thoughts of peace, and not of evil, to give you an expected end. Then shall ye call upon me, and ye shall go and pray unto me, and I will hearken unto you. And ye shall seek me, and find me, when ye shall search for me with all your heart."* When I read this, the Holy Spirit urgently pressed upon my heart what I should do. It was as if God had asked me the question, "Will you let Me be Lord of your life?" When I heard Him, everything within me became still. I seriously contemplated these matters for a few moments. How else could I respond to such a good and wonderful God but with the answer, "Yes"? Right then, I resolved within my heart that I would let Christ be Lord of my life and not only Savior. I was not entirely sure how to do this, so I asked God to help me allow Him to be Lord, instead of me being the lord.

God heard my prayer and, without my awareness, He began to orchestrate events in my life that drew my interests to focus more on Christ, so that I could come to experience a life with Him more abundantly.

God began to place several godly individuals into my life. These new friendships spurred a desire within me to know God more and to live a life that pleases Him. I witnessed men whose lives exemplified that of Jesus Christ. They lived a testimony that was pleasing to God (Hebrews 11:5), that benefited people, and that was irreproachable before the scornful. Furthermore, the abundant life was seen in them; they were full of Christ's presence. They possessed joy and peace, and they lived with a meaningful purpose in life. Their lifestyle and communications whetted my appetite to yield more of my self and interests over to God. As a result, God began to draw nigh to me as I drew nigh to Him, and little by little the lives of the people around me began to be benefited as well.

It was at the age of 25 that I began to relinquish my will and determination over to God. God was exceedingly gracious, and soon I began to see Him reward me with more outstanding friendships and indescribable joys. Whenever I would put Christ and others before myself, God just gave me more than I could ask or imagine. And when at times I was stubborn and placed myself first, God showed Himself patient toward me. He continued to chisel the selfish nature out of me by the hearing of His Word and the witness of His Spirit through my friendships with godly men and women. Despite my shortcomings, God's patience and the blessings of godly friendships and His Word helped me to learn to trust Him more. Meanwhile, I was in awe that God would use me to be a blessing to others. I began to understand that life is not about me but is about the Lord Jesus Christ.

As I look back now, I am exceedingly amazed at what God has done. The rewards of seeing Christ honored and glorified through me and others have gone beyond my wildest imagination! It has been a divine privilege to live for Christ. It has been a divine privilege to serve people, even at inconvenient times, and see them edified and encouraged. It has also been an encouragement and a joy to see God do many things through me by His strength. I am weak, yet He is strong. I can truly say that it is exciting and fulfilling to live for Jesus Christ. He truly offers and gives life more abundantly.

Living with Christ certainly is awesome and more abundant! But why are so few experiencing it? Perhaps the reason is shown in the words of Jesus Christ. Jesus warned, saying, *"...strait is the gate, and narrow is the way, which leadeth unto life, and few there be that find it"* (Matthew 7:14). Jesus spoke for our admonition and understanding. His words do not only apply to the lost. They also apply to believers of Christ.

After one takes a step onto the narrow way with Christ for eternal life (salvation), Christ calls each believer by name and invites each one of us to take more steps with Him in service before the world. Jesus explained, *"For many are called, but few are chosen"* (Matthew 22:14). This is a great sorrow. Christ calls many believers to join Him in greater exploits, but few believers will rise up and become disciples of Christ. Few are willing to surrender their priorities and interests, and even surrender their lives to Christ in order to be honorable vessels available and useful for the Master's purpose.

Nonetheless, yesterday is gone, today is fleeting, and tomorrow is not here. We live in the *now*. Anything that we have or have not accomplished for Christ is behind us and our focus must be toward Christ in the *now*! Praise God for His great grace shown toward us when we have declined in the past to labor with Him. And praise God for all the things He has privileged us to do for Him in the past. Any good deeds we have done in the past are a mere smidgen of what God can and still desires to do through us. We simply must yield *now*, yield each day, and allow our hearts to be in reverence and awe of

Christ. As Paul asked Christ immediately after his conversion, we too should ask Christ, *"Lord, what wilt thou have me to do?"* And do what God instructs.

Essentially, we must focus our attention on God and His Word and obey Him. We must empty ourselves before God by yielding all our presumptions, ideas, wants, and selfish interests at the foot of His cross. Then God can fill us with more of Himself, and the desire to fulfill His interests will blossom in our hearts. Then we can be set ablaze by the fire of the Holy Ghost, and become ministers burning for the glory of Christ before the world (Hebrews 1:7c). As the prophet Jeremiah exclaimed, *"But his word was in mine heart as a burning fire shut up in my bones, and I was weary with forbearing, and I could not stay"* (Jeremiah 20:9). May we beg God to set our bones on fire for Him. May our souls burn for God so much that our bones will burn to see Him glorified through us. When we are set on fire for God then we will not be able to spend our time in self-pity but will go out into the world and minister to others

One such great minister of God who made the firm determination to be set ablaze for Him was a man named Charles Finney. He lived during the 1800s and was one of this world's great revivalists. Finney himself explained in his testimony that at the age of 29 on October 10, 1821, he headed out into the woods near his home in Adams, New York to find God. He said, "I will give my heart to God, or I never will come down from there." After many hours of lying prostrate on the wooded ground, he returned to his law office where, as he explained, he experienced a blaze of fire throughout his "body and soul" by the Holy Ghost. He later shared his experience, saying, "I could feel the impression, like a wave of electricity, going through and through me. Indeed it seemed to come in waves of liquid love, for I could not express it in any other way." He was caught on bright fire for God and was consumed with the intense desire to share Christ's gracious and merciful love with others.

Throughout Mr. Finney's life, people heard him beg God to once again set his soul on fire. He begged God to keep his soul ablaze so that he might be of continued use to mankind in the rescuing of souls from the damning eternal fires of Hell. He accepted his role as God's instrument in the demonstration of holiness. God heard his supplications. God honored his prayers, and today we have testimonies of God using this man to influence millions of people to submit their lives and serve Christ. God used this man to bring about a great revival in the 1800s because he was determined to empty himself before God and to be filled solely with the influence of the Holy Ghost.

When any believer is filled with the Holy Ghost, he will be a shining light glorifying Christ, because the Holy Spirit testifies of Jesus Christ (John 15:26). But in order for you and me to be led by God's Spirit, we must daily empty ourselves before God and allow Him to fill us with Himself. Then Christ will have the pleasure to accomplish anything He desires through us. Then our selfish ambitions, aspirations, and personal preferences will melt away by the awareness of the presence of Jesus. Then our lives will be influential to others for the cause of Christ, and Jesus will receive the honor He is worthy of.

Now back to my personal testimony. Not too long ago, after reading the *Radical* book, I opened my Webster's 1828 Dictionary and looked up the word "radical." I wanted to understand its implications better. I must admit, I had a preconceived idea of what the word means; but *boy*, thank God for a handy 1828 Webster's Dictionary inspired by the Holy Bible. God sure opened up my eyes to better understand it.

In Webster's 1828 Dictionary, you will discover that "radical" goes beyond meaning an extreme or passionate move or service. It further pertains to the root or origin of something, the fundamentals, as in "a radical truth." By this definition, Mr. Noah Webster himself was radical in his painstaking labors to provide us with an excellent dictionary. His meticulous effort to supply us with detailed definitions of over 70,000 words was a *radical* service. Mr. Webster diligently worked in extreme detail to bring about a clear understanding of each word's meanings and usage in the English vernacular. The result of his radical labors has now positively affected billions of people, helping them to properly communicate in English for almost 200 years. Furthermore, his legacy of service has placed him in high honor around the world. Most importantly, his faithful testimony brings honor to Christ and encouragement to others.

Unlike Mr. Webster, most likely neither you nor I are called to elucidate languages. God seems to be finished with that great task. Nonetheless, God retains a glorious calling for us. And the gifts and callings of God are without repentance (Romans 11:29). God is not going to change His plans for our lives.

You and I are called to have life more abundantly *in* Jesus Christ, one that is joyous and brings honor and glory to His name. We are called to be radically loyal to Christ and His wonderful cause. We are called to give all of our devotion, aspirations, time, and possessions—our whole life—to Christ, and consecrate our lives as an expression of gratitude and praise to Him. A more abundant life is the whole package Christ offers in and of Himself.

Now some might hear the above statement and make the comment that it is impractical and impossible. Impractical? No. Because the more we yield ourselves to Christ the more of His strength we discover. Impossible? No. We simply need the influence and strength of God, and that comes through

8

knowing Him better.

To sum it up, in order for us to have access to life more abundantly we first have to be saved, to be justified in God's sight. This is best pictured by the empty cross; Jesus once and for all paid the penalty for our sins at Calvary. Once an individual's salvation is accomplished, it is only through sanctification that it is possible for us to have life more abundantly. This is best pictured by the empty tomb. Jesus did not stay dead. A life more abundant is available to us because He rose again. Paul said, *"That I may know him, and the power of his resurrection"* (Philippians 3:10). The ability to know God is found in the resurrection, not the crucifixion! Knowing Jesus—a growing personal relationship with Him—is what gives you and me access to a life more abundant.

This transformation is the amazing miracle God desires to do within each one of us. However, we must first die so that Christ can live through us. Christ did not die to change our lives; He died so that He could exchange our lives! Paul wrote, *"For me to live is Christ, and to die is gain"* (Philippians 1:21).

Likewise, anyone who desires to have life more abundantly must on occasion step away from his responsibilities in life and do a self-examination. Second Corinthians 13:5 instructs us to *"examine ourselves...unless you be a reprobate."* We must look at ourselves and determine whether we are dead or alive. If we are dead to ourselves and alive to Christ, then the potential for us to be used by God is there. If we are dead to Christ and alive to ourselves, then we need radical change so that we can become useful to God and people.

What is your daily testimony before people? Do the people near you observe an individual who is trustworthy in the concerns of Christ? For example, does your mouth draw people's attention to Christ or mostly toward yourself? Do your choices and lifestyle bring attention to you, or to Christ? Are the possessions that God gives you used to encourage and help others? Do your day-to-day decisions create an atmosphere for people to want to hear the gospel and know Christ? Overall, what do people say about your walk with God?

Who is preeminent in your life—you, or Christ? In considering this question, here are a couple other questions that you might find useful: What things in your life do not draw people's awareness toward Christ? What things in your life do not influence people to seek God? All-in-all, does an encounter with you move people to consider Christ?

I understand that some of these questions are difficult to fathom. However, we must not only consider them, we must also understand the reality of their effects in the course of life. As we answer and understand our choices, we can make better decisions that influence people for the kingdom of God. We must live a life that shines a good testimony before our fellow men.

God has given each one of us ample room to make fundamental choices that determine who we are in decisions of vocation, residency, and the mundane routines of life. These choices in life, such as your job or where you live, help shape who you become, but the principal objective in God's heart involves you coming to know and understand God (Jeremiah 9:23-24). So, is Jesus Christ preeminent in your life? Or is it someone else or something else? Is your career, your possessions, or some *thing* more important than living a life that glorifies Christ and benefits others?

What are you known for? If you died tonight, what would people say in your eulogy? Would they describe you as a person who loved Christ and people? Or as a person who loved his things, his status, or his personal aspirations? Do people have a hard time differentiating you as a Christian from any worldly individual? Is Jesus Christ and His kingdom a passion in your life, even at work, amongst family, friends, and all the other mundane necessities of life? Or do you have some other passion? Just what is the truth about you? Do not cheat yourself, and quickly skim through these questions. Do not dismiss their importance. A fool is not vigilant in examining himself before God. On the other hand, a wise man will attentively seek God, and when sin is revealed, he will diligently seek God for help to turn away from sin.

It is not my purpose here to accuse or belittle, but to point out dangers. We are all objects of the malicious hatred of the devil and the lackadaisical indolence of our carnal flesh, and we are safe only as we are willing to humble ourselves and honestly accept help from each other, possibly even from one who is as weak and who stands daily in as great peril as this writer. I know how sensitive this matter is, and while my writing this will not win me many friends, I hope it may influence people in the right direction, toward Jesus Christ.

It is my prayer that you will be stirred to seek wisdom and then examine yourself before our merciful, faithful, righteous, just, and loving God. I understand that when you and I honestly examine ourselves in light of God's Word, we tend to not like what we discover. It is not a pretty sight. Nonetheless, a wise man will still look at himself in the mirror of God's Holy Bible with the determination to correct what he sees. God's Word acts as the wounds of a friend, and it reproves, corrects, and instructs us in righteousness; and this is for our good, so that we may walk in a manner that is righteous and honorable in the sight of God and man (Proverbs 3:1-4).

Sadly, I witness so many Christians who are mere pew warmers. They faithfully attend church services. They faithfully sit in their comfortable, cushioned pew; they keep it warm, listen to sermon after sermon from the pulpit, but never do anything with what they hear after leaving the church building; they go out into the world and attempt to do nothing for the Lord. Then the next week they do exactly the same thing. Their practice is their habit and their habit is their lifestyle: week, after week, all year round.

For such individuals, my heart fervently grieves. They are missing the abundant life Christ promises to give if they would only desire and seek to have it.

Jesus declared in John 10:10, *"I am come that they might have life, and that they might have it more abundantly."* The *"they"* is speaking about you and me. Jesus Christ offers an abundant life to each and every Christian who makes himself readily available to receive and live in His promise.

Now salvation is an eternal, everlasting life, and it is freely given to all who want it. Salvation is a gift bestowed upon anyone who repents and believes in the Lord Jesus Christ. However, as I mentioned before, salvation is only the beginning in an enjoyment of God. If a person merely believes in Christ for salvation and does nothing else with this exceedingly great gift, then he is a fool. He is a fool because at the judgment seat of Christ he will *"receive the things done in his body, according to that he hath done, whether it be good or bad"* (2 Corinthians 5:10), and his reward will be nothing. The demonstration of his unfaithful stewardship on this earth will result in zero rewards to glorify God and cast before King Jesus on His Coronation Day. What a remorseful day that will be for him! Therefore, knowing the terror of the Lord, I seek to persuade you to make use of your life and be a wise and good steward over the glorious salvation you have in Christ Jesus.

God wills to impart much more to you than just a comfortable eternal home. God desires for you to experience and enjoy life more abundantly with Christ, even now as we live in this terrestrial home. However, a more abundant life is only bestowed upon those Christians who suffer for it (2 Timothy 2:12); meaning, those who are willing to die to themselves and surrender their all to Christ, and walk in submission to His guidance.

Normally, surrender is associated with loosing or ceding one's will. It usually lowers an individual in some way. Surrender to God, however, is gloriously quite the opposite. It is good, and it is for our best. Surrender to God elevates a believer with increase, but never an increase for self-regard or self-indulgence which is regrettably unfruitful. God's increase is joyously fruitful and comes without sorrow (Proverbs 10:22) with a purpose to benefit others and promote His kingdom while here on earth.

The added riches of God in a believer's life are always for the honor of Christ and the benefit of others. God is good and He is an abundant giver with the best intentions for our lives and the lives of others. God wills to load us daily with benefits by His goodness that He works in us through Christ Jesus our Lord (Psalm 68:19).

Now the Christian who is willing to go the extra mile and surrender all of himself to God is the one who dies to himself. *"For to me to live is Christ, and to die is gain"* (Philippians 1:21). Furthermore, Jesus explained, *"He that findeth his life shall lose it: and he that loseth his life for my sake shall find it"* (Matthew 10:39). *"For whosoever will save his life shall lose it: and whosoever will lose his life for my sake shall find it"* (Matthew 16:25). As the scriptures explain, *"[I]f we be dead with Christ, we believe that we shall also live with him"* (Romans 6:8). *"For ye are dead, and your life is hid with Christ in God"* (Colossians 3:3).

It is a blessing to live no longer for self-gain but for the gain of Christ and others. This abundant life—dead to ourselves and alive toward Christ—makes us complete in Him and exalts us to become pleasing vessels useful for the Master's purposes.

Therefore, we must do as Christ said to his disciples, *"If any man will come after me, let him deny himself, and take up his cross daily, and follow me"* (Luke 9:23). Occasionally, you and I will come to forks in life's road where we must choose between the flesh and the Spirit, between our will and God's will. At these forks, we face our cross—*daily.* New duty will demand, as it were, a new death and resurrection. Therefore, as someone once said: "We are to die daily, but we ought not to take all day to die."

Most Christians understand the cross of Christ; we have been given salvation by His suffering. Our sins are completely washed away and forgiven. Our Father in Heaven is satisfied and we are made perfect in Christ Jesus (John 17:23). But what about the personal cross we are commanded to bear through this present life? It is the daily personal self-sacrifices of turning from sin and obedience toward God that produce a life more abundant. The experience of daily dying to ourselves is worthy beyond description. Our personal crosses produce the propagation of the gospel and our sanctification, to be purposefully used of God.

I like how James "Jim" Elliott, a martyred missionary to the Auca Indians in Ecuador, described our daily death for Christ's abundant life. In the 1950's he said before his final sacrifice, "Our faith is not worth living for unless it is worth dying for." How true that is! Just as the scriptures say, *"According to*

[our] *earnest expectation and* [our] *hope, that in nothing* [we] *shall be ashamed, but that with all boldness, as always, so now also Christ shall be magnified in* [our] *body, whether it be by life, or by death"* (Philippians 1:20).

Likewise, is your faith in Christ demonstrated by daily choices that deny yourself and raise up Christ in the eyes of others? Would anybody want what you have?

Another worthy individual who gave her life for Christ was Cassie Bernall. She was a 17-year-old junior at Columbine High School in Littleton, Colorado. Two years before she was martyred for her faith in God, she was an atheist angry with God. But when she met Christ she not only gave her soul to Him; she became so enamored with Christ, she also surrendered her *all* to Him.

After she was martyred for God in the Columbine shootings, her brother found her personal diary wherein he found beautiful entries describing her wonderful relationship with God that her community only caught glimpses of through her countenance and character.

In one entry, dated April 18, 1999, she wrote these words, "Now I have given up on everything else. I have found it to be the only one way to really know Christ and to experience the mighty power that brought Him back to life again, and to find out what it means to suffer and die with Him. So, whatever it takes I will be one who lives in the fresh newness of life of those who are alive from the dead."

What glorious words that clearly describe the abundant life Christ yearns to give each believer! God gives each of His children a choice. Will you follow in Cassie's personal footsteps and yield your faith to a determined spirit of love and surrender to Christ?

Christ is calling your name too, and He offers to share with you life more abundantly. You may not physically have to die as a martyr for Christ, as in the testimonies of Jim Elliot and Cassie, but daily you will have to die to yourself if you want to partake in His exceeding rich blessings.

The daily death of yourself before God opens the door for God's riches to be poured through you. But do you desire this? If yes, then what *thing* must you give up today and tomorrow for your life to be more abundant with Jesus Christ? It is going to be tough to your flesh, but you must daily do this. Your spirit will rejoice. Christ said, *"Enter ye in at the strait gate: for wide is the gate, and broad is the way, that leadeth to destruction, and many there be which go in thereat: Because strait is the gate, and narrow is the way, which leadeth unto life, and few there be that find it"* (Matthew 7:13-14).

When you walk that narrow way with God, you shall find innumerable joys from God that most Christians will never experience or comprehend. Hallelujah! A more abundant life with Jesus is filled with rich encounters with Him each day. It gives you confidence of your completeness in Christ. This life makes a clear path of freedom from sin—suffering for righteousness' sake. This life gives the opportunity for a Christian to now have an unwavering foundation for choices and decisions, rather than basing them on the ever-shifting sands of expediency and self-centeredness. We can enjoy God's supernatural ability to guide us, and help us to transform from death to life and be conformed to the image of Christ as we follow Him. *"The night is far spent, the day is at hand: let us therefore cast off the works of darkness, and let us put on the armour of light"* (Romans 13:12).

Now, just as belief in Jesus Christ does not eliminate adversities in life, neither does walking with Him in a rich, more abundant life do away with troubles. On the contrary, more tribulations probably will arise, because a more abundant life in Christ is a threat to the world's ways of darkness, depravity, and death. The world does not understand this abundant life and therefore scorns it. Consider what the apostle Paul wrote, saying, *"Now thanks be unto God, which always causeth us to triumph in Christ, and maketh manifest the savour of his knowledge by us in every place. For we are unto God a sweet savour of Christ, in them that are saved, and in them that perish: To the one we are the savour of death unto death; and to the other the savour of life unto life. And who is sufficient for these things? For we are not as many, which corrupt the word of God: but as of sincerity, but as of God, in the sight of God speak we in Christ"* (2 Corinthians 2:14-17).

God makes known here that a life which is honorable toward Him is a sweet fragrance to Him. Either way, whether our lives encourage others to live just as honorably, or reprove others of sin, God is pleased with the sweet savour that rises from our testimony. Whether the people receive or reject our message, God is honored still because we exemplify and speak Christ!

If you are a child of God, there certainly will be troubles to meet. For the Christian who believes Christ and endeavors to walk with Him there will surely be more trials and temptations to encounter. However, Jesus tells us not to be surprised when they come: *"In the world ye shall have tribulation: but be of good cheer; I have overcome the world"* (John 16:33). Hear God's promise in Isaiah 41:10: *"Fear thou not; for I am with thee: be not dismayed; for I am thy God: I will strengthen thee; yea, I will help thee; yea, I will uphold thee with the right hand of my righteousness."* Hence, there is nothing to fear.

A more abundant life in Christ comes with great promises from God and gives us the comfort and encouragement to carry out Christ's mission. We can live without fear and in courage go out and share Christ with people under any circumstances. This life down here will have difficulties and turmoil, but the sweet presence of Christ will continue to encourage and comfort us even in the midst of this miserable world corrupted by sin.

A more abundant life with Christ gives the believer rest in knowing that his obedience to God is the right and best decision; for God has his best interests at heart. The believer understands that he has nothing to lose and everything to gain by committing himself to Christ and His purpose. Furthermore, the believer lives with a conviction that the greatest reason to submit to Christ is because He rightfully deserves all allegiance, obedience, and worship (Revelation 4:10-11).

Now God indeed calls us to a life consecrated to Christ. We have a worthy vocation. We are called to live above this world's ungodly system. We are not to walk according to the course of this world's pride of life (Ephesians 2:2; 1 John 2:15-17). We are to be radical and ambitious in following Christ and making Him known. Moreover, we are to have a determined mindset in our choices and actions to demonstrate a holy life before our fellow man—a life that walks particularly close to God.

God has shown in the Holy Bible what is good: *"and what doth the LORD require of thee, but to do justly, and to love mercy, and to walk humbly with thy God?"* (Micah 6:8) A close relationship with God always provides us the means to walk meekly and humbly with God. A humble walk with God keeps our confidence in Him alone, thereby giving us the opportunity to enjoy Him and be in awe of God's love, sovereignty, and glory.

A determined Christian doesn't just get to enjoy a more abundant life the Savior promises to give, he also brings glory and honor to God. His selfishness and vain desires just melt away before the presence of God. This type of Christian gets God's attention as he humbly makes himself available to be valuable in the winning of souls! Christ is being exalted, and he (the Christian) is being made low. As John the Baptist explained it to his disciples, "[Christ] *must increase, I must decrease"* (John 3:30).

My friend, are you determined to have life more abundantly with Jesus Christ? Are you determined to let Christ richly pour His abundance through you? Or are you so charmed by this temporal world that you are merely existing for yourself, and then one day hoping to fly onward to Heaven?

If that is you, friend, then with tears in my eyes I beg you to consider the words of Christ and allow God to make a change within your heart. Christ said, *"But if thine eye be evil, thy whole body shall be full of darkness. If therefore the light that is in thee be darkness, how great is that darkness! No man can serve two masters: for either he will hate the one, and love the other; or else he will hold to the one, and despise the other. Ye cannot serve God and mammon"* (Matthew 6:23-25).

Who will you love? Yourself, or Christ? You cannot serve both God and yourself.

As Lamentations 3:40 instructs, *"Let us search and try our ways, and turn again to the LORD."* As you continue to read, I hope this book will encourage you to consider your ways and make the appropriate changes to become an effectual servant of God who is determined to walk in the glory of Christ and enjoy Him in a more abundant life.

God lovingly has warned you and me, saying, *"See, I have set before thee this day life and good, and death and evil; In that I command thee this day to love the LORD thy God, to walk in his ways, and to keep his commandments and his statutes and his judgments, that thou mayest live and multiply: and the LORD thy God shall bless thee in the land whither thou goest to possess it...I call heaven and earth to record this day against you, that I have set before you life and death, blessing and cursing: **therefore choose life**, that both thou and thy seed may live: That thou mayest love the LORD thy God, and that thou mayest obey his voice, **and that thou mayest cleave unto him: for he is thy life**, and the length of thy days"* (Deuteronomy 30:15-16, 19-20).

Chapter Two

WHAT IS YOUR PURPOSE?

THE GLORIOUS NEWS OF THE GOSPEL is that Jesus Christ, *"who being in the form of God, thought it not robbery to be equal with God* [God the Father]: *But made himself of no reputation, and took upon him the form of a servant, and was made in the likeness of men: And being found in fashion as a man, he humbled himself, and became obedient unto death, even the death of the cross"* (Philippians 2:6-8). The Holy Bible further tells us that, *"Christ died for our sins according to the scriptures; And he was buried, and he rose again the third day"* (1 Corinthians 15:3-4). This was Christ's passion for coming and walking upon this earth. *"For Christ also hath once suffered for sins, the just for the unjust, that he might bring us to God, being put to death in the flesh, but quickened by the Spirit"* (1 Peter 3:18).

This is a most wonderful gospel to hear; and not only to hear but to believe, trust, proclaim, and live for. It is a saving gospel with eternal dividends.

If you believe this gospel (for it is good news) with all your heart and trust Jesus Christ as your Savior, then you have only entered the beginning of your life's purpose. Now, many individuals hear this gospel, and they believe it and are born again (John 3); however, sadly, they stop right there with God. They do not grow in grace and in knowledge of our Lord and Savior Jesus Christ (2 Peter 3:18). For when the time comes that they ought to understand the deeper principles and precious promises of God, they still need someone to teach them again. Their growth is stunted and they do not go beyond learning the first principles of the statutes of God, such as the doctrine of Christ and the foundation of repentance and of faith toward God (Hebrews 5:12-6:2). This is very grievous to God. God does not will for someone to become a child of His and yet stay ignorant of His countless promises and blessings.

How excellent it is to know that, as born-again believers, we Christians are adopted into the family of God. This is significant because we have been positioned by God to receive and enjoy Christ's inheritance as God's children. We are forever members of the Royal Family of God, chosen to be kings and priests of God, and furthermore will reign with Christ forevermore (Revelation 5:10; 20:6; 22:5). We are Christ's and His inheritance is a most precious gift with everlasting life.

God has a lot more for believers than just to save them and then further down life's road take them to Heaven. If that were all there is, then God would slay you and take you on to Heaven the moment you repented and trusted in Jesus Christ for salvation. But God did not kill us as soon as we were saved. Marvelously, God has *"saved us, and called us with an holy calling, not according to our works, but according to his own purpose and grace, which was given us in Christ Jesus before the world began"* (2 Timothy 1:9). With this glorious salvation, God is now entrusting you with a great responsibility to humbly walk and labor with Him to make Christ known! Furthermore, God wills for you to help other believers learn how to do the same (discipleship) so they too can experience life more abundantly!

Therefore, we are to grow beyond the basic principles of our faith and hope in Christ, and we are to go on toward perfection (Hebrews 6:1). Our time, energy, and resources are to be used to make Christ known and to help others become rooted, built up, and established in the faith (Colossians 2:7). When we do this, we will experience life more abundantly, which Jesus Christ offers.

This exceedingly abundant life is only accessible by grace through faith in Christ Jesus (1 Timothy 1:14), because faith moves an individual into action that glorifies God and benefits people. Therefore, a Christian who possesses a more abundant life is one who is bearing fruit. But not fruit in personal gain, earthly wealth, materialism, covetousness, or recognition. These are mere rudiments of the world and entice us to vainglory. Christ's fruit is that which is holy, harmless, undefiled, and separate from the world unto God. It has nothing to do with ourselves but has all to do with the esteem of Christ and the benefit of others. Christ's fruit through a believer serves to bring people and Christ closer together in fellowship.

The giving of ourselves is exciting and rewarding. We are here for God's splendor. We are given many opportunities to please God, to see Him move mountains, and to witness people grow in the knowledge and will of God. Nonetheless, a more abundant life is only possible to those Christians who determine within themselves that they will live a life that is more than just about "me, myself, and I." It is for those who live in obedience to His commands: *"Thou shalt love the Lord thy God with all thy heart, and with all thy soul, and with all thy mind. And the second, Thou shalt love thy neighbour as thyself"* (Matthew 22:37-39). Thus, you cannot experience a more abundant life if your focus is on yourself or the things of this world. Your aims must be focused on God and others.

Therefore, we have a joyful, confident expectation—*hope*—that we may be used of God through Holy Ghost boldness, so that Christ may be magnified in our bodies. Moreover, we ought to give the more earnest heed to the glorious matters which we have heard, lest at any time we should let them slip (Hebrews 2:1).

It is very sad that many Christians are unaware of this abundant life, and are missing out on fulfilling their God-given purpose. Worse, there are many other Christians who are aware of Christ's glorious promises, but are not committed to having even a smidgen of the more abundant life He offers. This is a dreadful thing in the sight of God. Nonetheless, this is the generation we live in. We live in a so-called "Christian" generation that has a form of godliness but denies the power of true godliness (2 Timothy 3:5).

Jesus warns these people, saying, *"I know thy works, that thou art neither cold nor hot: I would thou wert cold or hot. So then because thou art lukewarm, and neither cold nor hot, I will spue thee out of my mouth. Because thou sayest, I am rich, and increased with goods, and have need of nothing; and knowest not that thou art wretched, and miserable, and poor, and blind, and naked"* (Revelation 3:15-17). We should take heed of Christ's warning, lest a worse thing happen to us.

In the same chapter, after this rebuke, Christ then proceeds to encourage believers with good reasons to obey. Jesus appeals, saying, *"I counsel thee to buy of me gold tried in the fire, that thou mayest be rich; and white raiment, that thou mayest be clothed, and that the shame of thy nakedness do not appear; and anoint thine eyes with eyesalve, that thou mayest see. As many as I love, I rebuke and chasten: **be zealous therefore, and repent**"* (Revelation 3:18-19). I love His next statement: *"Behold, I stand at the door, and knock: if any man hear my voice, and open the door, I will come in to him, and will sup with him, and he with me"* (vs. 20).

Wouldn't it be good if God could testify that you are a zealous believer for His sake? (Take a look at Numbers 25:11 as an example of how being zealous for God can influence people.) Even with an abundance of sin around us, we should be zealous for God without murmur or complaint about what is occurring in our generation. God said it would happen! On our part, we should repent and forsake our own sins (Proverbs 28:13) and not focus so much on the sins of others. Do not worry. The snare of sin will overtake those who take pleasure in ungodliness. So let God handle the mess that is beyond our control. He is very capable of sorting it all out (Matthew 13:30). Let *us* focus on the Bible, heed its words, and live a holy and honorable life for God.

Likewise, we are instructed by Christ to *"watch...and pray always that* [we] *may be accounted worthy to escape all these things that shall come to pass, and to stand before the Son of man"* (Luke 21:36). Accordingly, we should continually be in a mindset of prayer; we should consecrate our lives to Christ. We should give Jesus the preeminence that He so rightfully deserves.

God has a purpose for our lives and we ought to humbly position ourselves by sanctifying the LORD God in our hearts so that we may partake in His excellent calling. God makes this clear, saying, *"For I know the thoughts that I think toward you, saith the LORD, thoughts of peace, and not of evil, to give you an expected end. Then shall ye call upon me, and ye shall go and pray unto me, and I will hearken unto you. And ye shall seek me, and find me, when ye shall search for me with all your heart"* (Jeremiah 29:11-13). In addition, God expressly says in Jeremiah 33:3: *"Call unto me, and I will answer thee, and shew thee great and mighty things, which thou knowest not."* How wonderful that God invites you and me into His counsel! We live in His counsel without worry because surely, *"the counsel of the LORD standeth for ever"* (Psalm 33:11). God's plan, mission, and counsel do not change! Therefore, the question now for you is, how will you respond to God's counsel?

God has called each believer to a worthy vocation. God desires us to walk worthy of our calling. He desires that we fulfill all the good pleasures of His goodness in the work of faith with Holy Ghost power (2 Thessalonians 1:11). It is God who authorizes you and me to accomplish His divine commission; and that commission is the ministry of reconciliation—*the making of disciples.* Second Corinthians 5:18 says, *"[A]ll things are of God, who hath reconciled us to himself by Jesus Christ, and hath given to us the ministry of reconciliation."*

Forty days after the resurrection of Christ, He left us a motivating reason to enjoy living. He left instructions, saying, *"As my Father hath sent me, even so send I you. All power is given unto me in heaven and in earth. Go ye therefore, and teach all nations, baptizing them in the name of the Father, and of the Son, and of the Holy Ghost: Teaching them to observe all things whatsoever I have commanded you: and, lo, I am with you alway, even unto the end of the world. Amen"* (John 20:21; Matthew 28:18-20).

Most people know these words of Christ to be the Great Commission. God has bestowed upon us this glorious, honorable, and great commission so that we should know how to live and experience a life more abundantly with Him: a life which extends God's heart for reconciliation to our neighbors. This is the whole package, as stated in Christ's Great Commission.

Shortly after giving these instructions, Christ ascended back to Heaven. As you have noticed by now, He left you and me here on this earth. He did not forget us, nor did He leave us here by accident. Jesus kept us here for a very special purpose. That purpose is for God-fearing individuals to go out and tell others about the true living God—Jesus Christ. Our purpose develops still further as we are given the opportunity to serve individuals in discipleship. After someone repents and believes God's message, we then are to serve them the Word of God in a proficient and effectual manner (by example in our life, and by teaching) so that they too can be encouraged to know God more intimately and get on board to live their divine purpose.

God desires all to learn and come into a more abundant life experience with Him. This is so important to God that He will even use a babe in Christ to reach lost people who perhaps older Christians might overlook.

One example is of a man who met Jesus in the country of the Gadarenes. Two men possessed with unclean spirits came out of the tombs (Matthew 8:28). Jesus delivered these men from their bondage of devils. In that moment's time, as they met Jesus, Christ literally revolutionized their lives! The story of one of these men is continued in the gospels. After being delivered, it is written that he sat clothed and in his right mind and desired to follow Jesus. The gospels of Mark and Luke tell us that he became a believer and worshipper of Jesus. Later, when Jesus had gone into the ship to leave Gadarenes, the testimony of this man is that he begged the Savior *"that he might be with Jesus"* (Mark 5:18). *"Howbeit Jesus suffered him not, but saith unto him, Go home to thy friends, and tell them how great things the Lord hath done for thee, and hath had compassion on thee. And he departed, and began to publish in Decapolis* (The Gospel of Luke's record says *"throughout the whole city")* how great things Jesus had done for him: and all men did marvel"* (Mark 5:19-20; Luke 8:38-39).

Unless a person is dying on their death bed, it is not usually God's method to save an individual and immediately call him home to glory. Neither is it normally God's method to steer a new convert into the forefront of ministry.

God looks out for our best interests lest a novice be lifted up with pride and fall into the same condemnation as the devil (1 Timothy 3:6). Accordingly, when a person is saved, God simultaneously supplies him with the indwelling of His Spirit: In the same token, God calls a new believer to go be a witness before the people within his sphere of influence, as was the case in this man's testimony in the region of Gadarenes. This man met Jesus; he got saved and became filled with great enthusiasm to leave his homeland and go follow Jesus in full-time ministry. However, Jesus had wiser plans. Though this man desired to be absent from home and present with the Lord, Jesus understood that the whole region of Gadarenes needed salvation too. So Jesus, with great compassion, looked this man in the eyes and directed him to stay in his own country and be a witness for Christ!

And you know what? The man obeyed! He went about publishing Christ and sharing his testimony throughout the whole city. He told everybody what great things Christ had done for him. And because he was obedient to Christ's command, Mark 5:20 tells us that *"all men did marvel."* Some Bible students even believe that Mark 7:31-37 gives evidence that when Jesus at a later time returned to this region, He came upon more believers and followers of Him. And all because one man was willing to obey Christ and stay, and be a witness to family, friends, and countrymen.

Likewise, would you care for your neighbors enough to go *today* and share Christ with them just as this brand new convert did? If not, why do you not have the motivation to do what you know you should? What changes should you make to become an active witness for Christ? No matter what you decide, you must know that God calls you *today* to go into your community and serve them with the good gospel news of Jesus Christ! Perhaps your motivation can simply be to obey Christ's command and *go*. *"Behold, to obey is better than sacrifice"* (1 Samuel 15:22).

Our Lord's great commission privileges you and me with the great purpose of taking the hands of God and men to join them together in Christ's name. Moreover, as we should walk humbly with God, our main interest among our fellow man should be to guide individuals to Christ and help them come to know God in a wonderful close relationship; in other words— *discipleship.* Like a schoolteacher, we need to know a great many things; but just as the schoolteacher must know about children, and how to proficiently educate them, so we must know about souls, and how to win and guide them into a dynamic, intimate love relationship with Christ.

When Jesus walked upon this earth, His goal was to do nothing but the will of His Father (John 8:29). Now He wants you and me to do the same.

Jesus has deputized you and me with His power to continue the work He began. Jesus has set the example of what we are to do to accomplish His work. He leads from the forefront (John 10:4). For example, observe how Jesus did not demand that we fulfill His cause. Rather, Christ exemplified the work with twelve hardheaded young disciples for three and half years. From the forefront of the work, He directs you and me to follow His example and do as He has done (John 13:15).

Like our Lord, our devotion must solely be what His will is. Jesus is no longer walking this earth in bodily form; however, He is walking in this world through us, *believers*. Ephesians 1:22-23 explains that we are His body and He is the head. That means our lips are the lips of Christ. Our hands are His hands; our eyes, His eyes; likewise, our hopes, our aspirations, and goals should be what His hopes, aspirations, and goals are. Everything of ours belongs to Jesus. While we remain on this earth, we are to be purposed for God: We are to get up, walk humbly with God, and go get involved in people's lives!

As we examine our God-given purpose in life, it is encouraging to not only understand what it is, but to have a perfect model Person to learn from and emulate. The Lord Jesus exemplified what life's principal purpose is all about: the making of disciples—that was the pursuit that weighed so heavily on Christ's heart; so that His influence on the world should be permanent; that His kingdom should be founded on the rock of deep and indestructible convictions in the hearts of individuals, not on the shifting sands of superficial evanescent impressions on the minds of many.

Jesus carefully and painstakingly trained His twelve disciples how to effectually invest their lives into the lives of others, so that the training might plainly behooved them to wholeheartedly carry on His mission. Through their successes and failures they eventually learned how to completely surrender to God, depend on Him, and best serve people their whole lives.

For example, several times the gospels depict Jesus giving orders for His disciples to go among the people and do what He taught and demonstrated before them. Jesus gave them many opportunities to go implement their learning. On many occasions they would go into towns and proclaim His word, heal the sick, and cast out devils as commanded (Mark 3:13-15). They ministered to the people.

Sometimes their unbelief would get the best of them, and they would mess up. On several occasions they went out, but could not achieve what they had set out to do, such as in Matthew 17:16, where they failed to cast out a devil using the name of Jesus. Other times they would become discouraged and weary in the work. Jesus understood their frailty; nonetheless, He allowed them to experience failure. Christ even let their emotions rule them rather than their faith. Their emotions ran dry a few times and this would cause them predicaments. Jesus would quietly watch them work themselves into a frenzy only to prove to them their depravity and need for total dependence on God. Their trials and adversities were good for their longevity in service to God and people. Their mishaps became a foundation for great lessons to be learned from. Later, they would build upon these lessons and establish great works that would help them carry out their God-given purpose.

Before Jesus ascended back to Heaven, He addressed several important matters with His disciples. Normally, the last words of a person nearing his death are associated with something of grave importance, something that is dear to the person's heart such as fond memories, or a last instruction or blessing for those he or she is leaving behind. When people speak their last words, we pay careful attention and remember them. As we do with dying people, we also should give great heed to Christ's last words before His departure.

One important theme He spoke about concerned our purpose in life. As I mentioned before, Christ said, *"All power is given unto me in heaven and in earth. Go ye therefore, and teach all nations* (The Gospel of Mark's version says, "[P]reach the gospel to every creature."), *baptizing them in the name of the Father, and of the Son, and of the Holy Ghost: Teaching them to observe all things whatsoever I have commanded you: and, lo, I am with you alway, even unto the end of the world. Amen"* (Matthew 28:18-20). Just as it was important for the early disciples to understand and observe these instructions, any Christian today who is resolved to walk with God and be greatly used by Him must highlight these words in his heart. He must determine to make application of them by word and deed (1 John 3:18).

Everything a Christian does should first be filtered through the Great Commission. This is to ensure that a Christian's decisions, words, and actions can correctly be positioned with God's interest of heart. God is worthy and He should have the preeminence and precedence over all that we think, say, and do. Though we sometimes fail at aligning ourselves with God's order, God remains faithful; and, with great longsuffering, He will remind us of the needed essentials for our obedience, *if* we listen.

If you are like me, I imagine your heart is encouraged when you witness other Christians giving their efforts and time to serve others in Jesus' name. I applaud Christians for such involvement; and I appeal for more to be done. Nevertheless, there is a grave error made by many believers who do serve.

Numerous Christians are ready to get involved in almost any activity that looks spiritual and that seemingly brings about some type of social reform. However, we Christians are not called to attack the social ills of our day to bring about good change. Like the prophets of the Old Testament, any labors of ours are to be done first with the priority of attacking causes of spiritual decline in order to lift people up to God. Then, if any social reform happens, this graciously occurs as a secondary benefit of the expansion of Christ's gospel among our communities.

Our intentions and all our efforts should first focus on service to accomplish Christ's Great Commission. Christ's words in this commission do not allow us to be merely builders of comfort, physical rescue, or nurturing. No, Christ's words speak directly toward what we are to do as believers: oppose sin and promote righteousness.

Notice Jesus did not say, "Go ye therefore and make church buildings," or "Go ye therefore and develop bus ministries," or "Go ye therefore and get converts." True, all of those activities are wonderful, in proper context. However, they should not be the focus of our lives. Instead, notice what Jesus instructed: *"Go ye therefore, and teach all nations, baptizing them in the name of the Father, and of the Son, and of the Holy Ghost: Teaching them to observe all things whatsoever I have commanded you: and, lo, I am with you alway, even unto the end of the world. Amen."* Jesus used simple language in directing what we are to accomplish in our relationship with Him. A close relationship with Jesus will always result in the work of proclaiming His gospel message and the making of righteous disciples. This is the more abundant life!

Jesus Christ's work is not a project, program, or curriculum. We are not commissioned to win the attention of people by erecting church buildings, hospitals, schools, or any other development. Again, these are wonderful, but only in their proper context. We are commissioned to publish Christ's gospel and spread its truths to all people, and our methods must be according to the Holy Bible. Jesus commissioned us to go out and invest our lives into the lives of others for eternal matters. We are not to be busying ourselves trying to solve temporal social concerns nor are we to be beautifying this world that is soon to burn up by the fiery judgment of God (2 Peter 3:7, 10,12).

We know this because Jesus used several action verbs in this Great Commission. The first action verb He used in directing us to accomplish His mission is the command, *"Go."* Jesus tells us that we are to go. That means we who are bodily able, are to go where the nonbelievers are. It does not mean to hang up a sign in front of our church, home, or office that reads, "If anybody wants to know Jesus, inquire within." It does not mean to place a bumper sticker on our cars and tell ourselves that we are doing our duty for the gospel's sake. Neither does it mean to create flyers, brochures, or leaflets and mail them to a mass audience hoping that they will take the initiative to come to us and find God. These are only a fraction of its meaning. The word *"Go"* means that you are to move toward the nonbelievers, to go where they dwell, and to create opportunities to be around them.

I am very encouraged by the testimony of a faithful woman in the Midwest who is a quadriplegic. Although she is unable to move any of her body except for her head and mouth, she is a noble witness for Christ. She produces more fruit for Christ than most Christians will produce in a lifetime. Each week she makes time to drive her wheelchair (by the push of a knob with her mouth) to busy street intersections. Once there, she approaches individuals and asks if they would be so kind as to help her reach for her Bible in her backpack. She says, "I've been thinking about a Bible verse and I really want to see what the exact words of the scripture say." Then she looks them in their eyes and asks, "Would you mind reaching for my Bible?" Most help her—for who can decline to help a quadriplegic?

Then she asks the individuals on the street if they would hold her Bible in front of her mouth. She then proceeds to use her tongue and nose to move the pages in search of the passage. Once she comes to the text she wants, she has them read the verse to her slowly. What's amazing is that she next begins a conversation with them about sin, judgment, and the gospel of the Lord Jesus Christ. She simply looks them in the eyes and asks simple questions. For example, she might say something like, "Wow. Does it really say that?" They nod, and she continues, "Sir, could you help me with understanding that verse? What do you think that verse means?" Or she will ask, "What do you think that verse means for your life and mine?"

I love it! She makes opportunities out of the disability that God allowed her to have. Her focus in life is on perfect target. The exceedingly great thing is that she has literally won scores of individuals to Christ, despite not being able to walk like most of us. No, it is because she is determined to believe God, take Him at His Word, and go among people to try to communicate the gospel to them. Likewise, you and I are to *"Go."* Whether through looking people up on Facebook and tracking them down, or simply walking out of our comfort zones and reaching out to people within our communities in different ways, we are to go. This can and should be done because Jesus said in John 17:18 that He has sent us into the world; and since we are left in this world, you and I are to go where the lost are and communicate the gospel to them.

This means we are to go when it is comfortable and convenient. But guess what? It also means we are to go even when it is uncomfortable and inconvenient.

We are to go because the whole purpose of the gospel is to get you and me involved in another's life (as Jesus did), so that they can learn how to have fellowship with God and fulfill their God-given purpose in life too.

You cannot get involved in other people's lives simply by sitting at home and praying that God will drop some magical, miraculous package of revelation into their lives. No, God typically does not do that. Instead, God works in the majority of people's lives by using other people. Read Philippians chapter 1. God has chosen to use people in others' lives to accomplish His will. This is why God calls you and me to go!

The second action verb that Jesus used in His Great Commission is, *"Teach"* (the book of Mark uses the order, *"Preach"*). The term *"teach"* means to impart knowledge. The term *"preach"* does not mean to scream; it means to proclaim and make known knowledge, especially the saving knowledge of the Lord's gospel. These words are synonyms. We are to teach and preach at the same time, meaning we are to impart and proclaim the knowledge of the gospel to the world. If you teach or preach, you can win them!

However, this involvement is only the preliminary work of soulwinning in the lives of others. It is the initiative to be involved in the course of someone's life. Therefore, we are to take upon ourselves this preliminary responsibility and go out and tell them they are sinners and how they can be saved from the penalty of their transgressions. We are to go and tell them about sin, righteousness, and judgment.

To reiterate, the first thing Jesus commissioned us to do is—*"Go."* Then the second thing He commissioned us to do is *"Teach"* them the gospel and compel them to be saved.

The next action verb Jesus used is, *"Baptize."* After we compel them to be saved, we are ordered to baptize new converts. We are not instructed to sprinkle water on them but to completely immerse (baptize) them. It is that simple. (For a further explanation of baptism, read chapter 5 in my book *A Practical Approach in Doing the Great Commission.*)

Finally, Jesus left us the last order with His words: *"...Teaching them to observe all things whatsoever I have commanded you."*

Notice again there are four basic action verbs in the commission of the Lord Jesus: (1) *Go*; (2) *Teach* (or preach, compelling them to be saved); (3) *Baptize*; and (4) *Teach* them again. These are four divinely-authorized orders, and they are all simple to obey.

This fourth and final command tells us to continue our involvement in lives of people. It tells us to impart His truth by investing our time, energy, possessions, resources, and knowledge into the lives of His new converts. If this last command of the Great Commission is not executed, then Christ's whole work through you has not been accomplished. Your service in the Lord's work is incomplete. For you do not win the soul of an individual until you win the whole person. After people call upon the name of Jesus for salvation, we are commissioned to baptize them and to immediately begin serving them by teaching and training Christ's new converts in wonderful life-altering truths from the Holy Bible; that they develop an intimate love relationship with Christ.

The points we are to teach them are what Jesus said in His Great Commission, to *"...observe all things whatsoever I have commanded you."* He did not say to teach "whatsoever I have suggested to you." He said to teach them *"whatsoever I have commanded you."* It is not complicated at all. The truths that Jesus commanded us to teach are the three preceding points that He just commissioned. The details Jesus commissioned us to teach are (1) *Go*; (2) *Teach* (proclaim, preach the gospel); (3) *Baptize*; and (4) *Teach* them what He commissioned us to do. Accordingly, we are to teach our new converts to "go," and "preach," and "baptize," that they may rise up in the service of God and teach their new converts to "go, preach, and baptize," that they too may rise up in the service of God and teach their new converts to "go" and "preach" and "baptize," and so on. It's that simple!

In 2 Corinthians 11:3 God informs us that the gospel is simple. Anyone can go and speak it. In 1 John 5:3 God makes known that His commandments are not grievous, in other words, not burdensome. He made it simple. We are the guilty ones who tend not to believe His work is simple and we try to make it difficult. However, God ordained and designed our service with Him in the lives of people to be so simple that anyone could understand it and be involved in His mission. We have such a great commission, and unquestionably, can accomplish it. We just have to act upon what we hear.

Why should we act upon what we hear and do His work? Because, if we fail to do so, then it is sin—James 4:17. A Christian who does not act upon what God has commanded is violating God's commands, and in reality he is also violating God's purpose (2 Timothy 1:9), God's plan (John 3:16), and God's pleasure (Ezekiel 33:11).

Likewise, if we are not ministering to propagate and increase God's kingdom then we are doing the opposite—wasting God-given talents and behaving as prodigal sons. Christ warned, *"He that is not with me is against me; and <u>he that gathereth not with me scattereth abroad</u>"* (Matthew 12:30). A Christian who is not concerned with ministry is one who demonstrates a life contrary to that of Christ, and therefore is against Christ. To live a life that is against God, His pleasure, His plan, and His purpose is to live a life that is an assault toward God, and that, my friend, is treason. Therefore, God rhetorically asks the right question in Isaiah 14:27: *"For the LORD of hosts hath purposed, and who shall disannul it?"* That is, "Which one of you dares to live a life contrary to My purpose?"

We know God's purpose because in 2 Peter 3:9 the scripture tells us: *"The Lord is...longsuffering to us-ward, not willing that any should perish, but that all should come to repentance."* Thankfully, God is longsuffering toward us. Nonetheless, the truth of the matter is that many of us still stubbornly fail to invest our time, energy, and lives into the life of another person. Sadly, many Christians fail in merely exalting Christ by proclaiming His gospel. Some Christians live their lives and daily assault God and commit treason against Him and His kingdom by refusing to put into action any of Christ's orders. It would do us a lot of good if we would get down on our knees, repent of our self-centeredness, and thank God for being so longsuffering toward us. God promises in 2 Chronicles 7:14, saying, *"If my people, which are called by my name, shall humble themselves, and pray, and seek my face, and turn from their wicked ways; then will I hear from heaven, and will forgive their sin, and will heal their land."*

Because Christ's Great Commission is not a theory, we can live a determined life that honors God and brings Him pleasure in fulfilling His purpose through His plan. For a Christian to live a life that implements Christ's commission brings God great pleasure. A life that brings God pleasure is a life that demonstrates love for God. And love can only be demonstrated toward God by a life of obedience to Christ's plan (John 14:15).

God warns three times in the texts of Isaiah 29:13, Matthew 15:8, and Mark 7:6 that we are not to merely draw near to Him with our mouths or to merely honor Him with our lips. The Bible admonishes individuals who do such things that they have a heart which is far from Him. God wants more than lip service. God wants more than eloquent words of adoration and praise. God seeks for our hearts to draw near to Him (James 4:8). God yearns for hearts that abide in worship toward Him. He lets us know in 1 Samuel 16:7 that He is a God who pays attention to the attitude of one's heart rather than an outward countenance of show before men. God is not interested in your focus on mannerisms, or your appearance before men, or your church attendance. God is focused on the intents and purposes of your heart.

To draw near to God is achieved by choices and actions rather than merely words and expressions of Christian jargon. Jesus taught how we are able to draw near and honor God with our hearts. Jesus stated in John 14:15: *"If ye love me, keep my commandments."* Our actions prove where our heart truly is. Our actions are stimulated by thoughts and our thoughts are stimulated by the desires of our hearts (see Proverbs 4:23, Matthew 15:18-19, and James 1:14-15).

If we are to demonstrate our love toward Jesus by obedience to His commandments, then apart from the Great Commission what are other commandments He gave us? The commandments Jesus set forth can be found in Matthew 22:37-40, which direct us first to love God and secondly to love our neighbors. Jesus quoted Deuteronomy 6:5 when he said, *"Thou shalt love the Lord thy God with all thy heart, and with all thy soul, and with all thy mind. This is the first and great commandment."* Then Jesus continued, quoting Leviticus 19:18, *"And the second is like unto it, Thou shalt love thy neighbour as thyself. On these two commandments hang all the law and the prophets."*

Again, in Matthew 28:19, Jesus informed us what we are to do in order to demonstrate our love and to fulfill His commands: (1) *Go*; and (2) *Preach and Teach* all nations the gospel. Therefore, if we love God and if we love our neighbors then we will execute these commands by getting involved in people's lives and telling them the gospel. A determined Christian will set himself to go anywhere, even to the uttermost part of the world, and preach (communicate) the gospel to every creature (Mark 16:15). A determined Christian will speak of repentance and the remission of sins in Christ's name among all people, beginning with his neighbors (Luke 24:47). A determined Christian will follow up and disciple babes in Christ.

This is a divine order. But sometimes Christians forget that we are *first* to love the Lord our God, before we love our neighbors. If we love God, we will most certainly go speak the truth of the gospel to others; and in keeping with the second commandment, we will speak to them "in love." Let us not offend our God with a supposed love of our neighbors in not telling them the gospel or discipling them. A Christian who does not go and get involved in others' lives, at least to speak the gospel, is being disobedient to Christ's commandments; and this is a demonstration of a lack of love for Jesus.

On the other hand, a Christian who does rise up and involves himself to minister to people is the one who opens himself to experience life more abundantly with Christ. He is the one who experiences God in a grand wonderful way. Perhaps it can best be explained through the words of the psalmist. He wrote, *"They that go down to the sea in ships, that do business in great waters; These see the works of the LORD, and his wonders in the deep"* (Psalm 107:23-24).

Therefore, will you be one who merely sits on the shore and does not get involved in Christ's gospel work among people, missing out on living life more abundantly? Or will you be one who goes out to sea and gets into the trenches of people's lives, experiencing God in wonderful ways beyond your wildest imagination?

Likewise, are you determined to render yourself ready and available for the Master's use? Where are you not demonstrating your love for Christ? What do you need to change in your life in order to please God?

In light of these questions, please take heed of the Lord's admonition in Matthew 15:8: *"This people draweth nigh unto me with their mouth, and honoureth me with their lips; but their heart is far from me."* Please prayerfully consider before God what you must do to have a heart that is tenderly close and yielded to His.

Chapter Three

WHO ARE YOU LIVING FOR?

AS YOU AND I READ THE BIBLE, we will come upon particular scriptures that are jam-packed with doctrine and truth. I call these scriptures "dynamite verses." *Dynamite*, because if pondered on and put to use they are sure to have an explosive impact in the life of a believer. They contain so much insight that you could write a whole book and still not cover every aspect God aims to communicate through them. These are scriptures which I believe every believer should memorize and make time to mediate on for better understanding and personal application.

One dynamite verse that revolutionized the course of my life a number of years ago, and which I still continue to ponder on, is Galatians 2:20. It says, *"I am crucified with Christ: nevertheless I live; yet not I, but Christ liveth in me: and the life which I now live in the flesh I live by the faith of the Son of God, who loved me, and gave himself for me."* This certainly is one of the most powerful verses in the Bible, in my opinion. Many men have endeavored to explain and expound this verse in literature, books, preaching, and teaching. I will only briefly touch on a few aspects that have revolutionized my life.

As you read Galatians 2:20, you should get a little sense of what the apostle Paul, the writer, was trying to convey. Under the inspiration of the Holy Ghost, it is apparent Paul was writing to express that he is no longer the same person as he was before he met Christ. Yes, those who saw Paul after his conversion would know that he looked physically identical to the individual they knew before his encounter with Christ. Someone would not need to study him, or any other Christian for that matter, to find that nothing has changed physically.

However, Galatians 2:20 does convey the reality that a great transformation has indeed taken place in a Christian disciple's life. That change is not necessarily one that is observable on the outside (unless a cleanup is needed in a believer's manner of dress or hair). The revolutionary change Galatians 2:20 speaks of is the change within a person (Luke 17:20-21). The new life within an individual is the evidence.

For example, if someone began to interact with me (Lawrence Bowman), and if the person knew me before I met Christ, he would find that when he now interacts with me it is not going to be the same. My whole character has taken a major alteration. Christ has gloriously done a wonderful transformation in my nature. What has happened is that I, like the writer Paul, came to know Jesus Christ as my Savior as well as Lord. Christ's indwelling within me has compelled me to yield myself submissively to Him. As I learn to relinquish control of myself to Christ—such as my preferences, desires, and purpose for living—He at the same time has been doing some wonderful works inside me.

Jesus has been allowing me to experience an abundant life as I choose to walk more closely with Him. My walk with Christ has influenced my character to become more like His. It has not happened all at once. Nor is Christ finished transforming me. It is an ongoing metamorphosis.

For instance, Jesus first started to change the way I view things in life, such as the general ideals I had before I conceded to Christ. What I once thought was important, and what I once purposed to attain, I now have come to understand were not the best. My former standards, morals, and principles of life have been surpassed by One greater in character and perfection. The ideals I used to hold changed when Jesus became the Lord of my life.

The things I used to value in my life are not the same anymore, either. I used to have a value system that was instilled within me based on my experiences—my upbringing, what I had seen and heard (whether good or bad), my religion, my family, my surroundings. All these had an impact on me and helped me to create a personal value system. However, as I have yielded to Christ, He has transformed my values. They are no longer based on my sentiments but are now based in the prominence of God's Word, with Christ as the preeminent, far above the strata of what is important.

My expectations changed, too. Before, I used to have expectations of people and events, again, based on how I felt or perceived situations. My expectations used to be focused on me first. Meanwhile, my expectations of others were unfairly imbalanced. It was certain that people were going to fail me because I would put a demand on them in my mind that they could never achieve. Therefore, I was always mentally frustrated with people. However, when I allowed Christ to be my Lord, my expectations were thrown out the window.

Christ has redirected me into a different approach in life: one of humility, gentleness, and servanthood. Christ has taught me no longer to put high expectations on people. I am now more sensible. Moreover, if someone does not meet a hope of mine, Christ has taught me to be meek, patient, and longsuffering with the person. I now go to God in prayer instead of charging toward someone with a strong demand, complaint, or accusation.

Furthermore, my relationship with people has changed. It is no longer based on what advantage I could get out of a relationship. Now my relationships with people are based on how I can serve them. Now my hope is not in what people can give me or do for me but instead what can I give or do to better enrich their lives.

Another aspect of my life has changed similar to what Paul described in Galatians 2:20. My faculty of mind to judge things in life, how I perceive people and events, has been reformed. In times past, I used to jump to quick conclusions without taking the time to seek understanding about a matter. I used to decide matters based on how I felt, what I had seen and heard. When Christ became the Lord of my life, He changed all of that. He changed who I am. The real me inside this physical body you look at is one who no longer takes pleasure in merely benefiting my flesh. Now I enjoy walking through life in the presence of Jesus with submission to His grace of love, joy peace, longsuffering, gentleness, goodness, faith, meekness, and temperance (Galatians 5:18-23).

Galatians 2:20 makes known that when you allow Jesus Christ to be your Lord and you begin to walk humbly with God, you experience a more abundant life with God because Christ cleans up your home—that body you are housed in. Christ does this because as a believer you are now a temple of God and the Spirit of God dwells within you (1 Corinthians 3:16). Second Corinthians 6:16 asks a good question, *"And what agreement hath the temple of God with idols? for ye are the temple of the living God; as God hath said, I will dwell in them, and walk in them; and I will be their God, and they shall be my people."*

We are living, walking buildings of God (1 Corinthians 3:9). God has chosen to dwell inside of us fragile vessels of clay (1 John 4:15) so that He should be glorified through us. God makes His dwelling inside us Christians and calls our bodies living temples of God (2 Corinthians 6:16).

Now God does not take pleasure in dwelling in a dirty home. Sin causes our temple to be defiled. Therefore, God begins to do a cleaning within us. He works to clean the ungodly views, beliefs, and ideals that our culture has ingrained into our minds. One prominent viewpoint that today's culture strives to ingrain in our mindset is that of entitlement. Each one of us has been brainwashed by this world, which says we are entitled to life, liberty, and a pursuit of happiness toward whatever we may fancy. We have been culturally programmed to seek and get what we want and desire. Our carnal flesh expects certain things and therefore it insists on and strives for personal entitlement. But may we not forget that the only thing we rightly deserve is Hell.

This entitlement mentality is erroneous and detrimental. This is the reason people battle so much with one another. This is why people argue and contest over silly matters, and why conflicts erupt. The pride within us expects that we be given certain treatment and comforts by others. Our pride causes commotions and conflicts because we believe a lie and are convinced we deserve better. This is an entitlement mentality and it is destroying people.

Therefore, one of the first issues Christ serves to change within us is our thinking. When Christ enters a person's life as Savior He immediately exposes to us that He must be Lord. He reveals to the new believer that the sins and hindrances they have been comfortable with for so many years are actually destructive and therefore need to be forsaken. Jesus introduces Himself as Lord and demonstrates that a great change needs to take place. Furthermore, the Lord Jesus then begins to reprove our wrongful attitudes and thinking. He does this because He cares too much for us to allow us to stay in a contemptible position of sin and dishonor. Jesus wants to wash our hearts clean so that He may raise us up to become useful individuals for honor and glory.

A foolish Christian offers rebuttals to Christ's plea for change. On the other hand, a wise Christian appreciates Christ's purging, and he submits himself to Christ's sanctification. Because *"If a man therefore purge himself from* [sin], *he shall be a vessel unto honour, sanctified, and meet for the master's use, and prepared unto every good work"* (2 Timothy 2:21). This individual shall be free from the power of sin and its influences. Because of sanctification (a setting apart of ourselves to God), we do not have to daily live under the dominion of sin.

Furthermore, Hebrews chapter 12 makes it known that the one the Lord loves He chastens and He scourges every son whom He receives. Therefore, we should not despise the chastening of the Lord nor faint when we are rebuked by Him. If we endure God's chastening, we will live and come into a fruitful life. *"Now no chastening for the present seemeth to be joyous, but grievous: nevertheless afterward it yieldeth the peaceable fruit of righteousness unto them which are exercised thereby"* (Hebrews 12:11). We should thank God for His reproof and correction, and embrace His chastening with an attitude of obeying His instruction in righteousness.

Christ comes to bring about a revolution in our mindset. Where there once was chaos in the mind, Christ now offers peace through submission to Him. Where there once was frustration in the mind, Christ now offers joy to the believer by yielding to Him. Jesus patiently works within us to get our viewpoints off temporal matters and onto eternal matters. He begins to enlighten us so that we can focus on the important issues of life rather than concentrate on ourselves.

When Jesus Christ is the Lord of our life then our mindset is reformed. Christ expects us to become so overwhelmed with the grace of His life that His abundance flows out of us like a well of water springing up into everlasting life (John 4:14). Christ expects us to become so thankful for a life with Him that we express our thanksgiving by good deeds toward mankind with the proclamation of the gospel.

Therefore, our mentality soon changes to become one of gratitude and service. We do not deserve what we have been graciously and mercifully given the opportunity to enjoy: a relationship with God, a new life, and an unselfish wonderful purpose toward mankind.

Moreover, when you live in the state of gratitude, that means you do not live anymore (Galatians 2:20). Instead, Christ lives in and through you! When people interact with you, they will notice that you indeed have changed and become a better, more beautiful person *in* Christ. They will see Christ's abundance flowing through you.

A more abundant life with Christ helps you to let go of what you think you deserve. It helps you to confront the impossible and give up your ideals, your value system, your judgments, your beliefs, traditions, and feelings. Virtually, it helps you to give up the whole makeup of yourself, and learn to naturally yield your whole life to Jesus Christ. A more abundant life with Christ gives you the understanding to renounce everything of yourself and the wisdom to receive everything of Him.

Most wonderfully, a more abundant life with Christ helps you and me to correctly relate to God. You and I mainly relate life from a three-dimensional perspective. We are impacted by relationships, events, and things, by what we feel and see. However, God is not three-dimensional; He is eternal. Therefore we should not try to relate to God by feelings and emotions. We cannot physically touch or see God. Nevertheless, we can sense God; and the way we should properly relate to God is by willing obedience to His Word.

A more abundant life with Christ enables you and me to do *just* this: to love and enjoy God through obedience. The love we have for God is not to be a love of feeling, but the love of willing. Love is within our power of choice, otherwise we would not be commanded to love God nor be held accountable for not loving Him.

Our culture has given us a false understanding of what it means to love. It teaches that we "fall in love," and this notion deceives many to believe they are manipulated victims and have no control over their affections. Such a belief has been very injurious to many Christians, because loving God is not expressed by any sentiment or feelings; neither is it to seek to embrace God with a kiss, hug, or some sensory act of feelings.

The idea that we should "fall in love" with God is ignoble, unbiblical, and certainly does no honor to Almighty God. We do not come to love God by a sudden emotional visitation. Love for God results from repentance, amendment of life, and a fixed determination to obey Him. As God moves more perfectly into the focus of our hearts our love for Him may indeed magnify and enlarge within us until like a flood, it sweeps everything before it.

But we should not wait for this intensity of feeling. We are not responsible to *feel* but we are responsible to *love*, and true spiritual love begins in the will. We should set our hearts to love God supremely, and go on to confirm our love by careful diligent and happy obedience to His Word. Jesus said, *"If ye love me, keep my commandments"* (John 14:15).

Therefore, if you are resolved to love God and correctly express your love to Him, you should seek to find out what He requires of you. If we are to be Christians who experience a more abundant life that Christ offers, then we must be determined to walk in obedience to that which our Lord has commanded.

For example, Jesus instructed in Matthew 5:16, *"Let your light so shine before men, that they may see your good works, and glorify your Father which is in heaven."* Notice that Jesus did not state we are merely to let our light shine before men. No, Jesus added emphasis to the command that we are to let our light *so shine* before men. By adding this little two-letter word *"so"* into His directive, Jesus made this order a whole lot weightier and more important.

This word *"so,"* though tiny in length, has a great reach. It impresses upon its hearers that they must do as instructed. *"So"* is an adverb expressing a higher degree of petition and a sense of urgency. Hence, Christ is speaking imperatively that we are to let our light *so shine* before men—that is, purposefully living the gospel in deed and word. We are to let our light so shine in a way that God may allure sinners' hearts to turn from darkness to light, and from the power of Satan to God, that they may receive forgiveness of sins and enjoy an inheritance that is by faith in Christ Jesus (Acts 26:18).

We were created in the image of God (Genesis 1:27). God is light (1 John 1:5). We are light-bearers; therefore, we should let the light (Jesus, who is the light [John 1:9; 8:12]) inside of us so shine out from us before men that the world may properly see God through us (Matthew 5:14).

When a Christian proceeds in life with a purpose of glorifying God, then the world *may see our good works*—that is, our labors in the ministry of reconciliation. And so *"they will glorify our Father which is in Heaven"*—lost individuals coming to repent and believe in the Lord Jesus Christ so that we see lives transformed.

Seeing lives transformed before us is possible as we give our lives in service to people. God has provided the means for us to be fruitful and effectual in our labors. God has provided the instructions on how we are to go about being productive. For example, 2 Timothy 2:24-26 teaches an important principle. The scripture says, *"And the servant of the Lord must not strive; but be gentle unto all men, apt to teach, patient, In meekness instructing those that oppose themselves; if God peradventure will give them repentance to the acknowledging of the truth; And that they may recover themselves out of the snare of the devil, who are taken captive by him at his will."*

Fruitfulness always boils down to the fact that our priority must be to proclaim God's Word in all methods of ministry. Meanwhile, as we teach, we are to do it without strife; that is, we are to have a disposition of gentleness and be longsuffering towards people. Our demeanor always speaks louder than any other voice. We need a character that draws people in to hear the words from our lips. Gentleness and patience are attributes that can lure in a person's attention to hear the gospel message of Christ's love, sin, righteousness, and judgment (John 16:8). Remember, the gospel in and of itself is provocative and it alone can prick someone's heart; we do not need to put any other unnecessary pains upon a person by our pride or a lack of love.

It is imperative whenever we communicate about sin, righteousness, and judgment that our spirit should also be at rest in His perfect peace. If our spirits are at *rest* then the words out of our mouths and the mannerisms of our bodies will naturally demonstrate meekness and gentleness. This is important because sometimes people attempt to test our faith by deliberately pushing our buttons; nevertheless, we must abide and rest in the cleft of God's Rock and yield to His gentleness.

"For we wrestle not against flesh and blood, but against principalities, against powers, against the rulers of the darkness of this world, against spiritual wickedness in high places" (Ephesians 6:12). The people we serve with the gospel are not our enemies. *"The god of this world hath blinded the minds of them which believe not, lest the light of the glorious gospel of Christ, who is the image of God, should shine unto them"* (2 Corinthians 4:4). Many individuals whom we encounter are unaware that they are in bondage to sin. They unknowingly oppose themselves and are in the snare of the devil. Therefore, these people need the Spirit's reproof from God's Word spoken to them in a character of gentleness, meekness, and patience.

Now teaching God's Word is not a formula or a step-by-step event. Neither is it going out and conveying a plan to people. Teaching God's Word is first telling lost people about the Person Jesus Christ, why they need Him, and how they can allow Him to be intimately involved in their lives. Then, for those who respond to Christ, it involves discipling them in biblical teaching and training.

The initial part of introducing people to the gospel of Jesus Christ can seem to involve a type of methodology. Nonetheless, we must keep in mind that we are not introducing a method to people; we are simply guiding them to understand their need for the Savior. The gospel does cover a spectrum of important points. Christians do not go out to introduce a religious plan to the lost. Christians go out to tell someone the gospel: the message of the Person Jesus Christ.

The initial great work of sharing the gospel is first telling the bad news to others that they have offended a very holy God by breaking His divine law and that their sin merits them worthy of Hell. Then, once we cover those points, we are to tell the good news: that people can call upon the Lord Jesus for the forgiveness of their sins. Once an individual is sorrowful for their sins and confesses unto Jesus for salvation, discipleship comes in and we are to train and teach a babe in Christ about their new found Love. To sum it up, the initial part of fulfilling the Great Commission is fundamentally telling the news that God has chosen to use a nobody to tell everybody about Somebody who can save anybody. I like how I once heard a preacher describe it—the gospel is one beggar telling another beggar about a great Giver.

The modern-day lifestyle evangelism, also known as friendship evangelism, does not appeal for Christians to initiate any kind of gospel conversation with people. It says that if we just simply befriend people, hopefully one day in life the opportunity will arise for the lost sinner to ask about their need of salvation. My friend, this is a misconception. It is a wolf-in-sheep's-clothing idea concocted by the devil cunningly whispered into the ears of many ignorant Christians.

The preliminary area of Christ's Great Commission, by definition, demands that we open our mouths and preach. Most often you must be the one who initiates the gospel conversation. While lifestyle can either hinder or enhance the message we should be telling, it clearly does not preach it for us. Jesus did not say, "Go ye into all the world and live the gospel before every creature." No. He said, *"Go ye into all the world, and preach* [purposefully tell] *the gospel to every creature"* (Mark 16:15).

In our living, we are to be doing the Great Commission. Whether we are proclaiming, sermonizing, preaching, ministering, serving, proselytizing, evangelizing, outreaching, helping, witnessing, mentoring, or discipling, we are to guide souls toward Christ. Though all these terms have semantic differences in reference to the methods of winning the lost for Jesus and guiding people closer to God, it can be agreed that all these descriptions absolutely have the same great concept in bringing the gospel of Jesus Christ to people.

We are not to be a defense attorney nor a salesman for God. God does not need anyone to defend His case. His case was settled long ago on the cross of Calvary. God does not need anyone to sell His gospel. His gospel is free without charge to anyone who will hear, believe, and receive it. What God wants is for a *nobody* to go and preach His Word to *somebody*. You and I are to speak and guide people to Christ and let God win souls for Himself as we go about our daily responsibilities in life.

We can witness to people just about anytime and anywhere. We Christians are testifiers of the Lord Jesus and therefore we can share the gospel by witnessing. When Jesus becomes your personal Savior, you at once become qualified with the Holy Spirit's indwelling stamp of approval to be a witness on Christ's behalf. Therefore, as a witness you have the responsibility to testify before people what you know about the CHRIST JESUS (1 Peter 3:15). What an awesome privilege! But some baby Christians might say, "I don't know anything about Jesus just yet." And I say, "That's not true." You know that Jesus is the Savior and you know that He saved you! In addition, you can testify about your personal experiences with Jesus, such as your salvation experience of what Jesus has done within and for you.

Another good reason why you should testify about your personal experiences with Jesus is that there are many times in life when you cannot pull out a Bible with someone, such as at work. Your personal testimony, just like the Word of God, is compelling evidence. You can use it to present the proof that they are lost and have a need for the Savior too (Revelation 12:11). The Word of God certainly does stand alone in convicting a person; but in the many times when you do not have a Bible, you ought to use your personal stories as persuasive evidence. You, as a witness, can use your stories because you have encountered the Savior, and you absolutely know what He has done *personally* for you. And no one is able to refute your testimony of whom you have met and know—the Lord Jesus.

The Bible reveals in John 6:29 that proclaiming Christ's truth is God's work to bring a lost sinner to a saving knowledge of Christ and come into reconciliation with God. It is our supreme duty to do so. God saved us, and the result of our love and appreciation for Him is to reach out to our fellow men and assist in guiding them to God (1 John 3:23).

Indisputably, you and I cannot save anybody—only Jesus Christ can save! *"Salvation is of the LORD"* (Jonah 2:9). The God of all time and space will save anybody who believes in the Lord Jesus Christ! It is fascinating to know that God Almighty wants all Christians—yes ALL CHRISTIANS—to be active gospel laborers in their daily lives.

God has given the ministry of reconciliation to all Christians. Paul, under the inspiration of the Holy Ghost, wrote, *"All things are of God, who hath reconciled us to himself by Jesus Christ, and hath given to us the ministry of reconciliation"* (2 Corinthians 5:18). Notice that the scripture says, *"us,"* and not "them." You, and I, and other Christians, each have a ministry of reconciliation given by God. Furthermore, 1 Peter 3:15 instructs all Christians, *"to be ready always to give an answer to every man that asketh you a reason of the hope that is in you with meekness and fear."* This instruction is not written only to pastors, missionaries, or evangelists. It is written to each one of *us.* Therefore, I repeat, because the Bible reiterates the point, that fulfilling Christ's Great Commission is NOT only for pastors, missionaries, and evangelists. It is for every individual who has trusted Jesus Christ as LORD and Savior!

The exceedingly great news is that God entrusts this wonderful responsibility to ALL disciples of Jesus Christ. This includes clergymen as well as the laymen. God makes this very clear in several passages. For example, 2 Corinthians 5:18-20 repeatedly explains, *"And all things are of God, who hath reconciled **us** to himself by Jesus Christ, and <u>hath given to **us** the ministry of reconciliation;</u> To wit, that God was in Christ, reconciling the world unto himself, not imputing their trespasses unto them; and <u>hath committed unto **us** the word of reconciliation. Now then **we** are ambassadors</u>*

for Christ." Another reference, 1 Thessalonians 2:4 explains, *"...<u>we were</u> <u>allowed of God to be put in trust with the gospel</u>, even so <u>we</u> speak; not as pleasing men, but God, which trieth **our** hearts."* In particular, this passage shows that God entrusts all of us with His gospel message. God does not entrust His gospel to the angels, seraphim, or the cherubim, nor any of the millions of other species that exist on this planet and out in the heavens. Amazingly, God chooses to use human beings to reconcile human beings.

If you are a saved, born-again believer, then you are an authorized agent of the Lord, and you are commanded to be a shining light for all to see. And with God's command comes aptitude. God has already gifted you with all the abilities you need to accomplish His purpose through your life. Therefore, it is our responsibility and our extraordinary privilege as children of God to go teach our friends and strangers the glorious news of God's Word. I strongly exhort you to go out, get involved in people's lives, and guide them to Jesus Christ by the opening of your lips, and tell them the good news.

So then, the next question that arises in one's mind is, "Who are we to teach?"

The answer: We are to teach the gospel of Jesus Christ to lost sinners. We are to show them God has given His law for us to live by and we should help them to understand that they have broken that law. We are to teach them that they are guilty before God and He ultimately will hold them accountable and judge them at the end of their life in accordance with His law (Matthew 12:36-37). We are to teach them about God the Son—Christ Jesus; that He came to this Earth; that He lived a sinless life without breaking one command of God's law; that He vicariously paid the punishment of death by being gruesomely sacrificed and nailed to a cross for our sins. Then we are to teach them that He was buried and that on the third day Jesus literally and physically resurrected from the dead and now sits at the right hand of the throne of God the Father. Then we need to tell them that Jesus is now urging sinners, like themselves, to repent and believe on Him and to receive Him as their personal Savior.

Next, we should baptize them in the name of the Father, and of the Son, and of the Holy Ghost (Mathew 28:19).

Then...and it is a big *then*, we are to teach those whom we guide to Christ how they can continue to get to know God in a vital, personal, alive, active, growing, intimate, dynamic love relationship. We are to teach and train them how they, too, need to get involved in others' lives and effectually win others to Christ by word of mouth and a holy lifestyle that brings glory, honor, and pleasure to God.

What a thrill and a joy it is to proclaim the gospel of Jesus Christ and to be involved in people's lives! How greedy and selfish it would be for us to withhold this treasure from new converts and impede them from learning that they, too, can experience a more abundant life with Christ and take part in the joyous, awesome work of soulwinning.

Just as it was the responsibility of the disciples in the Lord's day to teach the gospel to all nations (all people), it is our responsibility to do the same today. In the disciples' time, when someone became a believer and follower of Jesus Christ they would help that new convert grow in the Lord and fulfill God's purpose in their lives. This is God's divine plan to win the lost to Christ. We are responsible!

I must say that sin is no trifle. It is not taken lightly in the sight of God. The God-inspired work to *"let your light so shine"* takes an enormous effort. It takes the combined efforts of the Triune God to keep someone out of Hell— God the Father to provide the plan of salvation; God the Holy Spirit to convict; and God the Son, Jesus Christ, to redeem an individual by His blood. The saved believer's part is to go and tell the lost sinner. The unsaved individual is to repent, believe, and accept the gift of eternal life. In other words...

God the Father's Part	— PROVIDE the plan of salvation
God the Holy Spirit's Part	— CONVICT the people of their sins
God the Son's Part	— REDEEM the people through His blood
Christian's Part	— GO and TELL the people
Lost Sinner's Part	— BELIEVE on the Lord Jesus Christ

Now the question is: Will you make yourself readily available for Christ and His gospel work? Who will you go to and communicate this wonderful message of God's good news?

Chapter Four

WOULD YOU
JUDGE YOURSELF?

BEFORE YOU GO ON WITH THE REST OF THIS READING, would you stop for a moment to think about something? I ask you to first probe yourself and think for a moment about what qualities you would choose for an individual to posses whom you would ordain to speak on your behalf to a great multitude of people. Surely you would not choose just any Joe or Suzy off the street to represent you to the world and declare the important message you have on your heart. Think for a moment. What qualities would you desire in a person who is going to represent you?

Go ahead, think about that, and write those qualities down this space.

If you did that exercise, then I am sure you chose some significant characteristics and attributes in one's speech, behavior, mannerisms, habits, or even lifestyle, that you would desire for them to demonstrate. Why would you want an individual to have such qualities? If you are like me, you desire someone to have qualities that you deem most accurately represent your heart and can bring the results you desire.

We know from Deuteronomy 10:17 and Romans 2:11 that God is no respecter of persons as we often are. Nonetheless, the great God, the Creator, the Lord and the Savior of the world—Jesus Christ—has an important heartfelt mission to be accomplished among humanity. God has chosen to use people, in particular believers in Christ, to fulfill His mission. Jesus said it plainly, *"Ye have not chosen me, but I have chosen you, and ordained you, that ye should go and bring forth fruit, and that your fruit should remain..."* (John 15:16) We as believers are ordained by God to accomplish His mission by involvement in the lives of people. We are to publish His gospel and to go make disciples (1 Corinthians 1:21 and Titus 1:3).

Since God has chosen to use people as the medium to publish His message, God is particularly inclined to use individuals who possess the qualities He deems clean, honorable, and acceptable in His sight for the greatest usage in His work. Every wise workman uses a specific tool for a job that will accomplish the purpose he has in mind. As an example, a construction worker uses a jackhammer, not a nail gun, to break up cement. Certainly, both can bang on cement and cause a lot of noise and commotion, but only one—the jackhammer—has the make and mold to deliver the results the worker is trying to achieve, namely the destruction of cement.

As we look at this simple example in light of God's Word, we learn foremost that none of us is worthy to speak on His behalf. We are all transgressors of God's law and fall short of His glory. Nevertheless, because God has chosen the foolish things of the world to confound the wise (1 Corinthians 1:27), God through His own precious blood atones for our sins (Romans 5:9-11), and commits to us Christians the privilege of being His tools to represent and speak His Word (1 Thessalonians 2:4; Titus 1:3).

The Bible says clearly in Romans 6:13 that all of God's blood-bought children are as tools in His hands. The verse indicates we are either instruments for righteousness—the right way of doing things—or instruments for unrighteousness—the wrong way of doing things. Even in the midst of blood-bought individuals, what would be some core qualities that God would naturally look for in His people for His service? What qualities would He be likely to approve and most likely to use to a greater extent?

It is these questions that we look into at some depth within the rest of this book to help you become more aware of how to partake in Christ's wonderful abundant life. We will examine some qualities of character that God would use in His service. Hopefully, this should provoke you to become a more useful instrument for God in this wicked and evil generation.

As we examine these qualities, I would also suggest that you examine yourself in the light of God's Word and find out if God would desire to use you more. The scriptures exhort us, saying, *"Let a man examine himself"* (1 Corinthians 11:28). Why? The reason can be read in 2 Corinthians 13:5: *"Examine yourselves, whether ye be in the faith; prove your own selves. Know ye not your own selves, how that Jesus Christ is in you, except ye be reprobates?"*

Furthermore, God warns, *"For the time is come that judgment must begin at the house of God"* (1 Peter 4:17). Likewise, *"if we would judge ourselves, we should not be judged"* (1 Corinthians 11:31).

As you read the remainder of this book, will you please allow the Holy Spirit to probe your heart, your thoughts, and your daily decisions? Let the Holy Spirit instruct you in righteousness toward a holy manner in which you should execute your life as one who brings honor and praise to God. As Paul said to the church in Rome, I too express the same sentiment to you: *"I beseech you therefore, brethren, by the mercies of God, that ye present your bodies a living sacrifice, holy, acceptable unto God, which is your reasonable service. And be not conformed to this world: but be ye transformed by the renewing of your mind, that ye may prove what is that good, and acceptable, and perfect, will of God"* (Romans 12:1-2).

If you see an area of your life that needs some change, obey God and right away implement the necessary change in your life. Then you will be able to have better communion with God and experience life more abundantly, which God so greatly desires for you to enjoy. The abundant life Christ gives is not a life that is just personally fulfilling; as well, it is very influential.

God certainly desires to use your life. Nevertheless, you must properly align yourself with what God deems good and acceptable in His sight. God says in Jeremiah 29:11-13 *"For I know the thoughts that I think toward you, saith the LORD, thoughts of peace, and not of evil, to give you an expected end. Then shall ye call upon me, and ye shall go and pray unto me, and I will hearken unto you. And ye shall seek me, and find me, when ye shall search for me with all your heart."* Do you believe God? Then how will you respond to His Word?

Chapter Five

———————◆————————

WHAT ARE YOU SEEKING?

WE, CHRISTIANS, ARE AN EXAMPLE of God's magnificence to His enemies. God often leads His people into trials to thwart and challenge His enemies. God, who is not willing that any should perish, orchestrates events so that it might be possible for all, even His enemies to come to understand and know Him. This is why revival happens most in dark times.

God has been demonstrating His great love toward the world so much for so long that history is replete with the blood of God's children. We read about many followers of our Lord who endured extremely great hardships and severe suffering for their faith. Many were savagely tortured, killed, and fed to lions; others had trials of cruel mocking and deadly scourging, bonds and unbearable imprisonment. Still others were stoned; countless numbers wandered about, destitute, afflicted, and tormented. The world was not worthy of them. Therefore, God in His rich wisdom and great counsel chose them, and made them vessels for honor, whom the world reviled. They proved themselves to be God-fearing ambassadors, as mouthpieces of God, standing as flint to proclaim His glorious gospel.

A great multitude of believers died in faith, not having received the promises, but having seen them afar off, they were persuaded that the gospel of the Lord Jesus Christ was worthy to bear (Hebrews 11:13). They embraced their afflictions and trials, and understood that we Christians are strangers and pilgrims on this earth. They understood that life is a vapor, that appears for a little time, and then vanishes away (James 4:14). Accordingly, their determination to live by faith and obey God rather than man enabled them to endure great afflictions, by which they obtained a good report in the sight of God (Hebrews 11:2).

We believers in this generation read about their stories. We are admonished to learn to follow Christ as they did, and to persevere through our own battles.

One exemplary brother in Christ who endured such harsh treatment from the rulers and people of his day was none other than the apostle John. Many writers of history write that John was boiled in oil for his faith, but miraculously survived. Sometime afterwards John was exiled to the island of Patmos as punishment for his faithful witness of Jesus Christ and the Word of God. He was summoned to wait there away from his friends until Rome figured out what to do with him.

Whenever I think about the apostle John awaiting the end of his life on this earth on that tiny island, I try to consider how he might have been feeling. I wonder what thoughts might have run through his mind. I would imagine that John's first days on that sheltered island might have been spent in much prayer. Perhaps he wondered if God would ever use him again to be an encourager to the brethren. Perhaps he wondered if he would ever be used as a big witness for the gospel of his dear Lord again. Certainly, such thoughts must have run through his mind. When we are put in situations that seem troublesome, it is easy to inquire if we are of any more use for God and His glory.

Thankfully, no bewildering circumstance is above our God's sovereignty and ability. One would think that to be exiled away from home would be the end of one's usefulness. However, God is not bound by time, space, or man's devices.

Sometimes it is God who purposes that we should go through troubles and perplexities. Although we might be troubled on every side, yet we are not distressed; we might even be perplexed, but we are not in despair (2 Corinthians 4:8). Why? Because we know with confidence that God is absolutely in control. Nothing takes Him by surprise. God is sovereign.

In the case of the apostle John, it was God who orchestrated the events of his life to lead him into a place away from the familiarities of home and comfort. God was thinking of future generations. God had a special ministry for John, and it would require him to be alone in order to give God his complete attention. During this time, God granted John a special revelation of the Lord Jesus Christ, for Christ gave him the Revelation. The Lord Jesus Christ extended grace to John to see and write about important matters that would shortly take place. God gave John the ability to write a divine message to seven distinguished churches, which would also provide counsel to future generations.

When we read Revelation, it is only appropriate that we should take it seriously and heed its prophecy as from the mouth of the Amen, the faithful and true witness—the Alpha and Omega; for it is indeed from the Lord Jesus Christ Himself.

Within the first chapters of the Revelation, Jesus addressed each church with a solemn message. As a concerned God, He revealed His omniscience by saying, *"I know thy works..."* And He did not stop there. He appropriately diagnosed the errors of each church, and then, as a loving God, He reproved their errors and provided them with correction and instruction in righteousness.

In His last address to the church of Laodicea, Christ mentioned some significant contemptible matters: concerns that also are widespread within our own generation. It would be wise for us to briefly look into Christ's words and contemplate how today we might heed and apply them.

Jesus said, *"These things saith the Amen, the faithful and true witness, the beginning of the creation of God; I know thy works, that thou art neither cold nor hot: I would thou wert cold or hot. So then because thou art lukewarm, and neither cold nor hot, I will spue thee out of my mouth. Because thou sayest, I am rich, and increased with goods, and have need of nothing; and knowest not that thou art wretched, and miserable, and poor, and blind, and naked: I counsel thee to buy of me gold tried in the fire, that thou mayest be rich; and white raiment, that thou mayest be clothed, and that the shame of thy nakedness do not appear; and anoint thine eyes with eyesalve, that thou mayest see. As many as I love, I rebuke and chasten: be zealous therefore, and repent. Behold, I stand at the door, and knock: if any man hear my voice, and open the door, I will come in to him, and will sup with him, and he with me"* (Revelation 3:14-20).

Christ had much to say to this church of Laodicea. This was a real church in history. One could write a whole book expounding on the significance and implications of this passage. Nevertheless, the poor characteristics and attitudes of this church remain today, and thus are relevant to us too.

A lack of love for Christ is prevalent among many Christians today. Many of us have taken our eyes off Christ and have forgotten our first love. Christianity as a whole today resembles a big social club. Many believers have a "churchianity" mentality instead of a Christ-centered focus. So many believers display a concern for their own happiness instead of God's joy and delight. Still others exhibit a social demeanor of tolerance, as if the world is not going to Hell. Therefore, Christ entreats us to abandon all covetousness and temporal desires and view the world from an eternal perspective.

When we read Revelation 3, we should not merely view it as a statement made by God to Christians in times past; we should view it as a warning to us, too. Today, God is calling each of us out by name. God is reproving us of sin, and pleading for us to repent and renounce all self-seeking, self-indulgence, self-pity, and wrongful attitudes. Likewise, what are you forsaking for the cause of Christ? Are you a disciple of Christ or a self-seeking individual concerned about your own comforts?

If we are to be Christians who desire to live more abundantly, then we must die to self and be determined to live with the aim of bringing honor and glory to Christ Jesus and possess an earnest concern for people. We must determine within our hearts to live righteously before a lost world that is going to Hell. We must empty ourselves before God and give Him our all.

There is no room for apathetic, half-hearted service to God. He is too holy and too wonderful for that. He made a way for us to draw near and be reconciled to Him by the shedding of His Son's blood. God deserves our best and our all. God is not interested in second-best. It makes Him want to spew us out! (Revelation 3:16)

Jesus made it clear in Revelation 3:15 and 17 that He is not interested in any of our efforts, good works, or religious traditions. You might wonder why. God explains the reason in Isaiah 64:6. He exclaims that all of our *"righteousnesses* [good works] *are as filthy rags."* Anything of our own doing, even what we think is good, is tainted with the stain of sin, and it is a stench before God.

The matter that God is interested in is our worship of Him. *"For the Father seeketh such to worship him. For God is a Spirit: and they that worship Him must worship Him in spirit and in truth"* (John 4:23-24). The only way you can walk with God in a manner of worship is by truth. Likewise, Jesus clarified this point by explaining, *"I am the way, the truth, and the life: no man cometh unto the Father, but by me"* (John 14:6). Therefore, if you and I are to walk with God and worship Him, it can only occur through the Lord Jesus Christ. Not through good works or by riches that some think they can give to appease God. God desires our hearts to draw near to Him and to be consecrated in communion with Him. *"The LORD is nigh unto all them that call upon him, to all that call upon him in truth* [in Jesus Christ]*"* (Psalm 145:18).

Mark chapter 7 depicts a warning for us to learn from. Jesus was rebuking the religious people of His day because they valued their traditions and good works above their worship of God. Jesus rightly quoted the prophet Isaiah in His stern warning, saying, *"Well hath Esaias prophesied of you hypocrites, as it is written, This people honoureth me with their lips, but their heart is far from me. Howbeit in vain do they worship me, teaching for doctrines the commandments of men. For laying aside the commandment of God, ye hold the tradition of men"* (Mark 7:6-8). Further along in the passage, Jesus proceeded to rebuke some of their particular man-made traditions. Their great error was that they had emphasized other things above God's Word. This should never occur! We should heed Christ's rebuke and make sure that we also do not value or put emphasis on any of our traditions, methods, or abilities higher than God's Word. Lifting self or anything before God is an indication that one's heart is far from God, rejecting the power of the Spirit and the Word of God.

God is not one bit interested in using entertainment or amusement to draw people into the fold of Christ. Sadly, this is the popular method of the day, but it is a sham to the cross of Christ. For that by which you draw people in is that to which they belong. If you draw them in for entertainment then they will surely be followers of entertainment. But if you draw people in by conviction of sin, judgment, and righteousness then they surely will be followers of Jesus Christ.

Jesus makes it clearly known in Revelation 3 that God is not interested in using any approach mingled with worldly characteristics or humanistic efforts, even if it is stamped with the name of "Jesus." These concocted ideas indeed fail to bring Christ absolute true glory; and they only demonstrate the capability and ingenuity man can accomplish in his own might. Any hopes or desires for the true power of God to be shown will never come to fruition by the means of money, business techniques, human ideologies, or confidence in man. These are merely smokescreens that conceal the reality that those who partake in such acts really are wretched, miserable, poor, blind, and naked (Revelation 3:17).

God admonishes Christians to make the firm determination to forsake such ungodliness and turn to dependence on Christ, in God's ways, and in the Holy Spirit's power. God counsels Christians to determinedly refuse contemporary manners of the world and follow Him. Christians who abide in Christ are the ones whose eyes God opens to understand the depth of His riches in wisdom and knowledge. They are the ones who get to enter into God's rest as they cease from their own works and efforts (Hebrews 4:10).

Thank God for His immeasurable love. Thank God that He is willing to rebuke and chasten us so that we may repent of our godlessness and turn to become zealous for Christ, and learn to depend on the Holy Spirit and God's Word in our labors with God. Thank God that Christ stands at the door of our hearts and knocks. Praise God that He seeks us to abide in a closer, intimate relationship with Him. For when we are in love with Christ and captivated by Him alone, then God with delight can do that which we are not capable of doing: those abundant mighty works that glorify and honor Christ.

Likewise, we should not be impressed by anything of ourselves, because God is not. It is only when we are empty of ourselves that we can see God do magnificent glories through us. To this purpose God calls us by name to walk humbly with Christ and be as He is (Micah 6:8; Galatians 5:25). Why? Because you and I **cannot** live the Christian life in our own power. No matter how hard we try to do better, only Christ can live the Christian life! You have to stop trying and let God do the work. That's grace! Grace is when God does the work; religion (*Law*) is when man does the work. If you are striving to do what you should, you will ultimately fail and lose your joy, and not experience an abundant life. However, if you let God do what He wants to do, joy is certain.

Let's look at Christ for a moment. Second Corinthians 13:4 says Christ was *"crucified through weakness."* In light of this, do you find yourself "weak with Him?" Or, do you unconsciously try to shun the cross and continue asking for baptisms of God's power? It is only as "the *Crucified*" that God pours His Spirit upon us.

Christ emptied Himself, becoming the poorest of the poor. Should you avoid this likeness of Christ? How have you made yourself poor for His glory and the benefit of others? Do you find it difficult to give a significant measure of your funds to support missionaries? Do you find it easy to purchase unnecessary accumulations for yourself?

Hebrews 2:17 tells us Jesus was made in all things like unto His brethren. It behooved Christ to be made such in order that He might be a merciful and faithful servant. Have you ever been poured into the mold of your neighbor's misery? Does it behoove you to get under the burden of a neighbor in order to be his servant and help him in life? If not, then I encourage you to think about it and try it. Such may be your cross. Jesus explained, *"If any man will come after me, let him deny himself, and take up his cross daily, and follow me"* (Luke 9:23).

Our Lord was set at naught. Jesus Christ was disregarded, despised, and unappreciated. How many times has somebody valued you as nothing and found you to be uncomplaining? Or do your feelings get hurt when you are disregarded by someone? If so, then remember the statement that God makes in Psalm 138:6: "[God] *hath respect unto the lowly: but the proud He knoweth afar off.*"

Christ was willingly classed with criminals. Do you seek the better society? If so, then take heed that it is only for a season. Life is as a vapor (James 4:14). Moreover, remember the words of the psalmist, *"men of high degree are a lie"* (Psalm 62:9).

Philippians 2:7 tells us that Christ made Himself of no reputation. Are you seeking in any way to make one? Do you have a concern for public opinion, your rights, or your entitlements which you believe should never be violated? Such hopes will cause you to lose joy and peace.

Christ and all the apostles were *"made a spectacle unto the world and to angels and to men"* (1 Corinthians 4:9). Do you shun the path of becoming a laughingstock? Do you honestly esteem Christ's reproach as greater riches than the smile of the world, even the religious world? Or do you still count yourself among the respectably proper?

Matthew 26:39 tells us Jesus went a little farther and fell on His face. Then in the next chapter, Jesus proceeded to the place where He would be crucified. Have you certain limits where you say, "Thus far and no farther will I follow the Crucified?" What are your limits after which you will endure no more and utterly become a disaster in the presence of the holy God? Are you unwilling to speak for Christ at work? Silent at school? Quiet in your community?

Jesus felt the pang and agony of the cross all His life. The cross was His passion (Hebrews 12:2). Do you glory in the cross, or do you just talk about it?

My friend, all such thoughts on their own can overwhelm and cause us to become weary or faint. Nonetheless, any Christian who desires to experience life more abundantly with Christ must first be determined to regularly look within himself and perform a diligent self-examination. It is only fitting for us to first look into the mirror of God's Word that we might judge ourselves correctly and make the necessary adjustments.

As you think about such important matters in light of the Savior, be encouraged by the words of the writer of Hebrews, who said, *"let us lay aside every weight, and the sin which doth so easily beset us, and let us run with patience the race that is set before us, Looking unto Jesus the author and finisher of our faith; who for the joy that was set before him endured the cross, despising the shame, and is set down at the right hand of the throne of God. For consider him that endured such contradiction of sinners against himself, lest ye be wearied and faint in your minds"* (Hebrews 12:1-3).

Let's now look further at an admonishment God gives in 2 Corinthians 6:1 through 2 Corinthians 7:1. Please read it slowly and consider the words that are written. By the writing of the apostle Paul, God provides us valuable practical insight, saying, *"We then, as workers together with him [God], beseech you also that ye receive not the grace of God in vain. (For he [God] saith, I have heard thee in a time accepted, and in the day of salvation have I succoured thee: behold, now is the accepted time; behold, now is the day of salvation.) Giving no offence in any thing, that the ministry be not blamed: But in all things approving ourselves as the ministers of God, in much patience, in afflictions, in necessities, in distresses, In stripes, in imprisonments, in tumults, in labours, in watchings, in fastings; By pureness, by knowledge, by longsuffering, by kindness, by the Holy Ghost, by love unfeigned, By the word of truth, by the power of God, by the armour of righteousness on the right hand and on the left, By honour and dishonour, by evil report and good report: as deceivers, and yet true; As unknown, and yet well known; as dying, and, behold, we live; as chastened, and not killed; As sorrowful, yet alway rejoicing; as poor, yet making many rich; as having nothing, and yet possessing all things . . . . <u>Wherefore come out from among them, and be ye separate, saith the Lord</u>, and touch not the unclean thing; and I will receive you, And will be a Father unto you, and ye shall be my sons and daughters, saith the Lord Almighty. Having therefore these promises, dearly beloved, let us cleanse ourselves from all filthiness of the flesh and spirit, perfecting holiness in the fear of God."*

Thank God for those important words. This extensive admonition demonstrates that regardless of the circumstances, situations, or conditions of life, praise the Lord, a Christian can still be an effectual laborer with God (1 Corinthians 3:9). One point the passage teaches is Christians can and should possess distinctive characteristics, no matter what the situation is in life. This is encouraging because it clearly reveals the principal guidelines for success: godly character. It is the provision that God uses to sustain a Christian. Godly character enables a Christian to align himself with God in order to be useful for God's kingdom work through all the ins and outs of life's complexities.

Although Christians might aim to possess godly qualities within our own character, we should remember that we are just *"dust"* (Psalm 103:14). Dust is a nuisance, and we as *"dust"* certainly have shortcomings, which indeed are nuisances in this life. God knows we are short of perfection. God knows our frame: we are frail. God simply wants us to do all with all our might (Ecclesiastics 9:10). Likewise, one must determine to prayerfully aim for character that pleases and glorifies God; even though we all have shortcomings.

The concept of being a determined servant of God shows that we must be committed to follow God's guidance in order to obtain a character that best glorifies and obeys Him. If the learning attitude is there, then the character qualities and disciplines will eventually manifest, but not all at once, and not in any predictable order or at any prescribed rate. There are just too many variables involved. All we can say is that they will become evident in a Christian's daily walk with God. As they become more and more evident through his life, a Christian who willingly lays down his life to be a determined servant of God will demonstrate continual transformation, conformation, change, and growth. However, as sobering as it is to realize it, no Christian will ever "arrive" at a perfect state of godly character while he remains in this flesh. The Lord will continue to expose areas where He wants him to grow deeper in character.

As a Christian goes about his normal duties of life, the principal requirement to bring some growth in his character is first to set himself apart for truth; he needs to not live according to the sinful customs and traditions of man. This world offers many ungodly attractions, but in comparison to what God offers the world's attractions are just temporary hype, emotionalism, and sensationalism. As my pastor says, "just glitter." On the other hand, God offers eternal infinite riches in Christ Jesus.

This is why a Christian who is determined to be a partaker of life more abundantly with Christ will put himself in the truth—the Holy Bible—and daily discover what God would have for him. This Christian is promised an intimate and satisfying knowledge of God. And surely he will learn to delight in God's presence and taste and know the inner sweetness of God Himself in the core and center of his heart. Without a doubt, God will then be able to perfect His work through him because his heart has come to understand God's heart. You and I are natural composites of our surroundings and the input we receive. Without God as Lord of our life, we will merely be ungodly composites of this world. This is why you and I need a revolution of God; we need a transformation within our hearts that only God can do to make us who we ought to be in Christ. This definitely occurs by spending much quality time with God.

The evidence that you are a Christian is that people should be able to notice that you have been with Jesus. The emphatic reason many Christians are not making any impact in the world is because they do not spend time with Jesus. Hence, they do not *know* Jesus, for they lack understanding of Christ's heart and mind. They are unwise. When your neighbors see you, can they recognize that you have been with Jesus?

The power of the gospel is demonstrated through a Christian who has been with Christ. The Lord Jesus has promised to be with each believer always, but you must give up the world and be with Him instead (Matthew 28:20). Jesus is calling His followers by name to come closer to Him (Mark 3:13). Will you come closer to Christ? If you do, the world will take notice that you have been with the Savior (Acts 4:13). But this can only occur when you determinedly set yourself apart from ungodly affairs, wants, and lusts. When a Christian sets himself apart for the Lord in this life, then he will have a right fellowship with Christ. Then God has the liberty within that Christian to manage his life. In addition, when God is given the liberty to manage a person's life, then God will make him of greater use, even if the Christian is unaware of it (John 17:15-19).

Thus, I have not written this book to teach you how a nominal Christian can occasionally influence the world for the cause of Christ. That would do you and many others a disservice and would waste our time. Any regular Christian can be an occasional laborer who partakes in rescuing a soul here and there from Hell. However, a Christian who determinedly chooses to align his life with God's priorities will develop into an effectual servant of God in rescuing many souls from Hell. This will quickly get God's attention—and the devil's attention as well.

Going out and involving yourself in bringing people closer to God is indeed an arduous task. It is more difficult than singing, attending conferences, cleaning church property, giving money to the church, and driving people around. Although these are wonderful services God allows many to do, they are only a smidgen of the heart of God. The fullness of the heart of God is expressed in unconditional love and committed involvement we can give in the lives of others for the purpose of bringing people to know Christ and His Word more.

The devil is keenly aware of this and he will let Christians comfortably have an easy time in their "works" up until the point that he notices a Christian gets up and starts focusing on winning souls for God. The devil will allow any Christian to regularly attend church with ease and even sing for God at ease. However, when he notices that the Christian starts to sing for God or to drive people around town with the focus of winning souls for Christ, then the devil will bring a battle against such a Christian. But our faithfully loving God will bless you, Christian, even through the devil's attacks. God will encourage you to do more, while the devil will offer you all the flimsy excuses not to serve God. Focus on the race. The battle has been won!

A sluggish Christian is content with a lower standard of telling people about Christ only occasionally. A determined Christian who is resolute in accomplishing God's work is not content with such a lukewarmness. He recognizes that the Lord Jesus has the right to demand the very best that we should offer Him. A determined Christian recognizes that we will never be truly yielded in God's sight unless we offer to Him all the potential of our ransomed selves—body, mind, soul, and spirit; our functions, thoughts, desires, and attitudes. Then and only then can we experience the power of God to fill us with His Spirit and to raise us up to be influential servants of God in the lives of others.

It is true that we can all be nominal Christians who occasionally see God's influence through us. But if you and I desire to be mightily used for the kingdom of Christ, then we must determine to be active and effective instruments who are faithful and consistent in investing in the lives of people. God does not require intelligence, beauty, talent, or skill, for not everyone can have those characteristics. God requires faithfulness: a faithfulness that is consistent, reliable, steadfast, and trustworthy, even when the times get tough. Everybody can be faithful (1 Corinthians 4:2). No matter if we are ugly, beautiful, weird, or outstanding, anyone can be faithful and that is what God looks for in a Christian. Therefore, we must be faithful even when we do not feel like it.

The greatest vocation under the sun is that of the kingdom of God, and we ought to give serious consideration to our preparation for it. In preparing ourselves for this utmost holy vocation, it would be wise and useful for us to determinedly seek Christ and His kingdom first.

This is what Jesus said in Matthew 6:33. He stated, *"But seek ye first the kingdom of God, and His righteousness; and all these things shall be added unto you."* What shall be added to us? Everything we need. Why is that? The answer is explained one chapter earlier. If you turn your Bible to Matthew chapter 5, we get a glimpse of the first public sermon of Jesus. In this address, Jesus said, *"Blessed are the poor in spirit: for theirs is the kingdom of heaven."* Some understand Jesus to be teaching the necessity of humility. Others understand Jesus to have started His public ministry on a fundamental point, teaching that we are all spiritually bankrupt. We are poor. We cannot help ourselves, nor can we help others. Therefore, we need to seek the One Who can help.

Christ's words bring us awareness of our deep problem and of our great need for Him. We are poor. Poor people do not have anything to offer or use, yet the rich King wants to pour His riches upon us destitute saved sinners!

When we recognize the state of our poverty, then we can cry out to God, and plead with tears, "Lord, help Thou mine impoverished state!" Then we can readily look to Christ alone, and the riches of His kingdom can be poured upon us.

You and I are so spiritually poor that we do not have it within ourselves to have any of the qualities that God deems necessary in service for His kingdom. We do not even have the means to possess faith. It is God who gives us the simple ability to believe. It is God alone who gives us the ability to surrender, to obey, and to serve.

Therefore, it is so important that we determinedly seek Christ first before anything and everything else in life. That means we must submit our wills, desires, thinking, and emotions over to Christ. We must surrender our love of social popularity, desire for power, personal opinions, our reputation, influence, affairs, and friends over to Christ as well. We must empty ourselves before Christ, *daily* (Luke 9:23). As we yield everything of ourselves to Christ and seek Him first to be the number one priority, then Christ can begin to demonstrate all that is needed in order to be an effectual instrument in the service of God. Then Jesus will live the qualities that He takes pleasure in through us, and we will see the amazing evidence of His abilities through us (Galatians 5:22-23).

As a result, may we have the mindset of Galatians 2:20, saying, *"I am crucified with Christ: nevertheless I live; yet not I, but Christ liveth in me: and the life which I now live in the flesh I live by the faith of the Son of God, who loved me, and gave himself for me."*

Chapter Six

IS YOUR LIFE BEARING LASTING FRUIT?

ONE CHRISTIAN ACTIVITY THAT THRILLS MY SOUL is to go out with other Christians and proclaim the gospel of Jesus Christ to neighbors within the community. I just love walking up to people on the streets or knocking on people's homes with the intention of engaging them in a gospel conversation. One reason is that it is our mandate from God to do so (Mark 16:15; Luke 24:47). Second, I am encouraged to do so because of the countless examples written in His Word. Another reason is that doing the work of evangelism is excellent schooling. God always teaches me something I need, and quite often He recalls to my mind important doctrine and principles that I might forget.

In addition, public evangelism is a way to get out of our comfort zones and meet various kinds of people. As we meet more individuals, the intensity of our problems within our minds lessens as we discover greater struggles and troubles others face on a daily basis. You will surely become more appreciative of how God has orchestrated your own journey when you see the difficulties of others. You will take better notice of God's love for you and you will gain a clearer understanding of God's grace as you meet and minister to others.

Not too long ago, I approached a young man on the campus of San Diego State University. In our conversation, he asked me why I love Jesus. In response, I briefly explained my testimony and some of the many things the Lord has done for me. I do not think he was sincerely interested in hearing what Jesus has done in my life because several times he interrupted me with cynical questions. Whether he wanted to know the truth or was only interested in a debate, I simply stayed focused and persisted in telling of my experiences with Jesus. I straightforwardly told him what the Bible has to say regarding some of his questions. Eventually, I had enough of his skepticism and unwillingness to be reasonable in his thinking, so I kindly brought an end to our conversation. I thanked him for his time, and departed.

I knew that God brought the two of us together as I walked away from my encounter with him. It had been a divine appointment. Anytime we are given the opportunity to share Christ with someone, no matter what his or her response, it is a divine appointment orchestrated by God. As I walked across the campus, I quietly prayed for him. I asked God to give him repentance, to open his eyes, and to send another disciple to proclaim the gospel again to him.

Even more, I realized that God brought this skeptic into my life not only for his good but also for my edification. When I walked away from our conversation, the memory of his first skeptical question, *"Why do you love Jesus?"* lingered in the forefront of my mind. I found myself continuing to ponder on this question for the next several days.

It really is fascinating to think about God's love for us and ours for Him. Several times Jesus addressed this matter while He walked this earth. In all of His teachings, Christ never taught that we should express our love to God by words. Neither are there any commands or instructions in the Bible that direct us to *tell* God of our love. That would be effortless, superficial, and quite frankly, meaningless. Words are easy to come by, but actions are the costly pearls of our heart. The Bible sadly explains that many people with their mouths broadcast much love, but their hearts go after their own covetousness (Ezekiel 33:31), therefore proving their lack of love for God, or the complete absence of it.

In view of that, as you might imagine, Christ told us how we are to love Him. He stated, *"If ye love me, keep my commandments"* (John 14:15). Jesus directed us to express our love to Him by actively doing something; to obey His commandments. If you love God, then you will seek to please Him. And if you love Him, then you should seek to know what pleases Him so that you may do those things which please Him, thereby demonstrating your love to Him.

First John 3:18 affirms what Christ said, saying, *"My little children, let us not love in word, neither in tongue; but in deed and in truth."* So again, our love toward God is not substantiated by words; instead, it is proven by good deeds extended toward people.

On one occasion, a lawyer came up to Jesus and asked, *"Master, which is the great commandment in the law?"* Jesus answered his question, saying, *"Thou shalt love the Lord thy God with all thy heart, and with all thy soul, and with all thy mind. This is the first and great commandment. And the second is like unto it, Thou shalt love thy neighbour as thyself"* (Matthew 22:37-39). Notice that Jesus did not recite to him a collection of rules; neither did He quote any of the Ten Commandments. No, because Jesus came to reveal the grace of life and expose the shortcomings of the law of Moses (John 1:17).

The Ten Commandments, a *law of sin and death*, were given by God the Father—and no man is able to keep His law (Romans 8). It is a law written on stone, serving to bring transgression to light (Exodus 24:12; Romans 3:20), having a shadow of good things to come (drawing men to God through love). It is our schoolmaster to bring us to Christ, that we might be justified by the law of Christ: faith in Him to experience a love relationship with God.

Nevertheless, when Jesus walked this earth, He magnified the law and made *it* honorable (Isaiah 42:21). Jesus demonstrated God's great love to us, fulfilling the law in His life's example. Now the righteousness of the law may be fulfilled by Christ in those who have been born of His Spirit, *"who walk not after the flesh, but after the Spirit"* (Romans 8:4).

In Christ, the prophecy of God in the book of Ezekiel is fulfilled in born-again believers. God promised: *"A new heart also will I give you, and a new spirit will I put within you: and I will take away the stony heart out of your flesh, and I will give you an heart of flesh. And I will put my spirit within you, and cause you to walk in my statutes, and ye shall keep my judgments, and do them"* (Ezekiel 36:26-27).

The scripture says that, *"Love worketh no ill to his neighbour: therefore love is the fulfilling of the law"* (Romans 13:10). So when this lawyer asked Jesus which *"is the great commandment,"* Jesus correctly answered that we are to love God with all of our heart, soul, and mind by an outward expression of good deeds toward our neighbors. If we call ourselves Christians, should we not be demonstrating our love to God by lives engaged for His glory extended outward for the benefit of people?

I think so! This is what puts a smile on God's face: Christ's righteousness and love being demonstrated by actions to people before God.

Moreover, although we are commanded to love Him, our love toward God is only a result of His love first shown toward us. Our own love for God is not a result of anything within us. The primary reason we are even able to have thoughts, feelings, and actions of love for God has all to do with God Himself. If God had not determined to first love us, we would not love Him, nor would we even consider looking to Him. The Bible expressly tells us, *"We love him, because he first loved us"* (1 John 4:19). Thus, the fundamental reason we consider God and seek to look into His eyes of love is that He first placed His attention on us and chose to love us. Because *God* is the great Seeker!

There has never been an individual on this earth who took the initiative to seek God or who desired a love relationship with Him (1 John 4:10). It is true that we sinners *ought* to seek God, but we do not. In Romans 3:11 are these words: *"there is none that seeketh after God."* No, there is not one. There are multitudes who seek after pleasure, and seek after wealth and social popularity, but there is not one person who seeks after *God*. The sinner *ought* to seek God, for he needs Him badly enough. He ought to seek Him, for God commands him so to do: *"Let the wicked forsake his way, and the unrighteous man his thoughts: and let him return unto the LORD"* (Isaiah 55:7). In Isaiah 55:6, the scripture also commands, *"Seek ye the Lord while he may be found."* This is God's command; but fallen man, the sinner in his natural state, never does and will never seek the Lord (Psalm 10:4).

Let's look at a couple examples from the Bible to understand our depravity. How was it with the first sinner? When Adam sinned, in the cool of the evening of that first awful day, the voice of the Lord was heard through the paths of that beautiful garden of Eden. What did Adam do? Did he hasten to the Lord and cast himself at His feet and cry for mercy and love? No, he did not seek the Lord at all; he fled. The first sinner did not *"seek"* God—the Lord sought him and called to Adam: *"Where art thou?"* (Genesis 3:9) And it has ever been thus.

Another case in point, Abraham. How was it with Abraham? There is nothing whatsoever in scripture to indicate that Abraham sought God; there is not a little evidence to the contrary. He himself was a heathen, and his parents were idolaters worshipping other gods, as the last chapter of Joshua 24:2-3 tells us. Nevertheless, the Lord suddenly appeared to him in that heathen city (Acts 7:2-3; Genesis 12). Abraham had not been seeking God. It was God who sought him. And so it has been all through time. When the Savior came here He declared, *"For the Son of man is come to seek and to save that which was lost"* (Luke 19:10).

The Bible explains in Ephesians 3:19 that God possess a love for you and me that is beyond human comprehension. God has loved us with an abundant, unfathomable love even before the foundation of the world. Way before the creation of time and space, God's heart determined to love us and to demonstrate His love by the sacrifice of His only begotten Son, for us rebellious and wicked creatures.

Nevertheless, there are some Christians who say to themselves, "I cannot deny my own experience. I know quite well there *was* a time when I sought the Lord." We do not deny it; what we would call attention to is that there was something *before* that. But what *caused* you to "seek" the Lord? If you would be honest with yourself, you would agree that you sought God because He first sought you—just as you love God because He first loved you. It is not the sheep that seeks the Shepherd; it is the Shepherd who seeks the sheep (Matthew 18:11-12); and having sought the sheep, He created in the heart of that sheep a desire for Himself. Then it begins to seek Him.

Furthermore, Jesus stated in John 15:16, *"Ye have not chosen me, but I have chosen you, and ordained you, that ye should go and bring forth fruit, and that your fruit should remain."* If there is any desire within us to serve God it is because He first chose and drew us to Himself. For *"no man can come to Christ, except the Father which hath sent Him draw him"* (John 6:44). Now all that the Father gives Christ will come to Him (John 6:37). But the Father only gives to Christ those who repent and lift up Christ.

God loves and draws people to Himself; God desires to pour His grace upon us. Therefore, may we have a contrite spirit toward sin and renounce any self-centeredness so that we can draw near to Christ (James 4:8). Then, as obedient Christians, we can experience life more abundantly and witness Christ bearing much fruit through us for His honor.

We who have believed the gospel of the Lord Jesus Christ are to walk worthy of this love relationship. Christ saved us, and by His love He has called us with a holy calling, but not according to our personal preferences. Christ has called us by name and made us accepted in the beloved in order to make known His good pleasure. Therefore, if we say that we love God, then we ought to partake of His love by walking humbly with Him to glorify and honor Christ before others.

Being drawn to Christ in a love relationship always brings about a tendency for the believer to go and bear fruit, and fruit that remains (John 15). God has ordained you and me *in* Christ Jesus. Our ordination is a valid authorization from God, giving each believer the jurisdiction to go and labor anywhere in the world with the purpose of bringing souls to Christ. Jesus commanded, *"Go ye into all the world, and preach the gospel to every creature"* (Mark 16:15).

The world is God's harvest field (Matthew 13:38), and the harvest truly is plenteous. Therefore *"They that sow in tears shall reap in joy. He that goeth forth and weepeth, bearing precious seed, shall doubtless come again with rejoicing, bringing his sheaves with him"* (Psalm 126:5-6). Sheaves are people. God wants us to bring people to Him. God desires for us not to be barren, but for us to be productive and fruitful in our labors.

Jesus taught that a laborer in God's harvest field can bring in results of 100-fold, 60-fold, or 30-fold (Matthew 13). If you are not a laborer then you will bring in a zero-fold; however, Jesus spoke of laborers, and all laborers shall bring in some type of harvest. Do you aspire for God to bring about a great harvest through your life? If so, what results are you bringing to God?

Please keep in mind that the Bible does not emphasize quantity. God is not necessarily interested in a numbers game. God wants you to simply rise up to your potential and be the effectual laborer He created you to be. God's desire is that you become a laborer who acquires the greatest results He has designed for you to produce: a 100-fold harvest of fruit that remains; this is accomplished only through doing both evangelism and discipleship. Jesus stated, *"Herein is my Father glorified, that ye bear much fruit; so shall ye be my disciples...ye should go and bring forth fruit, and that your fruit should remain"* (John 15:8,16). Jesus spoke of laborers, and if you are not a laborer then you are not one of His disciples.

So how can you and I in our lives have much fruit that remains? The answer can be found in John 12:24. Jesus explained by comparing us to a corn of wheat. Jesus said, *"Verily, verily, I say unto you, Except a corn of wheat fall into the ground and die, it abideth alone: but if it die, it bringeth forth much fruit."* You and I cannot expect to bear much fruit in our lives until we die to ourselves. We must become empty of who we are, what we aspire, dream, and hope to become. We must surrender as disciples to God and allow Him to raise us up to be laborers wherever He so chooses.

Jesus wants you to have much fruit that remains, to have a 100-fold harvest in your kingdom undertakings. Nonetheless, you are the one who gets to decide how productive your life will be to minister souls into the fold. Do you desire to have a life that gives God the greatest potential? What are you doing about it?

It does not matter if you are a pastor, a layman, a housewife, or a child. God has pre-destined you with all the gifts you need to bring the greatest results you are capable of achieving. God has given *"to every man according to his several ability"* (Matthew 25:15). God reckons with each believer not to be slothful but to be faithful with the abilities He has distributed to us.

Likewise, we should not compare ourselves with each other. Some are given more grace than others, but all have God's influential Spirit. Some have more troubles than others, but all have God's comforting Spirit. Listen to what the scripture says in 1 Corinthians 12:7: *"But the manifestation of the Spirit is given to every man to profit withal."* Meaning, God has enabled you and me to accomplish a 100-fold result in our lives because He has given us His Spirit.

There are important concerns we need to uphold in order to experience a life that reaps an abundant harvest. Initially, we must learn some necessities (as you are doing by reading this book and hopefully studying the Bible), and to prepare ourselves for the work. Then, we must immediately put into active practice what we learn in order to attain the abundant results God desires (Jeremiah 7:23). That is one reason God commands us in 2 Timothy 2:15, *"Study to shew thyself approved unto God, a workman that needeth not to be ashamed, rightly dividing the word of truth."*

Christians who bear much fruit have no shame, except for their own inadequacies. For we all do fall short of the glory of God (Romans 3:23). The Christians who labor to guide people toward Christ instead are filled with much joy and enthusiasm. They experience God's joy and pleasure through seeing people come to know Christ and be transformed. It is these experiences in God's service which motivate us to learn more about how we can advance God's kingdom in even greater abundance.

God has given the Holy Bible so we may learn how to accomplish His mission. Second Timothy 3:16-17 informs us that, *"All scripture...is profitable...[so] that the man of God may be perfect* [or complete]*, thoroughly furnished unto all good works."* In the Old Testament, Job is quoted as having asked a good question. He asked, *"Can a man be profitable unto God, as he that is wise may be profitable unto himself?"* (Job 22:2) The answer is, "Yes."

God wants us to be profitable. Any enterprise of the world that does not earn profits soon goes out of business. The same applies in God's kingdom, and therefore God wants the revenues of many souls [being made into disciples]. The harvest truly is plenteous, but sadly, the reality is that the laborers are few.

Therefore, we need to rise up and go labor in God's harvest field—the world. God is waiting for His laborers to go bear much fruit (accomplished through evangelizing), and that our fruit should remain (accomplished through discipleship). As a good husbandman of the field, God has supplied His laborers with all the tools we need to serve effectually, and to be profitable. The best tools God has given are *prayer*—direct communication with Him— and His instruction manual, the BIBLE—Basic Instructions to Bring Lasting Effects—in order that we may learn how to be profitable.

Sadly, a major hindrance for most Christians is the lack of efficient personal work in using these tools. Most Christians are like guinea pigs in a clear plastic ball: Lots of activity, but accomplishing nothing. God's plan does not require a Christian to participate in fundraisers, or run a rummage sale, or manage entertainment events. These are man-made ideas. God's plan requires Christians to put forth a definite, determined effort to prepare themselves by spending time with Him in prayer and His holy Word. Sadly, there is a lack of communion with God and therefore a lack of fellowship with Him.

God's plan also requires Christians to put forth a definite, determined effort to go out and compel people to receive the Savior right now! But once again there is a great lack of witnessing.

Finally, and of equal importance, God's plan requires Christians to put forth a definite, determined effort to assist and guide other Christians closer to the Lord Jesus. But, tragically, there is a lack of discipleship.

Secular politicians faithfully work harder to get one vote than most Christians work to have men brought to Jesus Christ. Perhaps one reason is that these Christians have not been at all prepared for this work in the first place. What is even more heartbreaking is that many are ignorant of the importance of God's eternal mission.

It is tragic, since an ignorant Christian will most likely not be a useful instrument for God. A man who only knows that he is a sinner and that Jesus Christ is the Savior may be very useful to others in the same condition as himself, and it is his duty to do the best he can with what little knowledge he possesses. Yet, as a whole, it should not be expected that such an ignorant man would be largely used of God in winning and discipling souls. If he would endure the hardship of widening and deepening his experience in studies, human investments, and service to God, he would become, in the highest sense, a learned man. He could then use his knowledge for the life-saving influence of others; but being, to a great extent, ignorant of the things of God himself, it is likely that he cannot and will not make God's Word known to other people outside of his limited range. He possesses very limited influence.

The man who is almost or altogether ignorant, whatever the desire and will he has to do good, must be left out of the ranks of effectual soulwinners. His lack of labor in preparation disqualifies him from being recognized by our Heavenly God as an able soldier to be effective in influencing the sheaves of God's harvest.

Second Timothy 2:3 warns that we must endure hardship to be a good soldier of God. You do not become a good soldier by just signing up (getting saved). You have to daily decide to stay in the process as life unfolds.

A Christian who determines to be one of God's faithful and good soldiers must understand that he will suffer and endure troubles and snares. He must be determined to persevere through each and every attack from the devil, his enemies, family, friends, and his carnal flesh. He must steadfastly look unto

Jesus and avoid admiring and entangling himself with the things of the world (1 John 2:16).

If one can be a good soldier of God, then one must assume that he can be a bad soldier or a mediocre soldier of God too. One type of hardship is the diligent perseverance in preparations, experiences, and studies. This is the hardship that derails more Christians than any hardship this world presents in warfare. Many Christians have too much leisure and are undisciplined to keep their flesh down and prepare themselves today in studies of God's Holy Bible.

The few Christians who are willing and determined to discipline their flesh today and resist being lovers of pleasure find an enjoyment in walking the narrow, abundant road with Christ. It is therefore imperative that *today* we choose to well prepare ourselves in prayer and in doctrine and instruction of God's Word. The glorious results will be that we will become further rooted, built up, and established in the faith of God. Then and only then will we be able to influence others to live bountiful and productive lives in service of our Lord. This is what brings lasting results in bearing fruit for God. It is a great joy not to labor for our own account before God but also to serve others that they too may abound with much fruit that remains for the Savior.

In proper perspective, are the decisions in your life *today* lasting ones for the Lord? If not, what would God have you change? And what are *you* going to do about it?

Chapter Seven

HOW ARE YOU SEPARATE FROM THE WORLD?

AS WE BEGIN OUR LOOK into different qualities, attributes, and characteristics that we need to posses in order to experience the full extent of abundant life with Christ, let us begin from the bottom and work our way up to the top. All qualities stem from a common root—a gracious *godly separation.*

God gives instructions in 2 Corinthians 6:17, saying, *"Wherefore come out from among them, and be ye separate."* Come out from where? From among *them*—the world. We are to come out from among the world and be separate.

If we will pay attention to this wise instruction then we will better understand the walk that can lead a Christian to prosper and experience life more abundantly. The Christian who seeks to separate himself from being choked by the lusts of things (Mark 4:19), the pleasures of the world (Luke 8:14), and the pride of life (1 John 2:16) will thrive in Christ and naturally live as Christ would. Godly characteristics and qualities only flourish when we keep ourselves separate from the world.

Therefore hope for all of us lies not in huddling up to the human race but in renouncing allegiance to the world altogether. Separation is to move away from the world and closer to Christ. However, to be separate does not mean to physically be away from the world (John 17:15-17). We cannot arbitrarily break off all contact with those who refuse Christ (1 Corinthians 5:10). This would be unbiblical, not Christ-like, and unproductive. Cults do this.

Hebrews 12:1 tells us that we are surrounded with *"so great a cloud of witnesses."* One group of witnesses who are watching us all the time is the people of the world who we interact with on a daily basis. They observe us and seek a reason for the hope that is within us. Since we live among people of the world, we ought always to be ready to give them an answer whenever asked about our hope (1 Peter 3:15).

One aspect of putting our faith in Christ is this: we should aspire to keep ourselves unspotted from the world (James 1:27), because this is what Christ taught us. How is this possible? Galatians 5:1 provides the answer: *"stand fast therefore in the liberty wherewith Christ has made us free, and be not entangled again with* [any] *yoke of bondage."* God wants us to experience liberty—being free in Christ and not bound up in legalism, pharisiticalism, or sinful bondage. Therefore, we as wise servants of God need to separate ourselves in a godly manner from the world's entanglements, passions, and lusts.

We, Christians are in the world and while we live in the world we are to conduct ourselves with a somber and spiritual attitude that exemplifies Christ. For example, we are to graciously separate ourselves from our preferences because the love of God compels us to forsake all self-regard (2 Corinthians 5:14-15). Not living for ourselves obliges us to give others preference over ourselves (Romans 12:10). Separation helps us to willingly be put into uncomfortable circumstances (such as yielding our "rights") so that we can learn to yield ourselves to Christ's instruction to be meek and lowly like Himself toward people. And as we go along in life we will be filled with this heartfelt determination: *"For to me to live is Christ, and to die is gain"* (Philippians 1:21).

Whatsoever we do is to be done to God's glory (1 Corinthians 10:31). Our attitude, spirit, aim, and actions should be contrary to the world's ways; they should be aimed toward God Himself. A separate Christian gets His example from Christ—He was holy, harmless, undefiled, and separate from sinners (Hebrews 7:26), even while among sinners. Likewise, we should be the same, because the individual *"that saith he abideth in him* [Christ] *ought himself also so to walk, even as he walked"* (1 John 2:6).

There are numerous character qualities that a determined Christian who desires to be of great service for God must possess. The Christian who embody these godly characteristics is the one who can be a profitable and good success for God's Kingdom. However, it is important to understand that all character qualities only manifest themselves when a Christian exhibits a life that is graciously separate from the world and set apart for the Lord Jesus Christ. Jesus stated it precisely, *"But seek ye first the kingdom of God, and his righteousness; and all these things shall be added unto you"* (Matthew 6:33).

We Christians must seek Christ and His kingdom first. Christ must be preeminent in our thoughts, our words, our actions, and lifestyle. Jesus Christ must be the first priority if we are to experience the richness of Christ and enjoy life more abundantly.

In the following chapters, I will cover only some of the many character qualities that the Holy Bible points out. These character qualities seem to rise above all other qualities, characteristics, and attributes. It is my hope that as you continue to read this book you will develop a firm determination to *be* the Christian that God is urging you to be.

May you be encouraged to seek the Lord for guidance and strength, because none of us can live a life that is pleasing in the sight of God on our own. We, in and of ourselves, are simply incapable of exhibiting godly character without God's assistance. We need the power of God to manifest Himself in and through us.

Please be willing to spend extra time to study and thoroughly understand each of these qualities. Some of the things we will examine may be hard to swallow at first. But as you read, ask God to help you understand these truths and to give you the grace to apply them to your life.

Through reading, God may expose a sin or a hindrance in your life. If so, I hope you may be encouraged to yield to God's Holy Spirit and submit to anything God reveals or instructs you to do. It is my prayer that you will open up your Bible and sit at the Master's feet each day. For God's *"word is a lamp unto* [our] *feet, and a light unto* [our] *path"* (Psalm 119:105). If you seek Him, He will be found by you (2 Chronicles 15:2). By doing so, you will find an enjoyment of Christ that many Christians never experience, even after years of living for God.

Chapter Eight

HOW IS YOUR LOVE
EVIDENT BEFORE OTHERS?

THE LORD JESUS, while walking this earth, displayed perfectly what it is like to be in communion with the Father. His demonstration entailed prayer with the Father. He was as accustomed to praying alone with His Father as He was to praying with people. His prayers honored God the Father and reflected the fellowship He enjoyed with Him. Their love for one another was naturally demonstrated before mankind in their communion as they took great pleasure in being one in perfect harmony. The Father's honor was evident both in every inquiry and in every response to Christ's prayers.

The prayers of Jesus to the Father allow us a glimpse of their perfect union. In John chapter 17, Jesus prayed one last time with His disciples nearby. In that late afternoon, Jesus lifted up His eyes toward Heaven and prayed to the Father. His prayer expressed adoration to the Father in a perfect lexis of glory. Jesus reported to the Father the work He had accomplished, which was the fulfillment of all that the Godhead predestined Jesus to do while on earth. In addition, Jesus interceded to the Father with great vigor on behalf of all His present and future disciples' needs!

While interceding for us, Jesus prayed that the Father should not take us out of the world, but that He should keep us from the evil [within this world]. We believers in Christ are not of this world, even as Christ is not of the world (John 17:15-16). We are not to be enamored with the things of this world nor charmed by its customs, traditions, or manners. On the other hand, we are not to guard ourselves by secluding ourselves in the woods or some religious monastery. That would be fruitless and unprofitable for the kingdom of God.

Most believers would agree that to hide behind the physical walls of a monastery is counterproductive. Thankfully, we find very few believers today leaving the world and joining a religious faction. Nevertheless, we still have Christians hiding themselves away from the world, but in a more subtle modern way. Many Christians immobilize their witness in a reserved manner. They hide behind computerized gadgets. These devices are distracting people from having an awareness and concern for others nearby. Many individuals keep themselves engaged with unnecessary continuous meddling with technology, cutting themselves off from contact with other people. Many times these gadgets keep Christians from opportunities to share the gospel with those around them.

I understand that at times there are important reasons to use our electronics. Nevertheless, there is no real need to use them every single minute while we are among other people. A couple decades ago we got along quite well without them, and I am sure today we could still get along well without them. We simply need to make time for people around us, and to turn these devices off or mute them while out among people. In this age of technology, we need to be vigilant not to shut ourselves away from people, so that we do not decrease the prospects of getting the gospel out to individuals who may be just inches away.

This world is going to continue to wax darker and darker. Jesus said that because iniquity shall abound, the love of many shall wax cold (Matthew 24:12). Therefore, we need to maximize our opportunities to shine the light of the gospel to people around us. We are to live as shining lights in this dark and cold world (Mathew 5:16). We are to keep ourselves available and not distracted with *things* so that we may be an effectual witness for Christ.

As we live in this world, we are constantly being bombarded by its wicked elements and ungodly influences. Sometimes there is no way to avoid particular evils that this world presents. However, we should be determined and vigilant to make no provision for the flesh. Instead, we are to put on the Lord Jesus Christ so that we may not fulfill the lusts thereof (Romans 13:14). The world's manners can easily distract any Christian who is not careful to be blameless and undefiled.

The lust of the flesh, the lust of the eyes, and the pride of life can entangle us with hindrances and sins that can so easily enslave us. These enticements seek to gain our attention. Once a believer takes his attention off God and onto them, they enter into his heart and choke God's Word. Then, he, like a slave, yields to bondage and becomes unfruitful. Like a thirsty dog that will drink even dirty water set before him, we too can easily take in any thing this world sets before us: clean or dirty, godly or ungodly.

You and I must separate ourselves from the many evils disguised as good that this world has to offer. Not all things before us are pure and right. Ungodly appeals draw attention toward the lust of the flesh, the lust of the eyes, and the pride of life; they can steal our joy, kill our hope, and destroy our lives.

Though we walk in the flesh, we do not war in the flesh. A determined Christian must, through the power of God in Christ Jesus, cast down ungodly imaginations and every high thing that exalts itself against the knowledge of God. You and I must bring into captivity every thought to the obedience of Christ (2 Corinthians 10:3-6). If you do not, your eyes, your heart, and your thoughts will soon become filled with lusts for ungodly delights, and your appetite for more sin will continue to increase. You will crave more and more of what this world slyly offers, and you will be robbed of your joy by the greed of covetousness.

Likewise, you and I need to regularly examine ourselves in the light of God's Word to better understand sin and its devices. We are instructed by the Holy Ghost in the writings of the apostle Paul: *"Examine yourselves, whether ye be in the faith; prove your own selves. Know ye not your own selves, how that Jesus Christ is in you, except ye be reprobates?"* (2 Corinthians 13:5) Consider the following questions to help you examine yourself so that you might make wiser decisions in the stewardship of life.

How often do you close your eyes and dull your ears to unnecessary delights and ungodly choices from this world? Do you set boundaries or limitations on your eyes and ears? Whether you answered yes or no, what boundaries should you make to protect yourself from unwanted and unnecessary conflicts with your soul?

If you and I desire to be wise, profitable, and a good success, we need to courageously consider such questions; then we need to regularly make an honest assessment of ourselves in light of God's Word and make appropriate adjustments based on what He reveals to us. It should be a natural habit to examine ourselves and seek God for improvements in our walk with Christ.

Furthermore, do the people of the world have a hard time distinguishing you (the Christian) from themselves? Or are you so enamored with the world's way of life that you have no desire to be less like the world and more like Christ?

We Christians should live as far on the side of godliness as possible. There should be a clean-cut line of demarcation between Christians and the world: *that is*—a gracious separation that distinguishes the world's ways and God's way. Is this evident in your life? Keep in mind the testimony of the

Christians in Thessalonica. At one time they lacked godly separation, and this caused them much grief. Therefore, it was necessary for God to reprove them, and in 1 Thessalonians 5:22 we read that God commanded them: *"Abstain from all appearance of evil."*

The same applies today. God is the same yesterday, today, and forever (Hebrews 13:8). God's attitude on matters has not changed.

With this said, do your communications, your appearance, and your daily decisions resemble those of people of the world or those of a holy God? Remember, we should dress to avert lustful temptations (Matthew 5:28), we should communicate to minister grace to hearers (Ephesians 4:29), and we should make decisions to glorify God (1 Corinthians 10:31).

Therefore, as obedient children of God, we should not fashion ourselves according to the former lusts in our ignorance: *"But as God which has called you is holy, so be ye holy in all manner of conversation; Because it is written, Be ye holy; for I am holy"* (1 Peter 1:14-16).

If you struggle to separate yourself from the world, then you will surely find yourself failing to demonstrate godly characteristics. If you struggle with godly separation, then you may want to close this book at this time and go spend time with God in prayer. Confess your sin aloud to God; tell Him you are charmed and enamored by this world's system and the lusts it contains. Then forsake your sin, and beg God to enrich your heart with a fervent love for Him and for people's souls (Jeremiah 20:9). *"Set your affection on things above, not on things on earth"* (Colossians 3:2).

Confession to God is good and very important. The scriptures tell us, *"For godly sorrow worketh repentance to salvation not to be repented of: but the sorrow of the world worketh death"* (2 Corinthians 7:10). Keep in mind that *"if we confess our sins, he is faithful and just to forgive us our sins, and to cleanse us from all unrighteousness"* (1 John 1:9). These are promises from God that you can truly claim; however, you must confess, meaning you must acknowledge and take full responsibility for your sins and then immediately forsake them in order to receive the cleansing that only God can do within your heart. For *"[h]e that covereth his sins shall not prosper: but whoso confesseth and forsaketh them shall have mercy"* (Proverbs 28:13).

Godly separation from the world is the first move in devotion toward God; it opens the opportunity for a Christian to have life more abundantly with Christ. Separation from the world is like the root of a tree. Just as a sapling will grow stems and eventually have branches and bear fruit, so godly separation gives a Christian the ability to grow in love and eventually develop Christ's righteous fruit. Therefore, if being separate from the world is the root, then the main stem growing straight from the root of godly separation would be—*love*.

Love is the most excellent quality that extends higher than any characteristic in all respects; love is supremely necessary. Love is the first fruit of the Spirit (Galatians 5:22). It is love that enables you to produce every other fruit of the Spirit and to carry out everything else. It fills you with the vigor to get involved and do something in the lives of others.

The Lord has been suffering for the souls of mankind for a long time. The believer who loves God joins in the sufferings of Christ, watching with Him in seeking the redemption of lost men. Jesus said, *"tarry ye here, and watch with me"* (Matthew 26:38). Likewise, may you and I be found watching with Christ in lifting souls up to God in prayer; may we *not* be found as the ones of whom Christ asked, *"What, could ye not watch with me one hour?"*

When you make the determined decision to be in love with Jesus Christ, then you will naturally express that love by obedience to His word. There is no such thing as to *fall in love* with God. No, you must make a determined choice to obey Him, and your obedience is the proof that you love God. If you are partakers of Christ's sufferings, you will also be partakers of the consolation (2 Corinthians 1:5-7). Commit to memory the words of our Savior: *"If ye love me, keep my commandments"* (John 14:15). Later in the same teaching, Jesus expounded, saying, *"Ye are my friends, if ye do whatsoever I command you"* (John 15:14).

So are you a friend of Jesus? If you say you are, then are you doing what He commands? What is the proof of your familiarity with God?

In the context of John 15:14, Jesus was speaking to His disciples, and He made clear the truth about friendship with God and loyalty to His commandments. Jesus said, *"This is my commandment, That ye love one another, as I have loved you. Greater love hath no man than this, that a man lay down his life for his friends. Ye are my friends, if ye do whatsoever I command you. Henceforth I call you not servants; for the servant knoweth not what his lord doeth: but I have called you friends; for all things that I have heard of my Father I have made known unto you. Ye have not chosen me, but I have chosen you, and ordained you, that ye should go and bring forth fruit, and that your fruit should remain: that whatsoever ye shall ask of the Father in my name, he may give it you. These things I command you, that ye love one another"* (John 15:12-17).

Love causes your relationship with God to blossom into a friendship rather than just servanthood. You no longer serve God because it is your duty. You serve God because He is your most loved friend.

Love dispels every doubt and fear (1 John 4:18). It is love that enables a believer to get close to God. When you love someone you will seek to understand what his or her heart is after; therefore love for God transforms the believer to become trustworthy with the matters on God's heart. It is love that gives you the natural desire to take part in the works of God because your heart becomes aware of the thoughts of God's heart: therefore, your heart desires the best for people in Christ's honor instead of worrying about the negatives that may hinder your outreach.

Love is natural, and grows from being in the fertility of Christ. To love is the first and most important quality that a Christian must obtain from God in order for his soul to touch others' lives in a godly sense. Subsequently, a believer should seek love from God if he finds himself lacking; for no other influence of God's Spirit will be visible through him without evident love.

Have you ever acted contemptible toward another when faced with a stressful, troubling situation? There is no love, nor profit in that behavior. God exhorted us to love, and to exhibit His love from the bowels of our heart (Colossians 3:12-13).

Oftentimes people will do things that cause us pain. Seldom does someone willingly set forth to injure us; but people do hurt us out of ignorance without considering the effects of their words or actions. We can be tempted to become angry, bitter, or resentful. This is when we need the fruit of the Spirit—love—the most. Love manifests itself by forbearing and offering forgiveness, even when we would judge forgiveness is not warranted. Is not this what our Savior did before His enemies? He who was guiltless opened not his mouth when accused by false witnesses. Jesus, when smitten on the face and spit upon, refrained from wrath and showed love toward His enemies. From the cross, Jesus declared, *"Father, forgive them; for they know not what they do."*

Because of the hurts people will bring upon us, we should daily beseech God to fill our hearts with His unconditional love. Then when we are forced into an altercation, we stand in His strength to forbear and demonstrate love and forgiveness rather than succumb in weaknesses to act unbecomingly.

Likewise, Colossians 3:12-14 commands: *"Put on therefore, as the elect of God, holy and beloved, bowels of mercies, kindness, humbleness of mind, meekness, longsuffering; Forbearing one another, and forgiving one another."* Then it continues to explain that *"if any man have a quarrel against any: even as Christ forgave you, so also do ye. And above all these things put on charity, which is the bond of perfectness."* Therefore, love can be explained as the adhesive that completely bonds everything together.

It would be inappropriate to discuss love without taking into consideration the words of 1 Corinthians 13. Many consider this to be the love chapter of the Bible.

This magnificent chapter portrays in detail the many undertakings which you and I are capable of in our efforts to help people in this world: such as having eloquent speech in many languages, great understanding to serve in diverse ways, mighty faith, the surrendering of all our possessions, and dying as a martyr. These are impressive feats. Yet without charity—*love*—they are nothing. Therefore, we learn that every great exploit we might be capable of achieving is considered of no value before God when accomplished without love.

First Corinthians 13:3 explains that if we do not have love, then all that we achieve is in essence unprofitable. A lack of love yields no eternal dividends in the lives of people. You might be busy doing profound things, but your lack of love hinders you from influencing people with eternal results. Despite mountain-moving faith and impressive feats, a person without evident love in actuality has succumbed as a slothful servant who offers no genuine help to others. He is unprofitable because his endeavors are not aimed toward the most sublime objective. And why should we spend a lifetime doing something good when God wants us to do His best?

If you desire to be an effectual servant of God then you must have an evident love expressed toward others: a love that is concerned for people's eternity as well as their temporal needs. God gives His definition of what real love is, expressed through *charity,* in 1 Corinthians 13:3-8. Review the list and its explanations below and see how you compare in the light of God's Word:

Charity…

> **suffereth long, *and* is kind**: puts up with inconveniences
> **envieth not**: lifts up others rather than self
> **vaunteth not itself, is not puffed up**: is not proud or stuck up
> **doth not behave itself unseemly**: does what is right
> **seeketh not her own**: looks for ways to help others
> **is not easily provoked**: responds properly
> **thinketh no evil**: thinks correctly
> **rejoiceth not in iniquity**: doesn't enjoy what is not right
> **rejoiceth in the truth**: does get excited about what is right
> **beareth all things**: carries the weight
> **believeth all things**: gives the benefit of the doubt

hopeth all things: always hopes for the best
endureth all things: keeps on keeping on
never faileth: works every time!

If we are honest, we would have to admit that our service to others does not always manifest itself in actions and reactions of love. Sometimes we do achieve this level. But other times we behave with self-centered motives as we try to do good things in our own abilities. Why does this occur?

One explanation is that we do not recognize the importance of love; therefore, we consciously or unconsciously yield to our selfish flesh rather than to God. For this reason, it ought to be a routine prayer of ours to seek God for love and then for more love. The more love we possess, the more of a willing heart we will have to give ourselves to God and people. He is able to place genuine love inside our hearts, which can only come by the working of His Holy Spirit.

There is no other act that is given the honorable prestige of royalty besides love. Love is the royal law (James 2:8). God has given us His law, and 1 Timothy 1:5 explains that the end of the Lord's law *is charity*. Faith is the foundation of our Christianity and love is the end of our Christianity. You cannot make it a law that someone must love. Love is royal because it is the spontaneous and natural outflow of actions birthed from within one's heart. Therefore, the whole of our Christianity is love.

What's more, God is love. First John 4:16 tells us, *"And we have known and believed the love that God hath to us. God is love; and he that dwelleth in love dwelleth in God, and God in him."* The context further explains, *"He that loveth not knoweth not God; for God is love. In this was manifested the love of God toward us, because that God sent his only begotten Son into the world, that we might live through him. Herein is love, not that we loved God, but that he loved us, and sent his Son to be the propitiation for our sins. Beloved, if God so loved us, we ought also to love one another"* (1 John 4:8-11). God is love personified.

We are to love each other. It is that important. In John 13:34 Jesus gave a new commandment, *"That ye love one another; as I have loved you, that ye also love one another."* This is reaffirmed in 1 John 3:16, which says, *"Hereby perceive we the love of God, because he laid down his life for us: and we ought to lay down our lives for the brethren."*

In writing about the topic of love, author Christopher Adsit in his book *Personal Disciplemaking*, asked several influential Christian leaders about love. In one reply, I like how Bob Vidano of the Navigators responded to the question. In part of his answer, he stated, "As I love God and people, I will seek people's best at my expense." Now that is how we are to love people! That's true Bible love!

Similarly, the apostle Paul described his love for the Corinthian church, saying, *"And I will very gladly spend and be spent for you; though the more abundantly I love you, the less I be loved"* (2 Corinthians 12:15). You and I are to have a mindset that we are indebted to people and owe them love. Love enables us not only to speak the gospel, but also to serve and disciple people.

Love is so important that God looks for you and me to love as He loves people. God sought our best at His costly expense: *"For God so loved the world, that he gave his only begotten Son"* (John 3:16). *"Hereby perceive we the love of God, because he laid down his life for us: and we ought to lay down our lives for the brethren"* (1 John 3:16). We may not have to physically die for someone; however, we should demonstrate our love by seeking others' best.

Each one of us already knows how to seek one's best. We do it all the time—for ourselves. The thing man loves more than anything else in the world is himself. *"For no man ever yet hated his own flesh; but nourisheth and cherisheth it"* (Ephesians 5:29).

Each one of us is naturally ingrained with the element of love because every single day we feed, clothe, and bathe ourselves without being told to do so. We want the highest benefit for ourselves. Likewise, there is no room for you to say you cannot love and seek the best for others, because you have been practicing it your whole life. Just think about how good you are toward yourself. Now implement that same love toward others: Feed people. Clothe people. Bathe people with the truth and goodness of Christ. If you do these things then I am sure many lives around you will be changed gloriously for the better.

But the critics argue we are unable to love as God does. Most certainly, I agree with them, because in and of ourselves this is true. For I know that in me (that is, in my flesh) dwells no good thing (Romans 7:18). However, when a man is in Christ, he now has the Spirit of God dwelling within him; the Bible teaches that now he is a clean vessel that God can flow His love through to people (Galatians 5:22; Romans 8).

If we abide in Christ and yield to His Spirit, then the love of Christ can be demonstrated through us by what we do to others: good deeds. We are instructed, *"And walk in love, as Christ also hath loved us, and hath given himself for us an offering and a sacrifice to God for a sweetsmelling savour"* (Ephesians 5:2).

Love is a willing, sacrificial giving of oneself for the benefit of others without any thought of return, because love is self-denial. That is how God loves, and it should be how we love. In His power we will be capable of giving ourselves through our time, energy, possessions, and resources.

Philippians 2:7-8 explains how God demonstrated His love toward us, saying, *"But [He] made himself of no reputation, and took upon him the form of a servant, and was made in the likeness of men: And being found in fashion as a man, he humbled himself, and became obedient unto death, even the death of the cross."* As we look at Jesus Christ's example of self-denial and sacrifice, it should cause us to examine our own ways. Consider the following questions: How can you today be a sacrifice for others in a practical sense? How can you demonstrate your love toward people by denying yourself benefits? How can you shun your rights and your comforts for the benefits of others? In other words, how can you give your life to others for their benefit, *today*?

Philippians 2:4-5 is a good place to begin to answer such questions. God supplies us with instruction in how to demonstrate sacrificial, self-denying love toward people. He commands, *"Look not every man on his own things, but every man also on the things of others. Let this mind be in you, which was also in Christ Jesus."*

The love that Jesus possessed while walking this earth was a love that came from the heart; it showed itself through unselfish good actions. Hence, we should seek God for a love that is deeply rooted in concern for people. We too ought to express our love by putting people before ourselves.

First John 3:18 admonishes that we are not to love merely in word, neither in tongue; but we are to love in deed and in truth. When we have love for people, our love will be demonstrated by actions. Then people around us will take notice, and they will be compelled to give attention to the gospel that proceeds from our lips. Actions bathed in love really do open doors for us to communicate the gospel and more influentially help people.

If we love people then we can tell them anything. Even if what we say is inadvertently offensive to them. If people sense our love, they might simply think, "This Christian has no idea what he is saying, but at least he loves me." But if we do not have love for people, no matter how truthful our words are they will not receive them. They may simply think, "This Christian just wants to convert me."

Therefore, love is the issue. John 1:14 reveals, *"And the Word was made flesh, and dwelt among us, (and we beheld his glory, the glory as of the only begotten of the Father,) <u>full of grace and truth</u>."* When Jesus (the Walking

Truth) physically walked on this planet, He gave the truth; He also spoke it with grace. Truth given without the grace of love more often than not is rejected. However, truth spoken with perfect love is alluring and captivates its hearers to take notice of the message.

We are encouraged by the apostle Paul to follow Christ's example: *"And walk in love, as Christ also hath loved us, and hath given himself for us an offering and a sacrifice to God..."* Engaging people in Christ's love is so powerful that it arrests people's attention. If we can seize their attention, we just might be able to lead them to Jesus Christ. A Christian's love must be deep enough to bear the burden for souls to be rescued from the flames of Hell. A determined servant of God who has evident love will spend most of his time encouraging his hearers to look to Jesus Christ. He will care for them so very much that he will look through their faults and sins and will compassionately address their sinful condition and tell them about the saving grace of Jesus Christ.

Titus 3:3-5 addresses the miserable truth about each one of us; and for this reason, we ought to be compelled to love all people. The scripture says: *"For we ourselves also were sometimes foolish, disobedient, deceived, serving divers lusts and pleasures, living in malice and envy, hateful, and hating one another. But after that the kindness and love of God our Savior toward man appeared, Not by works of righteousness which we have done, but according to his mercy he saved us."* As the passage points out, today's Christians were once foolish and deceived and in times past did not know the Savior too. But, thank God! He was longsuffering toward us! Thank God, He extended His love toward us, even when we were disobedient, malicious, and hateful. Just as God showed kindness and love toward us through people, we too, *now*, should extend God's love to others so that they might be reached with the gospel too (Luke 6:31), no matter how seemingly far away from God they are.

A Christian who is determined to have a great influence in winning souls to Christ must have a real desire for the good of others. Whether it be in season or out of season; Whether the people make it easy or difficult, we are to love them.

People can easily perceive when a cold-hearted man is speaking, and they instinctively want to reject that man's message just because of his lack of genuine warmth. Who wants to be near a cold-hearted person? Not me. Nonetheless, nonbelievers easily become attentive listeners to those who speak with hearts filled with love and a sincere concern for them, even when they disagree. Sadly, many zealous Christians fail at sharing Christ with others because of the coldness of their own hearts. Instead of a puny, cold heart, we ought to have a great big hot heart so that all people could desire to be near us. People long to be around others who genuinely care about them.

Any Christian can enjoy life more abundantly by possessing a loving heart for the folks around him. Likewise, effectiveness in service for God, such as the winning and discipling of souls, is proportionate to the amount of love and genuine care you possess for people.

King Solomon asked for understanding and wisdom. God granted him both knowledge and wisdom and in addition God enlarged his heart to care for the people (1 Kings 4:29). Likewise, a wise Christian must have a big heart full of love if he is to do any good in people's lives.

Most people cannot stand to be around someone who is graceless and has a "holier than thou" demeanor. I know that I certainly do not enjoy it, and I am a disciple of the Lord Jesus. It is plainly foolish to attempt to be so perfect and holy or to think you have all the answers so that you have no humanness within yourself. This is a disservice toward people and is a downright misrepresentation of Jesus Christ. We can better serve people if we have some humanity within ourselves. People like to see at least a trace of humanness in Christians. Nonbelievers get along better with Christians who are compassionate than with overbearing, fanatical, dogmatic, religious Christians. Human nature, in many aspects, is an awful thing; but when the Lord Jesus takes hold of it and joins His own divine nature to it, He makes a grand masterpiece of it. Human nature becomes a noble thing when it is united with the Lord Jesus Christ.

Those men who keep to themselves apart like hermits, and live a supposedly sanctified life away from others, are not likely to have any influence among people or to do any good for their community or the world. Nevertheless, a Christian with zealous compassion for humanity and abundant love for others is an instrument that can mightily be used to that influence people to follow Christ.

A determined servant of God must love people and intermingle with them if he is to be of service to them. Not to the extent that he is consumed with their affairs, but he should be around them and be available to serve them and communicate the gospel to them. Look at Jesus—was He ever found in the theater? Did he ever go to the Olympic Games? Or did He go to any local horse or camel races, or to any of the Herodian court amusements? No. He was not found at such amusements. He was *"holy, harmless, undefiled,* and *separate from sinners"* (Hebrews 7:26). He did not go to the world's places of amusement, but He certainly did mix with the world in morally safe social environments such as the local synagogues (Mark 6:2), marketplaces (John

5:1-2), people's homes (Matthew 9:10-13, Luke 7:36-49), social engagements (John 2:1-2), important celebrations (Leviticus 23, Matthew 5:17-18, and John 2:23), and national feasts (John 10:22-23). Jesus understood that He must mix with sinners of the world in order to reach them, but only in unadulterated environments. Jesus never crossed the line of His integrity, nor did he seek to use popular methods that His religious peers might be doing. Jesus knew better and abstained from such defilement.

Each time the Lord associated with people, an opportunity arose for Him to impart His message to them. Christians would do themselves a lot of good to mingle with the world as Jesus did and watch the doors open to share the gospel.

Some Christians really are much better men than others are, yet they do not accomplish as much good as those who go and sit down with people, making themselves available to people as much as possible. Ecclesiastics 7:16 teaches that it is possible for a Christian to appear to be just a little too *"righteous over much* and *over wise,"* so that people feel that he is an altogether celestial being, and more fit to preach to heavenly creatures than to fallen men. A Christian of this sort should get a reality check; he should humble himself, and beg God for a heart that is filled with genuine love for people.

In God's Spirit and power, just be men among men, recognizing your faults and vices, but mingling with others in love and sympathy. Feel that you would do anything (godly, of course) to bring people to Christ (2 Corinthians 12:15). In His power, go out of your way and visit someone. In Luke 19:1-10, Jesus went to spend time with a sinner named Zacchaeus at his home. Jesus did not sin by hanging out with a lost man and his companions. Jesus noticed that this lost man desired to know the truth. For that reason, Jesus went to spend time with the man in the comfort of the man's surroundings. Because of that visit, Jesus was able to explain his need for Christ, and Zacchaeus believed on the Lord and was saved!

We absolutely need to love people with a genuine compassion and concern and warmth for them. God's love in us should compel us to live and be among people, so that our friendship might attract them to Christ.

As the apostle Paul said in 1 Corinthians 9:19-22, *"For though I be free from all men, yet have I made myself servant unto all, that I might gain the more. And unto the Jews I became as a Jew, that I might gain the Jews; to them that are under the law, as under the law, that I might gain them that are under the law; To them that are without law, as without law, (being not without law to God, but under the law to Christ,) that I might gain them that are without law. To the weak became I as weak, that I might gain the weak: I am made all things to all men, that I might by all means save some.*" Now this was real love. He was determined to go the extra mile to befriend and lead someone to Christ. Might you do the same?

If you decide to be a determined Christian with a heart overflowing with God's love, then your heart will become overwhelmed with a desire to go to great lengths to guide someone to the Lord Jesus. A heart filled with His love will compel you to express that love through godly actions of kindness toward people all around you. Then the results of His love flowing through you will allow you to proclaim His gospel and see people come to know Jesus Christ.

So now, will you seek to understand the matter which is greatest on God's heart: the reconciliation of mankind to God? The Lord has been suffering for the souls of mankind for a long time. Will you make yourself available and get to know God more by being in prayer and the Bible each day? Will you go out and suffer with God for souls? Or will you grieve God by forsaking the concern on His heart?

We believers have been given the Holy Ghost; the power now resides in us to love God and to love our neighbors; therefore, we are capable of walking with Christ and partaking of His sufferings to seek what He seeks. This is *love*.

Chapter Nine

WHY DO YOU PRAY?

ONE THING THAT IS COMMENDABLE in the eyes of God is to live a life that is separate unto the Lord. This is honorable and is something that one seldom sees nowadays. Narrow is that path, and few choose to live near to God.

We have seen that godly separation produces love. Right next to and almost equal to love is another important quality: *prayerfulness*. Praying itself must be the work of the individual. I highly endorse prayer and exhort all to its practice. But prayer cannot be taught; it can only be done. A determined Christian who seeks to experience life more abundantly with Christ must be one who is in continual communion with the Lord Jesus through prayer.

It is not part of the life of a natural man either to love or to pray. This is why a man needs to consecrate (separate) himself to the Lord. A consecrated life shapes a Christian with the capacity to commune with God. It also enables a Christian to speak honestly and frankly with God and to express love in prayer.

Love and prayerfulness, two godly qualities, stem from having a life separated unto God. They are the two prerequisites for every other quality that serves to help a Christian to be useful for the Master's use. All other qualities certainly will fall into place when a Christian is filled with love and walks in communion with the Lord.

I think the best two definitions of prayer I have heard came from one of my mentors, Paul Drake, and the old-time anointed preacher, John Bunyan.

Paul Drake defines prayer as "Communion with God the Father through faith in Jesus the Son, by the power of the Holy Spirit, according to the will of God (the Word), to the blessing of others, my fulfillment, and to the glory of God the Father." According to the book *Disciplines of a Godly Man*, John Bunyan defined prayer as: "A sincere, sensible, affectionate pouring out of the heart or soul to God, through Christ, in the strength and assistance of the Holy Spirit, for such things as God has promised, or according to the Word of God, for the good of the church, with submission in faith to the will of God." Think about those definitions for a moment. Maybe even reread them. Are they not so true?

Prayer is absolutely a privilege that God has liberally granted His children so we may be in communion with Him at all times. Communion refers to God's communication and presentation of Himself to us, together with our proper response to Him with joy. We say "with joy" because it would not be communion if God revealed Himself only as a total wrathful God; then we would be simply terrified. That would be a *true* revelation and a *proper* response, but it would not be communion. Communion assumes that God comes to us in love and that we respond joyfully to the beauty of His perfections and the offer of His fellowship. He may sometimes come with a rod of discipline; but even in our tears, we can rejoice in the Father's loving discipline (Hebrews 12:6-11). Communion with God may lay us in ashes or make us leap. But it never destroys our joy. It *is* our joy, because He is our joy.

Without prayer, it is impossible to engage in communion with God, have confidence in Jesus, or experience an out-flowing power of the Holy Spirit. Without prayer, it is impossible to possess the proper attitude to be determined to live a consecrated life in Christ's service. And without prayer it is certainly impossible to have any other characteristics that are needed in order to glorify God, to bless others, and to live life more abundantly.

Sadly, it grieves the Lord not to find more of His children engaged in prayer. And for one reason in Matthew 9:37-38 the Lord Jesus instructed us to ask God for more laborers. And what a worthy duty it is to engage in the vocation of prayer.

Continuous prayer is needed which is very much possible through communion with God. Continual communion with God gives us a rich, intimate awareness and consciousness of God and His presence that goes deeper than any expression of words. Because it's impractical and impossible to carry on a continuous dialogue with God while engaging in the mundane responsibilities of this life, we need constant communion with Him.

This is one reason God does not so much as look at the expression of our words. He looks at the posture of one's heart (1 Samuel 16:7). God is not only looking for us to participate in some designated religious "quiet time" that we might daily have with Him in the mornings. God also desires that we partake of Him in fellowship and communion around the clock: in the morning (Mark 1:35), during the daytime (Psalm 55:17), in the evening (Matthew 14:23), and at night (Luke 6:12). Continual communion—defined as moment to moment fellowship and awareness of the Lord—is imperative!

Certainly God desires for us to speak to Him, and He to us. And this is best experienced when we abide in communion with the Lord, because a Christian who is engaged in fellowship and communion with God will naturally articulate the words that need to be spoken to Him at the appropriate times.

In Proverbs 16:1 the Lord declares to us, *"The preparations of the heart in man, and the answer of the tongue, is from the LORD."* There are two matters that can be learned from this scripture. First, *"the answer of the tongue"* is a form of work. It takes work—energy, thought, motivation—to speak. It *"is from the LORD"* because He is the One who allows us to breathe, speak, move, and learn how to be more effectual in our labors with Him. Jeremiah 29:11-13 tells us that God has a plan for our lives. God invites us to seek Him so that we may learn how to effectively carry out His plan.

Second, *"the preparations of the heart in man...*[also] *is from the LORD."* Once again, all things, great or small, are made available from the Lord. God is the One who prepares our hearts to receive the faith He places in our hearts to believe Him and to stay in communion with Him by prayer. Prayerfulness is not even of us. It is of God, who gives us the ability to partake in prayer with Him. Furthermore, any type of labor that we partake in (that is in accordance to God's Word) is first established by God in the thoughts of our heart. It is God who confirms what we should do according to His will. God always prepares us for work before He accomplishes any plan through us. The arena in which He prepares us is inside our hearts.

Jeremiah 17:9-10 warns, though, saying, *"The heart is deceitful above all things, and desperately wicked: who can know it? I the LORD search the heart, I try the reins, even to give every man according to his ways, and according to the fruit of his doings."* Our hearts are deceitful and full of trickery. Therefore, we must test our thoughts and desires, no matter how "Christian" they seem to appear. We must verify our plans to see if they are in accordance with the Holy Bible. If a thought or plan is not in accordance to God's statues, principles, and instructions, then it must be forsaken because it is proven not to come from God.

On the other hand, if a thought or plan is in agreement with God's Word, then we may proceed further under the guidance of the Holy Spirit. No matter what, we must follow God according to His ways that are set forth in the Holy Bible and not according to the inspirations of our deceitful hearts or the popular methods of man's ideals today.

Prayer is given by God as a way for us to bring our hearts into rich communion with Him. Communion with God is only possible when we are in prayer with Him; but not according to man's traditions. Man deceives himself when his focus is not on God but instead on the particulars, such as where, how, when, or what he thinks he should pray and do. These conditions are trivial and immaterial to the glory of God. God does not want us to center our thoughts on what our physical stance should or should not be before Him, or to be overly concerned about the location where we think we are to pray. God's concern is that we have our minds in a continual state of awareness and our hearts in fellowship with Him.

Being a Christian is an inward experience, not an outward appearance. Yes, the inward experience progresses toward an outward demonstration before all to see, but this is not one's doing, but only of God's doing. For example, in Exodus 34, Moses, after spending quality time with God came down from the mountain. As he walked down the mountain, the skin of his face shone. He was unaware of the transformation. However, the people noticed the change of his appearance, and they recognized that he had been with God. People can notice when you or I have partaken in quality time with God; it is reflected by one's countenance.

If a Christian is not engaged in prayer, he lacks communion with God. Moreover, there is no rest within him because his spirit lacks closeness with God. Communion with God is of utmost importance for us to enjoy Him (Psalm 43:3-4). It positions our hearts to be engaged with the matters that are on God's heart. Closeness with God will get us aligned to His best. It draws Christians into an intimacy with God, such that they hunger more for His Word; choosing to saturate themselves by meditating on God's Word, allowing them to learn His mind, to understand His heart, and to be inspired to become involved more with His work.

Prayer allows us to be in communication with God. God desires for us to speak honestly, boldly, and frankly to Him as we would with any other respected friend. Prayer is like a partnership. Through prayer we are given opportunity to bring to God the concerns on our hearts! Through prayer we are given opportunity to take hold of God's sentiments and absorb what is on His mind. As we are in communion with God, He will communicate with us about what to pray and what to do. Prayer positions our hearts to come into agreement with God (Matthew 18:19), helping us Christians to show humility before one another.

Because of our lowly state we do not know how to properly draw near to a holy God, and before His holy throne we really do not know what we should pray for as we ought (Romans 8:26). Thank the Lord that He has graciously given us His Spirit. During prayer, a supernatural phenomenon occurs while we express our concerns to God. The Holy Spirit makes intercession for us, and He impresses upon our hearts what we ought to pray.

It is because of the Holy Spirit's participation that our prayers can be appropriately presented before God. Apart from the Holy Spirit's assistance, our prayers are very limited by our own reasoning and intuition. However, with the Holy Spirit's help our mental faculties become informed by Heaven. As we engage in communion with God and seek His help, the Holy Spirit will speak to us through the Holy Bible, to remind us of God's mind regarding matters.

The influence of the Spirit should move our hearts to consider God's perspective, to believe His Word, and to think in a holy manner. Then God's desires will become our desires, God's motives our motives, and God's fruition our fruition. God will reveal to our hearts the things which we need to pray and meditate about. Then the confirmation of God's peace will envelop us as we pray according to His revealed will discovered in the Holy Bible.

Prayer arouses us to offer praise and adoration to God, for He truly is worthy of all honor and admiration (Acts 4:24; Revelation 4:11). When we extol the virtues of God's greatness, it helps us to see life through His perspective. Praise helps us to be content with what we have and not desire what we do not possess. Praise holds our minds in peace, even if the present conditions are troublesome. Praise restrains us from ungratefulness and complaining. Praise makes space in our hearts to be filled with thanksgiving; it mortifies unappreciative attitudes, dissatisfaction, and complaint. Therefore, we ought to spend time praising and adoring our awesome and wonderful God. When we do so, we can be filled with a sprit of faith, thanksgiving, and contentment instead of being doubtful, unthankful, and complaining.

Prayer helps us to possess more faith in God and it stops us from slowly sinking into the self-absorbed quicksand of self-reliance. It helps us to see ourselves in proper relationship with God. We are His servants. He is our God. We are sinful and God is holy. We are imperfect. God is perfect. We are needy and God is abundant. We have questions and God is the answer.

Prayer is so wonderful because it is a two-way communication with God. We talk to God and He talks to us. We listen to God and He listens to us. We do not merely bring our cares, worries, and frustrations to Him; God also speaks and gives guidance and instruction. God reveals Himself to us in prayer.

There have been times when I have been confused and bewildered over a particular concern. Nonetheless, through prayer God calmed my fears and uncertainties (Matthew 11:28) and He answered my requests (Philippians 4:6), further building my understanding and trust in Him. Through prayer God helps you and me to recognize that all things are possible with Him. God gives rest to those who seek Him wholeheartedly and fervently through prayer.

One individual who was a man of prayer in the Holy Bible was the apostle Paul. Quite often in his writings, he would mention how he labored in great heaviness before God in prayer for people (Romans 9:2). Ephesians 1:17-19 is one of those examples. Here, he wrote his prayer out for the brethren to read. I can imagine that, as the pastor of the church in Ephesus read aloud Paul's letter, the words of Paul's prayer must have been a great encouragement to them. Today it still continues to enlighten and encourage us. The passage says, "[May] *the God of our Lord Jesus Christ, the Father of glory,* [give] *unto you the spirit of wisdom and revelation in the knowledge of him: The eyes of your understanding being enlightened; that ye may know what is the hope of his calling, and what the riches of the glory of his inheritance in the saints, And what is the exceeding greatness of his power to us-ward who believe, according to the working of his mighty power."*

What a beautiful prayer! God wants to give you and me wisdom. God wants to reveal Himself in a greater depth of understanding. God wants our perception in life to have more godly insight concerning all matters. God wants us to have a lively hope, and partake in His wonderful calling. God wants us to share in the greatness of His power by being effectual vessels of honor for the Lord Jesus Christ. These are just some of the many significant blessings we can obtain through prayer, and some of the matters about which we can pray for people, and for ourselves, that we may obtain them by God's grace and sovereignty.

The opportunity to be in communion with God is a sure blessing, and it only happens with prayer. Probably one of the greatest blessings prayer offers is the channel to give us full access before God's throne. There we find the presence of God, for surely, He sits on His throne. In God's presence, we can pray and receive divine wisdom, instruction, and direction. God desires to genuinely give wisdom to His children, but we must seek and ask for it. James 1:5-6, says, *"If any of you lack wisdom, let him ask of God, that giveth to all men liberally, and upbraideth not; and it shall be given him. But let him ask in faith, nothing wavering.*" Therefore, spend time with God in prayer and the Holy Bile and you will find knowledge and wisdom and get good understanding.

Problems, setbacks, and troubles are bountiful in supply. These can discourage or dishearten a servant if he is shortsighted; but a servant who is filled with wisdom and understanding trusts in the LORD and leans not on his own reasoning. Likewise, prayerfulness gives a Christian a deeper understanding of the riches of the glory of God's inheritance in the saints. Prayer is the channel God uses to give Christians discernment with spiritual enlightenment. God gives discernment to a Christian so that he may arise from his prayer chamber and be of genuine service to mankind. If we are going to be ministers (servants) to men, we must be equipped with His understanding so that we can recognize how to best serve individuals according to their needs. Discernment helps a Christian to better understand the principal causes of people's afflictions.

Discernment, wisdom, and insight are gifts from the Lord. God supplies gifts so that we may appropriately use them to lift up the brethren in times of need. God never gives a gift, such as discernment, to be used as a tool to hurt someone or to exalt ourselves. God gives gifts to believers so that we may humble ourselves and be good and wise servants unto others.

Not only does spiritual enlightenment help us to serve people effectively, it also provides us with clearer insight into problems and dilemmas. As God supplies a Christian with more discernment, wisdom, or understanding, the believer will soon become aware that his sorrows begin to grow as well. Ecclesiastics 1:18 explains, saying, *"For in much wisdom is much grief: and he that increaseth knowledge increaseth sorrow."* Thankfully, God will not load us with a burden we cannot bear. The Lord balances sorrow by supplying a believer with joy in the Lord as well. Although sorrow might persist because you see man's problems and understand their underlying causes, meanwhile you can experience the joy of the Lord by resting in assurance that God's sovereignty in His timing shall work it all out for the good.

Spiritual enlightenment certainly is a blessing because it also is given to help believers to better appreciate God's grace of longsuffering. Spiritual enlightenment helps you see God's gracious hand working among people in the depths of their problems. As we empathize with others, we are drawn closer to the Savior because our own need for God's grace is made ever more real to us. God patiently works to help us see and understand more of His greatness and holiness.

This is why we need prayer. Prayerfulness serves to expand our understanding of God's holiness. When you see His holiness you will be arrested with conviction by God's Spirit of your own sins and weaknesses. Then your mind will be moved to consider your own frailties, rather than the shortcomings of others. As you better see the glory of God, you will certainly be in awe that God would even call you and permit you to partake in His Kingdom service.

God's holiness causes us to consider all the goodness of God's grace within our own lives. His holiness brings a humbling to our minds. Our disposition is transformed into a likeness and meekness of Christ. We find that we can no longer be critical of others, but instead we must aspire to esteem others. We come to understand that we must yield ourselves more to Christ; then, if the Lord chooses to call us into more service, we will be better prepared because our hearts and minds are blessed to have been smitten by the Lord.

Hebrews 12:2 instructs that we are to look unto Jesus. However, all too often, we Christians find ourselves mistakenly focused on the works of God rather than on the Lord Himself. For this reason Jesus on one occasion had to reprove His disciples. He said, *"Behold, I give unto you power to tread on serpents and scorpions, and over all the power of the enemy: and nothing shall by any means hurt you. Notwithstanding in this rejoice not, that the spirits are subject unto you; but rather rejoice, because your names are written in heaven"* (Luke 10:19-20). In verse 19 Jesus identified some of the great works that are possible through His powerful name. But please pay careful attention to verse 20. He immediately directs the disciples attention that our concern should be focused on the intimate relationship we have with God. We are not to seek delight in our labors, but we are to delight in the LORD (Psalm 37:4). God is more interested in communion and fellowship with us than any good labors for Him.

Many times God must correct our improper perspective or viewpoints in matters. Correction always precedes direction. Once our attention is properly on God and our perception is as Christ's then God can direct us into a specific work. Therefore, we ought to welcome God's probings and convictions, so that we can be aware of any sin lurking within our hearts. We ought to give God the liberty to deal with any issue, whether good or bad, holy or sinful. If a matter in our life is a hindrance to our fellowship with God, then we should not murmur or resist; we should thank God for His probing, immediately confess sin, remove it out of our lives and abandon it.

God is holy and righteous and He deems His children to be too (1 Peter 1:16). Although our standing is holy and righteous in Christ, sometimes our present state becomes tainted with sin. Prayer is one of those mechanisms that God uses to often clean us up. Prayer brings about convictions, not so that we should run away from God, but that we should draw nearer to Him. If we come to God in prayer with the hope of being made more like Christ, then we will certainly be made more aware of any sins unconfessed to God. For in God no sin is hidden; He wants it recognized, confessed, and forsaken.

Some sins, such as selfishness, gossip, overeating, ill attitudes, doubt, or unforgiveness may be unseen by man, but God sees them. This is why we need to come into the light of Christ and dwell there. The individual who comes to the light, surely, his deeds will be made manifest (John 3:21). As the scriptures says, *"But all things that are reproved are made manifest by the light"* (Ephesians 5:13). The light of Christ shows and reproves all sins, and they must be renounced. If we confess and forsake our sins, then we can enjoy the wonderful presence of God and recognize His merciful blessings poured upon our lives.

Jesus taught an important principle in Mark 11:25-26. He said, *"And when ye stand praying, forgive, if ye have ought against any: that your Father also which is in heaven may forgive you your trespasses. But if ye do not forgive, neither will your Father which is in heaven forgive your trespasses."*

We have all been mistreated by someone. But we must forgive. So when was the last time someone wronged you and therefore you needed to forgive him or her? Did you pray for that individual? Jesus did. He prayed for His wrongdoers, even while hanging on the cross after a brutal vicious beating by them. Jesus prayed, *"Father, forgive them; for they know not what they do"* (Luke 23:34).

At another time, Christ spoke concerning prayer, saying, "*[I]f thou bring thy gift to the altar, and there rememberest that thy brother hath ought against thee; Leave there thy gift before the altar, and go thy way; first be reconciled to thy brother, and then come and offer thy gift*" (Matthew 5:23-24). An important principle we need to understand is that before it is possible to engage in true fellowship with a holy God we first must be clean in a practical sense. If we have offended anyone, we need to seek to relieve it. This is the reason we should be in a good habit of asking the Holy Spirit to examine and reveal any sins, faults, or offenses that grieve Him. We can be assured that He will make them known to us. Then our conscience can be at rest by confession to God so that we may seek correction and instruction in righteousness.

If we do not deny God but allow His holiness to bring to our attention sins that hinder our communion with Him, God will certainly bring them to our awareness. Therefore, before we even try to pray for someone, God might cause us to leave the prayer and go seek forgiveness and reconciliation.

This is why many times prayer brings mourning and a holy remorse upon us (Daniel 10:2, 12), because before we try to enjoy communion with God, whom we cannot see with our eyes, God demands that we offer reconciliation to individuals whom we can see. When we confess our faults to one another and to God (James 5:16), then we can draw near to God and engage in a wonderful fellowship with Him.

Sin hinders communion with God (Isaiah 59:2 and Psalm 66:18). We do not want anything obstructing our communion with God. He will not give attention to the prayers of a Christian who has unconfessed sin. Neither will God engage in fellowship with a Christian who will not take responsibility to confess and abandon his sin.

When the Holy Spirit brings to our attention any sin, we immediately need to confess it to God (Ezra 10:1 and Daniel 9:4) and get it behind us—or, should I say, behind the Lord's back. And forsake it forever! Then we can come into a wonderful fellowship with God, and be thankful that He is infinitely longsuffering and willing to bring us into a higher level of enjoyment with Him. Proverbs 28:13 tells us, *"He that covereth his sins shall not prosper: but whoso confesseth and forsaketh them shall have mercy."*

God is recorded in the scriptures as saying, *"Come now, and let us reason together, saith the LORD: though your sins be as scarlet, they shall be as white as snow; though they be red like crimson, they shall be as wool"* (Isaiah 1:18). Our holy God so much desires to commune with sinful men that He condescends Himself so that we may reason with Him. However, God is not saying we should try to reason with Him so that He might compromise His holiness. No, God pleads with us so that we should see our sinfulness, understand its depravity, and turn from our ungodly deeds. We are the ones who are to compromise our wrong ways and turn from them. Only then will God refine us from our sins like fullers' soap (Malachi 3:2), so that we may experience righteousness and enjoy the abundance of His goodness.

God gives a magnificent promise in 2 Chronicles 7:14, saying, *"If my people, which are called by my name, shall humble themselves, and pray, and seek my face, and turn from their wicked ways; then will I hear from heaven, and will forgive their sin, and will heal their land."* This promise comes with a condition on our part, though. We must have a holy reverence in response to our holy God's calling. The work of God must be done in us first before it can be done in others. Only then can a determined Christian who is in communion and fellowship with God be *fully* engaged in the great spiritual battle over people's eternal souls.

Therefore, we should engage in the battle with a seriousness of mind. It is our life or death. This is why our spirits need to be quieted within us, so that our minds may be sober and our hearts may always watch in prayer (1 Peter 4:7); meaning, we need to live in awareness of God's presence and be in tune with His Spirit so that we may appropriately respond to each new circumstance that buffets us.

God reiterates in 1 Thessalonians 5:6 that we are to watch and be sober. The pattern for us to *pray and watch* is emphasized in the scriptures. Colossians 4:2 instructs that as we go about our day we are to continue in *prayer*, and *watch*. One example is that of Nehemiah and his faithful team. Nehemiah understood that prayer and watchfulness must go hand-in-hand. When Nehemiah and his team made their prayers to God, they set a watch against the enemy day and night (Nehemiah 4:9). They were vigilant and focused on their responsibilities as they continuously sought God for His guidance.

Another example is that of the prophet Habakkuk. When he was perplexed over the evil events taking place around him, he separated himself from men for serious prayer time, and he watched with readiness of mind to hear an answer from God (Habakkuk 2:1).

The best example for us to learn from is that of the Lord Jesus Christ. On one occasion, found in Matthew 26:38-41, the Lord Jesus took His three closest disciples into the garden. In their private time together He charged them to *watch and pray,* so that they should learn to keep their eyes on Him and learn God's plan for coming face to face with sin, so that they should know how to take heed when temptation is at hand, lest through indolence they would be overcome by the desire of the flesh. Christ's disciples should have done as He has exemplified. Christ went a little further before them to vent His grief and pour out His soul unto the Father that He, as the Son of God and Son of man, should fulfill His destiny as the Savior of the world. Christ's agonies as the Son of man would be the example for His disciples to learn from in how to bear the load of His sufferings and drink of the bitterest cup which God should put into their hands, so that their minds should be in perfect peace to understand and do God's will when encountering temptations and sin. Christ knew it would be an hour of temptation both to Him and them, and so He advised them to watch and observe how it would go with Him, and what should befall Him. This submission to the Savior's will was to embolden them with God's grace in the face of greater temptations and agonies that they would suffer for His sake. Sadly, their flesh was weak and they yielded to the temptation at hand (self-indulgence in sleep) and missed this particular opportunity to become aware of God's plan.

Nevertheless, Christ's submission to the Father's wrath displayed before all the world would pierce the disciples' hearts and minds; and only by God's grace, after Christ's resurrection and ascension back into Heaven, would they overcome self-indulgence and passionately labor in God's plan. They would turn the world upside down for the Kingdom of God and persevere through great temptations.

May you and I learn from their hour of trial that we too need to be *praying* and *watching*, seeking to understand the Father's will, for we know not what battles we are soon to encounter. Listen to the scripture: *"Thou therefore endure hardness, as a good soldier of Jesus Christ. No man that warreth entangleth himself with the affairs of this life; that he may please him who hath chosen him to be a soldier"* (2 Timothy 2:3-4).

You and I are in a war, and to survive our spirit must be at rest in the presence of God in prayer, even in the midst of great temptations and sufferings. Prayer enables us to *"endure hardship as a good solider of Jesus"* because it helps us to trust God's sovereignty, rest in assurance that He is in control, and become aware of His plans. People are watching us and observing our warfare. As people observe you, what do they say about the war you are ordered to fight? Most importantly, what would God say about your efforts in the war you are supposed to be engaged in? Can God acknowledge you as a good and faithful soldier who does not entangle himself with the affairs of this life? Are you a wise soldier resting and trusting in the sovereignty of God or are you a slothful, unfaithful one?

' Prayer is the life and oxygen of a Christian. Without prayer in the Christian's life, there can be no power in his testimony before the world. God gives us orders through His written Word. We are given clarity as to His orders by prayer. A prayerless Christian is a powerless Christian. Likewise, a prayerless Christian cannot be an effectual servant of God. You might be a believer in Christ, but without prayerfulness you certainly cannot be one who is correctly positioned in the Lord's work; your communications with God are deprived.

Prayer does not so much change things around us as it changes *us* in the situations of life. God has so constituted things that prayer on the basis of redemption alters the way in which a man looks at things. Prayer brings about wonders in a man's disposition.

Just as the body is deprived when it does not have food, the spirit is deprived when it does not have prayer. Prayer is the way the life of God is nourished within a believer. Prayer is the food that makes you less self-sufficient and more God-sufficient. We can either starve or nourish our relationship with God.

The scriptures exhort us in Romans 12:12 to continue persevering in prayer. Ephesians 6:18 instructs us to be *always* in the mindset of *prayer and supplication.* That word supplication means coming to God pleading for something; such as asking God to reprove people of sin, righteousness, and judgment, or entreating God to raise up and send forth more laborers into His harvest. This is intercessory prayer and we are to intercede for others who do not know to pray (1 Timothy 2:1).

In Genesis chapter 18 when the Lord revealed to Abraham that He was going to judge and destroy the wicked cities of Sodom and Gomorrah, Abraham was immediately concerned for his family dwelling in Sodom. The scriptures tell us that Abraham *"stood yet before the LORD"* (Genesis 18:22). He began to intercede before God for Lot's family. Abraham steadfastly continued to intercede for them until God made it clear that they would be saved from judgment.

We need to be steadfast in our prayers for people as Abraham was for his family. We need to be determined in asking the Lord to extend mercy toward people. We need to stand in the gap before God and people as intercessors and pray that God would extend more kindness, grace, and longsuffering toward them. For the Lord's work of wrath and judgment is His strange act (Isaiah 28:21), and although God eventually metes out righteous judgment, the Lord delights to demonstrate longsuffering, mercy, and grace, especially in response to believers' prayers.

May we be found engaging bountifully in prayer; So Philippians 4:6 will be true of us: a people careful for nothing. How good it is to be free from anxiety and worry, and to live in peace of mind! Then, no matter what our present state is, we can thank God for what He is doing and will do in the future. We do not have to worry about anything. We do not have to be anxious, but we can live in peace of mind with thankfulness through both the good and perplexing situations, waiting patiently to see what the Lord will do.

Prayer assists us in embracing what God's sovereignty presents in this life. It enables us to accept even those troublesome unexpected circumstances that come our way. Prayer helps us to be patient and not to ask God to remove baffling conditions, but instead to ask God for the grace and perseverance to walk with Him through the dark valleys and shadows of death.

A determined Christian living life more abundantly learns to seek God in prayer to understand how God may be best glorified (John 14:13-14, 15:16, 16:23-26). He seeks God's interests instead of the things that interest and comfort him. His prayers become more God-centered and less self-centered. Soon, he finds himself thinking less much about himself and much more about the things of God.

If a Christian desires to be useful for the kingdom of God, then he must decide to be an individual who uses the tool of prayer frequently. We can be greatly encouraged by the many testimonies in the Bible of people who sought God in prayer for strength, wisdom, knowledge, and direction. We see Moses pleading with God for a deeper revelation (Exodus 33), Samuel crying unto the LORD for his people (1 Samuel 7:9 and 1 Samuel 12:23), Elijah casting himself down before God (1 Kings 18:41-46), and Daniel communing with and thanking God (Daniel 6:10). Each man regularly sought God in prayer; they cast their burdens upon the LORD, and God sustained them so that they were not moved.

These examples should grip our hearts and inspire us toward more prayer with the Lord, *always*. They illustrate how powerful prayer is and how essential it is for man. Prayer helps our hearts to be positioned in agreement with God in what He says and does. God is pleased to use the prayers of His people to accomplish His purpose in this world. Prayer does not bend the unwilling God to be favorably disposed toward us. Prayer, however, is the means that God uses to accomplish many of His plans through us. Prayer bends us.

Prayer is a supernatural divine privilege. It is a precious gift God gives us. The responsibility of this gift is filled with the satisfaction of helping the helpless, and of seeing the purpose of God fulfilled and the strategies of Satan thwarted. The real work of God is executed in the unseen arena of prayer. We are often given opportunities to see the results of our prayers in this visible world; however, God is also doing much more behind the scenes of life, acting in response to those who labor daily in prayer.

Exodus 17 vividly illustrates this reality. As the Israelites engaged in a pitched battle with the Amalekite army on the plain of Rephidim, Moses stood atop a hill overlooking the battlefield. Whenever he held up his arms with the rod, Israel prevailed. But when he lowered his arms, the Amalekites would gain the advantage of the battle. The clear principle emerges from this account that God acts in response to the prayers of His intercessors, supernaturally enabling those He has called to accomplish the assigned task. Moses' part in the victory of the battle, though it was probably unseen and unnoticed by those in the fight, without a doubt was vital.

Our role in the work of God throughout the world may be unnoticed, unseen, or unappreciated. This is alright. Like Moses, God calls you and me to "hold up the rod of prayer before God." God sees those who faithfully come before Him in prayer. He takes account of individuals' faithfulness behind the scenes in prayer.

The dilemma is that there needs to be more intercessors. Ezekiel 22:30 declares that God is searching for Christians who will stand in the gap as intercessors between Him and people. The scripture says, *"And I* [God] *sought for a man among them, that should make up the hedge, and stand in the gap before me for the land, that I should not destroy it: but I found none."* There is indeed a gulf between God and His creation, and that gulf is *sin*. The destructive effects of sin in the lives of people saddens God; therefore, God seeks individuals to share His care for them. God seeks Christians who will prove their love for man by involving themselves to intercede on people's behalf before God. How sad that in Ezekiel's day God had difficulty finding intercessors. Today, we believers *in* Christ are given the same opportunity to do what God could not find anyone to do in Ezekiel's day—to demonstrate our love for man by being intercessory prayer warriors. The question is, will God today find you involving yourself in intercessory prayer?

May God not look at you or me *today* and say He cannot find us standing in the gap, prayerfully interceding for people. We must take our part in God's program seriously and intercede for others through prayer (1 Peter 4:7). We need to be determined to develop the same attitude that Samuel had for Israel. He exclaimed in 1 Samuel 12:23, *"[God] forbid that I should sin against the LORD in ceasing to pray for you."* What an attitude! What a stance to take upon oneself before the Lord!

Remember, God is not an explanation; God is a revelation. In our prayers, we need to implore God that He will reveal sin, judgment, and His righteous plan of salvation to people. It does not matter how well or eloquently we can explain the gospel. If God does not reveal the truth, then there is no way in Heaven or Earth that we will be able to make the gospel clear to them. The gospel makes its appeal to a person's sensibility, not their intellect. The way into the kingdom of God is the heart first, not the head. Therefore, when we try to witness and persuade people to trust the truth, we also need to stand in the gap and pray for them.

God reminds us in the Bible that if we are to be effectual servants of God then it is extremely important that we labor in prayer. It is so urgent that more than 500 times in the Holy Bible God emphasizes it, exemplifies it, teaches on it, and commands us to pray. (See the command in 1 Thessalonians 5:17 for just one example.)

So, as a recap, the Bible teaches that our prayers should consist of:

- Praising and adoring God for who He is (Hebrews 13:15)
- Confessing our sins to God (1 John 1:9)
- Petitioning God for our requests (Matthew 7:7-8)
- Interceding on the behalf of others to God (1 Timothy 2:1)
- Thanking God for the things He has done, is doing, and will do (Ephesians 5:20)
- Listening to God (Psalm 46:10)
- Obeying God (Jeremiah 7:23)

As I mentioned earlier, there is a bountiful supply of individuals' prayers recorded throughout the Bible. Each prayer contains valid points to learn from. I encourage all believers to seek, find, and study all the prayers mentioned in the Bible. It will surely keep you busy and be a valuable study for you to gain much insight in how to rightly come before God's throne.

Among all the characters in the Bible, the best individual to learn about prayer from is our Lord Jesus Christ. One specific prayer that probably stands out above all others is in Luke 11. One day after Jesus was praying in a certain place, one of his disciples said to Him, *"Lord, teach us to pray."* Jesus acknowledged his request and responded to him and the other disciples, saying, *"When ye pray, say, Our Father which art in heaven, Hallowed be thy name. Thy kingdom come. Thy will be done, as in heaven, so in earth. Give us day by day our daily bread. And forgive us our sins; for we also forgive every one that is indebted to us. And lead us not into temptation; but deliver us from evil"* (Luke 11:2-4).

Jesus was not teaching what specific words to recite to God each day. Jesus was teaching something more valuable and personal. He was giving an example of a manner and discipline of thoughts that should cultivate an intimate dialogue with God. In brief words, Jesus gave an aid, an outline of how we are to pray. These words exhibit the fervency with which we are to engage in prayer with God: to confess sin, to petition our requests, to intercede on behalf of others, to worship God, to listen and obey Him. The Lord's example demonstrates many important truths about prayer. I would like to briefly mention only seven of those important truths that we must consider.

The first is seen in Luke 11:2 when Jesus said to His disciples, *"When ye pray."* Jesus started by first implying that if you are a disciple of Christ then you will pray; not that you perhaps might pray, but that you ought to be, and without doubt will be, engaged in fellowship and communication with God. Christ's assumption is correct because it is impossible to be a disciple of Jesus without interacting with God.

As a case in point, the scripture texts of Acts 6:4, Acts 12:5, Romans 12:12, Ephesians 6:18, and Philippians 1:4 all teach that we are to be in continual fellowship with God. Prayer needs to be a priority in our lives. It should be our first response to any question, concern, or blunder in life. Prayerfulness is to be part of our makeup as Christians, so much that its evidence is manifested through our lifestyles. Therefore, Jesus taught His disciples that as they go along in the daily nuances and responsibilities of life, they are to be in continuous communion, fellowship, and prayer with God.

Jesus then continued to explain how and what our prayers should engage us with so that we may continue this communion with God. Our prayers should engage our bond with God. We pray because we have a relationship with God. This is one reason Jesus begins His model prayer with the words, *"Our Father..."* By trusting in the Lord Jesus Christ, God is no longer solely our Judge, or the Creator; He is now our Father. Because God is our Father, Jesus explained in Luke 11:11-13 that *"If a son shall ask bread of any of you that is a father, will he give him a stone? or if he ask a fish, will he for a fish give him a serpent? Or if he shall ask an egg, will he offer him a scorpion? If ye then, being evil, know how to give good gifts unto your children: how much more shall your heavenly Father give the Holy Spirit to them that ask him?"* Likewise, we can continuously be in communion with our Father by prayer because we have a deep bond with Him. We can come to Him about anything and He will hear us. God is faithful and He is good and desires to commune with us.

Next Jesus said, *"Hallowed be thy name."* Whose name? God's name. Our next essence of being in continuous prayer with God is to worship God for who He is. He is the *I AM*, and the *I AM* is all-sufficient in all matters. God is to be worshipped. Jesus said in Matthew 4:10b, *"Thou shalt worship the Lord thy God, and him only shalt thou serve."* We are to engage our minds and hearts with God alone and nothing else. Some people ask, "How so?" How are you and I to constantly engage with God while we are occupied with the obligations and affairs of life? The answer: Look unto Jesus; He is the answer.

In the following words of the Lord's model prayer we find the key. Jesus said, *"Thy kingdom come."* Three simple words, yet powerful and important in significance. As we go about life's mundane tasks and responsibilities, we are to be in constant communion with God; this is worship. Worship causes us to allow God's kingdom to come into our lives by the simple act of being aware of His presence and understanding that God is the Owner. He has complete ownership of all that we have, all that we do, and all that we engage with in life belongs to God. There is nothing we can do without His knowledge. We cannot even take our next breath without His goodness and permission; God owns and gives even the air we breathe (Isaiah 42:5; Daniel 5:23). He owns it all, visible and invisible.

However, I am not talking about intellectually recognizing that God is in ownership. We all intellectually recognize owners of different estates in this world; but, with this intellectual knowledge we still have little to no understanding of the owners. Therefore, I am speaking of a more divine recognition and understanding of the Owner of all owners over all things, properties, and estates. I am speaking about having a heart-recognition of God. When we have a heart-recognition then we will engage in communion with God, so that we may come to a better relationship and personal understanding of Him. With a heart-recognition of God, we will choose to surrender, be sensitive, and submit to His official right over everything of ours: our thinking, choices, actions, habits, and lifestyles that should honor and glorify God. Jesus taught in Matthew 6:33 that we are to *"seek ye first the kingdom of God, and his righteousness."*

Jesus' prayer then continues with the words, *"Thy will be done."* This is Lordship. God wants not only to be our Savior—God also wants to be our Lord. Have you ever asked God, "What is *Thy* will today?" Have you ever told God, "I will do whatever *Thou* saith"?

Our communion with God through prayer should bring about a daily repentance within our hearts. It should move us to seek God's will, and then do it. Prayer is not bringing or pulling God to our will; prayer is the aligning of our will to the will of God. Prayer brings to light our selfish wants and ungodly desires. Then it breaks us so that our ambitions can be correctly aligned with God's will and desires. Prayer draws us to decrease so that Christ should increase (John 3:30).

Proverbs 3:5 tells us that prayer is our acknowledgment that we need direction. The simple truth is that we know nothing, and therefore prayer is our acknowledgment to God that He is the Director of our path. Ephesians 5:17 commands us, *"Wherefore be ye not unwise, but understanding what the will of the Lord is."* Do you understand God's will for you, *today*? Then submit to prayer.

Our prayer life should be a lifestyle in which we are joyfully seeking to know God's will and relinquish control of our own wills; it is showing to God that we desire to know and do His will. We have a great example of how we can do this from the life of our Lord. In John 12:27, the soul of Jesus was greatly troubled. However, He did not ask the Father to save Him; instead

Jesus accepted the Father's will and embraced it. Jesus submitted to the will of the Father and went on to the cross. His obedience in yielding to God the Father enabled Him to pray, *"not my will, but thine, be done"* (Luke 22:42).

Prayer helps us to learn to die to self. Prayer enabled Jesus to do what His human flesh did not desire; He endured the cross, despising the shame. Like Christ, we too by prayer can accept God's will, then yield our will to Him and embrace whatever He gives us.

James 4:7 instructs us, *"Submit yourselves therefore to God."* Mark 8:35 teaches how we can do this: *"whosoever will save his life shall lose it; but whosoever shall lose his life for my* [Christ's] *sake and the gospel's, the same shall save it."* The reason we engage in prayer is so that we can be close to God in fellowship and experience the best life that God wants for us, the most glorious and abundant life; and this only occurs when we reckon ourselves to be dead indeed to sin, but alive to God through Jesus Christ our Lord (Romans 6:11).

In the next part of the Lord's model prayer, He said, *"Give us day by day our daily bread"* (Luke 11:3). In essence, Jesus was teaching that our prayers are to assist us to recognize that God is sovereign. God is the Supreme One and He is supremely capable of orchestrating events to bring about His desired results. God is the One who produces the outcomes in life that are intended to be. Not us—God! For this reason, Jesus taught in Matthew 7:7: *"Ask, and it shall be given you; seek, and ye shall find; knock, and it shall be opened unto you."* We are to ask, not because God does not know what is needed, but because it puts us in our proper perspective. Prayer helps us not to have a false humility. Prayer helps us to recognize that we really do need to come before God, and ask Him for what we need.

When we pray we are acknowledging that we need God. Our petitions and requests are designed to help us understand that we absolutely do need to trust Him. We need to beseech God for help every day. Proverbs 3:5 says, *"Trust in the LORD with all thine heart; and lean not unto thine own understanding."* Why? Because our Father knows what things we need before we ask Him (Matthew 6:8). In Matthew 6:33 and Philippians 4:19 it is promised that our Heavenly Father—the Supreme and Sovereign One—will provide all that we need through Christ Jesus our Lord.

In the next part of the Lord's model prayer, Jesus said, *"forgive us our sins."* How wonderful is that! We can seek forgiveness and we can forgive others. Not only is God our Father, God also wants a friendship with us. God yearns to have a deep, intimate friendship, and this is made possible through forgiveness.

Jeremiah 23:23 demonstrates that God is not a God far away but He is very near. God is as near as in our mouths and in our hearts (Deuteronomy 30:14). Wow! What close intimacy! Such closeness should spur us to seek forgiveness, but not from Him alone, for we are already forgiven by the blood of Jesus. We are to seek forgiveness from others, too. Our prayer life should compel us not to have one unsettled issue between God and us, such as an ill heart toward another man.

First John 1:9 teaches that we are to confess our sins and seek cleansing. Oh, how we need constant confession and cleansing of poor attitudes and bad thoughts. If we have the slightest animosity or resentment toward another man, then our fellowship is hindered with our Friend—*God*. And we need to remove this obstruction as soon as possible!

Mark 11:26 teaches that we are to forgive those who have trespassed against us. First John 3:16 says, *"Hereby perceive we the love of God, because he laid down his life for us: and we ought to lay down our lives for the brethren."* John 15:13 asserts, *"Greater love hath no man than this, that a man lay down his life for his friends."* Therefore, may our prayers direct us to love our fellow man and not have an iota of sin between God and ourselves.

Next, Jesus spoke the words, *"Lead us not into temptation..."* These words teach us how we are to commune with God in prayer. Here, Jesus was showing that we need to recognize and submit to the Leader. We need leadership. We are not the leader. Jesus is the Leader, and He shows His leadership by His Word. We are to follow truth so we may be led by truth and lead others to truth. Jesus instructed us in John 8:31-32, *"[If] ye continue in my word, then are ye my disciples indeed; And ye shall know the truth, and the truth shall make you free."* Therefore, our prayer lives ought to provoke our minds to be in the Holy Bible as much as possible every single day, and to live by the truths of the Word. Our prayers ought to urge us to saturate ourselves with the Word of God.

Jesus is the Word (John 1:1, 14), and His Word is truth (John 17:17). Jesus lives inside of us by His Spirit (1 Corinthians 3:16), and the Bible says in John 16:13 that we are to be led by the Spirit of truth. Therefore, it is wise and essential to follow the guidance of the Holy Spirit. If we do not, major problems arise. For example, all too many people read their Bibles but they still are not led by truth. Even cults such as the Jehovah's Witnesses and the Mormons read and quote Bible verses (sometimes), but they are not following truth. They are not under the Leadership of the truth—God. Why is this? The reason is that they are not being led by the Spirit of truth. The Spirit always directs us to God the Son—Jesus—not to an individual, not to another book, not to an organization, not to a method, nor to anything but Jesus Christ alone.

The Holy Spirits guides us; but we can quench the Spirit when we do not act in obedience to what we are instructed to do. He certainly leads according to the truths and principles found inside the Holy Bible; but many believers quench God's Spirit because they do not obey His direction to read, study, or meditate on the scriptures. If one will not submit oneself to the Word, one will not submit oneself to the Spirit. We are not to grieve the Holy Spirit (Ephesians 4:30), but we are to be in submission to Him.

Submission to Holy Spirit leadership will always guide us in how to best bring glory to Christ. The Holy Spirit does not contradict the Word. The Holy Spirit is in communion and in agreement with the Word of truth. John 16:13 says, *"Howbeit when he, the Spirit of truth, is come, he will guide you into all truth: for he shall not speak of himself; but whatsoever he shall hear, that shall he speak: and he will shew you things to come."* The Holy Spirit always points us to the Word (John 15:26; 16:13) because He manifests to us the mind of Christ (Philippians 1:27; 4:2; 1 Corinthians 1:10), as the Word (which is the mind of Christ) always points us to Jesus—for Jesus is the Word (John 1:14). So in prayer, if we are in tune with the Holy Spirit, He will guide us toward what to pray for in accordance with God's holy Word.

Certainly, we can quench the Spirit, and in doing so we hinder God's influence in our lives. However, when a believer begins to intertwine his thoughts, time, and lifestyle with prayer, he discovers that his communion and fellowship with God is enriched, and he finds that he is no longer the one living but God's Spirit is living through him. Galatians 5:16 best explains it: *"This I say then, Walk in the Spirit, and ye shall not fulfil the lust of the flesh."*

Our flesh, our natural reasonings, and our common rationalizations will keep us away from communion with God. Nevertheless, when we are walking in the Spirit and engaged in communion with God by the tool of prayer, then the power of prayer will accomplish all these vital points that Jesus spoke about in His model prayer.

As we consider prayer in our own character, it would be wise for us to be like Daniel in Daniel 9:3. He set his face toward the Lord God. He was determined to be in communion with God, no matter the consequences. Like him, we should have a determined, faithful spirit of prayer. Then we can position ourselves and keep a blessed stance toward God with confidence all day long, no matter what good or bad occurs in our lives. Thus, we are given the glorious promise in Hebrews 4:16: *"Let us therefore come boldly unto the throne of grace, that we may obtain mercy, and find grace to help in time of need."*

It is my personal prayer that you may see and understand the necessity of a continual communion with God by prayer. Without it, neither you nor I will be able to abide with God and we will be found lacking with little to no fruit (John 15:1-8). As the disciples asked Jesus in Luke 11:1, let us also ask Jesus to teach us to pray, not how to pray, but TO PRAY, so that we may continually abide in wonderful fellowship and intimate communion with God. For these reasons should we always pray and not faint (Luke 18:1). Amen!

Chapter Ten

WHO ARE YOU SUBMITTING TO?

SURRENDER—according to the Noah Webster 1828 Dictionary—means to give in; to relinquish; to give up; to resign; to submit; to yield. This is what the dictionary paints as the picture of surrender. Normally, the word is seen in a negative context. For example, people in the criminal justice system have to "surrender in the name of the law" when they are in trouble. Or, in wars, one side surrenders to another. Surrender is a sign one has given up any hope for victory. Hence, to surrender is to yield or give up something to the authority or power of another, such as rights.

I have shown in the earlier chapters that we need to separate ourselves for the Lord so that we may live in a spirit of prayer. The next attribute a determined Christian needs to take upon himself is to be resolute in a spirit of surrender to God. Surrender, meaning to forsake sin and yield ourselves to Christ's righteousness.

Romans 6:16 asks a good question: *"Know ye not, that to whom ye yield yourselves servants to obey, his servants ye are to whom ye obey; whether of sin unto death, or of obedience unto righteousness?"* You and I are able to yield ourselves as servants for righteousness because of the love of Christ which is abundantly bestowed upon us. The scripture explains: *"For the love of Christ constraineth us"*; because Christ died for all, that we who live should not henceforth live for ourselves, but for Him who died and rose again for us (2 Corinthians 5:14-15). We know how to surrender and submit to God because we have this example: *"To wit, that God was in Christ, reconciling the world unto himself"* (2 Corinthians 5:19). God has given to us who are in

Christ Jesus the ministry of reconciliation; also, God has committed to us the word of reconciliation. Hence, we are ambassadors for Christ, as though God did beseech people by us (2 Corinthians 5:18-20).

The scriptures make this clear, saying, *"If any man be in Christ, he is a new creature: old things are passed away; behold, all things are become new"* (2 Corinthians 5:17). Therefore, we should walk in newness of life; and this can only come by total surrender to God: a complete yielding of our wants, desires, hopes, aspirations, and *all* to God. You will never walk as Christ walked until you yield and submit your all to God.

The day of your salvation was the beginning of your involvement in the glorious victory over the enemy. You chose to abandon the enemy's side and enlisted yourself as one of God's soldiers. Therefore, what kind of soldier are you choosing to be?

You will never launch into the deep with God or understand the precious concerns on God's heart if you do not relinquish yourself entirely to Christ and His mission. There is a spiritual battle, and if you are to be part of the conquest you must surrender yourself entirely to God for His service. We are commanded to *"endure hardness, as a good soldier of Jesus Christ"* (2 Timothy 2:3). If you are to be a good soldier then you must discipline yourself daily to yield to God. *"No man that warreth entangleth himself with the affairs of this life; that he may please him* [God] *who hath chosen him to be a soldier"* (2 Timothy 2:4).

Normally there are anxieties and worries that come along with surrendering to another, but not in surrender to God. The good news is that, as Christians, worry and anxiety are absent when we yield to God. Surrendering to God is absolutely positive, not negative. God's commandments are not grievous (1 John 5:3), they are liberating; they keep us in the boundaries of safety and protect us from sinful choices that cause harm and lead to death.

Surrender to God grants a believer the opportunity to enjoy God because He is our exceedingly great reward (Genesis 15:1). The believer who is enjoying God is the one who is living life more abundantly. If a Christian surrenders to God, he does not do so under forced subjugation by God. God does not force anyone to walk with Him. The true character and nature of God allows individuals to make their own decision to submit to Him.

As we seek to surrender our all to God, we seek to yield all our life's ownership; we are to relinquish control of all that we consider ours: not only our possessions, but also our time, ambition, choices, influences, friends, prestige, and self-entitlements, including "perceived rights" and the striving for selfish wants. When we surrender to God, we are simply acknowledging that what we "own" actually belongs to Him. In other words, a surrendered Christian realizes the truth that what he thinks is his actually belongs to God and not to him. Thankfully, God is so longsuffering and shows much mercy toward us, because we certainly on occasions find ourselves handling matters incorrectly.

God is the giver of all good things (James 1:17). We surrender because we understand that we are responsible to properly care for what God has given us. We are stewards of the time, property, resources, and life that God has given to us. A surrendered decision helps us to acknowledge that we need His intervention in the stewardship of matters He allows us to be involved in. We admit that God is ultimately in control of everything, including our present circumstances, whether good or bad, when we are surrendered to God. We let go of whatever has kept us away from wanting God's ways first by yielding to God. Surrendering to God helps us to let go of whatever has been holding us back from God's best.

God requests us to submit all to Him. This submission then allows us to experience a joyous love relationship with Him, as well as being used by Him for His pleasure and glory. Moreover, God has demonstrated how we should give all to Him by the example of the Lord Jesus Christ. *"For God so loved the world, that he gave his only begotten Son. Though he were a Son, yet learned he obedience by the things which he suffered"* (John 3:16; Hebrews 5:8).

God's love toward us constrains Him so much that Christ delightfully took on a body of flesh. The scriptures tell us, saying, *"He made himself of no reputation, and took upon him the form of a servant, and was made in the likeness of men: And being found in fashion as a man, he humbled himself, and became obedient unto death, even the* [sacrificial] *death of the cross"* (Philippians 2:7-8).

The scriptures also explain the amazing reason God became man. It says, *"For ye know the grace of our Lord Jesus Christ, that, though he was rich, yet for your sakes he became poor, that ye through his poverty might be rich"* (2 Corinthians 8:9). God, who was rich, became poor for our sakes—that is, poorer than any human has ever been, so poor that He occupied a manger (Luke 2:7)—so that one day we might occupy Heaven. He was so poor that He had nowhere to lay His head (Luke 9:58)—in order that you and I, who are among His favored ones, might rest our heads forever in His sacred bosom.

There is an intimation of the wonder of God in the eighth chapter of Proverbs. In this chapter we are taken back into the eternal counsels of God and are permitted to witness something of the relationship that existed between the Father and the Son before earth's foundations were laid: *"Then I was by him, as one brought up with him: and I was daily his delight"* (vs. 30). Further in the next verse, we read the words of Christ, spoken prophetically, or in anticipation, saying, *"...and my delights were with the sons of men."*

The verse says, *"My delights"*. Not only were we present in Christ's thoughts, not only did we stand before His mind in eternity past, but His heart was also concentrated on us; Christ's affections went out to us. We were His *"delights"* even then. We cannot truly comprehend this, how God delights to be with such sinful worms of the earth! Truly, the writings of the Prophet Isaiah, inspired by the Holy Spirit, were accurate in describing God's thoughts, saying, *"For my thoughts are not your thoughts...For as the heavens are higher than the earth, so are my thoughts than your thoughts"* (Isaiah 55:8-9).

Not all the mysteries of God are revealed and understood during this present dispensation. Right now we behold the glory of the Lord as if looking at it in a glass (2 Corinthians 3:18). The delight of God is glorious beyond comprehension when we try to take in the fact that God the Son stepped out of eternity into space and time on this tiny speck of dust called Earth. When Jesus took on flesh and walked upon this earth He took upon Him a glory of a more humble fashion than what He shared with the Father in eternity. We are given some insight into this in the Gospel of John. Just before Christ went to the cross He prayed to the Father, saying, *"And now, O Father, glorify thou me with thine own self with the glory which I had with thee before the world was"* (John 17:5).

Even more remarkable is Christ's comparison to that of a lion. Jesus is the Lion of Judah (Hosea 5:14). The amazing glory of God is that the Lion made Himself into a Lamb; nevertheless, He still is a Lion. Today, the Lion who has the power to execute His wrath upon sin presents Himself as God's gentle Lamb, reckoning the world to be alive to God through Jesus Christ our Lord. For the power of God is not best demonstrated by what He can do but is best demonstrated by what He can do yet does not by choice. Second Peter 3:9 makes known that the *"Lord...is longsuffering to us-ward, not willing that any should perish, but that all should come to repentance."*

Jesus Christ through His incarnation was made a little lower than the angels to suffer death so that He by the grace of God should taste death for every man (Hebrews 2:9). God became man, and in a body of flesh and blood He who knew no sin was made sin for us, *"that we might be made the righteousness of God in Him"* (2 Corinthians 5:21).

"Seeing then that we have a great high priest, that is passed into the heavens, Jesus the Son of God, let us hold fast our profession. For we have not

an high priest which cannot be touched with the feeling of our infirmities; but was in all points tempted like as we are, yet without sin" (Hebrews 4:14-15). Now this is the love of God! It is a wonderful love that passes all knowledge. Christ is our perfect example and by His willingness to lead by example gives us confidence and hope. Christ's love, our example, now constrains us, that we should walk in Him: *"rooted and built up in Him, and established in the faith"* (Colossians 2:6-7).

As we first had to place our trust in the Lord Jesus Christ for salvation, similarly, we are to daily place our reliance in Christ for sanctification. God daily invites believers to abandon worldly affections: the lust of the eyes, the lust of the flesh, and the pride of life; in other words, the lust of our senses, the lust for more stuff, and the desire for status. God beckons believers to renounce restless vain pursuits for more pleasure, popularity, and worldliness—things of the world. God daily bids believers to *"Set your affection on things above, not on things on the earth"* (Colossians 3:2). For if you are in Christ, then you must renounce your allegiance to the world altogether and transfer all your hope upon Christ alone.

So many Christians look around themselves and boast about how sanctified they are because they do not consume drugs, or drink alcohol, or engage in explicit sins such as extortion or adultery (Luke 18). They unwisely compare themselves with others, and because they seemingly appear better, they foolishly deceive themselves into believing they are godly and not worldly. May I remind you that some of the worst deceptions are not what can be seen but what we may not see? Our hearts are *"deceitful above all things and desperately wicked"* (Jeremiah 17:9). Jesus explained that from out of the heart *"proceed evil thoughts, murders, adulteries, fornications, thefts, false witness, blasphemies"* (Matthew 15:19). Worldliness is a sin before God, not people. Therefore it does not necessarily have to be detected by people, but it is always seen by God. Worldliness for the most part has crept into our lives without us even noticing it.

When is the last time you quietly humbled yourself before God and asked Him to show you if you are worldly? There are subtle forms of worldliness which, if not forsaken, gradually lure us into destruction and wreck our Christian testimony.

One of these is the dread of seeing other individuals' faces—this is a fundamental lack of love for people. If we do not love individuals, we surely will not become servants to them. The moment we forget that we are servants of the Lord and of people, we are in great moral peril. If we decide not to be someone's servant, then we are full of self-respect and conceit. This is not the heart of God.

Another subtle form of worldliness is the needless time a person can spend over some trifling hobby instead of *"redeeming the time,"* as the Bible commands us to do (Ephesians 5:16; Colossians 4:5). Our viewpoint has become friendly toward our sin and modernized it by giving it a name: we call it relaxation, but there may be still much worldliness in it. Nowhere in the Bible does God instruct us or give permission for us to relax. He does make it clear that we are to rest, but not to relax. Relaxation in general means to slacken, to abate in attention and possess an emptiness of mind. This is not good because it always leads to lasciviousness—a looseness or irregular indulgence of something in life. Lasciviousness is a work of the flesh (Galatians 5:19) and a sign of the last days, *"for men shall be lovers of pleasure more than lovers of God"* (2 Timothy 3:1,4). However, rest is to be in a state of quietness, peace, to be still, and a state of reconciliation and dependence in God (Matthew 11 and Hebrews 4:10), not an emptiness of mind, because the scriptures tell us, *"Thou* [God] *wilt keep him in perfect peace, whose mind is stayed on thee: because he trusteth in thee"* (Isaiah 26:3).

Here's another subtle form of worldliness that we all are guilty of: The ease with which we can listen to and talk about the world's news instead of giving the "good news" to lost men. We find it so easy to talk about any thing of this world, yet find it difficult to speak about the most important issue of the day—the gospel of our Lord Jesus Christ. We refuse to endure hardness as good soldiers of Jesus Christ. We forget that *"no man that warreth entangleth himself with the affairs of this life."* Why? So that as soldiers, we may please God, who has chosen us to be soldiers (2 Timothy 2:3-4). This world has certainly encumbered us.

A worldliness that not many Christians are concerned about is a lack of time in fellowship with God in His Word and prayer. We cheat ourselves in our preparation to fight the world by not daily spending ample amounts of time with God. We lie to ourselves and say that we do not have time for God in His Word, yet have a lust for unnecessary things such as television, surfing the internet, or wrongful eating habits. Instead, we should make weekly habits of fasting and meditating on the Word so that we may be prepared to face the world. But sadly, all too many of us walk right into the world every day stripped of our armor—all because of our own secret inner worldliness; and we wonder why we have no influence to lead people to Christ.

Ineffective are we in our preparations to contact those in the world to win them to Christ, because we yield ourselves to the opinions of others. Many

Christians are regulated by public opinion, and even religious opinion, rather than scriptural principle. Instead of being concerned with what man says, we should be concerned with *"thus saith the Lord."* Proverbs 29:25 warns, *"The fear of man bringeth a snare: but whoso putteth his trust in the LORD shall be safe."* Do you agree with men, or God? Do you seek to please men? If you still seek to please men, you would not be the servant of Christ (Galatians 1:10).

How rarely we count it a privilege to suffer shame for Christ's name. We forget that for Christ's sake we are given the esteemed privilege not only of believing in Him, but also of suffering for His sake (Philippians 1:29). For Christ pleased not Himself but, as it is written, our reproaches fell on Him (Romans 15:3). How great a privilege it should be for you and me to bear reproach for Christ's name at our jobs, schools, and before our community! However, fear broods over the church like some ancient curse. Fear for our living, fear of losing our jobs, fear of becoming unpopular, fear of each other. With this said, do your fears hinder you from being Christ's living and verbal witness? Do you withdraw yourself from being despised by your peers for Christ's sake?

Billions grope in darkness. Millions still have never once heard a clear presentation of the gospel. God is calling thousands if not millions of Christians to give up their comfortable lifestyles and go reach a lost and dying world for Christ. Sadly, many Christians sacrifice the best for the good. They do not want to suffer for Christ and help reach the forgotten. Many Christians have an incorrect expectation that they are to have happiness from earthly comforts rather than the contentment of obedience to Christ. They are fond of nice things and luxuries, and they are unwilling to forego them for the sake of sending the gospel to the lost. Many live as individuals whose ears are dull of hearing. Their own comforts have blinded their understanding and they are unaware that God has called them to arise and go shine His light in a dark place.

God graciously warns us in 1 John 2:15-17, saying, *"Love not the world, neither the things that are in the world. If any man love the world, the love of the Father is not in him. For all that is in the world, the lust of the flesh, and the lust of the eyes, and the pride of life, is not of the Father, but is of the world. And the world passeth away, and the lust thereof: but he that doeth the will of God abideth for ever."*

We are to deny ungodliness and worldly lusts. We should live soberly, righteously, and godly in this present generation. We are only able to do this by looking for that blessed hope—Jesus Christ. God gave Himself for us, that He might redeem us from all iniquity, worldliness, and purify for Himself a peculiar people, zealous for good works (Titus 2:11-14).

For that reason, God invites us to walk daily in faith with Him that we might enjoy Him. We are to anchor our hearts to the values and concerns on God's heart. This is what is meant by the *love of the Father*. Christians must determine to happily abandon their will over to Christ alone. In so doing, Christ can extend their love back to the Father and then back out to others. The practicality of walking with God occurs by choice each new day in giving love to the Father and out to people. To reiterate, Jesus not only wants to be our Savior, but our Lord too. Lordship is the need of the day.

LORDSHIP—the happy abandonment of oneself and surrender to God on a daily basis. This is our sanctification and it is the will of God (1 Thessalonians 4:3). We need to give our lives as a daily living sacrifice to God. God wants our bodies as well as our lives to be a living sacrifice before Him. We hear God's plea for us to do so in Romans 12:1-2. God wants us to sacrifice our hearts, thoughts, minds, and bodies, as well as our time, energy, possessions, friends, work, status, and everything else that is ours. This is only our reasonable service to God.

God does not want a dead sacrifice. There was a time in Old Testament history when God was appeased by a dead sacrifice. Under the former Jewish law, certain animals sacrificed to God would appease God's righteous anger, but only for a time. Then they would have to offer another sacrifice, repeating this ritual before God month after month, and year after year. Thankfully, this is no longer the case since God demonstrated His love by giving His only begotten Son as a living sacrifice on the cross; meanwhile, the veil of the temple was rent in twain from the top to the bottom (Mark 15:38). God tore down the partition that was obstructing us from living in His holy presence. Now we can come boldly unto the throne of grace, we may obtain mercy and find grace to help live and enjoy God's holy presence by the blood of Jesus Christ (Hebrews 10:19). Hallelujah!

God wants our bodies while we are alive. God wants our hearts, souls, and minds, as well as our strength and focus. If you will empty yourself before God and give your complete self to Jesus as a sacrifice before Him, then you will partake in an experience of God's most wonderful glory. Galatians 2:20 reveals that *"I am crucified with Christ: nevertheless I live; yet not I, but Christ liveth in me: and the life which I now live in the flesh I live by the faith of the Son of God, who loved me, and gave himself for me."*

The decision to sacrifice (abandon) ourselves (our wants, ambitions, etc.) is a daily opportunity to surrender to God. With each new day, we get to decide on a new surrendering to such a wonderful and worthy God. Yesterday is gone, tomorrow is not promised, and today is here. The good news is that when a Christian surrenders to God, then that Christian receives the privilege of experiencing Christ in a more abundant life.

If you hold on to your perceived "rights" and to what you think you own or should have, you might be happy for a short time. You might even have some temporary or momentary relief from stress or longing. Nevertheless, temporal satisfactions eventually perish because they exist only momentarily. They never endure.

There are people who spend an excessive amount of thought and work on advancing themselves in a social position. Then there are those who endeavor to step up their reputations before friends or the community. Others exert themselves to acquire more things. These people might attain what their hearts set out to gain, but they still find themselves in want. There is never a satisfaction in wanting.

On the other hand, when you submit to the Lord Jesus Christ, you find that the desires for unnecessary things or longings for self-gratification gradually abate. I like how the psalmist explained it. He wrote, *"The LORD is my shepherd; I shall not want"* (Psalm 23:1). Living in the presence of Christ vanquishes all desires of our flesh for what this world can offer because the LORD's goodness surpasses anything our souls could ever crave or require.

The LORD is none other than the Lord Jesus Christ, because Jesus said, *"I am the good shepherd: the good shepherd giveth his life for the sheep"* (John 10:11). And to His sheep He promises, *"Peace I leave with you, my peace I give unto you: not as the world giveth, give I unto you. Let not your heart be troubled, neither let it be afraid"* (John 14:27).

Is the LORD your shepherd? Shepherd, meaning Christ is the only One you trust, fear, and want. Trust, because you know He has the best intentions and decisions for you; fear, because His goodness leads you to forsake sin and avoid its deceitful allurements through its temptations of your eyes, emotions, or senses.

As a result, the same psalmist at another time in life could write, *"O fear the LORD, ye his saints: for there is no want to them that fear him"* (Psalm 34:9). There is no want of anything when your heart is yielded to Jesus. Christ's presence brings peace and true satisfaction. What do you need besides Jesus?

Look at the parable of the prodigal son in Luke 15. Jesus gave us a perfect example of a man who foolishly thought he needed more than what his father provided for him. He went up to his father and insisted, *"Father, give me the portion of goods that falleth to me"* (vs. 12). How incredible! This son had everything he needed to live, yet without gratitude he demanded, *"Give me."* It sounds like many Christians today. Many pray, ask, and beg God for this and for that and more of this and more of that. They have forgotten that God shall *"supply all your need...by Christ Jesus"* (Philippians 4:19). Notice, God said, *"need,"* singular, and not need**s**, plural.

This prodigal son's father gave him all that was rightly due to him. At one moment in time this young man had excess galore, which soon brought his ruin. Excess without the need for it will generally ruin most individuals, just as it did with this son. Most of us are not capable of being good stewards over a substantial measure of money, things, status, or influence. These good things can soon get the worst of our pride, which leads us to become selfish, and foolishly take what God created for others' benefit and exploit them for our own personal gain.

This is not good. Without the Lord's guidance, an overabundance of any good thing can destroy any one of us. Therefore, you ought to be careful what you ask from God. In His omniscience, He just might give it to you, thus allowing a reproach against you. Instead, we ought to pray like Agur the son of Jakeh, who requested of God: *"Two things have I required of thee* [God]; *deny me them not before I die: Remove far from me vanity and lies: give me neither poverty nor riches; feed me with food convenient for me: Lest I be full, and deny thee, and say, Who is the LORD? or lest I be poor, and steal, and take the name of my God in vain"* (Proverbs 30:7-9).

Finally, the prodigal son was miserable in his sin of greed and covetousness. He found his self-indulgence, personal ambitions, and selfish wants had led him astray to a lonely, destitute place. He missed the blessings of His father's company, friendship, and familiarity. At the end of himself, he longed to return to his father's presence.

When he returned home, wrapped up in shame and guilt, he discovered that his father had all along been longing for his fellowship. Thankfully, God our Father is always longing for us to come nearer to Him. So, whatever area of your life you need to yield to God, I encourage you to do so. You will discover that the Father's arms are opened wide for you to come closer to Him in communion and fellowship. Nonetheless, you have to let go of what you are holding onto and in its place embrace the Father. You will find satisfaction in His presence, you will not want, and you will be joyful that you escaped ruin from selfish ambitions.

Victory through Christ is within your grasp if you choose to submit to God whatever has a hold on you. Surrendered Christians discover a genuine peace and satisfaction that comes only by yielding to God. As the scriptures say, *"Blessed is the man that trusteth in the LORD, and whose hope the LORD is...For they shall not be ashamed that wait for me* [God]. *For the scripture saith, Whosoever believeth on him shall not be ashamed"* (Jeremiah 17:7; Isaiah 49:23; Romans 10:11).

Surrender is not involuntary; meaning, it is not some instinctive inevitable choice that comes from being helpless; it is necessary to be aware of God and to purposefully give up one's personal will and personal control to Him. Surrender is not a matter of admitting helplessness; it is just that in times of helplessness, surrendering to God becomes a last resort when there is no more strength and no more hope in oneself. Thank God! In those moments, surrender to God just seems like a more practical alternative than at other times. After all, commitment and trust are never easy for us prideful men to give, especially unconditionally to God.

The heart of spiritual experience is faith in God. We discover the reality of God by complete surrender to Him. Total surrender to God is the greatest expression of faith. Surrender must come with eyes open and clear intent. Complete surrender should not just come at moments in which we face overwhelming circumstances, but in the calm when it seems we are personally in complete control of our lives. Through surrender, our ego is revealed.

When we yield to God, we obey God. Then those around us are benefited in a mighty way. For example, if Adam in the garden of Eden had continued to obey God, it is possible that our world today would be gloriously different, and it would not be suffering the consequences of his disobedience. Nonetheless, that is not the world we live in. We dwell in a world of sin.

In this sinful world, we Christians need to obey and yield ourselves to God. When you surrender to God, you are benefited because you will be more focused on Christ and His will. You will gain more godly insight and understanding; therefore, you will be able to make better choices each day. You will be enabled with more might and courage to serve God as well.

When you live submissive to God, people are benefited and encouraged as well. Along with the benefits of surrender to God, your heart will be moved to make more opportunities to serve and share the gospel with individuals. People will be drawn in closer with a desire to know God because of the witness of a godly testimony. Likewise, more people just might call on the name of the Lord Jesus for salvation and devotion to God.

Undoubtedly, God's desire for you is far better than any momentary advantage or pleasure you can obtain, but you can only know that victory if you submit yourself, your desires, and your perceived "rights" to God. Then Christ will be glorified, honored, and pleased through your life for all the world to take notice.

It is a glorious thing when God can be pleased and Christ can be exalted in and through a person. Are you living a life submissive to Christ right now? If not, what is hindering you from surrendering and permitting Jesus to be absolute Lord of your thoughts, emotions, and body? What tangible or intangible thing[s] in your life have you not entirely given God total control over?

Now, with these questions and this reading, what will be your response to what God would have you to do?

Chapter Eleven

ARE YOU LIVING UNDER THE CONTROL OF GOD'S SPIRIT?

WHENEVER I READ THE BOOK OF ACTS I am fascinated and filled with enthusiasm at all the Lord did through our first brethren. These believers were filled with prayer, faith, charity, fervency, and certainly much hope. They yielded themselves wholly to God; thus, they were sensitive to His Holy Spirit, and submissive to Christ's commission. And God blessed them for their faithfulness.

In the midst of persecution and great trials, the first believers were inevitably scattered among many nations. They had to run for their lives! Nevertheless, everywhere they went they still preached the Word and exalted Christ. The results of their faithfulness were that *"The hand of the Lord was with them: and a great number believed, and turned unto the Lord"* (Acts 11:21).

God's providence saw fit for His Word to be unstoppable during all this turmoil and confusion. An unprecedented number of people were reached with the gospel of Jesus Christ: Jews, gentiles, friends, and even enemies of the cross of Christ heard how Christ died for our sins, and that He was buried and rose again the third day (1 Corinthians 15:3-4). Fascinatingly, God even convicted a great enemy of the cross and gave him a new heart. This enemy, Saul, who then became Paul, went on to become a fervent servant for the Lord.

Paul, an apostle of our Lord Jesus Christ, had great difficulty getting everyone to trust that he had been genuinely converted by the Lord's calling and made into an apostle of the Lord. It took much time for some to believe that he was the real deal. Acts 9:26-27 gives the account, saying, *"And when Saul was come to Jerusalem, he assayed to join himself to the disciples: but they were all afraid of him, and believed not that he was a disciple. But Barnabas took him, and brought him to the apostles, and declared unto them how he had seen the Lord in the way, and that he had spoken to him, and how he had preached boldly at Damascus in the name of Jesus."* Years later, Paul spoke concerning some who had forsaken him. In a letter to Timothy he wrote, *"This thou knowest, that all they which are in Asia be turned away from me; of whom are Phygellus and Hermogenes…For Demas hath forsaken me…Alexander the coppersmith did me much evil..for he hath greatly withstood our words. At my first answer no man stood with me, but all men forsook me: I pray God that it may not be laid to their charge"* (2 Timothy 1:15; 4:10, 14-16). Then Paul went on to explain about the grace and faithfulness of God's involvement in his life, saying, *"Notwithstanding the Lord stood with me, and strengthened me; that by me the preaching might be fully known, and that all the Gentiles might hear"* (2 Timothy 4:17). It is a marvelous encouragement to know that God will stand by you and me when everyone else might forsake us.

God did open a great and effectual door for Paul to preach the gospel; he bore the name of Jesus Christ before the gentiles, kings, and the children of Israel. Paul strove with tears to preach the gospel and strengthen the body of Christ in many nations (Acts 20:31; 18:23 as examples). He did not hesitate to declare to people all the counsel of God (Acts 20:27). It was his hope and yearning to bring the light of the gospel to as many races as possible. He delighted to preach Christ to people who had not yet been told the wondrous story, *"lest he should build upon another man's foundation"* (Romans 15:20 for example). And because of God's hand upon him, many nations, tongues, and tribes of people heard the gospel and were converted.

The apostle Paul ministered to people in the Lord's doctrine along with using common sense. His priority was obedience to God. He understood that God's thoughts are not our thoughts, neither are our ways God's ways (Isaiah 55:8). If common sense said for him to do one thing, but God guided him to another, he turned away from his ideas and chose to obey God. Paul would rather trust in the Lord than lean on his own understanding. Even though sometimes this caused him to be considered a fool, nevertheless, for the gospel's sake he persevered and God honored his obedience.

In Acts chapter 16 Paul, along with some other believers, had a desire to go and preach the gospel in Asia (today it is Asia Minor). They had been ministering in some cities nearby. His rational thinking said that they should go on ministering toward Asia, since it was in close proximity. Although it seemed a good idea at the time, they still sought God about the matter, and the Holy Ghost forbade them to go (verse 6).

Some time later, they had been ministering in the region of Mysia. Once again, at the close of their work in Mysia they endeavored to minister in another nearby location known as Bithynia. Again, the Holy Spirit would not give them permission (verse 7). So they deserted their intentions and submitted to the Holy Spirit's guidance.

After they pressed forward to where the Holy Spirit was leading, Paul was given insight as to where they were to go. Following God's leading, they went on their next destinations, preaching Christ.

This testimony depicts some aspects of God's character that are shown throughout the scriptures. God often allows dilemmas in His servants' lives. Predicaments are given by the Lord to help us stay focused on God's broader purpose. God is doing a great work, and many times we do not clearly recognize all that He is simultaneously orchestrating in many lives. God uses remarkable means to compel us to move forward in the direction of the work that He wants us to partake in.

God may instruct believers that we are simply to *go*. Oftentimes God does not provide details upfront concerning the work. He may simply command us to *go*. Whether or not we understand the whole scope of God's instruction, we should simply act upon His command and obey. After God sees believers' obedience in *going*, using their faith, then further along the Lord does supply believers with better clarity in understanding His instructions.

It is as if God patiently waits to see if we will forsake our own intentions, presumptions, and plans and choose to submit to His Spirit's guidance. God did this with Abram in Genesis chapter 12. He did this with Moses in Exodus chapter 4. And God did this with most if not all of his men such as Joshua (Joshua 1), David (1 Samuel 17), Hosea (Hosea 1), and Saul, later Paul (Acts 9). God just might teach you about faith in the same way.

God tests our faith to see if we will trust and obey Him. God tests us so that we can learn to patiently wait, and then learn to wait some more for His right and benevolent providential guidance. Our ways can lead to death, because, as the scripture says, *"there is a way that seemeth right unto a man, but the end thereof are the ways of death"* (Proverbs 16:25). God's ways lead to life. God's timing is always right and always best. Therefore, it is good for us to wait on the counsel of God. God's ways are set before us in order to lead us into life and good, not death and evil (Deuteronomy 30). Although the Lord might not always provide light through the shadows up ahead, He does provide His servants with light to our feet where we should step forward right now. For *"Thy word is a lamp unto my feet, and a light unto my path"* (Psalm 119:105).

Obedience always takes faith, because certainly we will not always understand God's reasons for leading us one way or another. No matter what, we can always trust that God's guidance is best. God's plans always seek to glorify Christ and to benefit others. God always has our best interests in mind.

Yes, we might come up with good methods or produce valid plans to reach people with the gospel; nevertheless, we still must seek the Lord for His guidance. We are to do as the Bible says, *"Trust in the LORD with all thine heart; and lean not unto thine own understanding. In all thy ways acknowledge him, and he shall direct thy paths"* (Proverbs 3:5-6). The end of this passage is a wonderful promise from God; but we must heed its instruction. If God gives us the green light, then we can follow through with our plans. But if God sees fit that we should not act upon a plan, then we should reject it and seek His counsel for how and where He would have us serve.

If a question as to duty comes up, whether something is of God or not, then some good questions to consider while waiting on God's providence: Am I living close to Christ? Am I seeking His guidance? Am I renouncing self in what I undertake to do for Him? If we can say yes to these questions, then we may safely go into any path where duty lies (Luke 17:10).

Many people read the testimony in Acts 16 and wonder why God would divert someone from going to preach Christ to a group of people. Certainly, Paul had good desire and the means to do it, so why not go? I do not know the specifics of God's reason; however, the scriptures tell us, *"O the depth of the riches both of the wisdom and knowledge of God! how unsearchable are his judgments, and his ways past finding out! For who hath known the mind of the Lord? or who hath been his counsellor?"* (Romans 11:33-34)

Perhaps God was intervening for their safety, or maybe God was waiting for a better time to send the gospel when more could hear and would believe. Whatever the reason, Acts 19:10 does make known that several years later, on account of more persecutions of the church of God *"all they which dwelt in Asia heard the word of the Lord Jesus, both Jews and Greeks."* How awesome is that! The Bible says *"ALL"* in Asia ultimately heard the gospel!

Nevertheless, God is not on trial, so the issue of "why" should not be the focus. The important matter is confidence in the Lord. God's sovereignty knows best. Contrary to what you or I may perceive, the highlight of Paul and his team's testimony was their obedience. Their testimony should stir our faith to act in obedience toward God as well. We should continue steadfast in an unwavering faith to go proclaim Christ and get involved in people's lives. Furthermore, their testimony is comforting because it demonstrates that we really can trust and obey God.

We must learn to yield our intentions and desires at the altar of God; then we can appropriately walk humbly with God and thus become more receptive to the Spirit's guidance. Then we will witness God moving more mountains of unbelief for Christ's glory.

The Holy Spirit affirms God's counsel in the Holy Bible. If we will become more in tune to His guidance and proceed to where He would have us serve then we will be better positioned to bring more glory to Christ. We are the servants; God is the Commander-In-Chief. God is on a mission, and if we yield and submit to His guidance, then Christ will be appropriately glorified and honored through us. If He cannot control us, then how can He lead us into His greater tasks?

Although Paul was prevented from going into Asia Minor for a short time, God eventually did take the message of Christ to this people, but *in His time*. We know this not only because the Bible tells us in Acts 19:10, but also because history provides a vivid account that the gospel did spread throughout these areas—today's Turkey and the surrounding regions. History records that, as the centuries passed, sadly, other religions and factions came in. During this era, Biblical Christianity was still present in Turkey, but only existed underground in minority ethnic groups. The unbiblical "Christianity" that was shown before the Turkish people was cloaked by the Roman papacy with many pagan traditions, rules and customs. It was not a demonstration of the authentic Christ and the Holy Bible. Then, in the 1600s, Muhammadanism (Islam) conquered those regions and enslaved the people with greater spiritual darkness. Once again, many Christians were dispersed to other nations, and all Christians who were found in Asia Minor were killed.

And Turkey for the last nine-hundred years has had no historical evidence of a Turkish Church, as defined by the Holy Scriptures: genuine Christianity rooted in Christ.

This tragic example in history is a lesson for us to learn from. When Christianity becomes a culture or a routine of life, a belief of dos and don'ts, then the penetrating power of the gospel to bring light into people's spiritually dark lives becomes weak. When comfort and tradition are more valued than proclamation and regeneration, Christianity operates only as another religion. And what hope is that? None whatsoever!

However, there is good news! Within the last two decades, the Islamic nation of Turkey has seen a wonderful movement in the hearts of their people that had not been seen for many centuries. Missionaries in Turkey today are reporting that God is adding to His church, daily, and an unprecedented number of Muslims are finding Christ as their Savior and Lord. The light of the gospel is shining in that dark land because believers in Christ have decided to follow God's guidance and to go and preach Christ, despite the ramifications.

How is this possible? It is because of the work of God's Holy Spirit. The Holy Spirit guides us believers to do courageous acts of love beyond our abilities. Sometimes the Holy Spirit moves us into circumstances for Christ's sake, because when we are weak then Christ's strength can be more manifested (2 Corinthians 12:10). This is the reason we need to submit to what the Holy Spirit guides us to do. In due time, the Spirit's guidance will bring us into an adventure of sacrificial service to people beyond our ways and means. This is where we learn the strength of God, for we are not strengthened until we know our weakness and how frail we really are (Hebrews 11:34).

The strength of Christianity only holds power and channels an abundant life toward people when it is revealed through love. Love is revealed by sacrifice: A sacrifice of your desires, your will, your hopes, and your dreams. The apostle Paul could have disobeyed the Holy Spirit's guidance and gone on over to Asia. But all the great joy in of seeing people's lives changed by His omnipotence would have come to a complete halt; he would have been laboring through his own strength, ideas, and methods.

We do not serve God and see Him bring about great results without first emptying ourselves before God: a surrendering of our self-pity, personal aspirations, dreams, abilities, talents, and gifts to Him must occur before anything else. An emptying of ourselves at the altar of Calvary's cross always brings about an influential service with God, and serving with God always brings about an experience of Christ and living life more abundantly.

Thus, a determined servant of God must possess an attitude that constantly seeks the guidance and power of the Holy Spirit. God is looking to live through us in order to exhibit His power through our weaknesses. A believer who wants to know the influence and power of the Almighty God must be submissive to His Spirit. This type of Christian is the one who permits himself to be controlled and influenced by the Holy Spirit rather than by his aspirations, ideals, philosophy, or education.

I like how the old-time preacher Bob Jones Sr. summed up our daily need to be yielded to the Holy Spirit. He said, "There is always something to do with God...The great trouble is that you have not really given yourself up to be led by the Spirit. You want your way, your plans, and your purposes to be fulfilled. You cannot have your way if God has His way. You must let your way be lost in God's way." If you do as he plainly spoke, then you will find yourself walking with God in His way doing good works that move others toward God and bring honor to Christ. The scriptures tell us, *"For they that are after the flesh do mind the things of the flesh; but they that are after the Spirit the things of the Spirit. For to be carnally minded is death; but to be spiritually minded is life and peace. Because the carnal mind is enmity against God: for it is not subject to the law of God, neither indeed can be. So then they that are in the flesh cannot please God"* (Romans 8:5-8).

There is a difference between living under your own influence and living under the influence of the Holy Spirit. The believer who is under his own influence does not have a godly and genuine care for the things of the Lord. Although he might be among the brethren in church, or he might even talk about God occasionally, he finds his mind more often thinking about the things of the world than the things of God. For example, he might physically be in a church service, but his mind is elsewhere. Or he might be hanging out with some good Christian brethren, but his mind is privately craving to be with another crowd pleasing the passions of his flesh.

On the contrary, the believer who is under the influence of the Holy Spirit genuinely cares for the things of the Lord. Though he may be living in this body of flesh, he is circumspect in valuing the things of God. He seeks to please his holy God. He understands the importance of being with the brethren and therefore involves himself as much as possible to be near them and join in opportunities to minister to others and honor Christ.

Christ is to be admired and given the preeminence. No one else! Not even the Holy Spirit is to be revered higher than the Lord Jesus Christ. It is the Holy Spirit's nature never to draw attention toward Himself, but only to Christ (John 15:26).

By principle, the Holy Spirit never manifests Himself to people in physical bodily form. Such an act would demand an unprecedented exceptional occasion to honor the Lord Jesus Christ to the highest magnitude. And, my friend, this occurred only once in history while Jesus walked this earth (Luke 3:21-22).

In this one great occasion, the Holy Spirit manifested Himself in physical bodily form at the baptism of Jesus Christ. The Holy Spirit's physical presence, along with God the Father's voice, declared Jesus to have all the honor and glory of God before man, and confirmed before mankind the perfect union God the Father and God the Son and God the Spirit have eternally coenjoyed. The Holy Spirit's visible presence signified an affirmation to the world that this Man being baptized, Jesus of Nazareth, was indeed God the Son manifested in the flesh, who came into the world to seek and to save lost sinners. Therefore, believers can rest assured knowing that this Jesus is the Person chosen by God to be the slain Lamb before the foundation of the world.

The Holy Trinity of God has always been under attack by deceptive teachers, *"wolves in sheep's clothing"*, who proselyte with their erroneous teachings. In particular, some misleading teachers have come along and tried to undervalue the Holy Spirit. They lie and teach that the Holy Ghost is not a separate Person coequal with God the Father and God the Son. Rather, they teach that the Holy Ghost is merely a force or power of God. They dismiss the Holy Trinity of God. They ignore the hundreds of verses that attest to the trinity of God. Led by malevolent spirits they deceive unlearned students of the Bible and teach fake doctrine, using verses such as Romans 8:16 and 26 out of context to erect a fallacy, disregarding the entire contextual meaning of the scriptures. We must remember that a text without a context is only a pretext; and a pretext causes foolish beliefs and opens room for great errors and factions.

Romans 8:16 declares, *"The Spirit itself beareth witness with our spirit, that we are the children of God."* Romans 8:26 also says, *"Likewise the Spirit also helpeth our infirmities: for we know not what we should pray for as we ought: but the Spirit itself maketh intercession for us with groanings which cannot be uttered."*

These verses left to themselves do sound as if the Holy Spirit might be an *"it"* and not a Person. However, if one looks at the whole context of this chapter, one would understand the opposite. It is clearly evident in this chapter that God is expressly explaining the Holy Spirit's part in this world; specifically, His role among Christians. In the context of this chapter, the word *"Spirit"* is used nineteen times. Each occasion refers to the workings of the Holy Spirit, showing the evidence that Christians belong to Christ, and demonstrating how God's Spirit intercedes to help believers in their walk on this sinful world. Therefore, the word *"itself"* is referring to the Holy Spirit, as we would use the same pronoun regarding an unborn baby, but nevertheless still a person. It cannot mean that the Holy Spirit is an *it*, meaning that He is some impersonal, nonliving energy force with whom we may not have a relationship. This cannot be, because Jesus declared that the Spirit is indeed a Person. Several times Jesus mentioned the Spirit as "He." For example, at our Lord's inaugural speech, Jesus said, *"The Spirit of the Lord is upon me, because **he** hath anointed me to preach the gospel...**he** hath sent me..."* (Luke

4:18) Did you catch the use of he?

On other occasions Jesus referred to the Holy Ghost as *"He"* and *"Him."* This is clearly observed in John chapter 14 when Jesus said, *"And I will pray the Father, and he shall give you another <u>Comforter</u>, that **he** may abide with you for ever; Even the <u>Spirit of truth</u>; whom the world cannot receive, because it seeth **him** not, neither knoweth **him**: but ye know **him**; for **he** dwelleth with you, and shall be in you....But the <u>Comforter</u>, which is the <u>Holy Ghost</u>, whom the Father will send in my name, **he** shall teach you all things, and bring all things to your remembrance, whatsoever I have said unto you"* (John 14:16-17, 26).

In a couple other discourses of Jesus, the Gospel of John records Christ confirming the Holy Spirit to be a Person, saying, *"But when the <u>Comforter</u> is come, whom I will send unto you from the Father, even the <u>Spirit of truth</u>, which proceedeth from the Father, **he** shall testify of me"* (John 15:26), and also *"Howbeit when **he**, the <u>Spirit of truth</u>, is come, **he** will guide you into all truth: for **he** shall not speak of **himself**; but whatsoever **he** shall hear, that shall **he** speak: and **he** will shew you things to come"* (John 16:13).

It is clearly evident that Jesus without a doubt taught that the Holy Spirit is not some force, energy, or merely a power of God, but that the Holy Spirit indeed is a Person. The Holy Spirit is indeed the third Person of the triune God.

Therefore, the word *"itself"* in Romans chapter 8 is written to refer to the manifestations of the Spirit in His dealings among believers. The Holy Spirit dwells within each genuine believer. Each believer is given an awareness of His presence; the Spirit raises within our spirits sentiments answering to the filial relation already established between us and God. The manifestation of His inner dwelling within each believer is an affirmation that we are enabled to confidently express outwardly what has taken place inwardly.

God did the impossible! He, being an infinite God, made Himself finite for us to behold; infinite Spirit was made eternal flesh! (We simply can never completely comprehend an infinite God, even though He has manifested Himself in finite flesh.) When the infinite God the Son came and took on a prepared body of flesh, He did not bind His infiniteness to be pigeonholed by any of our preconceived notions or conceptions of what and who God is. The *I AM* showed Himself to us.

Similarly, God has done the impossible again! In this age of grace, God has revealed Himself to man by putting Himself into each one of us believers. Although He does not manifest Himself in bodily form, we still get to behold and know Him. The infinite God the Holy Ghost makes Himself known to us by manifesting His presence and influence, by working in us to will and to do of His good pleasure. His manifestations are the *"it"* in Romans chapter 8.

For example, we can recognize the Holy Ghost within us by His fruit of love, joy, peace, longsuffering, gentleness, goodness, faith, meekness, and temperance. It is these attributes that demonstrate that the Holy Spirit is alive, personal, and presently at work in and through us.

We know the Holy Spirit is a Person because He possesses a capacity to think. The Holy Spirit has a mind of His own. Romans 8:27 says, *"And he that searcheth the hearts knoweth what is the mind of the Spirit, because he maketh intercession for the saints according to the will of God."* Like God the Father and God the Son, the Holy Spirit has a mind; meaning, He has intention and purpose. The Holy Spirit is inclined to act in accordance with the will and Word of God. The Holy Spirit is a Person, able to will and desire in harmony with God. Thus, the Holy Spirit is able to make intercession for us that we might be consumed with a desire to esteem Christ and labor with Him to draw men to Christ; His thoughts are in perfect unison with God the Father and God the Son.

The Holy Spirit desires for believers to be in good communion with Him. As the third Person of the trinity, His ministry to us is guidance, teaching, recalling our memory, comforting, convicting, correcting and above all controlling our being through His filling. Through His ministry He influences and guides people closer to God the Father through God the Son. The Holy Spirit is coequal to God the Son—the living Word—and God the Father (Matthew 28:19; Romans 1:20). First John 5:7 explains that *"there are three that bear record in heaven, the Father, the Word, and the Holy Ghost: and these three are one."* The Holy Spirit is the Comforter and He guides believers into all truth, teaching us all things and bringing to our remembrance the words of Christ. Jesus, again referring to the Holy Spirit as a Person, said, *"for he shall not speak of himself; but whatsoever he shall hear, that shall he speak,"* such as reproving, correcting, instructing, guiding and assisting Christians in the sanctified life (John 14:26; 16:13).

The Bible teaches that while Jesus walked upon this earth He was filled and led by the Holy Ghost (Luke 4:1). Jesus was dependent on the Holy Spirit to guide Him to bring glory to the Father (Luke 4:18). So think about this: If the holy Son of God was dependent on and anointed with the Holy Spirit, surely you and I need the influential power of the same Spirit, too. Why? Because the Bible expressly states in Acts 1:8, *"Ye shall receive power, after that the Holy Ghost is come upon you: and ye shall be witnesses unto me both in Jerusalem, and in all Judea, and in Samaria, and unto the uttermost part of the earth.* " We are incapable of carrying out God's mission without the guidance and strength of the Holy Spirit. Are you living daily dependent on the Holy Spirit?

There are many points of interest in that verse, Acts 1:8. Three of them concern the amazing transformation that occurs within a new believer in Christ. First, the Holy Spirit immediately and simultaneously makes His abode inside a believer. Second, a new believer receives the Holy Spirit for the purpose of receiving His influential power. (Notice that the power is distinguished from the Holy Spirit and the power is a direct manifestation in a believer because of the Spirit's inner dwelling in the believer: In other words, the Holy Spirit is a Person and not a force of God.) Third, the Holy Spirit's power is given to a new believer to not just be an active witness for Jesus Christ, but a witness who is empowered to persuade people to trust the truth.

The Holy Spirit makes His habitation personally inside the temporal bodies of saved sinners who believe in Christ for salvation. It is inside our bodies of clay that the Holy Spirit reveals Himself. Not only does He manifest His attributes, but His gentle voice also whispers the words of Christ's love and God's conviction: reproving us of sin, righteousness, and judgment. He leads the children of God in the paths of righteousness for Christ's name's sake.

Acts 1:8 points out there is an exceedingly great work that takes place in a new believer's life—he shall be a witness for Christ. It does not teach that he shall first go learn the Bible and then become a witness. Nor does it teach that he had better get to understand God first and then witness. No, the scripture teaches something more profound than knowledge. It conveys the first duty of Christ's Great Commission—*Go,* go get involved in people's lives and *proclaim* the gospel.

I am afraid that all too often, Christians skip this important point. Many Christians tell new believers the truth that God now lives inside them, but fail to explain what this really means. All too often they indoctrinate new believers upfront with a bunch of rules and traditions. Many Christians immediately instruct about the importance of church, and the importance of doing this and that. They have it all wrong. Christianity is not a bunch of rules, customs, and traditions; it is a love-relationship with God. Certainly, participating in a Bible-believing church, learning, and applying other essential Bible doctrine is important; however, the major of all fundamentals a brand new Christian needs to learn and understand is that God, who now lives within him, is within him for the purpose of engaging a healthy, pure relationship with Him. It is imperative to have a vital, personal, alive, active, growing, dynamic, real relationship with the third Person of the Godhead, the Holy Spirit.

One of the immediate benefits of starting a relationship with God is that the Holy Spirit's presence empowers a believer with the ability to persuasively tell others about his profound love for Christ. Any Christian, whether he has known Jesus for ten years, one month, or one minute, is empowered by the Holy Spirit to be a servant and witness of God. This is the reason we should fervently exhort newborn babes in Christ to witness to others about their newfound relationship with the Savior. They are now ambassadors for Christ, and have been given the authority to represent the Kingdom of God; they are now empowered to plead with mankind to be reconciled to God (2 Corinthians 5:20).

The first way they can witness is by sharing their testimony. Second, they can positively speak on behalf of Jesus Christ and proclaim what He can and does do: He saves and cleanses people from sin! Then the process of getting to know Jesus will develop naturally in a new believer's life. We can certainly get to know Jesus by the Holy Bible, but we can also get to know Him more through our experiences of working with Him in evangelism and discipleship.

In John chapter 1, a man named Andrew got saved. He recognized and believed that Jesus is the Messiah. He then immediately went to find his brother Peter and led him to Christ. Peter got saved! Then, later that day, a man named Philip got saved (verse 43). The very first thing Philip did, shown in verse 45, was to go over and witness to his friend Nathaniel. Though none of them had any background in formal scriptural classes or soulwinning classes, they got up and went to their friends and showed themselves as witnesses for Christ. The Spirit of Christ influenced them so much that they simply reached out to their loved ones and confidently spoke the simplicity of the gospel they knew: that each one had found Him of whom Moses spoke in the law—the Lord and Savior JESUS. They knew little about Jesus, yet they trusted Him as the Lord and Savior of the world, and with that profound faith they were compelled immediately to go share their God with loved ones.

Thank God there was no one around telling them to first take soulwinning classes, then to go witness. This probably would have hampered their faith and they would have missed out on seeing loved ones get saved as soon as they did. Please note that I am not against doctrinal classes. I am simply making the point that we need to make sure that we do not emphasize schooling above obedience to God's Word: *"ye shall be witnesses"* (Acts 1:8). Remember, *"to obey is better than sacrifice,"* and schooling, as great as it is, still is a sacrifice, while witnessing is obedience.

As we consider these men's testimonies in light of Acts 1:8, it seems that each man had his attention correctly fixed on God. These men were not focused on who was around them or what the world thought about them. Neither were they concerned about what they did not know. Instead, they were alert about their loved ones' need for the Savior and therefore made known to them their need.

These passages should greatly inspire us to seek God and be sensitive to His Holy Spirit. We need a daily influence of God's Spirit so that we can mortify the deeds of our flesh and yield fruit unto righteousness (Romans 8). Consider these words from Galatians 5: *"This I say then, Walk in the Spirit, and ye shall not fulfil the lust of the flesh...Be led of the Spirit"* and *"If we live in the Spirit, let us also walk in the Spirit."*

One of the Holy Spirit's principal duties is to guide us into good works and supply us with the courage to witness for Christ. The writer of Psalm 51 understood that the only way he was going to be effective in bringing souls to God was first to be filled with the influence of God's Spirit. Therefore, the psalmist cried out to God, saying, *"...uphold me with thy free spirit. Then will I teach transgressors thy ways; and sinners shall be converted unto thee"* (Psalm 51:13).

The more we are influenced and controlled by the Spirit, the more alert we can be in perceiving His guidance as to whom we should serve the gospel; perhaps as the prophet Isaiah expressed it, saying, *"And thine ears shall hear a word behind thee, saying, This is the way, walk ye in it, when ye turn to the right hand, and when ye turn to the left"* (Isaiah 30:21). The Holy Spirit yearns for us to seek God and to be led by His gentle voice. He speaks, and we should listen. He guides, and we should follow. He instructs, and we should obey.

When we are led by the Holy Spirit, God is pleased to pour His wisdom into us and extend His power through us. Then more souls can be given the opportunity to hear the gospel from our mouths. There is no better way to glorify Jesus Christ than to bring salvation to those individuals for whom Jesus poured Himself out on the cross of Calvary. When we are attentive to the Spirit of God then we can teach and persuade transgressors to trust God's ways, and sinners will be converted. The Spirit's influence will lead us to the right individuals at the correct time to share the gospel.

We can do nothing without the power of the Holy Ghost. We lack the motivation; we lack the attitude; and we lack the strength. It is only by God's anointing upon Spirit-influenced individuals that anything can be accomplished for the kingdom of God in this world.

It is true that we can labor by our own reasonings and still speak God's Word to people. I even agree that perhaps someone can be saved that way.

This is only possible because God always honors His Word. In Isaiah 55:11 God declares, *"So shall my word be that goeth forth out of my mouth: it shall not return unto me void, but it shall accomplish that which I please, and it shall prosper in the thing whereto I sent it."* God may not be pleased with the instrument that His Word is coming out of, but His Word is holy and powerful, and no matter by what or whom it is spoken God always will honor His Word. God used a donkey (Numbers 22). God used babes (Matthew 21:15-16). God is not opposed to using rocks (Luke 19:40), and He certainly is capable of using even a heathen or ungodly man's mouth to bring forth His Word.

This is why I am not opposed to gospel tract distribution. Some people have been saved simply by reading a gospel tract. They have read God's scriptures on a piece of paper with no human involvement, and the Holy Spirit convicted and convinced the person by the power of the written Word. God honored His Word, and people have been saved.

God's Word is faithful and true. It can be counted on. God reveals to us in Psalm 138:2: "[F]or thou (God) *hast magnified thy word above all thy name."* This verse makes it clear that God magnificently honors His Word. Of all the visible and invisible matter that is in creation, God has chosen to exalt His Word above everything else, including His own name. God magnifies and honors His Word because it is life (John 6:63), it is perfect (Psalm 19:7), it is eternal (Matthew 24:35), it is pure (Psalm 19:8), it is complete (Revelation 22:18-19), it is living (Hebrews 4:12), it is powerful (John 8:32), and it is transformational (Romans 12:1-2). Even if it comes out of an unholy sinner or a lackadaisical Christian, or a donkey's mouth, or off a piece of paper, God's Word tells us all we need to know. It is important to God and it ought to be exceedingly important to us.

Amazingly, God invites you and me to be used by Him along with His Word. He has given us the Spirit of His Word; and the Spirit of God seeks to interact with us each day. Likewise, our hearts need to be yielded and sensitive to the Spirit's voice. If we seek His guidance and submit in obedience to His leading, then we may enjoy the presence of God as He works to accomplish His glorious plan through us.

If we are reluctant or our attitudes are not right, thankfully, God manifests grace toward us. God has a plan and He will accomplish it. It is true that God will not make you go against your will; but He may very well make you willing to go, just as He demonstrated in Jonah's life. No matter what, God and His plan will be honored.

During Israel's second wave of captivity under Babylon, Ezekiel was called to preach God's Word and reprove Israel of their sins. Ezekiel was not particularly fond of his divine orders. In fact, the scriptures record that he had a bitter attitude (Ezekiel 3:14). Nevertheless, he yielded to God's Spirit and still obeyed God's directive, even *in the heat of his spirit*. God extended grace toward him, and the hand of the LORD stayed strong upon him, not only to compel him in his work, but to fit him for it, to carry him through it, and to fortify him against the difficulties he would meet. Ezekiel experienced this, finishing the course before him. God and His plan were honored among the people, all because a yielded Ezekiel chose to apply himself to obedience.

Submission and obedience to the Holy Spirit's direction can bring about a mighty, unstoppable charge that God enjoys accomplishing through Christians before the world! Obedience does not necessarily mean a smooth-sailing course of life; on the contrary, it normally means a walk with God in tribulations, difficulties, and trials. *"Yea, and all that will live godly in Christ Jesus shall suffer persecution"* (2 Timothy 3:12). Nevertheless, obedient Christians can rest in knowing that the providence of God will use them to bring the sheaves of God into His storehouse. God's grace and mercy will always be available to them wherever He may send them. More can be accomplished for eternity in one moment through a man under the power of the Holy Spirit, than in a million hours of laboring in the flesh. A man who occasionally half-heartedly serves God only stumbles upon a blessing; but a man who yields to God's Spirit in obedience gains many blessings.

This great work has some warnings one must heed. The Holy Spirit's filling is not for some disorderly, emotional, or fanatical display. The Holy Spirit fills an individual so that he can be empowered to humbly walk and labor with God to reach lost souls by the proclamation of the gospel of Christ in this darkened world. Second Corinthians 3:17 says, *"Now the Lord is that Spirit: and where the Spirit of the Lord is, there is liberty."* His influence gives us the liberty, confidence, boldness, and peace of mind to reach out to people with the saving and transforming gospel of Jesus Christ.

In addition, the Holy Spirit's influence is not poured out for a prideful show of spiritual gifts before people, but rather, as mentioned, it is for the powerful exhortation of sinners in direct service to God. Thus, a determined servant of God needs to consistently yield to the Holy Spirit and His instructions. Sometimes He will tell us to do something; at other times, He will warn us to not do or say something. He does all this to exalt and glorify Jesus Christ, to benefit us, and to bring people into the saving knowledge of grace. The Holy Spirit seeks to keep us meek and humble so that we may best honor Christ. Christ said, *"he* [the Holy Spirit] *shall testify of me"* and *"he shall teach you all things, and bring all things to your remembrance, whatsoever I have said unto you"* (John 15:26; 14:26).

I can remember one evening when I was talking about the gospel with a young man. As I was showing him a particular verse from the book of Romans, I heard the Holy Spirit gently tell me to take the young man to another reference in the book of Hebrews. I praise God that I obeyed the Holy Spirit's voice. Immediately after we read the text in Hebrews, his eyes lit up. That verse in Hebrews turned out to be the exact words his heart needed to hear at that moment. It really gave him insight into what he had been doubting, and soon afterward I had the privilege of leading that young man to call upon Jesus for salvation. HALLELUJAH!

I share this experience with you to demonstrate the point that God is working in the lives of people around us before we ever meet them. Jesus pronounced this truth in John 5:17 when He said that His Father has been working, and now, He Himself has been working too. God knows exactly what each individual needs to hear for today, and if we are sensitive to the Holy Spirit's voice, we can be guided to say the exact word of edification that individuals need to hear at any given moment. Yielding to God's Spirit can give us the results God promised in Isaiah 50:4: the tongue of the wise used to speak a word in season to an individual in need.

What a joy it is to experience God enlightening and encouraging someone's heart when we speak the exact word he or she needs to hear! It is an unfathomable joy and encouragement to our faith when we see Christ do a work through us that the Holy Spirit guided us to do. It just makes you want to yield more to Him and listen more attentively so that you will be more influenced by Him in the lives of people.

Now, what must you do to become more aware of and attentive to the influence of God's Holy Spirit?

Chapter Twelve

WHAT ARE YOU DOING WITH GOD'S WORD?

HERE'S A RIDDLE FOR YOU—What is magnified higher than the name of Jesus Christ, is incorruptible, and can be summarized in one word?

Any guess?

How about another clue? It also is as honey, fire, a sword, water, bread, gold, and a hammer.

What's your guess?

Well, if you said, "God," then I am sorry but your answer is wrong.

The correct response should have been the Bible—God's Word—the Holy Bible. Psalm 138:2 expressly tells us that God magnifies His Word higher than the mighty and honorable name Jesus Christ—which, by the way, all shall one day confess and bow before. The Word of God is certainly incorruptible (1 Peter 1:23); and, what is more amazing, it has a theme threaded throughout all of its pages. The Holy Bible is written to reveal and make known the one Man—Jesus, the Son of God. The Holy Bible is Jesus Christ in print.

John 20:31 expressly says, *"But these* [the words of the Bible] *are written, that ye might believe that Jesus is the Christ, the Son of God; and that believing ye might have life through his name."* Jesus affirmed this, saying that the scriptures are they which testify of Him (John 5:39).

Given that the incorruptible, infallible Holy Bible is magnified higher than God's own name and is about God Himself, there is a great personal need for us to be inside this great valuable resource. The Holy Bible *is* the revelation of God. Therefore, a Christian who desires to know God and is determined to

135

experience life more abundantly with Christ must possess a thirst for God and a hunger for His Word. He must saturate himself with the Word of God. What you do with the Bible determines what God will do with you.

Jesus stated, *"It is written, Man shall not live by bread alone, but by every word that proceedeth out of the mouth of God"* (Matthew 4:4). Notice, Jesus said, *"by every word."* One attribute that distinguishes a nominal Christian from an effectual Christian is that he determinedly makes daily time with God in His Word. An effectual Christian spends time in the whole counsel of God—the Old Testament, the New Testaments, the Psalms and the Proverbs—to have a complete consumption of God's mind. He focuses his eyes to read and attunes his ears to hear from God. His heart meditates on what he reads with the anticipation of hearing instruction from God, that he may put into action what God makes known to him that day.

The Holy Bible is not an end in itself, but it is a means to bring men to an intimate and satisfying knowledge of God, that they may enter into Him and delight in His presence, and taste and know the inner sweetness of God Himself in the core and center of their hearts; and so be able to come to understand the matters most important on God's heart with a fervency to do those things.

There is not another book on the planet that appropriately represents God's heart apart from the Holy Bible. We can be confident of this because of the Bible's precise accuracy in science, history and fulfilled prophecies. Therefore we can believe it's claim in 2 Timothy 3:16-17 that proclaims it's scriptures are inspired by God and are profitable for humankind. The text tells us, *"All scripture* [talking about the Holy Bible] *is given by inspiration of God, and is profitable for doctrine, for reproof, for correction, for instruction in righteousness: That the man of God may be perfect, thoroughly furnished unto all good works."*

The word *"all"* is important in this passage. Here we learn that not one jot of God's Holy Book can be shunned because all of it is God-breathed. Bible students call this "plenary," which means entire, complete, and yes, *all*. All of the Holy Bible's scriptures are given from God. It was not amassed, compiled, or created by man's intellect, ideals, or reasonings. It is God-breathed, and it is to be received as God-breathed. It is the revelation of God.

Nothing has ever been more clearly established in the world than the Holy Bible. God blesses every individual, people, and nation who believes *and* lives by His Word. Because it is of God, the evil one has stood against it from the beginning (Genesis 3:1); still, the Holy Bible has stood the tests of time. Psalm 119:89 declares that God's Word *"is settled in Heaven,"* and no one is able to bring a railing accusation against it.

Now, the world has seen its fill of scorners; they have arisen countless times and sought to come against the Bible with immense hatred. They have extensively scrutinized, dissected, and cut apart the Holy Bible. Nonetheless, God's Word has stood all tests, because the words of the LORD *are* pure words: They are as silver tried in a furnace of earth, purified seven times (Psalm 12:6); *"The grass withereth, the flower fadeth: but the word of our God shall stand for ever"* (Isaiah 40:8). The Holy Bible is preserved *forever* (Psalm 12:7).

Jesus proclaimed in Matthew 24:35 that God's Word shall never pass away. His Word is indestructible. No other book has suffered even a small amount of the ridicule and attack that the Bible has endured and survived. All of the cunning philosophies and the physical brutalities of countless men have attempted to denounce the Holy Bible, all efforts which have been intended to destroy it, turned out, by the grace of God, for the furtherance of the Bible. The Holy Bible has withstood them all and will continue to be around forever. What an Almighty God!

Even with all the thousands of universities, colleges, and seminaries throughout the entire world, mankind has never been able to produce a book equivalent to the Holy Bible. Human reasoning would find it impossible to conceive that such a powerful, influential book of its magnitude could have been written and put together by any persons on their own accord. Thus, the Holy Bible did not come by any man's cleverness, philosophies, or reasonings. God was the Author behind the writers' inspiration, and these writers knew this.

In 2 Samuel 23:2, David, who wrote many of the psalms, stated that what he wrote came from God. Jeremiah stated the same thing (Jeremiah 1:4), as did the apostle Paul (1 Thessalonians 2:13). Peter says Paul's writings are *"scriptures"* (2 Peter 3:16). Jesus Himself testified about the Bible's purely divine character (Luke 16:17; 24:44; John 17:17). Jesus routinely considered all Old Testament stories to be trustworthy accounts, as evidenced in Luke 11:51 and Luke 17:26-33.

God has been behind all the countless individuals who have diligently and faithfully served to preserve His Word through the many generations. Second Peter 1:20-21 makes known that the Holy Bible's writings were composed as holy men of God were inspired by God to pen the words He pressed upon their hearts to write: *"Knowing this first, that no prophecy of the scripture is of any private interpretation. For the prophecy came not in old time by the will of man: but holy men of God spake as they were moved by the Holy Ghost."*

The Holy Bible was written by around forty men from all ranks of life and ages: a king, a prophet, a fisherman, a doctor, a herdsman, a teacher, to name a few. These men lived in three separate continents spanning an era of nearly 1,600 years—from the ancient historical writings of Moses to the 1st century prophetic writings of the apostle John. As the first writers began their work there was no collusion with those who were going to write centuries later, and yet when we put together all 39 Old Testament books with the 27 New Testament books, there is a perfect and complete unity of the whole Book (that is, speaking about the King James Version). Although the Holy Bible was transcribed by these multiple writers, it (KJV) exhibits phenomenal continuity throughout its pages and contains not a single contradiction. Thus, we are able to compare different parts of the Bible and find that they agree with, support, and clarify each other (1 Corinthians 2:13). We can go to any part of the Bible and know it is consistently trustworthy.

The Holy Bible is most extensive in its range because of its magnitude. It brings a more intense personal conviction than any testimony to a single fact. The most amazing evidence of the Bible's trustworthiness is the subjects that it discusses. The themes within the Bible are of matters that the Bible could speak on only if it were created by God. For example, the Bible states that Jesus claimed He is God (John 10:30); the Bible states that Jesus Christ's enemies asserted He claimed to be God (John 10:33); the Bible states that apostles of Jesus claimed He is God (John 20:28); the Bible states that the Father declared He is God (Hebrews 1:8).

The Holy Bible is the only book that talks in a precise magnitude about sin with an accurate assessment of humankind. The Bible presents a horrible picture. It offends us, and we are not happy to read it. This explains why some individuals find it so hard to believe that the Bible is true. The problem is not with the evidence but rather with our hearts. Who wants to know that he is a rotten, no-good sinner? Who welcomes the knowledge that he is spiritually dead in trespasses and sins (Ephesians 2:1) and that he is in rebellion against the God who made him?

Only God can be honest with us because only He knows the truth. Only God is willing to be honest with us as an expression of His love. Real love is not expressed by the words of people who try to make us feel good by means of vain flatteries, but leave us in our dire predicaments because they have no real hope to offer. Real love is expressed by the truth because it is the only thing that can help us. This is what the Bible does, because God is a Friend who sticks closer than a brother (Proverbs 18:24), and as a *Friend*, He speaks the truth to us.

What Are You Doing With God's Word?

There has never been a book written that came by luck or chance. Every book owes its existence to some being(s). Within the range and scope of human intelligence there are but three things that bring a book into existence—good men, bad men, and God. Speaking of all known and unknown knowledge, all that originates in intellect, and all that the intellect can comprehend, everything must come from one of the three.

The Holy Bible could not possibly have been the product of evil, wicked, godless, corrupt, vile men—for it pronounces the heaviest penalties against sin. The Bible, within itself, includes all men in the same condemnation, that *all* have sinned and deserve the same penalty of Hell. Like produces like, and if evil men were writing the Bible, they never would have pronounced condemnation and punishment against wrongdoing, for they would be condemning themselves. On the other hand, it is explained in 2 Peter 1:21 that many godly men of old *"spake as they were moved by the Holy Ghost."* These holy men did not attribute the simple, yet profound words to themselves, but only to God. Therefore, the only being left, to whom a sensible person could ascribe the origin of the Bible, is God.

Many other great men of history realized this truth and did not attribute these beautiful, matchless, and well-arranged passages in the Holy Bible to human intelligence alone, but to God. Such men, who even the world honors, highly magnified God as the Author and Designer of the Holy Bible. Great statesmen, inventors, painters, poets, artists, and musicians have lifted up their hearts in praise to God for the authorship of the Holy Bible. Some of the foremost scientists of our world, such as Sir Isaac Newton and George Washington Carver, as well as the inventor of the steam engine—James Watt; the inventor of the steamboat—Robert Fulton; the inventor of the telegraph—Samuel Morse; the honorable U.S.A. Lieutenant General William K. Harrison Jr.; former U.S.A. Presidents George Washington, Thomas Jefferson, Abraham Lincoln, Theodore Roosevelt, and Ronald Reagan; and thousands of other prestigious and honorable individuals all confirmed God to be the divine Author of the Holy Bible.

The Bible has always had such a conviction on men that many wars have been fought over it's truths; governments aiming to eradicate such divine precepts have even punished men by throwing them to beasts, torturing and imprisoning them, or burning them to death for having Bibles in their possession. Everything vile, dirty, rotten, and iniquitous have been brought to bear against the Bible because it reveals man's sin and declares need to repent and call upon God for salvation. Notwithstanding, it is still here and its power and influence are greater today than ever before. The sinful pride of men has viciously fought to obliterate it, but it is still here. Billions have been against it and have sought to destroy it, but it is the Word of God, and billions of others have come to know it.

With this said, the Holy Bible should hold the highest importance to us. It is of utmost preeminence because our living Savior Jesus Christ is the living Word. The Holy Bible is a tangible manifestation of God. John 1:14 makes known that the Word became flesh and dwelt among us. The Holy Bible is so important that John 1:1 tells us that the Word is God and God is the Word. First John 5:7 says that the Word, the Father, and the Holy Spirit are one. Our Triune God has manifested Himself in a Book (Hebrews 10:7).

If we are going to serve God, then we must serve the Bible. And we can only serve the Word by spending time in the Bible and getting to know it. We can only get to know and best serve God by knowing His Word.

Our Lord Jesus compared the Word of God to sustenance, *bread*. Jesus is quoted as saying, *"It is written, Man shall not live by bread alone, but by every word that proceedeth out of the mouth of God."* As we must eat physical bread to survive and live, we too must eat the spiritual bread—the Word of God—to survive and live. Since Jesus is that living bread which came down from the Father in Heaven, He was accurate in saying, *"Verily, verily, I say unto you, Except ye eat the flesh of the Son of man, and drink his blood, ye have no life in you"* (John 6:53). Jesus further explained, *"Whoso eateth my flesh, and drinketh my blood, hath eternal life; and I will raise him up at the last day. For my flesh is meat indeed, and my blood is drink indeed. He that eateth my flesh, and drinketh my blood, dwelleth in me, and I in him. As the living Father hath sent me, and I live by the Father: so he that eateth me, even he shall live by me"* (John 6:54-57).

Jesus is that bread of life (John 6:48)! Jesus declared, *"I am the living bread which came down from heaven: if any man eat of this bread, he shall live for ever: and the bread that I will give is my flesh, which I will give for the life of the world"* (John 6:51).

On a regular basis the Lord's method was to use physical things to teach spiritual matters. For example, in this passage Jesus spoke repeatedly of men *eating of His flesh*. What did He mean by this? Did He mean that men must eat Him in a physical, literal way? Obviously that idea is impossible, repulsive, and contrary to the Law (Leviticus 3:17; Acts 15:20). Some think, however, that Jesus meant to teach that we must eat of Him in the communion service; that in some miraculous way the bread and wine are changed into the actual body and blood of Christ and that in order to be saved we must partake of those elements. But this is not what Jesus said. The context makes it quite clear that to *eat* of Him means to **believe** in Him. When we trust the Lord Jesus Christ as our Savior, we appropriate Him by faith. We partake of the benefits of His Person and of His work. As someone once said, "**Believe and you have eaten.**"

The Lord Jesus was simply stating that unless we appropriate to ourselves by faith the value of His death for us on Calvary, we can never be saved. We must believe in Him, receive Him, trust Him, and make Him our very own.

The individual who hears Christ's words and believes, he is the individual who eats Christ's flesh and drinks Christ's blood. He is the person who appropriates (uses) his faith to believe Christ, receive Him, trust Him, and make Him his very own. He is the individual who partakes of Christ by receiving everlasting life, which means union with Him forever.

A very close union exists between Jesus and those who believe in Him. Whoever eats His flesh and drinks His blood abides in Him, and He abides in that person. Nothing could be closer or more intimate than this. When we eat literal food, we take it into our very being and it becomes a part of us. When we accept the Lord Jesus as our Redeemer, He comes into our lives to abide, and we, too, abide (continually dwell) in Him (John 6:56).

That's good news! Thank the LORD we have His words written in the Holy Bible; we have been given a more sure word of prophecy so that we may draw near with a true heart in full assurance of faith. He is faithful who has promised, and because of this our faith may be without wavering (Hebrews 10:22-23). We can take confidence in what is written in the Holy Bible because *"God is not a man, that he should lie; neither the son of man, that he should repent: hath he said, and shall he not do it? or hath he spoken, and shall he not make it good?"* (Numbers 23:19). God's promises are *"yea"* and *"amen"* (2 Corinthians 1:20). Therefore, God appropriately magnifies His Word higher than His name (Psalm 138:2d); He has a lofty regard for it.

We too should have high regard for God's Word. So often we Christians call on the name of Jesus for help, but God says that His Word is above His name (Psalm 138:2). It would do us a lot of good to study the Word, so that with the next problem we face, we can search His Word for an answer before we cry to Christ for an answer. Either way, He is going to point us to His Word. This is why we need constant exposure to God's Word. We need to make sure to read, study, and mediate on His Word. All answers for life are in the Bible.

This is why a determined Christian will make sure to seek for all of his answers to life's problems from the Word of God. The Holy Bible is so important that you and I must be inside it and observe its truths every single day.

Most Christians rightly proclaim that the Bible is the most important book on the face of this planet, but it is so sad that many never pick it up to read. What hypocrisy! So many Christians wonder why they have no power. So many wonder why they have unrelenting problems within their homes, and why they cannot lead anyone to Christ. These Christians position themselves as useless vessels for God and are a disgrace and an insult to His holiness; even so, the consequences and shame is the proof of their foolish decision not to be inside the Bible.

The opposite is true for the determined Christian. He experiences a life that is rich in an abundance of Christ's blessings because He commits himself to be in God's Word every day, whether in season or out of season. A determined Christian commits himself to apply what God's Word speaks for him to be and do. Why? Because he understands that *"All scripture is given by inspiration of God, and is profitable for doctrine, for reproof, for correction, for instruction in righteousness: That the man of God may be perfect, thoroughly furnished unto all good works"* (2 Timothy 3:16-17).

A determined Christian seeks not to be foolish or have shame in his life. He readily believes the Bible and allows its truth to transform him and benefit his life. God's Word says that the Bible is *"profitable for* [our] *doctrine."* That means it shows us what is beneficial; it is advantageous for our forward steps in life. It shows what is right. Further, 2 Timothy 3:16 explains that the Bible is *"profitable for* [our] *reproof."* In other words, it reproves and shows our false steps. It tells us what is not right. The Holy Bible points out our sins and brings conviction of sin. Not only is it profitable for the negatives, but also for the positives.

What's more, the Bible explains it is *"profitable for* [our] *correction."* This could mean our faltering steps. For example, the Bible not only shows us where we are wrong, it also shows us how to get right! It shows us the way back to closeness with God. Praise the Lord!

God wants us to grow in knowledge and understanding of Him, and for that reason He has given us the holy scriptures, *"for instruction in righteousness,"* to understand right living, and how to keep it right. Although in the sight of God we have imputed righteousness given to us by Christ, He also desires for us to be right and live right before our fellow man. We must seek to have a good testimony before all.

Second Timothy 3:16-17 ends with the words, *"that the man of God may be perfect, thoroughly furnished unto all good works."* This means that we should be mature and complete. Maturity and completeness can only come about in one's life by being in the Word of God daily. The idea here could be compared to our being fitted for a voyage as a ship is. The Lord saves us and fits us through the scriptures so we can effectively serve others in this voyage of life.

We have a grand holy Book! The Holy Bible is the only book that tells us of a God we can love and know, how to win souls for Heaven, how to disciple converts on earth, how to avoid a lonely and dark Hell, and how to know the Savior who saves. Furthermore, the Holy Bible is the only book that gives us exceedingly great and precious promises from God.

John 17:17 teaches that the Holy Bible can sanctify us from what is wrong and evil. If someone desires to understand what is evil and how to steer away from that evil, all he has to do is search the Bible, and God's Word will show him.

Romans 10:17 informs us that God's Word can increase our faith. Ephesians 6:17 lets us know that it is the Word that can fight off Satan's attacks. It can show us the depravity that is within our hearts, (Hebrews 4:12; Jeremiah 17:9) and how to get cleaned up (Psalm 119:9-11). In 1 Peter 2:2 and Isaiah 58:11 we learn that God's Word always can satisfy a believer. How important is that!

The Holy Bible is our shield and our buckler (Psalm 91:4); it is our protection. Hence, we should take hold of God's shield and buckler, and stand up with it in the battles of life (Psalm 35:2). We need to use it!

Psalm 119:11 shows that God's Word can keep us from sinning. Then we learn in Psalm 119:105 that God's Word can show us the safe steps to take and the right way to go in life. His Word, as shown in Psalm 119:165, can give us a peace of mind. And speaking of a peace of mind, we can rely on God's promise in Isaiah 55:11: God's Word will never fail in the task He has sent it out to accomplish.

After reviewing those wonderful promises given by God, now think about this amazing truth—God regarded us creatures of low estate and gave us the Bible so that we can know Him and enjoy life through Christ (John 20:31). How awesome is that! God thought about us (Jeremiah 29:11). He did not have to. Nonetheless, He does think about us and demonstrates His love toward us by inscribing thoughts of peace toward us in one little book called the Holy Bible.

It is amazing beyond comprehension that God would even consider thinking about us. Who are we in comparison to the cosmos? We are nothing in size to anything else in all the universe. NASA scientists state that the Milky Way Galaxy, which we live in, is not even a piece of dust compared to the enormous depth and size of the universe. With this said then, how absolutely nothing we must be in comparison to the universe! I once heard an estimate by a reputable public figure that the size of our universe is anywhere between 2.932×10^{21} light years and 5.864×10^{42} light years in diameter. That is beyond grandeur! However, I imagine this estimation is nowhere close to the actual magnificent size of the universe because God makes known in Jeremiah 31:37 that the universe can never be measured. Simply put, this immense number alone is an unfathomable magnitude of space and distance, yet that is reality. Such an immensely colossal grandeur proves how infinitesimal and minuscule we really are!

Many times I wonder who we are that God would even consider giving a millisecond of a thought about us (Psalm 144:3). Yet God, beyond all the immense size of the universe, sees us; He thinks about us, and involves Himself in each one of our lives every second of each day (Job 7:17). It is too overwhelming to understand, yet wonderfully absolutely true!

The grand love of God for each one of us surpasses all knowledge (Ephesians 3:19). God's irresistible love toward us compels Him to extend kindness and longsuffering toward us, not wiling that any should perish.

God's love compelled Him to manifest Himself in the volume of a book. This is why the Holy Bible is not just any ordinary book; it is the Word—the living revelation of God! Hebrews 4:12 lets us know that *"the word of God is quick, and powerful, and sharper than any twoedged sword, piercing even to the dividing asunder of soul and spirit, and of the joints and marrow, and is a discerner of the thoughts and intents of the heart."* That word *"quick"* can be understood to mean alive. The Word is alive. Because He, the living Word, is alive.

The Bible is so clear that it includes God's mission statement for its existence. John 20:31 states: *"But these are written, that ye might believe that Jesus is the Christ, the Son of God; and that believing ye might have life through His name."* What a mission! What an awesome reason to get a Bible and diligently study its truths! God has given us His Word so that we might have the privilege and opportunity of knowing and understanding Him (Jeremiah 9:23-24)!

Nobody reads a mechanical manual to learn how to train a dog. Nor does anybody read a cookbook to learn to drive a car. No, people read a mechanical manual to learn about how to fix a vehicle, and a cookbook to learn how to make food. In the same way, the Holy Bible is given so that we can learn to know and understand God. If you want to get out of a book what the author put in it, you must find out why it was written. That is the way to get good out of a book. We have the mission of God's Word, so that we may know Him; therefore, we need to be in it, daily!

Now God could have used the language of angels that no one could understand. However, He chose not to do that. Rather He chose to use words put down on paper in our understandable language so that we could search His precepts to gain His pure wisdom and rich knowledge.

God exhorted the children of Israel in Deuteronomy 32:46-47 to "[*Set*] *your hearts unto all the words which I* [God] *testify among you this day, which ye shall command your children to observe to do, all the words of this law. For it is not a vain thing for you; because it is your life.*" The nation of Israel is our example for admonition that we too should set our hearts in His Word, because the Bible is our life too! If we want life, especially abundant life, then we must be in the Word of God (John 10:10).

Thus, a determined Christian reads the Bible to know God and have an abundance-filled life. This is why the Bible was written; that you might read and believe that Jesus is the Son of God, and in knowing Him, that you may have life more abundantly.

Now the Bible was not intended as a history or a business guidebook. It was intended to keep you and me out of Hell and to direct us into a union with the Creator. The Bible was not intended merely to be a science book any more than a crowbar is intended for a toothpick. The Bible was written to tell men how they should live!

A person is misinformed if he does not believe that the Holy Bible (King James Version) is the Word of God from cover to cover. This includes all 66 books of the Bible, all 1,189 chapters, all 31,102 verses, and each of its approximately 788,280 words; and yes, every single dot, question mark, colon, semicolon, and comma. It is a heresy to say you believe the Bible is the Word of God yet proclaim that one or two commas are incorrectly placed in a particular location. Either it is the whole Counsel of God or it is man's incredible design of great stories and enlightening legends. So, which will you choose to believe? You cannot be in the gray. There is no room for middle ground on this point.

I personally determined within my heart a long time ago to agree with what God declares in 2 Timothy 3:16—that all of it is His inspired Word. ALL OF IT! As the Word of God, the Holy Bible exhorts us to study and seek to understand truth (2 Timothy 2:15). Meanwhile we can be at rest in knowing that we do not need to try to understand *all* the philosophies, dogmas, and any unclear precepts within it. We cannot (Deuteronomy 29:29). I personally would not attempt it and I would be a fool if I tried. None of us is that intelligent. We must believe it because it is from the mouth of God.

It is a divine privilege to partake with God in the Holy Bible. A determined Christian realizes this; therefore, he daily spends significant amounts of time with God in the Holy Bible. He is determined to be saturated and consumed with the Word. There are many things that you and I do not know. There are many things God desires to say, but we cannot bear them right now (John 16:12). However, if we patiently meet with God each day, God will teach them to us. God says in Jeremiah 33:3, *"Call unto me, and I will answer thee, and shew thee great and mighty things, which thou knowest not."*

Mark 4:34 lets us know that when Jesus was alone with His men He expounded all things to His disciples. Solitude with the Savior is important! Likewise, we must spend alone time with Christ, too. We must daily get away from the world, family, friends, and influences, and simply spend time alone with God in His Word and prayer.

Solitude with Jesus and His Word is important because it is where God can feed and nourish us. God will convict us of unknown sin and clean us up, too. Jesus can teach us or clarify truth to us while we are in His Word. He desires to expound on truth and give wisdom to us, but only if we make ourselves available to Him in the Word every day.

Solitude with Jesus and His Word produces many good results. You can discover a confirmation of sonship with the Father and a cleansing of doubt. You can develop a closeness of trust with God. You can be given comfort in the Word. You can sense a certainty of protection and be given a consolation from your enemies. You can experience a ceasing of the self. You can be given counsel for battles, a transformed heart, and feel contentment in the service of the King of kings. Plus you must not forget that solitude with Jesus in His Word is where satisfaction and peace is found (Psalm 145:15-16).

There are five things we must be determined to do in handling the Holy Bible. First, we must read it daily. The reason we read the Bible is to learn. There is much we do not know and we need to learn from the One who knows it all. First Timothy 4:13 and Revelation 1:3 exhort that we are to give attention to reading the Bible. Our focus in life should daily begin with meditating on the Word of God. If our thoughts are on the Word, then we will develop a disciplined attitude of presenting ourselves before the living Word (Jesus) each day. Hence we can be appropriately aligned with God to receive from Him convictions, decisions, applications, knowledge, management, insight, and a purpose for life.

Second, we need to make time in our schedule to study the Bible. The reason we study the Bible is for preparation, so that God may find us trustworthy and reliable and ready to be influential servants among people. We can only prepare ourselves by investigating and discovering biblical truths on important topics, issues, and doctrine on a consistent basis. Second Timothy 2:15 commands us to study the Word in order to present ourselves approved unto God, so that we may be laborers who do not need to be ashamed and who can rightly divide the Word of truth.

God looks for determined Christians who are reliable before He raises them up to be godly influences in other people's lives. God is not going to approve a Christian to carry out godly responsibilities if he is not preparing himself. There is a war going on (1 Timothy 1:18), and no commander is going to approve a soldier for battle if he does not first learn and prepare himself for what is out there. God wants us to study so that we can be prepared for understanding, transformation, tranquility, and longevity in the war (Proverbs 3:1-2).

Third, we need to memorize God's Word. It is good to learn and prepare ourselves in the Holy Bible, but we will be less effective if we do not know where to take someone in the Bible to prove truth as an offense against lies. The reason we memorize the Word is so that we can be able to store Bible truths in our minds and, more importantly, pull the Word down eighteen inches from our heads into our hearts when we meditate on it. God wants the Word in our hearts, not just in our heads. The world is dark, and more times than not we will need to rely on the Word stored in our hearts when we do not have a Bible near us. Deuteronomy 11:18 instructs us to lay up the Word in our hearts as well as our souls. The heart is where all the mental triggers and passions come from within us. Our soul is where our personal desires and our will come from. In addition, Deuteronomy 6:8 says we are to bind the Word as a sign upon our hands that it might be very close to us. How true it is that we need the Word very close to us.

Fourth, and of particular importance, we need to be determined to meditate on God's Word every single day. We should meditate on what we read, study, and memorize. Meditating on any one of these truths is exceedingly good for us. However, before we can experience the best benefits from Bible meditation, we should be reading the Bible every day for learning, studying God's Word for preparation, and memorizing God's Word for battle.

The reason we meditate on God's Word is to live. Meditation is most effective when we are doing the first three objectives. Joshua 1:8 commands that we are to meditate on the Word day and night. Not just in the morning. Not merely once in a while when we feel up to it. We are commanded to meditate on it, *day* and *night*.

In the same passage, God further explains the results of meditating on the Word day and night: we will be able to observe to do according to all that is written in the Bible, we will make our way prosperous, and we will have good success. That is a whole lot of blessings and a pretty good deal. Meditating on the Bible enables us to obey God, observing to do all that He commands. The prosperity and good success that Bible meditation produces are wisdom and understanding for health, strength, vitality, and nutrition (look at the principles of Psalm 1:2-3). If we have strength, vitality, and both physical and spiritual nutrition, then we are certain to have success in other areas, and all for Christ's glory! But only if we meditate on the Word *day* and *night*.

Therefore, if we read the Bible, we can then study the Bible more effectively, and then we can memorize and meditate on the Bible more effectively. If we learn the Bible, then we can love the Bible, and if we love the Bible then we can live the Bible. The Bible teaches us to learn to love in order to live the Bible. If we want to live the Bible then we will have to be determined to apply and implement the Bible's truths into our lives.

Applying the Bible is the final and most important matter we should do with the Word of God. Meditating most definitely can assist us to live the Word of God. However, if we want to live the Bible then we will have to apply the Bible. If we are living in it then we can implement it in practical ways in whatever God shows us. This is obedience. We apply His Word to our lives so that we may always do those things that are pleasing to God (just as Jesus exemplified [John 8:29]).

Applying the Word of God is simply taking counsel of scripture that speaks to your heart, meditating on it, and developing practical steps toward making it an integral part of your life. For example, a particular scripture might speak on an important principle that you find lacking in your life. Then you would want to meditate on that scripture and develop a way to apply or live out what the scripture speaks to you about.

One simple method that can help you apply scripture to your life is to ask yourself good discovery questions, and then to meditate on your answers. The seven I list on the next page serve as examples. There are many other questions you can ask yourself, but for now these are a good start. As you meditate on a scripture, these questions can help you develop an application for any verse or passage.

- What does this passage say to me?
- Where am I falling short?
- What are some specific examples?
- What am I going to do about it?
- What should I change in my life?
- Is there something God wants me to do or not do?
- How should I respond to what I have just read?

This approach takes the Bible out of the theological realm and places the Bible's emphasis on daily life, where it should be: *application.* This emphasis on daily life is extremely important, and this, rather than simply studying good theology, is God's main aim in giving us His Word.

All too often, God's truths in His Word are sadly left in the same categories as other things we admire and appreciate. We may be captivated by the majesty, beauty, and eternity of His Word, but mere appreciation of the scriptures is not God's full intent when He gave us the Bible.

God informs us of His intent in giving us His Word in John 20:31 and 2 Timothy 3:16-17. Once more, John 20:31 says, *"But these are written, that ye might believe that Jesus is the Christ, the Son of God; and that believing ye might have life through his name."* And again, I know I have shown this verse a few times before, but please pay careful attention and note what God says: *"All scripture is given by inspiration of God, and is profitable for doctrine, for reproof, for correction, for instruction in righteousness: That the man of God may be perfect, thoroughly furnished unto all good works."*

God's intent for the Holy Bible is for us to live, understanding and knowing God. A knowledge and understanding of God enables us to live life more abundantly with Christ. This abundant life can only be experienced by applying God's doctrine, His reproofs, His corrections, and His instruction in our lives. Application is the key.

It is God's desire that His Word be lived out in our daily affairs and that the Word of God find expression within us. God's desire is that we be walking and living BIBLES, demonstrating the beauty and validity of the scriptures in our homes, our jobs, our schools, our communities, and anywhere else we might find ourselves.

God's Word is not an abstract doctrine; it is the final authority on the whole life and being of man. For that reason, Romans 12:2 shows why we need to be reading, studying, memorizing, meditating on, and applying the Word of God. Romans 12:2 says, *"And be not conformed to this world: but be ye transformed by the renewing of your mind, that ye may prove what is that good, and acceptable, and perfect, will of God.*" Therefore, we need to:

- Read His Word to Learn
- Study His Word to Prepare
- Memorize His Word to Pull It Down into Our Hearts
- Mediate on His Word to Live
- Apply His Word to Please God

If you have any doubts about God or His Word, there is only one way to have the doubts removed—be in the Holy Scriptures and obey them. Some people say that they cannot understand them. Perhaps because *"the natural man receiveth not the things of the Spirit of God: for they are foolishness unto him: neither can he know them, because they are spiritually discerned"* (1 Corinthians 2:14). One must have the Spirit of God living within him to understand the rich treasures of God's Word. Jesus stated that it is the Holy Ghost who will teach us all things (John 14:26). He is the One who guides believers into all truth (John 16:13). The Holy Ghost desires to be our personal Tutor and to guide us in learning. How good are you at paying attention to Him?

When we do not understand something in the Bible, it's all right for the time being. However, we should seek God for understanding, and at the appropriate time, the Holy Spirit will teach us. Just like everything else in life, there are steps to learning. Everything in life has the ABCs of learning, and there is an A, a B, and a C with reading the Bible too. When you and I first started school, we learned the ABCs; soon afterward, we started understanding things we never thought we could when we started out. And so it is in spending time with God in the Bible every day. A Christian must begin with the simple things and faithfully continue, and in time he will come to understand more.

If you are someone who currently does not spend time daily with God in the Bible, then I wholeheartedly suggest that you start reading it on a consistent daily basis. Do not worry about what you do not understand. You will never understand everything. The more you learn, the more you will see the need to spend time with God to learn more of what you do not know. God inspired holy men to write the Holy Scriptures in such a way that you and I would be obliged to spend time with Him every day in order to learn more of Him and His Word, little by little for the rest of our lives.

I recommend a method that might assist you in gaining understanding of the Holy Bible. I encourage you first to start by reading the New Testament.

Perhaps start by reading at least one chapter a day. The New Testament begins with the Lord's life and His teachings, and this is vital reading. You could begin reading in the Gospels—Matthew, Mark, Luke, and John. These books will give you a broad and clear picture of Jesus: His life, death, and resurrection from four different viewpoints.

After reading the Gospels, move on to the book of Acts. This is written in story form and it tells how Christianity spread after the Lord's resurrection from the dead in spite of all the momentous persecutions.

Most of the other books in the New Testament were written to teach and instruct Christians in a basic understanding of God's character. In addition, they teach how we can live by His strength to demonstrate our love toward Christ in those things that please Him.

The two Testaments of the Bible can be compared to a lock and a key. The Old Testament is the lock and the New Testament is the key. They fit perfectly together.

After finishing the New Testament, go to the beginning of your Bible, to Genesis in the Old Testament, and begin to read from there. Your reading of the New Testament first will stand you in good stead for understanding the Old Testament. The Old Testament is filled with men and women's stories of successes and failures, and how God blessed those who obeyed Him and how God dealt with those who disobeyed Him. We can learn a great deal from their obedience and disobedience toward God.

I also suggest that you read another section of the Bible for additional wisdom and practical knowledge. For example, if you want to learn how to praise and worship God, read a Psalm a day. There are 150 Psalms in this book. If you read one Psalm a day, you would be able to read the whole book of Psalms twice a year.

All the Psalms are songs of praise to God and each one relates to the Pentateuch, the first five books of the Bible. Chapters 1 through 41 can teach you to praise God because of man and creation, as they correspond to the book of Genesis. Chapters 42 through 72 can teach you to praise God because of deliverance and redemption, as they correspond to the book of Exodus. Chapters 73 through 89 can teach you to praise God in worship and the sanctuary, as they correspond to the book of Leviticus. Chapters 90 through 106 can teach you to praise God through the wilderness and wanderings of life, as they correspond to the book of Numbers. Finally, chapters 107 through 150 can teach you to praise God in scriptures, as they correspond to the book of Deuteronomy.

If you desire to gain wisdom, read a Proverb a day. There are 31 Proverbs.

If you read a Proverb a day, you will be able to read the whole book of wisdom once a month; that is, twelve times a year. That's a whole lot of wisdom that you and I desperately need!

Be sure to read the Bible every day. Make sure you set aside a time in your schedule that will be God's time alone with you. No one else! No other distractions!

It is a determined lifestyle and habit of mine each day to start my mornings off with God and His Word. I prearrange my schedule as my first priority to meet God in the mornings immediately after bathing. I normally sit down on my recliner, and I spend time alone with God in His Word. I keep my phone turned off. I do not allow anyone to interrupt God and me. It is God's time for me to have intimacy with Him. No one else. This is precious time that God and I value and love to spend privately together every single day.

You may even find it helpful to keep a journal of what you read. While you read, I suggest that you have your journal next to you, and write down any observations you notice, any personal applications or points that stick out to you. As well, write down any questions you might have. Sometimes over an extended period of time you will come to notice that God is speaking to you on a broader level about something, and it will encourage you to review what God has been trying to show you.

I also strongly suggest that whatever you read, be sure to meditate on it and think about it all day long. It is great to read the Bible each day; however, it is so much more beneficial to meditate and ponder on His Word throughout the day, instead of musing on background noise from the radio or television. Thinking about God's Word withholds us from sin (Psalm 119:11, 116) and produces courage for our witness (Joshua 1:7-9). In addition, it is a good habit to sing the Bible and make melody in your heart to the Lord. You can do this by speaking to yourself in Psalms and hymns and spiritual songs (Ephesians 5:19). For instance, many scriptures can resonate in your heart by singing them. A few scriptures that I have learned to sing to the Lord and keep in the back of my mind are Galatians 2:20, Philippians 4:4, John 3:16, and 1 John 4:7-8. Galatians 2:20 is my favorite!

Among all of the biblical testimonies, proofs, and promises from God, it is amazing that people still resist believing its record. It is even more mind-boggling that Christians resist spending time with God on a consistent basis. Why is this? I have no definite answer, but perhaps the answer resides in an issue concerning *sin*: perhaps individuals know they will learn particular things that God disapproves of. Therefore, if people just try to ignore His Word, then they might be able to conjure up an excuse for their lack of obedience. Ultimately, that will not work with God, as God will bring all intentions into judgment (Ecclesiastics 11:9). Ignorance is not a defense in the eyes of God. (Just check out Leviticus 5:14-17 and notice how God handled individuals who unknowingly committed sin. In addition, look at Luke 12:47-48 and notice how Jesus, an austere Man, will judge people despite the fact that they sin ignorantly. The Lord is austere in His judgment seat [Luke 19:20-24].)

God counts it best for all to know His Word. God regards Christians as witnesses for Him, and if a Christian discounts time in the Word then God will compensate him with leanness of soul, just as He gave the Israelites when they lusted against what God judged best for them. Psalm 106:15 explains, *"And he [God] gave them their request; but sent leanness into their soul."*

Friend, might your soul be lean? How much more should you be in the Bible for nourishment and strength?

I surely agree with what one of my mentors has often said, "Most books are written for our information, but the Bible was written for our transformation." It is amazing what is said and how much is said in God's Holy Word. No words are put in the Bible just to fill space. If an individual reads the Bible, then it will talk to him or her, because it is *quick* (Hebrews 4:12). The Bible talks to us so we can understand and make appropriate changes within our lives to align with what God instructs.

Second Corinthians 11:3 informs us that the message of God's Word is simple. The gospel, the stories, the instructions, and its commands are written with simplicity for the reader to understand what God desires for us to know and do. Hence, we should apply its words because we are able to understand and do them.

To the critics who argue that there are topics in the Bible that can never be understood, and therefore conjecture that we should not read the Bible, God has a response to their foolishness. The remedy for these time-wasting arguments is Deuteronomy 29:29. The scripture tells us, *"The secret things belong unto the LORD our God: but those things which are revealed belong unto us and to our children for ever, that we may do all the words of this law."* Here God alerts us that there are indeed some secret matters God has chosen for us not to comprehend; they are for Him alone. Nevertheless, this does not justify anyone in not reading the Bible. The verse also explains that there certainly are matters God has made available for us to understand; such as sin, righteousness, and judgment; in addition, there are principles of the doctrine of Christ, the foundation of repentance, and faith toward God, which we can learn and understand (John 16:8; Hebrews 6:1-2). Therefore, we should diligently seek to understand the important truths in God's Holy Bible.

Then there is extra knowledge and deeper understanding about matters which God does make available, but only to those individuals who fervently seek to know them. God sees fit to only reveal more of Himself to those who reverence Him, as shown by their hunger for Him. Psalm 25:14 explains, *"The secret of the LORD is with them that fear him; and he will shew them his covenant."* Are you hungry enough to study your Bible and search out greater understanding of our infinite, fearful God?

Now we cannot understand all of God's deep treasures in His Word by simply hearing and reading it. The Bible can be compared to gold mines inside a mountain. Although people know there are gold mines in California, the fact of their existence does no good for anyone who just looks at these mountaintops. Only those who dig for and get the gold will gain the fortune desired. It is the same with the Bible. Only the people who dig—study and meditate—and spend extra time with God in the Bible find valuable knowledge and priceless wisdom. To do little beyond hearing the Word will provide little knowledge and minimal understanding of the Word. The truth is that you and I must spend precious time alone with God and passionately dig to find the priceless, joyous gems of truths.

First Corinthians 2:13-14 says, *"Which things also we speak, not in the words which man's wisdom teacheth, but which the Holy Ghost teacheth; comparing spiritual things with spiritual. But the natural man receiveth not the things of the Spirit of God: for they are foolishness unto him: neither can he know them, because they are spiritually discerned."* A hungry Christian will be a prudent student of God's Word. He will study by comparing spiritual things with spiritual things. He will study scripture in light of scripture, examining texts with the context of the whole Bible. He will seek the wisdom of the Holy Ghost to teach him doctrine that exalts Christ.

We can see in the Bible that God reveals truth to man, and when a Christian accepts this, then he can be content. Meditating on God's Word consistently and applying its truths will give a Christian a joyous spirit and peace of mind (Philippians 4:6-8).

God knows our every need. Jesus can and will fulfill our every need. The principal way Jesus accomplishes this is by showing us the answers to our needs from His doctrine found inside His holy guidebook. But the answers are only discovered when we spend time with God in the Word.

The Bible contains exceedingly great and precious promises running all through it and God wants you to appropriate them for your use (2 Peter 1:4). If we could make a comparison—a mundane one, I might add—God's promises are like money. They are of no value unless used. You might starve to death if you have money in your pockets but won't use it. Therefore, the promises of the Bible may not do you any good if you will not spend time in the Bible to find them and use them. The Bible is a galaxy of promises in the universe of God's love. The Bible contains a little over 20,000 promises from God that we Christians can claim and appropriate. We just have to get inside the Bible and find them. Then, when we find a promise, we can make use of it in our lives and see God glorified.

Here is just one fundamental promise from Jesus in John 15:7: *"If ye abide in me, and my words abide in you, ye shall ask what ye will, and it shall be done unto you."* If Christians received such a promise from Mr. Rockefeller or Mr. Trump, most of them would sit up all night writing out checks to be cashed the next morning. Yet such greater, more powerful, richer promises from God that we can liberally claim are at our disposal, waiting for us to use, such as, "Lord, give me souls to win." Or "Lord, give me wisdom and understanding." God's promises are more valuable than all of Mr. Rockefeller's and Mr. Trump's money put together. Sadly, most Christians let the Bible lie on the coffee table, and just sit, missing the opportunities to abide with Christ in appropriating His promises for us.

The Bible has personally taught me the way to live and it has taught me how to die (Galatians 2:20). The Bible has blessed me to know God, to have an understanding of His mind, and shown me how to live and die in Him. Likewise, will you be determined to get inside your Bible each day and get to know God? Will you implement a determination to learn God's Word by reading, studying, memorizing, and meditating? Will you be determined to obey what God says and to apply and implement God's doctrine into your life? The decision is yours. How will you respond?

Only you can answer such questions. In retrospect, what changes are you going to make in your life, *starting today*, as a result of reading this chapter? I exhort you to be determined to implement those changes *TODAY*. Otherwise you are just wasting the valuable life God has given you. Without applying these practical biblical truths in your life, you will miss out being an effectual servant of God.

Chapter Thirteen

WHAT DO PEOPLE SAY ABOUT YOUR SPIRITUAL WALK?

ONE OF THE PERSONAL ROUTINES of my daily life is to go exercise and lift weights at my local gym. On many occasions during my workouts God has given me opportunities to talk about the gospel with other members. It is a blessing beyond words.

On one evening as I was getting out of my vehicle to go into the gym, the parking lot security guard was not too far from my car. Although I had seen him countless times before, we had never greeted one another. That night I determined that I would say hi and see if I might be able to witness to him. I grabbed a gospel tract out of my car and put it in my pocket. Then I grabbed my gym bag out of my trunk and headed towards the gym. On the way, I made sure to walk by the security guard so I could give him the tract.

I greeted him and he replied "hello" back. Then I asked him if he had ever received one of my tracts as I pulled it out of my pocket. He accepted it and glanced over it. Then he smiled and asked if I was a Christian.

I gladly responded affirmatively. He responded with a smile, "I thought you were a Christian. My sister is one." The next thing he said to me just about gloriously knocked me off my feet. He continued, "I've been watching you for a couple of months now. I've wanted to know if your Christianity is real or not.... Every time I see you, I see you smiling and you just seem so happy like my sister." His statement quickly reminded me of what I sometimes forget: people really are watching us, whether we realize it or not. Then he confessed, "I want what you have."

I quietly thanked God for giving me a good testimony before this man. I then responded to the man by sharing Christ with him. We talked for twenty minutes and I had the privilege to answer many of the questions that he had been reluctant to ask his sister. Although, he desired to have what his sister and I have, sadly he was not committed to trust solely in Jesus Christ. He was not repentant to trust what he knew to be true. Since then, I have had numerous other occasions to share with him about Jesus, and to graciously contend with his doubts and worries.

I share this testimony with you not to make you think I always live as a bright shining light before the world. I wish I did, and I pray that I will become more of a witness for Christ, as you should too. I share my testimony to encourage you to make a determination within your heart *to be* a witness for Christ each and every day in your communications, mannerisms, and lifestyle.

There is a peace and joy that comes along with walking humbly with God and being a living testimony for Him. This peace and joy can be seen on your face as a witness before the world. Your face is a billboard for all to see. The scriptures tell us, *"Wherefore seeing we also are compassed about with so great a cloud of witnesses, let us lay aside every weight, and the sin which doth so easily beset us, and let us...look unto Jesus"* (Hebrews 12:1-2). People are watching you and me all the time. They are seeking to verify if faith in Jesus Christ is valid.

When people look at the billboard of your face, who do they see? Do they see your countenance, or that of Jesus Christ?

People are yearning to have an abundant life. If they understood it was free to enjoy *in* Christ Jesus, perhaps more might receive God's abundance of grace. Then they could enjoy the gift of righteousness so that they might reign (enjoy) life by One, Jesus Christ (Romans 5:17).

If a man is to experience life more abundantly with Christ, and be used as an effective instrument in God's hands, then he must have a spiritual life to a heavenly degree. Christ stated Himself in John 10:10, *"I am come that they might have life, and that they might have it more abundantly."* The world, and sadly many Christians, search for fulfillment through money, the arts, science, materialism, friendships, and many other things. Nonetheless, these are fleeting and only bring about a temporary reward of happiness that must be worked for; but Jesus liberally gives an abundant, fulfilling life to any Christian who simply yields to Him.

Jesus said, *"Peace I leave with you, my peace I give unto you: not as the world giveth, give I unto you. Let not your heart be troubled, neither let it be afraid"* (John 14:27). This is a promise, guaranteed by the Lord. Our hearts can rest in peace because Christ has promised that He will never leave us, nor forsake us (Hebrews 13:5). Likewise, Christ's presence encourages our hearts to face our troubles and perplexities, because He is with us (Deuteronomy 31:6-8).

Psalm 23:4 says, *"Yea, though I walk through the valley of the shadow of death, I will fear no evil: for thou art with me; thy rod and thy staff they comfort me."* The peace of Christ found in His presence gives our hearts the stability not to feel overwhelmed, troubled, or afraid. Christ's peace strengthens us, and gives us the ability not to avoid difficulties but to embrace unpleasant circumstances. This is why Jesus is the God of peace; He supplies His peace for us to walk with Him through uncertainties.

The peace of the world only can offer temporary relief to help you cope with problems and difficult circumstances, such as by drinking alcohol or practicing yoga. Yet again, this merely relieves you from your problems briefly, because eventually you must face your suffering, only to find yourself ill-equipped to endure what you preferred to avoid.

The peace that Jesus supplies is free. He gives it. You simply must receive it. You do not have to strive or toil for it. Neither do you have to sit in some type of posture and try to empty your mind (as offered by yoga). You must simply receive Christ's peace even in the midst of life's busyness and perplexities. You must not be anxious but be in prayer and communion with God; He most certainly gives attention to your heart and its requests. That is one of His promises (1 Peter 3:12).

You must yield your mind and heart to God; you must abandon your worries, and not succumb to anxious thoughts, but become consumed in affectionate thoughts on God. Then the peace of God, which passes all understanding, will keep your heart and mind through the power of Christ Jesus. This is how you can rest and enjoy God.

Christ's peace helps you and me to enjoy a priceless gift God has given to us: the entrustment of God's gospel. It is a splendid thought to try to understand that we have been allowed by God to take His gospel of peace and share it with people, even our enemies.

Not only is it an entrustment, it is our duty. We have the wonderful responsibility to use our mouths as well as our testimonies to demonstrate Christ before the world. Therefore, as the scriptures tell us, we are to stand fast in the liberty wherewith Christ has made us free. We are not to *"be entangled again with the yoke of bondage"* (Galatians 5:1).

What can we say then? Should we continue in sin, that His grace may abound? God forbid. How can we, who are dead to sin, live any longer in it?

The world is going to Hell, and we have been liberated from sin by the cross of Christ. Our old man is crucified with Christ; we are buried with Christ by baptism (baptism with the Holy Spirit) into His death, that as Christ was raised up from the dead by the glory of the Father, even so we also should walk in newness of life (Romans 6:1-8). Since we are new creatures, old things have passed away; we must understand all things have become new (2 Corinthians 5:17).

As Christ yielded Himself to the Father, we are to yield ourselves to Christ. If you are not experiencing this abundant life, then all you need to do is to submit yourself in obedience to God. This includes surrendering all areas of your life or ideals of your mind which you strive to control. Hesitating to give God control robs you of a more abundant life. Surrender gives you abundant life in Christ. As you begin living more abundantly with Christ, your Christian responsibility to so shine as a light will be better understood. Then God will raise you up to be a faithful instrument in His hands to help influence more people to consider and come to Christ.

If you desire your life to positively touch other lives in a spiritual sense then you must have a great deal of this abundant life yourself. Jesus said, *"He that believeth on me, as the scripture hath said, out of his belly shall flow rivers of living water"* (John 7:38). That word *"believeth"* is not referring to an intellectual belief or knowledge. It refers to a heartfelt belief, a conviction, reliance, and total trust. Jesus was saying that the person who possesses a fervent belief in Christ for remission of sins *is* the individual through whom the indwelling Holy Spirit can manifest God's grace. Heart belief gives the Holy Spirit the liberty to flow out from a person's heart (like a mighty river) the witness of God's grace by displaying a character of love, joy, peace, longsuffering, gentleness, goodness, faith, meekness, and temperance (Galatians 5:22-23). Such grace is captivating. It seizes people's attention and draws them toward Christ.

Now these are living waters, not the dead, murky waters of a stagnant life, but living! If you have ever been to a flowing river, you will notice that in the middle of the river the waters flow the fastest downstream. Any river is a physical representation of a determined Christian living an abundant life with Christ. He who is determined to live like Christ can discover a spiritual life to a heavenly degree. He is the Christian who seeks God daily. He is obedient to God's Word. He picks up his cross daily and dies to himself and lives controlled by the Holy Spirit. A determined Christian's life is filled with living waters flowing rapidly through him. The gospel flows from God's Word into his heart, then up and out of his mouth into the ears of people. God pours the river of living change through him into the lives of others around him. People are refreshed; they desire to know more of Christ, and sooner rather than later, people get saved and discipled. Such a life is so encouraging to people.

Furthermore, you may have been to a river where you might have noticed that some parts of it on the sides next to the banks contain stagnant waters. These stagnant parts of the river can be filled with sluggish water that just seems to be sitting in place. It does not seem to be going anywhere. It is the same with a Christian who does not have a spiritual life in the Lord. This type of Christian is just stuck in the self-absorbed affairs of his own life. He is not pressing toward the mark for the valuable prize of the high calling of God in Christ Jesus (Philippines 3:14). It is evident because he does not spend time alone with God each day in the Bible and prayer; or if he does, it is because it has become a daily routine, which he does to quiet his conscience. Neither does he serve God from love, but rather performs out of tradition, duty, or compulsion. He is not interested in God's work to bring people closer to the Savior, nor in bringing glory to God. No one is being rescued around him and his involvement in the lives of people is sluggish. God is not able to bring glorious change in his life or the lives of people around him because of his stagnant spiritual life. He is self-serving and self-indulgent. This type of Christian lacks influence in the lives of others around him.

Nevertheless, the water in the middle of the river is flowing. The part of the river that has movement is filled with life, nutrients, and oxygen. It is the same with a Christian who has an influential spiritual life. This determined type of Christian is naturally concerned with the eternal destiny of others. He is Christ-centered and focused in honoring Christ and bringing God the glory He deserves. He is filled with love, and he labors to guide people toward the Savior. Many are being reached around him. He has his priorities correct and aims to please God. People look at him and notice that God is doing a great work through his life, and others are attracted to him because of the presence of God in his life. He is full of the abundant life Jesus Christ gives. Many want what he has and seek to learn how to have that closeness with God.

Christians like this seem to be a rare find these days. But oh, how refreshing it is to be near them. Their determination to please and glorify God just emanates from the presence of God in them. You cannot come into contact with them without feeling the power of God's presence within and about them. They are determined within their souls to know God and humbly walk with Him. They love God and are in love with Him. They have an intimate spiritual life with Christ that shines God's love and hope toward people (Colossians 1:27). It is not merely while they are talking about religious topics, but even in the ordinary affairs and things of their lives you are conscious there is something about the person that tells you they live for God and Him alone.

Such determined individuals are used by God for the quickening of others. Many will come to know God by such people who allow Him to pour His abundant life through them. A Christian who desires to be a living, effectual servant of God will seek the Lord in order to know Him and to be deeply influenced by Him to a heavenly degree in every area of life.

The joy of our salvation should radiate from our countenances (Philippians 4:4-5). God does not use dead instruments to work living miracles in saving many souls from Hell. Rather God enjoys using men, women, and children who are filled with His Spirit, living His abundant life, and who are determined to be expendable for Christ's mission.

Therefore, what sort of Christian are you? There are many who are alive physically, but they are not altogether alive spiritually. If you want to be a shining, living, effectual instrument in God's hands, you must be determined to have a heartfelt passion, a Spirit-led attitude, and a determined will to obey God. You must pick up your cross *daily*, die to yourself, and humbly abide in Christ. Once you are firmly determined to do so, you can immediately cry out to the Lord and say with tears, "Lord, I'm determined; *'help my unbelief; make me into the manner of person I ought to be, in all holy conversation and godliness'"* (Mark 9:24; 2 Peter 3:11). Then God can do something with you beyond your wildest imagination.

The question is, will you lay aside every weight, hindrance, and sin that so easily besets you, and look to Jesus?

Chapter Fourteen

DO YOU ASPIRE TO BE AS CHRIST—*Holy*?

HAVE YOU EVER OBSERVED a couple in love with one another? If you have, then you might have noticed something fascinating: one's love for another always moves his heart to conform himself to be the person his darling desires him to be. Why? Because he wants his love to be pleased. His mind is not on himself but on his darling. Likewise, we believers in Christ are in a relationship with God. God desires for us, his bride, to be holy. All the more, should we not be so in love with God that we aspire to live and be as He is, *holy*?

This brings us to another quality a Christian needs if he is going to be determined to experience life more abundantly with the Lord. Jesus Christ is holy, and the abundant life He bestows on those who seek it only comes through a holiness of character.

I am not talking about seeking perfection, for there is no one righteous and none who does good (Romans 3). Neither am I talking about man-made ideals and traditions. God warns in Isaiah 64:6 that *"we are all as an unclean thing, and all our righteousnesses are as filthy rags."* Consequently, any holiness we attempt to bring about by our own self-righteousness, any deed one might regard as good, will in due course be revealed by God's righteous reproving as an essence of self. God will have nothing to do with the self, because our self is full of egoism, self-conceit, and pride: *vanity*. Therefore, we are in need of God-given holiness, which can only be produced by the indwelling Holy Spirit within us.

This biblical holiness that is entirely of God is rooted deep down in an individual's heart from the indwelling presence of Almighty God. It is expressed outwardly only because the heart is filled with genuine holiness (God), manifested through godliness in demeanor, speech, and actions.

A Christian who is determined to be exceedingly useful for the kingdom of God must realize that God is pleased to use clean instruments for His work. God would choose to use people who would not compromise His own holy character. Therefore, God enjoys selecting holy instruments to accomplish His majestic mission.

Yes, the blood of Jesus cleanses us thoroughly from all sin, and our eternal position is holy and settled in Heaven; but our daily disposition regularly needs to be cleaned up. In other words, our standing is perfect, justified, and holy *in* Christ before the holy God; but our state may not always reflect before people the holiness we have in Christ Jesus. Just like a little child playing in the mud, Christians sometimes get dirty on the outside. Sometimes Christians participate in sin and get ourselves dirty. Praise the Lord that 1 John 1:9 lets us know that God is there to clean us up from sinful tendencies.

Nevertheless, if someone continues to play in the mire of sin, then he continues to bring attention back onto himself for a re-cleaning of his disposition. If God's attention has to continually address the cleanup of a believer, then that Christian is not yet available for God to advance him for use in greater glorious works.

Sin draws attention inward toward ourselves. Holiness draws attention outward away from ourselves and toward God and people. God always meets individuals at their own spiritual levels. If a Christian continues to play in sin, then God patiently stays still and with great longsuffering works on that Christian's downfalls, strongholds, struggles, and sins. However, the moment a Christian decides he has had enough of sin and yields completely to God's abundant mercy and grace, he opens up his heart to express holy character in fervent love for others to see. And God can do something mighty with that!

A Christian who seeks to be effectual in his walk with God must determine to constantly be learning and meditating on the holy scriptures, for it is God's Word that feeds our souls, which can then enable our bodies to partake in God's holiness. Holiness is not a list of dos and don'ts that a Christian has to follow as a set of rules in his life. Instead, holiness is the evidence that one has become aware of God and aspires to be as He is. Therefore, his actions match the words of his lips as he is ever more inspired by the presence of God's Holy Spirit. First John 2:6 makes known that whosoever says he is of Christ should himself also walk as Jesus walked. Meaning, he must aim to have a lifestyle and communications that resemble the Lord.

God is not interested in a people who draw near to Him and honor Him with only their mouths or religious activities. This is vain worship, and merely man's ideals and traditions (Matthew 15:8-9). The Father seeks individuals to worship Him in spirit *and* in truth. Jesus said, *"God is a Spirit: and they that worship him must worship him in spirit and in truth"* (John 4:23-24). God wants men whose hearts are enamored with Him to walk with Him. This kind of heart is the instrument that naturally produces the holiness of character needed to extend the Kingdom of God on earth.

A determined servant of God realizes it is of no use talking about "the glorious life" on Sundays with church people, and then living a sinful life during the week. A Christian must be very careful not only to be innocent of actual wrongdoings but also not to be a cause of offense to the weak ones in the body of Christ (Romans 14:1-15:7). A holy Christian is sensitive to the needs of people and the Holy Spirit's guidance because he has a deep, genuine love for God and people.

Love produces holiness. Jesus quoted the law and emphasized what we are to do. He said, *"Thou shalt love the Lord thy God with all thy heart, and with all thy soul, and with all thy mind. This is the first and great commandment. And the second is like unto it, Thou shalt love thy neighbour as thyself. On these two commandments hang all the law and the prophets"* (Matthew 22:37-40).

A holy Christian is so in love with God that though he is freed from the law (Romans 7:6; 8:2), his love compels him to live a life in obedience to the law before mankind (Romans 8:4; 14:7; 15:2). A holy Christian lives by the principle that all things are lawful, but not all things are helpful and useful in service toward others (Romans 14). He lives thinking about others and therefore he lives a standard that moves him to receive others, just as Christ also received us to the glory of God (Romans 15:7). He seeks to do things that are right and just. He willingly abstains from things that might not be wrong in and of themselves, but that might be an occasion for stumbling to others (Romans 14:13). A determined Christian seeks to live in such a holy way that his life is always right before men. He has a good testimony before the world. He stands out!

A determined servant of God who wholly *"follows holiness"* reaps the promise of seeing His Lord (Hebrews 12:14). He realizes that if his actions do not match up to the gospel he preaches then those around him will reject his message. They will scorn him, and they will not repent, as they will ask him the same questions, "Where is your own repentance?" and "Why do I need your God if He can't clean up your life?"

This is why the world needs to see a holy character about us. Romans 6:22 makes known that Christ's holiness in you is the evidence that you have been made free from sin and no longer a servant of sin. His holiness is liberating! God, through death on His cross opened access for us to experience freedom from sin and its consequences. We simply must pick up our cross and die to ourselves each day to enjoy this grace of holiness.

When people see a Christian who not only preaches about holiness but is himself a holy man, these same people will be drawn toward the holy God by his character as well as by his words. Therefore, his mind is made up to obey the Lord and resist the carnal desires of his flesh so that God may be glorified and others may be guided toward the Lord. A determined servant of God spends much time in private intimate fellowship with God so that his public path of service reflects the holiness of God's character. This is the abundant life that Christ offers.

Let me ask you something: When is the last time you heard a Christian say, "I want to be holy"? Or how about this, when in your whole *lifetime* have you heard a Christian assert, "I aspire to be holy"? Probably not many times, if even once at all. There are few and far between who yearn to be holy. It is a rare occasion to meet an individual who truly aspires to be holy. Although God commands us to be holy, why are we not aspiring to be as He is, *holy*, during our pilgrimage on this earth?

Sadly, so many Christians are not picking up their crosses daily and dying to themselves. They are living unholy lifestyles that are deplorably below biblical standards of righteousness and holiness. Even worse, they are congregating together and calling themselves a church. These modern-day social gatherings that call themselves a church have become a third-rate amusement gathering. This unholy amusement is so much below mediocre standards that the world no longer even goes to the church of Jesus Christ for a type of morality check-up, as in the old days.

The world certainly needs to see a clean-cut line of demarcation between Christians and the world: A gracious separation that distinguishes God's ways from the world's way. Although many Christians' ways have changed for the worse, God still commands in Isaiah 52:11 for Christians to *"Be ye clean, that bear the vessels of the Lord."* Did you notice that God was not talking to the world? He was talking to believers. It is only believers who bear the vessels of God.

Sometimes the question arises in people's minds, "How do I know if my present state before mankind is holy or not?" Indeed, we should be concerned in knowing whether our character, conduct, and communications are really manifesting God's holiness. The thing to understand is what holiness really is according to God's Word. What is practical holiness on a day-to-day basis in this life we live? The answer is that true practical holiness is never self-conscious; it does not look at itself in the glass; and if it did, it would see only the beauty of Christ, not itself, reflected there. Holiness is God's beauty portrayed for all to see through us. We were made to the praise of God's glory, and this can be appropriately seen when we live a lifestyle which is pure, lovely, virtuous, and bears a good report. The scriptures say, *"That ye may be blameless and harmless, the sons of God, without rebuke, in the midst of a crooked and perverse nation, among whom ye shine as lights in the world"* (Philippians 2:15).

True beauty should draw a man's thoughts toward God and never away from Him. Take for instance a flower or a tree. They are beautiful because they exhibit only their created purpose, illuminating God's beautiful character. On the flip side, a woman dressed like a harlot defaces beauty because she has substituted her primal beauty for a facade of conceit and vainglory. But the woman whose character is one of integrity, meekness, and modesty is one who exhibits her created purpose, and this is beautiful: a showing of God's character. Any attention drawn to her reveals attributes of God's beautiful character. Beauty that is true outwardly radiates God's glory and the inner dwelling of God's presence (1 Peter 3:3-4).

The holiest individual is the one who loves righteousness most and eschews evil with a fervent passion. A holy person sets himself apart from his carnal desires and the world's manners. He makes himself presentable for God's use so that the works of God should be made manifest in him. He wholeheartedly believes God's Word and unwaveringly trusts God for however God may choose to use him. He lives a distinguished life with integrity and character, which gives him opportunities to glorify God and to seek to extend Christ's kingdom. His manner of life is right and clean; his temperament is good and his conduct is peaceful toward all men. He carries himself righteously and is charitable toward people. Therefore, his conscience is blame-free.

When people look at a holy man, they at once know they are looking at a new man. His disposition displays the promise of God's life transformation: *"if any man be in Christ, he is a new creature: old things are passed away; behold, all things are become new"* (2 Corinthians 5:17). Therefore, holiness makes evident before the world that Christ indeed makes a dead man into a new man alive in Christ.

God has commanded both in the Old and New Testaments for His children to *"Be ye holy, for I am holy."* He commands this in Exodus 22:31, Leviticus 19:2, and 1 Peter 1:16, to name a few. Any so-called unholy Christian is a disrespect to the world and a dishonor to God. Any so-called unholy Christian is a disservice to the world and is of no service to God.

God is pleased with and desires to use holy instruments in magnificent ways. This is greatly exemplified in the books of Exodus and Leviticus. God instructed Moses in how to make a holy tabernacle, holy clothing, and holy instruments for use by holy priests in the worship of the holy God. God commanded all holy things to be consecrated for His use only and no other (Leviticus 19). When one reads these instructions and the law in the books of Exodus and Leviticus, one notices that God emphasizes and repeats the word *"holy"* numerous times. The word is mentioned 45 times in Exodus and 77 times in Leviticus. Certainly, God has established that *"holiness"* is important to the Lord, wouldn't you say? Holy God wants holy instruments for His holy use.

Today you and I are God's instruments. Romans 6:13 says, *"Neither yield ye your members as instruments of unrighteousness unto sin: but yield yourselves unto God, as those that are alive from the dead, and your members as instruments of righteousness unto God."* Do your walk and communications exhibit holiness? Are you seen as a holy instrument for God before the world? Since God views us as instruments, it would be wise for us to be instruments that have holiness in character so that God can choose to magnificently use us for His cause in any manner He desires. Even if an ignorant man lives a holy life, God will honor him and use him to reach out to lost souls bound to Hell. Then he will not be ignorant; he will become a wise man. For *"the fruit of the righteous is a tree of life; and he that winneth souls is wise"* (Proverbs 11:30).

Let any man once become genuinely holy, even though he has but the slenderest of abilities, he will be a more fit instrument in God's hands than a man of enormous skills who is living a disobedient and unclean life in the sight of the Lord God Almighty.

A Christian might know how to speak well and even eloquently, but if a Christian does not have a life of holiness, then there will be few souls, if any, saved and discipled by him. An unholy Christian will probably come up with other reasons why people are not being saved and discipled by him, denying that the problem is due to his lack of holiness. He might blame other people, or the generation in which he lives, or anything except the true culprit—himself. Nonetheless, that will be the root of the whole mischief he encounters.

A Christian might even possess considerable abilities, be of significant industry, and increase in secular vanities and prides of life, but at the same time lack an increase in the winning and discipling of souls. I have seen it before and I am sure I will see it again. I recall one man who is abundant in money, diligent in his work, and can talk about any subject, yet his lifestyle stinks. By his own admission he has told me that he has difficulty winning people to Christ. His problem is that he does not have holiness of God in his life.

Christians need God's holiness upon their communications as well as their lifestyles. Sure, you can talk about Jesus, but if aspects of your lifestyle are questionable then nobody is going to heed the warning of the gospel from your lips. Even if people would listen to your gospel message with you living an unholy life, you still have a problem: you are not living before God as you ought to live. The issue really isn't your walk before man, but before God. Galatians 1:10 asks a good question, *"For do I now persuade men, or God?"* We need to be wise and walk circumspectly in holiness so that God is pleased, *not merely man.*

God wants to see holiness. Although man looks at the outward appearance, God still looks on the heart (1 Samuel 16:7). A Christian whose character is unholy needs a reality check before God. His priorities are not in order. He is shortsighted, looking at the vanities of life, which are physically seen. The visual matters are blocking his view of the invisible eternal matters of life. His focus is not correct. His long-term vision is blurred and dimmed. If he would stop looking at the visible matters of life, he could adjust his perspective and correctly see the invisible matters of eternal value (2 Corinthians 4:18). Unlike a determined servant of God who has the focus off of himself and instead on eternal souls, an unholy Christian deceives himself because he forgets to place Jesus as the number-one priority.

Holiness is a requirement for communion and fellowship with God. A Christian's holiness ought to show itself as what it is—living a life in communion with God, free from unnecessary distractions that come between himself and God. If a man delivers his own message, it will have the power that his own character gives to it. However, if he delivers his Lord's message, having heard it from his Lord's lips, that will be quite another thing; the great force of His message lies in the power of the Holy Spirit.

God's greatest delight is our joy in Him alone and in His ways. We have the choice to either resist God or cleave to Him. No matter what, or which way, God will receive the honor, glory, and praise that is due His name. Hopefully you will choose and experience the joy of God having His way with you, rather than resisting His will and purpose for your life.

In light of this, does your life reflect that of a vessel for the holiness of God? Or are you walking in resistance and indulging in self-gratification?

Whichever the answer, would you choose today to cleave to Jesus and aspire to be as your Savior is—*holy*?

Holiness costs much! It is a delusion to aim at holiness that costs nothing. Likewise, an effective servant of God must get ready for the whole service by private fellowship with Him, and real holiness in personal character. He comes to God and asks God for three things: He asks God: (1) "Lord, search my heart and know me (Psalm 139:23-24). Turn on Heaven's beam lights and reveal to me any hidden sin lurking in the crevices of my heart." (2) "Break me. Purge me. Clean me, and burn out any sin, pride, conceit, or arrogance existing within me" (Psalm 51:7). (3) "I'm listening, Lord. Instruct me in what I am to do, today" (Acts 9:6).

Can you ask God those three things? Will you? If you do, He will listen to your prayer and He will gladly do as you ask.

Chapter Fifteen

WHERE DO YOU FIND SECURITY?

ONE MORNING I WAS READING MY BIBLE in the comfort of my recliner, enjoying the presence of God's sweet Spirit consoling me with some precious scriptures from His Word. As I read, I came upon a question that caused me to pause for a moment and receive the wisdom that only God could impart to me. The text was 2 Corinthians 10:7, which poses the question: *"Do ye look on things after the outward appearance?"*

This text captured my attention and caused me to examine my way of thinking about a specific matter. The Lord revealed my need to better understand my reasoning so that my way of thinking would not become a stumbling block to myself or to others.

It is a good idea to examine and scrutinize ourselves often before our holy God upon reading simple but profound questions in the scriptures. We should consider and understand the intents, motives, and reasonings behind why we may or may not be doing something. Galatians 6:4 says, *"But let every man prove his own work, and then shall he have rejoicing in himself alone, and not in another."* This way we can be ready to abandon all ungodly intents or interests we discover within ourselves and embrace holy and acceptable service to God.

Getting back to 2 Corinthians 10:7, I think this question stood out for several reasons. First, it appears in a remarkable place in scripture. In the context surrounding this question, the writer Paul was pouring his heart out to some believers. He cautioned them to follow righteous instructors and warned against being swayed by external appearances rather than inward reality, such as following vain teachers who commend their own selves for the praise and respect of others. Paul warned against cunning teachers who seek men's approval rather than God's; they spoil the faith of believers by the use of eloquent words and destructive teachings after the traditions of men and philosophies of the world, and not of Christ. Paul took the extra humble effort to abase himself and rightfully warned the brethren of certain detractors of the ministry. Meanwhile, he dealt with them as a concerned father would with a son in a spirit of love and meekness. He vindicated his God-given right to be their minister, and in so doing, he correctly defended against those false accusers who were trying to lead believers astray from keeping their confidence in Paul's teachings about Jesus Christ. At length, he provoked them to have a readiness in body and have a sound mind so that they might fulfill their obedience toward God in Christ.

As I just mentioned at the opening of this chapter, the question in 2 Corinthians 10:7 brought a bit of conviction to my personal way of thinking. God smote my heart concerning a responsibility I had been overseeing. After deep meditation and personal probing in prayer, God altered my way of thinking in light of His Word. God provoked me to change my approach in ministry toward a company of nonbelievers. God used this question to fine-tune some particulars in my ministry that are important to Him. I am grateful to submit as He leads, because Christ taught, *"He that is faithful in that which is least is faithful also in much: and he that is unjust in the least is unjust also in much"* (Luke 16:10).

Perhaps, like me, you too have been guilty of making decisions based on an observation of the *outward appearance* (as mentioned in 2 Corinthians 10:7). We are not alone in this wrongdoing, and thankfully, we have examples to learn from.

For example, even the "father of faith," Abraham, sinned and caused a big uproar because of wrongful perception (Genesis 20). Abraham's mistaken observation could have cost his and Sarah's lives. Most certainly, it did cause them big problems before king Ahimelech and before God. Abraham and Sarah had been journeying and temporarily made a stay in the city of Gerar. As they arrived, Abraham thoughtlessly considered certain unfamiliar sights and sounds to be ungodly, and therefore quickly concluded that the fear of God was not in that place. His mistaken, hasty conclusion swayed Sarah to follow along: they both lied to the king and said they were siblings, rather than telling the truth that they were husband and wife. Naturally, the king took a liking to Sarah and brought her into his palace for marriage preparations.

Providentially, God intervened and made this sin known to the king (Genesis 20:6).

The king, rightfully fearful of divine judgment, arose early in the morning and confronted Abraham about his deception. Genesis 20:11 records Abraham's response, saying, *"Because I thought, Surely the fear of God is not in this place; and they will slay me for my wife's sake."* Abraham should not have come to a quick conclusion based on what he had seen and heard within the city. Abraham misjudged his own gracious God; therefore, God reproved him, and he learned that this king indeed was a man of integrity and faith in God's law.

First observations can certainly cause conflict or dilemmas down the road, as was the case for Abraham and Sarah. For one, an initial look on something can incorrectly be based on our personal viewpoints, values, or ideas. Second, our perception of something can be misleading, especially when based on feelings or emotions. This causes many problems! This is why the scriptures are adamant that we should walk by faith and not by sight (2 Corinthians 5:7). Feelings and emotions are temporary but faith lasts and helps you look past what you are feeling. Faith helps you to partake in the grace of diligence, virtue, knowledge, temperance, and patience. Grace helps us refrain from making hasty decisions. It also works to slow us down and help us carefully consider a matter with an eternal mindset rather than solely considering the temporary state of matters.

For example, in a farmer's field you have wheat and tares growing together. Wheat is the good crop, and tares are the darnel, the degenerate wheat. Tares so closely resemble genuine wheat that one cannot be distinguished from the other until harvest-time. It is only when both wheat and tares are fully ripe that a farmer can see there is no grain in the ears of the tares. Then the farmer can separate the wheat from the fruitless tares. But if a farmer prematurely tries to root up the tares from the wheat he will certainly cause injury to the good blades of wheat. Therefore, a farmer must use the grace of knowledge and patience, and wait until the end of the harvest to distinguish the good from the bad.

We too, like the farmer, must partake in God's grace in situations we encounter, so as not to make hasty judgments that can cause injury to people anytime. We Christians should use our liberty in Christ to add to our faith diligence, virtue, knowledge, temperance, and patience as ways to encourage others and avoid becoming a stumbling block to the weak. We who are strong should bear the infirmities of the weak, and not to gratify ourselves, lest we offend our brother (1 Corinthians 8:9, 13; Romans 15:1).

Merely looking at the *outward appearance* of a matter can cause our labors to become messy, or it can make us unfaithful in response to needful specifics that might initially appear unimportant but in the long run prove to be of great importance. Jesus said, *"Inasmuch as ye did it not to one of the least of these, ye did it not to me"* (Matthew 25:45). Although He was referring to serving people, the principle applies to serving God in every area of life as well. We ought not to overlook anything great or small, but minister and serve with diligence and attentiveness.

Thankfully, as I mature with age I am also learning to slow down and take my time in the decision-making process. Proverbs 14:29 says, *"...but he that is hasty of spirit exalteth folly."* Proverbs 21:5 also says, *"The thoughts of the diligent tend only to plenteousness; but of every one that is hasty only to want."* How true that is! Hasty decisions can sometimes lead to regretful moments later down the road. I am so glad that I am learning to pray more before jumping into a commitment or making an important decision. If I do not have the absolute peace of God, I have discovered I must stop and wait upon the Lord.

There are precious and valuable promises to those who wait upon the Lord. Isaiah 40:31 makes this clear, saying, *"But they that wait upon the LORD shall renew their strength; they shall mount up with wings as eagles; they shall run, and not be weary; and they shall walk, and not faint."* When we stay focused in the work God has for us today and patiently wait upon Him for direction to move forward into a new frontier then there is peace, enjoyment, and longevity (Proverbs 3:1-2). Normally time helps to adjust our sentiments and eventually it works out emotions and feelings, making it possible for a good decision to be made based on unbiased facts rather than temporary attitudes. So we should learn to happily wait on God. His timing is perfect.

There is no need to become frustrated, stressed, or anxious when we wait upon the Lord. The Christian who waits purposefully upon the Lord understands that no work of God is thwarted unless the Lord says so. Whatever the Lord has thought shall surely come to pass. Whatever the Lord has purposed, so shall it stand (Isaiah 14:24). Therefore we should consider the question God proposes in Isaiah 14:27, *"For the LORD of hosts hath purposed, and who shall disannul it? and his hand is stretched out, and who shall turn it back?"* The answer is, no one! This is why it is important not to be hasty or rash with our mouths, actions, or decisions. We need to seek the whole counsel of God before making important judgments.

Determined

Jesus taught, *"For which of you, intending to build a tower, sitteth not down first, and counteth the cost, whether he have sufficient to finish it? Lest haply, after he hath laid the foundation, and is not able to finish it, all that behold it begin to mock him, Saying, This man began to build, and was not able to finish. Or what king, going to make war against another king, sitteth not down first, and consulteth whether he be able with ten thousand to meet him that cometh against him with twenty thousand? Or else, while the other is yet a great way off, he sendeth an ambassage, and desireth conditions of peace"* (Luke 14:28-32).

If we do not count the costs and think through decisions before making them, then we stand a greater risk of making wrong choices. What we initially see with our eyes and hear with our ears is not always what is really happening. Our eyes and ears can improperly perceive a matter and misguide us into making great mistakes.

For example, years ago when I was checking out colleges to further my studies, I almost chose the wrong school. I had applied and been given invitations to attend several universities. One of the schools was nationally respected for its excellent academics and rigid disciplines, but its costs were very high!. My friends, counselors, and teachers with all good intentions expressed what a good pick it would be for me to attend this particular university. Their reasonings sounded persuasive, despite the fact that I could not afford it. Even worse, at the time I lacked discipline in good study habits. I almost made the error of choosing to attend this university simply because of its reputation and what people were advising. Who knows? If I had attended, maybe I would have flunked out because of bad study habits, or perhaps today I would be over $100,000 in debt. Only God knows.

I am grateful that God intervened and arrested my attention one specific week during my high school senior year. God caused me to pause and re-evaluate where I should attend. After good prayer, God showed me the school I was to attend for my undergraduate studies. When I visited the campus of the university He intended for me, God reaffirmed my decision by giving me His presence of great peace (just as Philippians 4:6-7 promises).

Nonetheless, there are times as I look back in life where I have made hasty decisions that still affect me today. For example, even though I received a generous scholarship from the university I attended, as a young man greed got the best of me and I still took out unnecessary college loans. My perception, blurred by greed, has caused me to spend many years making needless monthly loan payments.

I imagine if I would listen to your life story, you would also have some examples where you foolishly looked at the *outward appearance*, and without much thought you acted upon your initial perception and made a hasty decision, which later down the road came back to bite you. I hope that now you have learned to patiently seek the Lord, and wait for His counsel before you make another decision.

Proverbs 11:14 warns, *"Where no counsel is, the people fall: but in the multitude of counsellors there is safety."* And the greatest counselors are the sixty-six books of the Holy Bible. Psalm 119:24 expressly tells us, *"Thy testimonies also are my delight and my counsellors."* Whose? God's testimonies! His holy Word. For *"[w]ithout counsel purposes are disappointed: but in the multitude of counsellors they are established"* (Proverbs 15:22). Because *"in multitude of counsellors there is safety"* (Proverbs 24:6).

We need godly counsel and good understanding because things on the outside are not always what they are inside. Thankfully, God is not like us, and praise the Lord He does not look at the *outward appearance*. If He did, none of us would be saved. Our outward appearance would have inhibited any prospect for salvation. I do not know about you, but there was a time years ago wherein my heart was broken and yearning for Christ, but on the outside I portrayed myself before others as sophisticated and self-confident, acting as if I had no problems. The world was fooled, but the Lord saw beyond my pretentious *outward appearance*. He saw a sinful and vainglorious self-serving man, filled with confusion, who needed Jesus Christ. Thank the Lord that *"the LORD seeth not as man seeth; for man looketh on the outward appearance, but the LORD looketh on the heart"* (1 Samuel 16:7). Amen! And because He looks on our heart, salvation is possible!

In the passage above, God was speaking to the prophet Samuel. Samuel had an important judgment to make. He had to find God's next king for Israel and anoint him with God's blessing. Many men would have loved to be anointed with God's blessing as king. If Samuel had taken account of men seeking the duty, he probably would have made a grave error in choosing based on what his eyes and ears perceived. The men who were brought before Samuel were robust, valiant, and handsome. From a human standpoint, they appeared to be the intelligent choice for next in line to be king. Nonetheless, God does not look at the outward appearance. God is not captivated by a person's physique, intellect, or capabilities. God looks into the hearts of men; therefore when God was searching for a new king, He was seeking someone after His own heart (1 Samuel 13:14).

As each man stood before the prophet Samuel, hoping to be the one anointed king, Samuel discerned the voice of God's Spirit, saying, "These are not the ones. Continue searching." Samuel obeyed God, and saw beyond the natural sense. Samuel continued seeking. The scriptures tell us, *"And Samuel said unto Jesse* [the father], *Are here all thy children? And he said, There remaineth yet the youngest, and, behold, he keepeth the sheep. And Samuel said unto Jesse, Send and fetch him: for we will not sit down till he come hither. And he sent, and brought him in. Now he was ruddy, and withal of a beautiful countenance, and goodly to look to. And the LORD said, Arise, anoint him: for this is he. Then Samuel took the horn of oil, and anointed him in the midst of his brethren: and the Spirit of the LORD came upon David from that day forward"* (1 Samuel 16:11-13).

God has never been impressed with what man makes himself out to be. God never has called an individual for His cause based on a man's appearance, abilities, or knowledge. Not many men of great intellect, not many mighty men, nor many noble men are called. God most of the time chooses the foolish things of the world to confound the wise, and God chooses the weak things of the world to confound the things that are mighty (1 Corinthians 1:26-27). Jesus explained that many are called but few are chosen (Matthew 22:14), because many disqualify themselves by their pride, conceit, or self-confidence. God is not one bit impressed with what a man can seemingly give Him, whether it be business power, influence, money, love of the arts or science, things, or preferential self-sacrifice.

Thankfully, God is no respecter of persons (Acts 10:34). The LORD looks at the heart of man. God searches for a heart that is filled with ambition, passion, loyalty, and submission to Christ. The thing that pleases and draws God near to someone is the heart that humbles itself and seeks to let God be on the throne.

There is not one Christian who has done some *thing* to earn the right to be a servant of God. We all can serve because God by His grace calls us into His fold. Just as there is not one *thing* a Christian did to be saved by his own credit or merit, there is not one *thing* a Christian can do to maintain his salvation. None of us deserves salvation in the first place. We all should be burning in the lake of fire because of our guilty wrongdoings. Praise the LORD, God graciously called out our names and invited us into the fold. We Christians heard the voice of God's Spirit, and by faith we responded to His gracious call. All we did was to repent of ours sins and place total faith in the Lord Jesus, in *His* perfect work of atonement. It is Christ and what Christ did to pay for our sins that gives believers reconciliation with God the Father; we had nothing to do with it.

Salvation is OF GOD, not man (Jonah 2:9)! Therefore, why in the world would anyone conclude that a person has to maintain a certain level of fellowship or servanthood with God to keep his salvation? This is nonsense. Such a damnable belief is no less than a WORKS religion! If we cannot do any good works to become saved, then surely we cannot do any thing to maintain our salvation. Nor can any bad works make us unsaved.

Anyone who says you can lose your salvation by not behaving in a prescribed manner that God wants does not understand grace nor sin. For we are all sinners. Just think about it; when has your state been completely sinless? NEVER. We all have some amount of pride, conceit, vainglory, or ungodly thoughts within us. It is only because of God's great grace that He sanctifies us as well as justifies us and makes us righteous in Jesus Christ. God does it all (Philippians 2:13)!

Galatians 3:2-3 asks some good questions, *"...Received ye the Spirit by the works of the law, or by the hearing of faith? Are ye so foolish? having begun in the Spirit, are ye now made perfect by the flesh?"* The answer is an emphatic, "No!" We are never made perfect by the flesh—that is, any attempts to do good and appease God. God has freely given to us the earnest of His Spirit through the redemption that is in Christ Jesus our Lord.

It is God who draws a man to Himself. It is God who convicts a man of sin. It is God who convicts a man of judgment. It is God who enlightens a man in righteousness. It is God who convinces a man to repent and call upon Christ. It is God who saves! And most certainly it is God who keeps a person's soul unto salvation (1 Peter 4:19).

Psalm 55:22 says, *"Cast thy burden upon the LORD, and he shall sustain thee: he shall never suffer the righteous to be moved."* Do you have a burden of sin? Then cast it to the Lord. God sustains those who humble themselves before Him and He gives them the peace of righteousness.

The Lord Jesus is the Author and Finisher of our faith (Hebrews 12:2). Our salvation is settled in Heaven (read all of 1 Peter chapter 1), sealed by the Holy Spirit (Ephesians 1:13), and sustained by both Christ and the Father (John 10:28-29).

I explain this to establish another quality that a determined servant of God must possess if he is going to have a godly influence on this world. He absolutely must be convinced of God's promise—his personal salvation.

If we study history we can learn a lot from the first Christians and their beliefs and practices. The early church was being persecuted for preaching the name of Jesus Christ. In the midst of this persecution, Christians such as Peter and John were still determined and motivated to speak with boldness and confidence about the gospel. They had a firm determination within themselves that nothing was going to shut them up.

On one occasion, Peter and John stood up and confidently spoke the gospel to a group of discriminatory religious leaders who demanded that the name of Jesus not be preached. Acts 4:13 enlightens us on this occasion, saying, *"Now when they saw the boldness of Peter and John, and perceived that they were unlearned and ignorant men, they marvelled; and they took knowledge of them, that they had been with Jesus."* This passage clearly makes known that Peter and John were both without formal education. Although they did have knowledge and understanding of God's law because of their Jewish heritage, they lacked the formal rabbinical schooling (John 1:40-42; 2:17; 4:27; Luke 9:51-54; Acts 10:1-34).

They had just come out of a life of being fishermen before following Jesus for three and half years. Fishermen were citizens who generally did not have a formal education in Israel back in those days. They were considered by the populace as *ignorant*. Although they were *unlearned* men by the opinions of their culture's leaders, being considered of low social standing, they still possessed a boldness and confidence in their demeanor and speech. The reason is that they had been with Jesus! They assuredly knew of Christ's promises, and their security in Jesus enabled them to unreservedly speak His name with courage, to represent Christ's cause and to proclaim a case for truth and righteousness with conviction, even to those who would rather subdue liberty through intimidation and hold captives captive.

Today, God is still empowering Christians to proclaim Christ's name with boldness and confidence. As Peter and John had been with Jesus (Mark 3:13-14), we too must spend time with Him. God flows His power only through those Christians who daily spend time alone with Him. Spending time with God each day empowers us to have the Holy Ghost boldness and confidence we need to minister to people. *"Now the Lord is that Spirit: and where the Spirit of the Lord is, there is liberty"* (2 Corinthians 3:17).

This power of confidence and courage God gives is never for the intention of being rude or dictatorial in our speech. God supplies ample courage so that we may demonstrate charity towards all types of people with the purpose of imparting the good news and guiding them closer to Christ.

Speaking the gospel of Jesus Christ should always be done in confident humility. Confidence is not tumultuous, boisterous, or rude; it is calm, firm, and refined in speech and actions. It sometimes takes courage to love and show charity to certain individuals. Must I say more? Therefore, may we be determined with a perfect resolve to go and show charity and proclaim Christ to them.

Later that day, after Peter and John's ordeal with the hatemongers, they regathered with other believers of Christ. Acts 4:23-31 gives the account of their gathering together, and in verses 24-30 we read the words of their prayer lifted up to God. These verses give an insight into the pattern of their thinking and the conviction they possessed in the midst of great persecution. I encourage you to open up your Bible and read the words of their whole prayer.

You should notice that their prayer was not for the conversion of the hypocrites. Nor was it for deliverance from opposition. Neither was it that they themselves might speak more carefully or more lovingly. Instead, their prayer was of thanksgiving toward God, even though there were many troubles and tribulations surrounding them. They thought it not strange concerning the fiery trial which was to try them, as though some strange thing happened to them. (1 Peter 4:12) They understood that the things that were happening to them were for the furtherance of the gospel (Philippians 1:12).

Fascinatingly, they asked nothing for themselves; their only petition was for *"all boldness"* to speak God's Word (verse 29) so that they could continue the job that they were commissioned to do—thereby jeopardizing their lives even more. Why is that? Do you think that it was because they were totally assured of their salvation in Christ? Do you think it was because of Christ's promise that He would never leave them nor forsake them (Hebrews 13:5)? Do you think it was because Christ said in the Great Commission, *"and, lo, I am with you alway, even unto the end of the world"* (Matthew 28:20)? Certainly so! These Christians understood that they dwelt in Christ and He dwelt in them. They recognized that truly the winning side is the Lord's and they were sheltered within that side.

Hebrews 13:5 says, *"Let your conversation be without covetousness; and be content with such things as ye have: for he hath said, I will never leave thee, nor forsake thee."* These first brethren had a security in Christ. This security enabled them to recognize that this world is not our home; therefore, they did not run for anything of this world. They were not covetous for some comfortable, luxurious life, because they understood that Heaven is their permanent residency (Ephesians 2:18-19). They understood they were strangers and pilgrims on this earth and were fixated on accomplishing Christ's mission (Hebrews 11:13). The presence of Christ's Spirit gave them the refuge our souls need.

Security in Christ enabled them to see beyond the temporal situations and to focus on the eternal concerns of individuals around them. They were able to see beyond the physical realm and into the spiritual realm. They saw through the surface layer of grime and dirt in people's conducts and attitudes, and saw the real heart of individuals underneath; thus, the gospel was spread to all men!

The gospel was a glorious compound of a terrible, yet tearful, tenderness that caused these early Christians to go forth as a dreadful army bent on taking human hearts captive for their crucified and risen Savior. They knew the meaning of Christ's promise: *"Because I live, ye shall live also"* (John 14:19). They knew the empowerment of the Holy Spirit. They did not have a spirit of fear, but of power and of love and of courage—of *power*, to reach out to their neighbors and speak the gospel truth fearlessly; of *love*, because it constrained and drove out any fear; and of *courage*, to stand up against all the dreadful engines of torture mustered by the Roman Empire and the Jewish rulers. They were filled with God's courage and became the invincible army of Christ for all future generations to learn from.

Acts 4:31 describes the result of their prayers to God: *"And when they had prayed, the place was shaken where they were assembled together; and they were all filled with the Holy Ghost, and they spake the word of God with boldness."* First, notice that they had a prayer meeting. They were joined together in prayer. (It would do Christians a lot of good today to join together for prayer times often.) Furthermore, they left their prayer meeting united in Christ. They were encouraged and strengthened to go back into their community, being filled with the Holy Ghost to speak the Word of God with boldness. Prayer always strengthens the brethren for the work of God.

Likewise, any prayer meeting we have should strengthen and provoke us to go back out into the world and proclaim Christ too. If it does not, then most surely God was not part of our meeting and we only gathered for a social affair.

It was the apostle John, inspired by the Holy Spirit, who affirmed the profound promise of God in his writings of 1 John 5:11-13. He wrote, *"And this is the record, that God hath given to us eternal life, and this life is in his Son. He that hath the Son hath life; and he that hath not the Son of God hath not life. These things have I written unto you that believe on the name of the Son of God; that ye may know that ye have eternal life, and that ye may believe on the name of the Son of God."* What an awesome passage of scripture! It reiterates God's precious promise of assurance in Christ!

God repeats within three back-to-back verses that those who have Jesus have life. This life is eternal. This awesome passage makes known God's promise that believers in Christ can know with certainty they are saved and saved for good! God says here that the salvation of someone is in *"the record."* Meaning, God has registered his name by the ink of His blood in the chronicles of the Lamb's Book of Life within the throne room of Heaven's headquarters. The believer's name has been recorded and is now preserved forever. Christ's blood sprinkled on the mercy seat in the tabernacle of Heaven is a bonafide proof that we are reconciled to God the Father forever and ever without end (Hebrews 1:3; 9:11-12, 14, 23-26; 12:24). Christ's atonement and resurrection on our behalf is the genuine evidence that what God has joined together cannot be put asunder. We have a sure salvation that even God Himself cannot undo. We have been shut in Christ! Amen!

Now please take a moment and carefully understand this: Any Christian can only enjoy life more abundantly with Christ, and become an effective servant of God, when he is absolutely sure of his own personal conversion and what the Lord has done for him. A Christian must have a complete assurance that he is saved and adopted into the family of God, and that he can never lose or forfeit his God-given gift of salvation.

The believer who is unsure or has some doubt concerning his salvation— if he really is eternally right with God or not—will not be able to effectually invest his life into the lives of others. You cannot give assurance if you do not have assurance yourself. *"Can the blind lead the blind? shall they not both fall into the ditch?"* (Luke 6:39)

Doubts blur a believer's sight and cause disruptions in his walk with God. Doubts obstruct a believer from enjoying a relationship with the Father. Instead of resting in Christ, the Christian who doubts is consumed with thoughts of worry about the *work* of God. He is never at rest within his spirit that he has done enough for Christ, and therefore he only seeks to appease God by more works instead of total rest in the righteousness of Jesus Christ alone.

Doubt also affects a Christian's witness to the world. It hinders Christians from confidently and boldly proclaiming the gospel. Doubt reflects itself in our speech and conduct. Nevertheless, if you firmly believe, and without a doubt know that you are saved and your salvation is in Christ's hands, then you will have the potential to speak the gospel with courage and confidence. For you have been given the gift of the Holy Spirit to empower you to speak even when fear arises (Acts 1:8).

We have been given the earnest of God's Spirit as a witness of our salvation. Ephesians 1:12-13 gives peace to our hearts concerning our salvation, saying, *"That we should be to the praise of his glory, who first trusted in Christ. In whom ye also trusted, after that ye heard the word of truth, the gospel of your salvation: in whom also after that ye believed, ye were sealed with that holy Spirit of promise, Which is the earnest of our inheritance until the redemption of the purchased possession, unto the praise of his glory."* Praise the Lord, our salvation is earnestly and solemnly sealed and kept safe and secure in the promise by God's indwelling presence of His Holy Spirit. Second Corinthians 1:22 confirms that God *"hath also sealed us, and given the earnest of the Spirit in our hearts."*

In addition, Romans 8:16 makes known that the Spirit itself bears witness with the spirit of Christians that we are children of God. This witness of the Spirit absolutely gives us the assurance that our salvation in Christ is assured because there is a manifestation of the living God within us. *"[T]he fruit of the Spirit is love, joy, peace, longsuffering, gentleness, goodness, faith, meekness, temperance"* (Galatians 5:22-23).

It is true that after your salvation you did not turn into a perfect, sinless being. However, did you notice that you no longer took pleasure in sin as you used to? Now, whenever you and I sin we can feel God's sorrow. This is because we have a new Person living inside of us—He is the Holy Spirit. But unbelievers have no grief over sin because they do not possess the Spirit of holiness who is contrary to sin. They act and do according to what their sinful, carnal nature seeks to do: *sin.* But when a child of God finds himself in sin, the scriptures explain that the conviction he feels is because he now has the discernment to sense the grievance of God's Spirit. It is the Spirit that convicts us of sin; and praise God for this conviction, because when I do disobey God I sure am thrilled to be able to feel the Holy Spirit impress me of my wrongdoings. His inner persuasion (conviction) is the witness that I am assuredly a child of God.

The inner dwelling of the Holy Spirit in a believer is a confirmation that our salvation is assured in Christ. First John 4:13 says, *"Hereby know we that we dwell in him, and he in us, because he hath given us of his Spirit."* Thank God for that! In addition, Romans 8:9 affirms, *"But ye are not in the flesh, but in the Spirit, if so be that the Spirit of God dwell in you. Now if any man have not the Spirit of Christ, he is none of his."*

Therefore we ought to believe God's promise and not grieve the Holy Spirit, *"whereby ye are sealed unto the day of redemption"* (Ephesians 4:30). We ought to believe His promise, enjoy our secured relationship with God, obey the gospel, and go proclaim it filled with the power of the Holy Ghost.

All of those verses are such an encouragement to help us keep a steadfast mind in Christ concerning the confidence of our salvation in God. However, if they were not sufficient, we could further find rest and peace of mind

Where Do You Find Security?

concerning the assurance of salvation. In John 10:27-29 Jesus guaranteed that there is no one, not even God Himself who can or will ever remove the seal of our relationship with Jesus Christ (John 6:39). We have a sure salvation. Jesus stated, *"My sheep hear my voice, and I know them, and they follow me: And I give unto them eternal life; and they shall never perish, neither shall any man pluck them out of my hand. My Father, which gave them me, is greater than all; and no man is able to pluck them out of my Father's hand."*

These are the words of Christ and we can trust them. Christ is not a man that He should lie nor repent of what He has said. Numbers 23:19 rhetorically asks the questions, *"...hath he said, and shall he not do it? or hath he spoken, and shall he not make it good?"* The answer is an emphatic, "Yes!" Whatever the Lord has said, so shall it stand (Isaiah 14:24).

I once heard a doubter ask, "How can we be so sure that the words of Jesus in the Holy Bible are indeed reliable?" Okay, fair question. The answer: We can know that the Lord's words are trustworthy based on the works He did and the witness of the Father. First, Christ's works provided the evidence, yet the skeptics in His day still challenged the credibility of His words. Jesus was publicly confronted by them. He responded to their questions, saying, *"I told you, and ye believed not: the works that I do in my Father's name, they bear witness of me"* (John 10:25). (Jesus fulfilled over 500 prophecies proving His divinity. To learn more, please refer to the last two chapters in my book *Important Soulwinning Verses of the Holy Bible's Fundamental Doctrines*.)

Secondly, not only did His works bear witness, the Father bore witness of Christ as well. On another occasion Jesus explained, *"...for the works which the Father hath given me to finish, the same works that I do, bear witness of me, that the Father hath sent me. And the Father himself, which hath sent me, hath borne witness of me"* (John 5:36-37).

In addition, in case someone still does not believe Christ's words, He gave them this charge: ***"Search the scriptures;*** *for in them ye think ye have eternal life: and they are they which testify of me"* (John 5:39). So the next time you meet a skeptic of Christ, charge him to search the scriptures, and then be quiet. Let the Holy Spirit do His perfect work to reveal the truth of the gospel, instead of trying to argue someone into belief. Because *"he that seeketh findeth."*

You and I are able to have peace of mind concerning the reliability of the Bible's words based on God's nature, which is trustworthy. Second Peter 1:19-21 says, *"We have also a more sure word of prophecy; whereunto ye do well that ye take heed, as unto a light that shineth in a dark place, until the day dawn, and the day star arise in your hearts: Knowing this first, that no prophecy of the scripture is of any private interpretation. For the prophecy came not in old time by the will of man: but holy men of God spake as they were moved by the Holy Ghost."* This passage assures that the Bible's words are honorable and trustworthy because they are given of God. God cannot lie nor repent. God is not a man that He should repent for if we believe not, yet He abides faithful: He cannot deny Himself.

Individuals who hear God's Word and believe it are considered blessed (John 20:29). If God's Word says our salvation is secured in Christ (and it does tell us that) then it absolutely, completely, entirely, solely, and exclusively is secured in Christ Jesus alone. If God's Word says that we can boldly proclaim His gospel with confidence in the strength of His Spirit (and it does tell us that), then most certainly we can.

Nonetheless, there are those, such as babes in Christ, who are unaware of God's promises. Their minds are not yet strongly rooted in God's Word. Their hearts are short of confidence and are easily shaken because they are deficient in good understanding of God's Word. Thankfully, God is longsuffering and extends mercy and goodness to all His children. If a child is unlearned in God's Word, God still has given the earnest of His Holy Spirit. Needless to say, these Christians will struggle to enjoy their relationship with God.

For example, a person can be saved and on his way to Heaven but lack the assurance of his salvation. Such a Christian needs to be exhorted to be in his Bible and to be discipled (trained and taught) by a mature Christian from the sincere milk of God's Word. He needs to be enriched in the doctrine of Christ. Then he can decide to become rooted, built up in Christ and established in the faith. If he so chooses, then his faith will become complete in Christ, abounding with thanksgiving and strong assurance (Colossians 2:6-10). Then he shall discover that his salvation is not of him but is all of Christ's doing.

Colossians 2:4-14 says, *"And this I say, lest any man should beguile you with enticing words. For though I be absent in the flesh, yet am I with you in the spirit, joying and beholding your order, and the stedfastness of your faith in Christ. As ye have therefore received Christ Jesus the Lord, so walk ye in him: Rooted and built up in him, and stablished in the faith, as ye have been taught, abounding therein with thanksgiving. Beware lest any man spoil you through philosophy and vain deceit, after the tradition of men, after the rudiments of the world, and not after Christ. For in him dwelleth all the fulness of the Godhead bodily. And ye are complete in him, which is the head of all principality and power: In whom also ye are circumcised with the circumcision made without hands, in putting off the body of the sins of the flesh by the circumcision of Christ: Buried with him in baptism, wherein also ye are risen with him through the faith of the operation of God, who hath raised him from the dead. And you, being dead in your sins and the uncircumcision of your flesh, hath he quickened together with him, having forgiven you all trespasses; Blotting out the handwriting of ordinances that was against us, which was contrary to us, and took it out of the way, nailing it to his cross."*

God clearly makes known in great detail the believer's perfection in Christ. The apostle insists, and rightfully so, that we not be swindled by deceivers who use enticing words to lure us from the hope and assurance of salvation in Christ Jesus.

Our salvation is sure because *"we are complete in him"* (vs. 10), that is, we are complete in Christ. Our minds can rest assured that we have God and God has us because we now have the presence of God within us, and this is because of the work of our Redeemer—Jesus Christ—who is both God and man. In Christ dwells *"all the fulness of the Godhead bodily"* (vs. 9) and Christ partakes of our nature; Christ is bone of our bone and flesh of our flesh. Christ has declared the Father to us. Therefore Christ, who is the Proprietor and Mediator of our faith, is able to accomplish a holy matrimony between holy God and sinful man. We are perfected and justified in Christ before God because of our faith in the gospel revelation. We have communion with Christ through His whole undertaking for our sins, through His death, burial, and resurrection. Likewise God has inscribed His seal of salvation upon our hearts by His Holy Ghost—*"ye are circumcised with the circumcision made without hands"* (vs. 11). Our faith in Christ has made us alive to God the Father; and we now are partakers of the divine nature (2 Peter 1:4). Our sins in the past, present, and future are blotted out and forgiven. God's wrath has been justified, satisfied, and appeased when Christ was made *"to be sin for us"* (2 Corinthians 5:21). God took the law and nailed it to His cross. Thus God's law has been satisfied and canceled at the cross of Calvary for all who believe on Christ.

It is God who secures and holds our salvation. Not us. First Corinthians 1:8 substantiates this promise, telling us that it is God *"Who shall also confirm you unto the end, that ye may be blameless in the day of our Lord Jesus Christ."* Moreover, God expressly tells us in 1 Peter 1:5 that we believers *"are kept by the power of God through faith unto salvation ready to be revealed in the last time."* It is God who saves a soul. God is the one who upholds our salvation, and He is the one who keeps it by His power.

If we were given the duty to uphold our own salvation, surely we all would on some occasion let go of it and lose it. However, God is the One who preserves us. Psalm 37:28 says, *"For the LORD loveth judgment, and forsaketh not his saints; they are preserved for ever: but the seed of the wicked shall be cut off."* How do you know if you are a saint of God? The answer: It is of faith, that it might be by grace; to the end that the promise might be sure to all who believe in the Lord Jesus Christ (Romans 4:16). By God's grace your faith in Christ makes you a saint because the moment you believed on Christ for salvation, you were sanctified (set apart for God) and called to be saints *in* Christ Jesus. Read 1 Corinthians 1:2. The Corinthians were a bunch of carnal, sensual, and sinful individuals, yet they were still *saints* of God. Look at it this way: God has done the impossible. The unworthy have been made saints *in* Christ Jesus. We have nothing to do with it; therefore, Christ gets all the glory and we receive none.

Jesus said in John 5:24, *"Verily, verily, I say unto you, He that heareth my word, and believeth on him that sent me, hath everlasting life, and shall not come into condemnation; but is passed from death unto life."* Have you believed in God and His report concerning His Son? If so, then **you are** a child of God and have everlasting life (John 1:12).

Jesus plainly stated in John 6:47: *"Verily, verily, I say unto you, He that believeth on me hath everlasting life"* (John 6:47). This is one of the clearest and briefest statements in all the Word of God concerning the way of salvation. The Lord Jesus stated in words that could hardly be misunderstood—that whoever **believes** in Christ **has everlasting life.** John 1:12-13 explains, *"But as many as received him* [Jesus], *to them gave he power to become the sons of God, even to them that believe on his name: Which were born, not of blood, nor of the will of the flesh, nor of the will of man, but of God."*

Salvation is not of our own doing; it is in and of Christ Jesus! God is the One who has established and confirmed our salvation. God made a covenant through the shedding of His begotten Son's blood to give us eternal life. God, who cannot lie, validated this salvation by an oath made by Himself. We have a strong consolation and a hope set before us: Jesus Christ our hope, is as an anchor of the soul. Our hope is sure and steadfast in Christ Jesus who has entered into the covenant by His blood before God's holy throne.

God is the One who has sealed us and given the earnest of His Spirit in our hearts (2 Corinthians 1:22). God is the One who justifies His children to be righteous. We are adopted into the beloved. God does not one moment call you His child, then the next moment abandon you, waiting for you to get your act together so that later He may readopt you into the family of God. That is ludicrous. Our adoption is an official legal and binding covenant. *"For* [we] *have not received the spirit of bondage again to fear; but* [we] *have received the Spirit of adoption, whereby we cry, Abba, Father"* (Romans 8:15).

We do not have to fear losing our salvation because we have been consecrated into an obligatory relationship with God. Now we can cry out to God at any moment the intimate words, *"Abba, Father"*—meaning *daddy, Father.* We are now united together with God in a covenant blood relationship: Father and sons. How great is that!

Galatians 4:5-6 further explains that God through the work of Jesus Christ on the cross has redeemed us, who were under the law (which we never keep), that we might receive the adoption of sons. Christ purchased us from the curse of the law by being made on our behalf a curse under the law (Galatians 3:13). Christ abrogated the law by becoming subject to its curse; He made Himself perfectly acceptable to God by obedience to the will of God, under which it pleased God to crucify His only begotten Son that whosoever believes in Him shall be given eternal life.

God has positioned all believers in a full measure of sonship, guaranteeing us access to God the Father and giving us all rights that belong to Jesus Christ. The proof of our sonship is that God has sent into our hearts Himself—Holy Spirit. His inner dwelling imparts the vivid consciousness of sonship that we enjoy. The fact of the adoption qualifies us to be recipients of His divinely inspired consciousness: a peace and rest of mind because of His presence, knowing that we are partakers of the dearly beloved.

God does not want you to struggle about your union with Him. If you are a believer in Christ Jesus, then God is your Father. God is not as an earthly father who might deprive you of your rights. God is faithful and He cannot deny His promises. The reason God has reconciled and adopted us into the family of God is so that we can know and enjoy Him. God lovingly wants you to *personally* have a good understanding of Him. Then you may splendidly enjoy Him.

We can know that we are saved because of the witness of a new, regenerated heart. Where before we did not even think of talking about Jesus, now we cannot fathom a day passing by without including Him in our conversations. Now we desire to be in the Holy Bible; now we desire to be around other believers; now we desire to be a witness; now we desire others to know Christ. These new desires are a manifestation that Christ truly has permeated our hearts and now we are new creatures: old things are passed away; behold, all things are become new (2 Corinthians 5:17).

The Holy Spirit is the One enabling our hearts to be filled with surety so that we can go out and do the work of spreading Christ's gospel. God's presence assists us to confidently speak the truth unequivocally, and without apology, in love. When we do this, people will be able to see our hearts and the profound depth of our conviction. People will be able to tell we are certain that when God says He wants to give the gift of eternal life, He means what He promises. Our assurance can help us to convey God's Word with clarity so that others may receive the message accurately. We will be able to talk about the gospel with confidence and know that our gospel is the remedy that can bring true peace to the hearts of the individuals with whom we speak.

Christians who have a complete assurance that they are saved are empowered to speak the truth in such a way that their hearers can observe that they really believe it. Our assurance supplies us the boldness to proclaim God's gospel because we are certain that all the work of salvation was, is, and will always be of the Lord Jesus Christ. God gives peace of mind and a humble confidence in the security of Jesus Christ. It is of Christ, in Christ, and through Christ who has committed to us His eternal salvation. It is never of ourselves. Ephesians 2:8-9 clearly makes known: *"For by grace are ye saved through faith; and that not of yourselves: it is the gift of God: Not of works, lest any man should boast."*

We are empowered to approach people with boldness and proclaim the gospel to them because we know with certainty the promise God has given us. First John 2:25 says, *"And this is the promise that he hath promised us, even eternal life."* We know that God does not lie because He cannot lie (Titus 1:2). Since God has promised eternal life, we know we have it. No doubt about it! No ifs, ands, or buts about it. Settled! Done, and secured! And everlasting life is forever lasting; it not temporary, it's not short-lived, or fleeting; it is forever, eternal, and ceaseless. It's settled by God Himself!

A Christian who desires to be a useful and effective servant of God (to have life more abundantly) must know with complete certainty that his salvation is absolutely 100% secure in Christ Jesus and that he will never lose his relationship with God. Oh, his fellowship with God might be broken occasionally, but he will never be cut off from the blood-bought relationship with God. God just loves us too much.

In addition, it would be a good reminder for Christians not only to be absolutely convinced of their conversion, but also to attempt to keep the freshness and the wonder of our conversion experience. God forbid that we should ever come to regard it as one of the commonplace aspects of life. I personally can testify that ever since I met Jesus Christ and believed on Him for salvation many years ago, I have never gotten over it! It is a great thing to live with a constant sense of wonder that the grace of God has reached out to us and saved us. This joy and peace surpasses all understanding and enables an assured Christian to go speak the gospel with immense confidence and great courage in the spirit of love.

Now may you be rekindled with the fire of Christ in knowing that your salvation is as the Bible states: safe and secured *"in Christ."* Because God was in Christ, reconciling the world to Himself, not imputing our trespasses to our record (2 Corinthians 5:19). We have been justified freely by His grace through the redemption that is in Christ Jesus (Romans 3:24). We are the children of God by faith in Christ Jesus (Galatians 3:26).

God has *"saved us, and called us with an holy calling, not according to our works, but according to his own purpose and grace, which was given us in Christ Jesus before the world began"* (2 Timothy 1:9). *"That we should be to the praise of his glory, who first trusted in Christ"* (Ephesians 1:12). Now, to God be all praise in Christ's glory amidst this crooked and dark generation. Amen!

Chapter Sixteen

WHAT IS THE EVIDENCE THAT YOUR FAITH IS GENUINE?

HAVE YOU EVER SAID something to someone only to have to repeat it? I certainly know that I have. Hopefully, with patience, we look the person in the eyes and kindly reiterate our thought, hoping he or she comprehends what we are seeking to communicate. When something is important to us we attempt to properly convey the message so that our hearers accurately receive and understand our words.

The same occurs between God and us. Have you ever noticed in your Bible reading that God keeps repeating certain matters, themes, and subjects of importance? God does not have to repeat Himself, but He does so and for good reason. God reiterates because He seeks to establish a matter within our hearts, thus demonstrating His care for us. It is for our own good and safety. God knows that we are stubborn and hardheaded. If God did not repeat Himself about important issues, we most certainly would bring more trouble upon ourselves than we already subject ourselves to. Thankfully, God is patient, merciful, and longsuffering toward us, not willing that any should perish. God understands that we have the potential to destroy, ruin, or make a mess out of our lives; but Jesus came that we might have life, and that we might have it more abundantly (John 10:10).

It is a blessed peace to know that God is a friend who sticks closer than any brother (Proverbs 18:24). Sometimes a brother will become impatient and confrontational when someone does not receive his message. However, God is not like that. He cares for us so much that He demonstrates great longsuffering. God suffers through our stubborn mindset and reaffirms His heart to us.

Job 33:14 tells us, *"For God speaketh once, yea twice, yet man perceiveth it not."* What an interesting verse. God speaks, yet man seldom perceives what God is communicating. Perhaps because man loves darkness rather than light and our deeds are evil (John 3:19). God speaks by way of admonition and instruction. God speaks to awaken men out of their slumber; to those who listen God is graciously pleased to give and reveal the deeper treasures of Himself, that we may do all the words of His law.

God has His ways of speaking to man, which sometimes are not how man would expect God to speak. Certainly God uses His Holy Bible to plainly reveal His heart and speak to man; but if God chooses to convey a message by another approach, He certainly is able to do so. However, the Holy Bible is how God authenticates any message of His to assure man that a message is really from Him and not a fraud or a contrivance. Man must simply quiet his spirit and listen.

For example, God did not speak by thunders and lightning as Moses presumed He would, but He spoke silently and secretly (Exodus 19:16-20). When Elijah was up in a cave on Mount Horeb, he had to learn that God does not always speak through great strong winds, earthquakes, or fires, but that the Lord also speaks with a *"still small voice"* (1 Kings 19:11-12).

Man many times is guilty of presuming God will speak something startling and sensational. However, God's ways are greater than our ways. God is not bound to our wants or preconceived ideals and conceptions of Him. When God speaks, who shall disannul it? God's word stands. But if a Christian does not listen with a heart attuned toward God, then as the scripture explains, *"man perceiveth it not."* This individual through his own inadvertency, negligence, or dullness of hearing will not understand. Therefore, he has no reason to accuse God regarding His will or revelation.

Those who listen to God hear His voice. Jesus explained to Pilate, *"Every one that is of the truth heareth my voice"* (John 18:37). Are you of the truth?

God's gracious voice lovingly smites our spirits when we are in wrongdoing. God's voice compels us to repent daily and follow Christ. Jesus stated, *"My sheep hear my voice, and I know them, and they follow me"* (John 10:27). Do you hear God's voice? If not, you may want to examine yourself to see whether if you are in the faith. The scripture urges us, *"...prove your own selves. Know ye not your own selves, how that Jesus Christ is in you, except ye be reprobates?"* (2 Corinthians 13:5). For the Spirit of God reproves of sin, of righteousness, and of judgment (John 16:8). It is a most glorious, humbling blessing to hear God reprove us, knowing that He is drawing us closer to Himself.

In John 10:3 Jesus said that His sheep hear His voice, and He calls His own sheep by name, and leads them out. That is how familiar and devoted He is to each of His sheep. Moreover, Jesus continued, *"And when he putteth forth his own sheep, he goeth before them, and the sheep follow him: for they know his voice"* (John 10:4). Jesus compared believers to sheep. The evidence that you are in Christ's fold is hearing His voice, and then obeying it. If you hear God's voice but never obey and follow Christ, then you should examine yourself and find out why not. There is something wrong when a believer says he has a relationship with God yet lives a life that is defying God's law. Surely, such a one does not have the joy and peace of God. Nevertheless, if you hear God's voice and do obey and follow Christ into righteousness then *"happy are ye"* Jesus said (John 13:17).

We should take heed to God's warning written by the prophet Isaiah to the children of Israel. He said, *"Go unto this people, and say, Hearing ye shall hear, and shall not understand; and seeing ye shall see, and not perceive: For the heart of this people is waxed gross, and their ears are dull of hearing, and their eyes have they closed; lest they should see with their eyes, and hear with their ears, and understand with their heart, and should be converted, and I should heal them"* (Acts 28:26-27; Isaiah 6:9-10). God desires to make our lives whole. However, a wholesome life only comes to fruition through our sanctification, setting ourselves apart for God. The condition of having a wholesome godly life is that we must set ourselves apart unto God: we must open our eyes, hear with our ears, listen with our hearts, and *act!* Application is the key. We must do what the Spirit of God commands. For *"he that hath an ear, let him hear what the Spirit saith"* (God repeats this instruction seven times in Revelation chapters 2-3).

God gave instruction through the words of the prophet Jeremiah, saying, *"Obey my voice, and I will be your God, and ye shall be my people: and walk ye in all the ways that I have commanded you, that it may be well unto you"* (Jeremiah 7:23). In order for us to obey God's voice we must hear it, and in order to hear God's voice we must quiet our spirits and listen. Sadly, most Christians do not know how to quiet their spirits, be still, and listen to God. The idea of being quiet is a strange concept to many. Nevertheless, it is what is commanded. The scriptures instruct, *"And that ye study to be quiet..."* (1 Thessalonians 4:11)

We must turn off devices such as the cell phone, television, internet, and radio, and free our minds from unnecessary distractions that keep us from hearkening to God's voice. Then and only then can a Christian discover the words of God for his life (Jeremiah 15:16).

The words of God must be found. They are not emblazoned on the face of a mountain so that the most careless person may look around and see them. God's words are hidden treasures to be dug for, pearls of great price to be sought after.

Divine truth in nature is only discoverable after thoughtful observation and reflection—meditation. This is why it is so important for us to seek God in His Word by fasting, praying, and watching. God only reveals His rich, glorious treasures to those who labor and seek for them.

The words of God are not so hidden that they cannot be discovered by the earnest and prayerful seeker of truth. Jesus said, *"...he that seeketh findeth"* (Matthew 7:8). Many honest, earnest men pass through a season of doubt. Sadly, some remain hopeless skeptics all their lives. Those who never find the light are probably suffering from some moral or intellectual obstinacy which distorts their spiritual vision. Jesus warned, *"But if thine eye be evil, thy whole body shall be full of darkness. If therefore the light that is in thee be darkness, how great is that darkness!"* (Matthew 6:23)

At the same time, there are others who are not content to trust the measure of God's light that has been given to them. These individuals remain restless and continually question God because they desire satisfaction in a direction in which it cannot be afforded. They deny God's will for their sanctification, and they wander from the truth in search of a "better hope." They do not realize that the grass is never greener on the other side. They find themselves empty because they talk themselves into believing cunning philosophies rather than walking in the light of the truth (Colossians 2:8).

Thankfully, when any man forsakes doubt and unbelief and is a seeker for truth and righteousness, he may be assured that ultimately the Father of Lights will dispel his darkness and give him a journey in the light. Therefore, we ought to do as Jesus warned: *"Walk while ye have the light, lest darkness come upon you: for he that walketh in darkness knoweth not whither he goeth. While ye have light, believe in the light, that ye may be the children of light"* (John 12:35-36).

In addition, *"we have also a more sure word of prophecy* [the Holy Bible]*; whereunto ye do well that ye take heed, as unto a light that shineth in a dark place"* (2 Peter 1:19). God's Holy Bible is *"a lamp unto our feet and a light unto our path"* (Psalm 119:105). How wonderful God's Word is, that it directs us to lie down in green pastures of peace. Yes, though at times we walk through the shadow of death, we do not have to fear: for God is with us. God's

Word is a comfort for us as we quiet our souls to hear God speak (Psalm 23:1-4).

How sweet it is to hear the Lord. Jeremiah wrote, *"Thy words were found, and I did eat them; and thy word was unto me the joy and rejoicing of mine heart: for I am called by thy name, O LORD God of hosts"* (Jeremiah 15:16). God calls each of us by name to enter into an intimate, close relationship with Him and experience life more abundantly with Christ. James 4:8 reminds us, *"Draw nigh to God, and he will draw nigh to you..."* But sadly, few choose to draw near to God.

The individual who desires a close relationship with God will study to be quiet and be still. Not to be quiet audibly, but to be quiet within one's own spirit: to have a spirit that is yielded and close to God, no matter what life's situations are. Such a spirit is one that is at peace to let God be in control. Therefore, God rightfully commands, *"Be still, and know that I am God"* (Psalm 46:10).

God is faithful and He does speak. We simply must pay attention and hear what the Spirit says. The book of Hebrews urges us, saying, *"To day if ye will hear his voice, harden not your hearts, as in the provocation"* (Hebrews 3:15). Again, it is repeated, *"To day if ye will hear his voice, harden not your hearts"* (Hebrews 4:7). God repeats this admonition so that we may learn from the example of the nation of Israel. They heard God's voice but they did not perceive. They hardened their hearts in the day of provocation and went astray. May we not have ears dull of hearing, as the Old Testament Israelites had. May we learn to be quiet and hear what the Spirit of God says, particularly in matters which God states to be of great importance, which He repeatedly reconfirms in His Word.

If God says something one time in the Bible it is worthy for you and I to understand. If God repeats a matter twice, it is most worthy for us to heed. If God reiterates Himself three times, it is a matter of intensity and a high degree of importance. What about when God speaks a matter more than three times? Shouldn't that stop us in our thoughts and grip our minds to seriously ponder what He is saying? Matters repeated by God should compel us to seek and grasp understanding of the indescribable intensity of God's concern for us. Should we not halt all our presumptions and seek what God is saying, and seek how we should respond? I think so!

The issue concerning *"our faith in God"* is a subject that God takes quite seriously, much so that four times in the Bible God indisputably commands believers: *"the just shall live by faith."* He repeats this command in the texts of Habakkuk 2:4, Romans 1:17, Galatians 3:11, and Hebrews 10:38.

It is with great concern and interest that we should look into the faith that we have in God. Either you have faith or you do not; And if you have faith, then it is either growing or withering. Faith never stays static. Your faith is either greater than it was a week ago, or candidly, it is less. But it never is the same.

Hebrews 11:1 gives us a clear definition of what faith is: *"Faith is the substance of things hoped for, the evidence of things not seen."* In other words, faith is a quantifiable intensity of God's might through us right now at this moment. We can prove it; we can see God's strength in action through us at any given moment when we are using it. But the question is, are you doing things by faith? Are your works by faith? Or are you merely doing good things in the comfort of your own strength? Sometimes we can get comfortable doing good things without any faith involved; we at times unconsciously rely on good organizational skills, diligence, hard work, and a outpouring of ourselves into a work, without any faith involved. This is what unsaved people, cults, and great organizations do every single day; they do incredible things all the time simply because of diligence and hard work. Man can build great feats but that does not mean God is in it. But when faith is involved, achievements beyond ourselves will occur and God will certainly be glorified while man will be amazed at God.

It is impossible to overstate the importance of faith. Faith is the essence of every area of a Christian's life. Faith is the means God uses to justify a believer from the penalty of sin and to sanctify a believer from the power of sin. Faith is the mechanism that allows a believer to live freely in a bound world. Therefore, we need faith, and a faith that is evident. If a determined servant of God desires to experience and enjoy life more abundantly with Christ and succeed in the work of the Lord, then that Christian must possess a living faith.

James wrote, *"...shew me thy faith without thy works, and I will shew thee my faith by my works. Even so faith, if it hath not works, is dead, being alone"* (James 2:18-17). Faith is always demonstrated by obedience in actions. It is impossible to believe in the Lord Jesus Christ without using the faith God has given you to believe. Likewise, we must use that same faith and demonstrate outwardly God's work within us to show that we love Him. Then God will use this faith before the world as evidence of our ambassadorship, beseeching mankind to repent and be converted.

Every believer in Jesus has the God-given faith to live life more abundantly with Christ. Such a life is evidence of God's magnificence before the world. Christ promised to give life more abundantly (John 10:10). No

Christian lacks that faith. God has given it to him, and he simply must yield to it.

Sadly, many of us lack the obedience and zeal to put our faith into action. Many walk in the carnality of their flesh and regard not the things of God. They would do themselves a favor if they would get down on their knees and confess their sin (fear, selfishness, cold-heartedness, etc.), forsake it, and beg God to consume their hearts with His fire. Then they could confidently arise from their prayer chamber, and with Holy Ghost fire express their faith to a lost and dying world. Then the world could know that Christ has been sent to them, that God loves them, and He is calling their name, too.

We are commanded: *"the just shall live by faith"* (Hebrews 10:38). And *"the just"* can live by faith because God has dealt to every man a measure of faith (Romans 12:3). Therefore, we must live by faith and use it (Luke 17:6). There is no more time left to play and be preoccupied with ourselves any longer. Too many people have already gone to Hell, and too many are soon to die and become separated from God forever. Time is urgent, and the need is great!

It is by faith that we have peace with God through our Lord Jesus Christ, and it is by the same faith that God has justified us—meaning, made us right in Heaven before His holiness (Romans 5:1).

You and I are justified because *"without faith it is impossible to please him* [God]: *for he that cometh to God must believe that he is, and that he is a rewarder of them that diligently seek him"* (Hebrews 11:6). The use of our faith is the crossroads of life, or life more abundantly with Christ. How you use your faith determines whether or not Christ is living through you. If Christ is living your life, then it is because you are yielding to this belief and are acting on it in faith; you have moved on to a greater experience in your relationship with God. However, if you would rather yield to doubt in the face of adversity, your Christian life will experience defeat and be up one day and down the next.

Faith in God is the mechanism that moves us to invite God to do great exploits through us. God only rewards those who please Him, and faith in God is what pleases Him. Faith in God pleases Him because it ceases to have self-confidence and is Christ-centered. Faith in God is confidence in God. Faith in God is not concerned with self but is concerned with the esteem of Christ in the lives of others. Likewise, God's heart is moved to get involved in a Christian's faith when that Christian attempts to demonstrate his faith by doing good.

Any faith we have is a gift God has imputed unto us. Faith is not something generated of ourselves. It is given by God (Hebrews 12:2; Romans 12:3). Therefore, it is an urgent matter that we beseech the Lord with a broken heart, as the apostles earnestly requested Jesus: *"...Lord, Increase our faith"* (Luke 17:5).

In the context of this passage, the Lord Jesus had just rebuked and alerted his disciples about honorable characteristics that are expected of followers of Christ. When they heard these directives, the words pierced their hearts, and they found themselves realizing their inadequacies to do such divine acts as they beforehand thought possible. Their new understanding brought a clearer revelation of Christ and a good humbling dissatisfaction of themselves. Conviction grasped their hearts as they realized their need for more of Christ as they embraced Christ's mission given to all His followers. This new understanding compelled them to abandon self-reliance and united them to focus on Christ, petitioning Him to increase their faith; or, in other words, to help them use what they already had.

Jesus used this opportunity to teach them an important principle about the faith they possessed. In Luke 17:6, Jesus said to them, *"If ye had faith as a grain of mustard seed, ye might..."* and then continuing along His teaching, He gave them an example of what great exploits can be accomplished with a living faith. Christ used the comparison of a mustard seed, one of the smallest seeds on the planet, to emphasize an important lesson: it is not the possession of a particular size of faith that is important (for we are all given by God a predetermined measure of faith, as Romans 12:3 tells us), but it is the usage of our faith that is important. Meaning—the measure of faith God has given you should be full of life, as the mustard seed is. Then the power of using the living faith for a particular purpose (appropriation) will avail for all occasions.

If someone is himself a believer and follower of Jesus Christ then he has been given a grain of faith. Whether great or small, he has faith, and he is able to appropriate that faith for the edification of others to the glory of Jesus Christ. Faith always breeds hope and hope always begets charity (1 Corinthians 13:13; Romans 5:2), and charity always excites a person to extend himself for the benefit of others and God's honor and glory.

In another passage of scripture it is written that Jesus said, *"The kingdom of God is like to a grain of mustard seed, which a man took, and sowed in his field"* (Matthew 13:31). You as a believer in Christ have Christ's seed of faith, and you, as the man in this passage (for Christ lives within the believer), are to take that seed and use it in God's field. God's field is the world (Matthew 13:38). You are to go into the world and appropriate Christ into others.

If you say, "But I don't have much faith." That's not so, but only an excuse. Jesus said, *"If you have faith as a grain of mustard seed, ye shall say unto this mountain, Remove hence to yonder place; and it shall remove; and nothing shall be impossible unto you"* (Matthew 17:20). Again, the size or quantity has nothing to do with what God has given you. Jesus instructs that we are to use our faith. Rise up and get involved, do something for God and the benefit of others. Go get involved in people's lives and use your faith!

Any such excuse as that I just mentioned is evidence of a *mountain* of unbelief. Any *mountain* that appears before us always has a core of unbelief. We all face unbelief at one time or another. In the past, we all have doubted, questioned, and even rebelled against God. Nevertheless, as Jesus said to His mountainous temptation, *"Get thee behind me, thou art an offence"* (Matthew 16:23). May we have the same attitude, "Get out of the way! I'm moving forward."

Therefore, stand fast in your faith, and get involved in people's lives. Go speak the gospel to them. Remember, God said that to obey is better than sacrifice (1 Samuel 15:22). God is looking for loyalty to His high calling. You simply must take God at His Word, believe, trust, and *go!*

This is the reason we Christians need to come to an understanding that a slight and feeble use of faith does not accomplish anything in the Lord's work. A feeble use of faith had failed the twelve disciples before, and it would always bring failure again. In Luke 9:37-40, the disciples were not able to cast a devil out of a man's son because of their lack of faith (Matthew 17:14-20 gives the parallel reference). Perhaps this is one reason why they were so eager in another occasion to beg Christ in Luke 17 to increase their faith. They could vividly remember that a lack of faith simply will not suffice in the Lord's work. Only a faith that is living and is a growing power today will triumph over the difficulties that must be met and mastered in our lives. We must also understand that any former faith of ours, whether great or strong yesterday, may not be adequate for today or even tomorrow's unknown trials. Yesterday's faith was alive and sufficient for the past only, not necessarily for today too.

An important principle to remember is that the past is there for us to learn from and build upon. Although yesterday's faith can assist in increasing our faith for today and tomorrow, yesterday's faith should not be the focal point of our whole lives. We must not consider past faith to be sufficient for today—it may not be relevant. The past certainly can encourage us; nevertheless, it can also deceive and mislead us. For that reason, we must not live in the past. Our faith must be renewed day by day just as the Lord's mercies are renewed each morning (Lamentations 3:22-23). We must live today; therefore, our faith must be in Christ today and continually growing.

A feeble and weak faith accomplishes little for the kingdom of God. A weak faith sinks at the very height of our trials, as seen in Matthew 14:30: Peter walked on water while he looked upon Christ, but then when his attention veered off Christ he began to sink. The same occurs to you and me when our faith is frail and not attuned to Christ: we can shrink back from being bold and courageous faltering wherever the Lord leads.

Feebleness makes us do God's work in secret, with fear and worry, like Nicodemus and Joseph of Arimathaea. These two men believed in Christ but they followed Him in secret during Christ's earthly ministry (John 3:1-2; John 19:38).

A living, appropriating faith is the only effective power we have to experience life more abundantly with Christ and do the work of God here on earth. This kind of faith, like the mustard seed in the soil, puts forth the power of life, and appropriates to itself the riches around it in order that it may bear fruit—this is a power that will be seen. It accomplishes great and wonderful things.

A Christian who is determined to have life more abundantly with Christ must have a deeper faith in God than just any ordinary believer. He must rely on God and trust God's judgments, whether he understands them or not. Faith is not by sight, nor by feelings, and it is not totally based upon understanding; faith is trust in God that leads you into interaction with people.

If a Christian desires to be a good success in Christ's cause then he must believe that God can and will save souls through him. When a Christian firmly believes this, then God will reward that Christian with courage and confidence to speak His gospel. The determined servant of God will know that he is doing his work not because of any conceit or pride, but because he has a God-given commission to do it.

If you have an idea that you are possibly a nuisance, an intruder, or a bother to someone, then you will do nothing of any account in the Lord's work. You will be only a poor, limping, diffident, half-apologetic proclaimer of the gospel, whose message no one will care to hear. On the other hand, if you have genuine living faith you will be ready, you will be determined, and you will be heard.

In addition, we must also believe that the message we have to give is indeed God's Word. It would be so much better if a Christian believed only half a dozen truths of Bible doctrine whole-heartedly than a hundred truths only feebly. Christians should possess a firm conviction of what we believe, or else we will never persuade anybody else to believe it. If you doubt something, you are most likely to speak the gospel in a tentative manner such as, "I think—thisssss.....miiiight beeee—a truth...and....I aaask...your kind...attention to what I'mmmmm about to-to-to say." Then you will not easily be able to convince people of the truth but will instead breed doubters. We are not called to breed doubters but confident believers in Jesus Christ (1 John 3:18-23).

Do you desire to be an effective servant of God? Then you must have great faith in the Word of God. If you doubt, then your hearers will doubt, too. Your proclamation of the Bible must be without doubt, and then your response to any nonbeliever's questions can help encourage a soul for Christ.

A Christian will speak with confidence and boldness when he is firm in what he believes, and very likely others will be led to believe too. God takes pleasure in using the faith of His servants to breed faith in other people. For not all men have faith (2 Thessalonians 3:2), therefore, Romans 10:17 explains: *"faith cometh by hearing, and hearing by the word of God,"* and especially when someone speaks it convincingly, as we are called to do (Romans 10:14).

Paul wrote, *"For I am not ashamed of the gospel of Christ: for it is the power of God unto salvation to every one that believeth; to the Jew first, and also to the Greek"* (Romans 1:16). A determined Christian, like Paul, must believe in the power of the gospel message. Yes, God's Word stands alone in converting a soul. Nevertheless, God desires to produce much fruit through us by the use of His Word (John 15:5-8).

A Christian cannot believe it is possible that by some strange mysterious method through one in a hundred proclamations God might win a quarter of a soul. This will not do. God does not save just part of a soul. God is in the business of saving all of the soul and the souls of many people (1 Timothy 2:4 and 2 Peter 3:9)! This insecure type of Christian has hardly enough faith to keep him standing upright; how can he expect God to bless him? God just will not bless such believers. God will only bless those who will go out believing that the gospel is God's word and that they are going to deliver it to people in the powerful saving name of the Lord Jesus Christ.

God promises in Isaiah 55:11, *"So shall my word be that goeth forth out of my mouth: it shall not return unto me void, but it shall accomplish that which I please, and it shall prosper in the thing whereto I sent it."* This is a sure promise we can claim when we use God's Word before people. Therefore, a determined servant of God should become familiar with his Bible, and he should make it a practice to use the Bible as much as possible! A determined servant of God must believe that God's Word will not return to Him empty, but will produce the results God sent it out to accomplish whenever he speaks it. This Christian must believe that God's blessing is upon his obedience to proclaim the gospel and that God is bound to bless what He purposes to be done. The results are always up to God (Isaiah 14:24, 27). This is a living faith that brings an abundant life in Christ Jesus.

Faith is never found alone; it is always accompanied by expectation. The man who believes the promises of God expects to see them fulfilled. Faith is not the stuff dreams are made of; rather it is determined, practical, and realistic. Faith sees the invisible but it does not see the nonexistent. Faith engages God and takes God at His Word; faith works to lift our knowing of the facts into a higher level of reality. Where there is no expectation there is no faith.

Similarly, where there is doubt, there is a lack of faith. Romans 14:23 teaches that to doubt is sin and whatever is done with doubt is mingled in sin. God does not bless sin, nor does He have anything to do with it. As a result, God does not have anything to do with doubt. A doubtful Christian limits God from blessing him and the work he attempts to do when he doubts God.

For example, the people of Nazareth limited Christ's influence in miraculous blessings because of their doubt. When Jesus returned to visit His hometown, the people doubted who He said He was. Though they had heard the countless testimonies of His divine works, they doubted Christ. Jesus had the power to revolutionize their lives, but the Lord did not do many mighty works there because of the people's unbelief (Matthew 13:53-58). Today, some Christians resemble these doubters. They question why they do not see God's miraculous hand. Perhaps they should look at their sin. God rarely does many mighty works when people choose unbelief. If a Christian chooses not to believe, neither should he expect to be used of God. Therefore, a Christian must determine within himself not to doubt God or His Word but be resolved to believe and move forward in the work.

Where there is a determined attitude of living faith, God is welcome to do anything. Where there is living faith, God's power is not challenged or limited. As I heard a man say once, "Faith is not something that talks, but faith is something that walks." Meaning, God has given us faith not just to talk about something we hope for, but to move us into action so that God can miraculously bring it forth.

James 2:26 tells us that faith without works is dead. *"Even so faith, if it hath not works, is dead, being alone. Yea, a man may say, Thou hast faith, and I have works: shew me thy faith without thy works, and I will shew thee my faith by my works"* (James 2:17-18). A Christian must walk by faith, trusting God's promises, if he is to move forward in bringing honor and glory to Christ by good works.

Jesus stated, *"ye shall know them by their fruits"* (Matthew 7:16). Many profess they know Jesus but they show no evidence. Many profess they have faith but lack the evidence of the outworking of that faith (Hebrews 11:1). Most men will proclaim good: but who will be a man of faith? Broad is the way of lip service but narrow is the way of action.

The gift of salvation is given by simple faith in God's promise; so too, a believer in Christ must use the same simple faith to believe that God will use him *today* as an influence for others to come to Christ. Simply put, faith is to take God at His Word for today. God says, *"go"* and *"proclaim the gospel"* and *"teach them whatsoever I have commanded."*

Faith moves an individual to act in obedience to what God has commanded. Faith is authenticated when there is obedience, never without it, and faith only becomes faith in the act of obedience. Obedience is the evidence that there really is faith.

Therefore, faith always moves a person into action; faith always shows itself in faithfulness. Take for example Daniel in the Old Testament. The scripture says, *"Daniel purposed* [that means he made a determination] *in his heart that he would not defile himself with the portion of the king's meat, nor with the wine which he drank: therefore he requested of the prince of the eunuchs that he might not defile himself"* (Daniel 1:8). He had the faith to determine within his heart that he would not defile himself by eating royal foods even though the king of the nation required him to eat it. He would rather die of starvation than dishonor his God-given convictions.

Daniel used his faith by taking action to ask the prince if he could refrain from eating the king's portion of food but instead eat solely vegetables and water. He did not know what the outcome would be. He simply believed God and put his faith into action. His faith gave him the initiative to ask and believe that somehow God would intervene. As a result, we know from the story that God indeed gave his request favor and blessed him much more than he imagined would happen.

If you are a child of God, the Holy Spirit took residence within you the moment you believed in Christ. Your faith offers you great power, not in yourself but in God. This power is not because you know *about* God, but because you *know* Him. Daniel 11:32 says, *"...the people that do know their God shall be strong, and do exploits."*

A determined servant of God trusts God will do some exploits through him because he has a personal relationship with God. Therefore, he implements his faith into action by getting involved in people's lives. He does not know what the outcome will be; nonetheless, he trusts God will do something wonderful. For instance, he would believe that God will draw people to Himself when they hear the gospel.

Living faith put into action will always lead a believer to prayer. Hebrews 4:16 says, *"Let us therefore come boldly unto the throne of grace, that we may obtain mercy, and find grace to help in time of need."* God is a Father who is accessible, approachable, and touchable. We have a God who can be touched with the feeling of our infirmities. God understands our need. Living faith always moves an individual to humbly approach God with confidence and seek help and guidance.

In Matthew chapter 9 God demonstrates this point several times. A certain ruler had a daughter who was sick unto death. He believed Jesus could heal her. Therefore, he came to Jesus, worshipped Him, and asked Jesus to come heal her. Jesus accepted the invitation and followed the man back to his home.

Then, while Jesus walked on the way to heal this ruler's daughter, another woman who suffered from a blood disorder for twelve years put her faith into action for healing. She pressed through the crowds and finally reached Jesus; and then, barely able, she touched the hem of His garment. Her body was instantaneously healed! Right away Jesus turned around, looked through the crowd, fixed His eyes on her with a smile, and asserted: *"Daughter, thy faith hath made thee whole."*

Soon afterwards, Jesus arrived at the ruler's home only to find that the daughter had died. Jesus put out of the home those who disbelieved, and He touched the ruler's daughter and brought her back to life.

Then, later that afternoon, two blind men followed Jesus through the crowds, crying and saying, *"Thou Son of David, have mercy on us."* The crowds tried to hush them, but these two blind men had great faith. Jesus had never expressed in words that He was the Son of David. He only demonstrated the proof by His mighty works. These two persistent men, although physically blind, could spiritually see more than most. Their spiritual sight was precise in understanding who Jesus was. Therefore, without fear, they cried out to Christ.

Jesus saw their faith, and when they came into His presence He asked them if they believed He was able to heal them. They answered without hesitation, *"Yea, Lord."* Their faith was great; it proved that Jesus was their Lord. Then Jesus touched their eyes and said, *"According to your faith be it unto you."*

God gives you and me faith that we may request of Him to do that which we cannot, whereby the glory of His majesty is declared. Living faith provokes people to beg God and to seek for those things that only He can do.

Some more examples of faith may be read in passages such as Mark 2:1-12, Mark 5:35-43, and Mark 10:46-52. I encourage you to read these passages, as I do not have time to expound on them. However, they do demonstrate that we need to trust Jesus and believe He can and wants to do mighty works through us, too.

We need to use the faith God has given us to serve people meanwhile petitioning God to turn the hearts of men toward repentance. If we say we have faith, then we must do the works of God and show proof of our faith by our works.

Let us remember that any faith we have is faith that God has given us, and we need to humbly acknowledge and thank God for the faith He has provided. Romans 12:3 says, *"For I say, through the grace given unto me, to every man that is among you, not to think of himself more highly than he ought to think; but to think soberly, according as God hath dealt to every man the measure of faith."*

Jesus is the Author and Finisher of our faith (Hebrews 12:2). Therefore, let us not become haughty and foolishly think that any work we do is of our own accord. The faith God has given we need to exercise, and then we might just see more people brought into His kingdom. Then, after folks are saved, we should exercise it some more and serve these babes in Christ by discipleship and mentorship. As we disciple them, both their faith and ours will grow together, and we can then exercise our faith together (2 Timothy 2:2).

As we use our faith, may we keep in mind one caution: God never gives faith for the intention of glorifying someone or some thing. God freely gives faith to people for the purpose of knowing and understanding Him (Jeremiah 24:7; 9:24) and using it to bring glory and honor to Jesus Christ. For *"worthy is the Lamb that was slain to receive power, and riches, and wisdom, and strength, and honour, and glory, and blessing"* (Revelation 5:12).

As I mentioned earlier, Jesus taught: *"If ye have faith as a grain of mustard seed, ye shall say unto this mountain, Remove hence to yonder place; and it shall remove; and nothing shall be impossible unto you"* (Matthew 17:20). Therefore, all we need is just a little faith to do great works of God, which is primarily the saving and discipling of souls. However, if God asks a Christian, "Where is your faith?", that is an indication that there are mountains of unbelief hindering you from influencing souls to take up their cross and follow Christ.

If perhaps you might be an individual that God would confront with such a question, then I encourage you to seek the Lord for change. He is merciful and longsuffering (Numbers 14:18). Keep in mind that fear is the enemy of faith. Fear causes discouragement. Faith breeds courage. The way to experience the measure of faith that changes your behavior is not to ask for more faith, but rather to ask God for help in yielding to the faith that is already within you.

It all boils down to the fact that a determined servant of Christ must whole-heartedly believe God if he is to be a useful instrument in God's hands. God says it in the Old Testament and He repeats it three times in the New Testament, *"the just shall live by faith"* (Habakkuk 2:4, Romans 1:17, Galatians 3:11, Hebrews 10:38). God may permit some other things to be omitted, but the matter of faith must not and will never be. Because *"the just shall live by faith."*

It is true that God does not always measure His mercy by our unbelief, for He has to think of other people as well as us. Nevertheless, *"the just shall live by faith."* Therefore, looking at the matter with common sense, it does seem that the most likely instrument to do the Lord's work is the Christian who humbly expects that God will use him and who goes forth to labor in the strength of that conviction. When the success of guiding souls to Christ comes, he is not surprised, for he was already looking for it. He sowed living seed, and he expected to reap a harvest from it; he invested his life into others, and he means to serve and watch until the Christian babes in Christ are transformed into laborers. This is a determined Christian who is living the scripture, *"the just shall live by faith."*

Chapter Seventeen

WHAT ARE YOU
COURAGEOUS ABOUT?

THE UNITED STATES OF AMERICA has been on the frontlines of fighting two invisible wars within this last century, as have other nations: moral wars, that is. On June 26, 2013 the news broadcasters gave word concerning both these wars. My heart dropped in grief as I listened to the report from my living room that evening. National leaders once again chose to defy God and give sin precedence, contrary to God's law. Whoremongers who choose to defile themselves in abominable relations are now said by the U.S. Supreme Court to be allowed nearly one thousand rights and privileges.

As if that were not enough, my heart further plummeted in sorrow as I listened to the next broadcast concerning abortion. The news anchor reported that the slaughter of innocent unborn babies would continue to be upheld as law in many states, in particular in the state of Texas.

The righteous fight to close down abortion clinics has been a grueling war. As an example, it came to a climax in the summer of 2013 in the state of Texas. The opponents in favor of abortion brought on a great battle in the Texas State Capitol building on June 25th through the early morning hours of June 26.

This date will go down in infamy. Texan lawmakers had diligently worked on a bill that, if voted into law, would close thirty-seven of their forty-two abortion clinics, virtually banning abortion in this large state. The bill had more senators in support of it than opposed it. Therefore, early in the day it appeared as if Texas would become America's strictest state opposing abortion.

The only way the opponents could defeat the measure was by not allowing it to come to a vote. And this is what the challengers accomplished.

Members of the Texas State Senate were set to vote and sign the bill into law by midnight. However, early in the day at 11:18 a.m., a heartless and audacious senator walked up to the floor of the Senate and condemned the bill by filibuster. She began a speech that lasted over eleven hours and foolishly halted lawmakers from taking a vote to protect innocent lives. She did not consider innocent babies, but determinedly spoke out to keep abortion alive.

At last, her filibuster ended abruptly. She was near exhaustion. It seemed as if the legislators could finally take a vote and get the bill signed into law before the midnight deadline. As they hastened their work, writing the final details of the bill, with the deadline nearing, the House was suddenly interrupted by an unruly mob of people. As her evil feat was broadcast live on the internet, the senator had gained thousands of supporters who came down to cheer her on and shout their approval for murder.

The throng of people broke loose in the Senate House, disturbing the lawmaking activities. They made such a loud ruckus of cheers and yells that it drowned out attempts by the legislators to vote the bill into law. Amidst the chaos, the bill was not signed by the midnight deadline. Consequently, righteousness was rejected and the wicked rejoiced.

Indisputably, this is not the first time ungodly individuals have boldly risen and defied God's law. The wicked have always scorned God, thinking their deeds will not be judged. Nevertheless, they are foolish and do not understand that there are ways which seem right but eventually lead to the way of death (Proverbs 16:25). Although the wicked work in determination to defy God and boldly boast of their evil desires, God is not mocked. God keeps account.

We Christians are not to fret because of those who prosper in ungodly deeds and bring about great wickedness to fruition. We are to patiently wait, and in the Lord's timing the wicked shall not be. The Bible tells us that the wicked shall perish, and *"the enemies of the LORD shall consume away into smoke"* (Psalm 37:20). Just look at the numerous testimonies of the heathen in the Old Testament, such as many evil cities God eventually took vengeance upon and judged: Sodom, Gomorrah, Nineveh, Tyre, and Sidon. The LORD preserves all those who love Him: but all the wicked He destroys.

In the meantime, you and I are to continue to uphold righteousness. We are to be strong and very courageous in pursuing righteous deeds as well. We are not to be afraid, neither are we to be dismayed (Joshua 1:7-9). The LORD

God is with us, unlike the wicked. Therefore, we should determine to courageously be a light that shines in a dark place. We are to uphold God's law and bring glory and honor to the Lord Jesus Christ.

If your eyes are enlightened to what is happening in the world today you will notice that the times are becoming darker with each passing day. Evil is prevailing more and more. The hearts of men are waxing worse and worse. People's minds are becoming reprobate as they do not like to retain God in their knowledge, pursuing the lusts of their wicked hearts and doing those things which are not right.

As the wicked become more undaunted in their determination to prevail against righteousness, how much more should we Christians endeavor to uphold righteousness? If there is ever a time for your light to shine and your life to make a difference, that time is now! Tomorrow is gone. Yesterday is not promised. Right now you are alive, and you are given the glorious gift of life from God to make a difference.

God has called you to rise up and go make an influence in a godly manner, to bring good change to the lives of others. Your duty is to be obedient to God's command—*go* and simply reach who you can. Our generation is waiting for you. They need your help.

Will you arise and take the initiative to make a difference in someone's life *today*? Will you go touch another life *today* in Jesus' name?

But I hear many Christians timidly say, "...but I am fearful. I don't have any courage." Well, then I agree you do have a problem, but only a minor one. Nothing is too difficult for God that He cannot supply you with what you lack. You must simply ask God, and He will supply.

If a Christian determines within himself that he wants to have life more abundantly and make a good change in his community, then that determined servant of God needs to be filled with courage. Nobody can go before people and labor to make a positive godly change in the lives of others without first possessing some element of courage and bravery. It is simply impossible.

A courageous attitude is demonstrated in both the Old Testament and the New Testament. For time would fail me to tell of all the stories; but let's take a look at just a few examples written about in the holy scriptures: In the Old Testament, the book of Joshua describes of Joshua's bravery and how God used him to courageously lead the nation of Israel into the Promised Land. We read in the book of 1 Samuel that Jonathan on many occasions fearlessly saved his friend David from being assassinated by his father. We read in the book of Esther that this young lady (Esther) heroically came in before the king on his throne without invitation and advocated for the Jews, not knowing what would become of her. As a result, her courageous feat saved all Jews from mass genocide.

In the New Testament, we read about individuals who confronted the liars and perpetrators of their day and proclaimed the truth, such as John the Baptist and the apostle Paul. We also read about the many testimonies of Christians who ministered the gospel amidst trials and times of uncertainty, such as in the books of Acts, First and Second Thessalonians, and other writings like the book of James. We sometimes overlook the fact that these early brethren were real individuals who consistently dealt with real trials and adversities, similar to and most certainly more difficult than what you and I experience. However, these individuals, despite their challenges, believed and trusted God. They placed their confidence in God, and by this, they courageously influenced their generation, led thousands to salvation, and became examples for us to follow.

Now the book of Acts, I am in awe of it! What a book! This book encourages me so much. It provokes me to seek God for more courage, which He liberally supplies, and then to put that courage into action. This book is filled with so many stories of courageous men, women, and children who defied obstacles for God and valiantly served Him. If Hollywood ever needs a new exciting movie script, they should indulge themselves with this awesome book. But then, Hollywood just might get saved for looking into the Word of God, much like what occurred a few times in the book of Acts.

In Acts chapters 6 and 7, for example, God records the testimony of one such man who was courageous; he did not fear man even in the face of his death. This man was Stephen. It is written that he was a good and faithful man of the Lord. The Bible tells that he was not a clergyman but a simple layman who was determined to make known the gospel of Jesus Christ to the sphere of people in his influence. He was a man who labored with integrity and honesty in his lay job. He was also a man who was filled with the Holy Spirit and who understood his purpose in life—to be a witness for Christ. As a result, his life had great influence on many.

The Bible records on one occasion that Stephen took the extra effort to proclaim the truth of God's Word to a group of proud and arrogant individuals. Acts 7:54 records that while he spoke the gospel to these unreasonable men, God's Word cut to their heart, as it often does with anyone who hears it. And when it cuts, the results are either repentance or bitterness. As Stephen carried on the discourse and spoke the truth without hesitation, their annoyance turned into resentment. Nevertheless, Stephen continued steadfast in courageously speaking the Word that they needed to hear even as their resentment grew into violent wrath.

The Bible shows us how Stephen was able to persevere and speak the truth with courage, instead of being fearful and running away from those who aimed to brutally murder him. Acts 7:55 tells us that Stephen was full of the power of the Holy Ghost, and because of this influence his spirit was rightly positioned with God to receive the ample supply of courage he needed at that moment. Therefore, Stephen was able to proclaim the truth to these individuals who so dearly needed to hear it. Without the Holy Spirit's influence, he would not have had the courage or confidence to proclaim the gospel, especially to these wicked, bitter men, and God would not have been glorified.

Stephen's testimony portrays the reality that the service of God requires a determined effort. There is no harder labor and none that brings greater results than the winning and discipling of souls for Jesus. If you are going to be a Christian who brings adequate results, then you will need courage from God. I am not stating that God will call you to become a preacher before individuals who will seek to physically murder you, as in Stephen's case. Perhaps not, but God will indeed call you to be a living sacrifice in the pursuit of souls.

God invites you to renounce and die to your self-pity and self-interest. In their place, God promises to supply you with courage to daily pick up your cross and deny yourself (Luke 9:23). Few of us are called to experience physical martyrdom for Christ, but all of us are called to experience daily spiritual martyrdom on the behalf of others.

God calls all Christians to commit to the greatest act of martyrdom in the pursuit of making God priority: to love God first and love people second (Matthew 22:37-40). We can avoid making up our minds, but we cannot avoid making up our lives. If today you make your life's determination to serve God and not yourself, then you will be able to say as Paul wrote, *"I am crucified with Christ: nevertheless I live; yet not I, but Christ liveth in me: and the life which I now live in the flesh I live by the faith of the Son of God, who loved me, and gave himself for me"* (Galatians 2:20). God will supply you the courage if you are determined to live daily as a martyr for Christ by laying down your life for the benefit of others. We are to present our bodies as a living sacrifice, holy, acceptable unto God, which is our reasonable service (Romans 12:1).

Such determination and resolve is only born through courage. An apprehensive or doubtful Christian will not be able to commit to such glorious experiences with God. However, if you seek God and beg Him to supply you the courage, He will give it to you. Will you be determined to seek God for courage and then put it into action? Will you be provoked to move your walk with the Lord into a higher level of courage?

Now courage is not always the absence of fear; it is the perseverance *to still go* in spite of fear. If you lack courage, then the devil will most certainly use his ammunition of fear to attack you. If you are without courage, then you will notice all sorts of fears consuming you, and you will not speak the saving gospel to men. For example, when you try to talk to someone about the gospel, you will have fears and worries about what people think of you, such as if the person is going to get mad that you approached him with the gospel, or you might worry whether the person will receive the gospel.

These examples of fears are merely disguised lies from the devil. They are deceptions rooted in emotions. They seem to be reasonable, but they are attacks aimed to discourage you and cause you to quit. This is why the apostle Paul regularly reminded himself and the men around him to take courage and be fearless. He recognized that fears stem from lies of the enemy. He was well aware that these lies would manifest themselves through unstable emotions of doubt and worry (Philippians 4:6-7), and he was not going to have any part of being enslaved to deceptive emotions of fear.

Neither should you or I be enslaved to emotions, doubts, or fears; we should be courageous. This is the reason in 1 Corinthians 16:13 we are commanded: *"Watch ye, stand fast in the faith, quit you like men* [act manly], *be strong."* We are not going to get anything done if we slouch around and embarrassingly try to whisper the gospel to someone. God knows His work could never be carried through with cowardice. Therefore He commanded, *"quit you like men,"* meaning—be valiant like soldiers and act like men!

Read Joshua 1 and listen to God's continual exhortation to Joshua and his men: *"Be strong and of a good courage"* (vs. 6). Again, *"Be very courageous and be of good courage..."* (vs. 7). Yet again, *"Be strong and of a good courage; be not afraid, neither be thou dismayed..."* (vs. 9). And then, as the people followed God's example (vs. 18), you shout the encouragement, *"Be strong and of a good courage"*! This is moral support at its best!

Nevertheless, courage is never done in a defiant attitude or shown by signs of contempt. Courage is demonstrated with temperance. As an example, the whole life of our Lord exemplified courage. Of Christ it was said, *"He shall not strive, nor cry; neither shall any man hear his voice in the streets. A bruised reed shall he not break, and smoking flax shall he not quench, till he send forth judgment unto victory"* (Matthew 12:19-20). Christ achieved His tremendous purposes without undue physical exertion and altogether without violence. His whole life demonstrated temperance and restraint; yet He was of all men the most utterly courageous. For example, Jesus could send back word to Herod who had threatened Him, *"Go ye, and tell that fox, Behold, I cast out devils, and I do cures to day and to morrow, and the third day I shall be perfected"* (Luke 13:32). There is complete courage here, but no defiance, no sign of contempt, no extravagance of word nor act.

On the other hand, if we do not take God at His Word and show courage, then we will find ourselves to be like the man Gideon. Although Gideon's testimony demonstrates the necessity of faith in practice, it exposes some areas that can cause a Christian to lack a courageous character.

Gideon's story can be read in the book of Judges. In chapter 6, we read that Israel was greatly impoverished and oppressed by neighboring enemies. During this fearful time God came down and approached a pessimistic Israelite man named Gideon (whose culture considered him of low degree). God began to speak with Gideon about Israel's matters at hand. In their conversation, God informed Gideon that He would save Israel, and more astounding, He had chosen him to be the man who would save his nation from their enemies. In verse 14, God assured Gideon that the LORD had indeed called him to liberate his nation from their bondage. In addition, God later affirmed to him that he would not die in accomplishing this victory.

One would think that such guarantees verbally spoken from God would be the confirmation needed for anyone to rise up and fearlessly do a mighty work. Gideon had spoken with God face to face and was given this awesome privilege. However, in verses 15 and 27 we learn that Gideon still viewed himself inadequate to fulfill God's requests. He was apprehensive to follow through God's orders to go cast down the city's wicked altars.

Although he was naturally inclined to be hesitant and feared to take a stand for what was right and against wrong, we learn in verse 34 that Gideon's attitude did a complete turnabout when God filled him with the Holy Spirit. The Spirit of the LORD had come upon him and the Spirit's influence emboldened Gideon to gather key men to war with him against the enemies.

But later again (only two verses afterward) he questioned whether he was the right man to lead a defeat against the enemies. Once more he stopped believing in God's unseen promises. He focused on the seen problems, and very soon his attitude reverted to doubt again. Fear and worry once again consumed his mind and his doubtful state of thinking crippled his spirit.

Thankfully, God showed much grace toward him, and helped Gideon to believe the divine promises. Soon afterwards, Gideon once again stood up with God; he became filled with courage, and he victoriously lead a small group of men to drive away the enemies. Courage triumphed in victory!

Another encouraging testimony is that of Elisabeth, Mary's cousin. While Mary was courageously pregnant with Jesus, she went to visit Elisabeth. When

Mary met and greeted her, the Bible says in Luke 1:41-43 that Elisabeth's baby leaped in her womb and she was filled with the Holy Ghost. It is significant that while she was filled with the Holy Ghost the Bible explains, *"And she spoke out with a loud voice."* Though there is great joy in being influenced by the Holy Ghost, the prominent and most important outcome of His influence in a person is the divine capability to speak God's Word with persuasive confidence. Elisabeth was filled with the Holy Ghost and this influence empowered her to joyously speak prophetic words of God in a tone of voice that all could hear. The influence of the Holy Ghost will not only move you and me to speak the truth of God's Word, but His power will move us to speak it with boldness and confidence, without worry about what others might think.

I hear Christians sometimes say, "I can't tell the gospel to anyone. I am not educated." You know what I say to that? "That's a deception from the devil." Neither you nor I need to have any formal education to be empowered to speak God's Word. All we need to do is what the apostle Paul said in Ephesians 6:19: to beg God that He would give us the utterance so that we may open our mouths boldly to make known the Lord's gospel. We need not rely on ourselves but rely solely on the power of the Holy Ghost. When we are filled with the influence of the Holy Ghost, we will declare God's Word with conviction and power.

This same courageous influence of the Holy Spirit is what assisted (or should I say, "Who assisted") Peter and John when they stood before a resentful and vengeful religious council in Acts 4:1-22. Their Spirit-filled courage empowered them to publicly stand up and boldly declare what needed to be said—the whole gospel truth, and not some timid, watered-down, apologetic statement.

Acts 4:13 makes known that Peter and John were just ordinary *unlearned* men; yet they possessed a boldness in their speech that got the religious men's attention. Peter and John had never been educated in how to conduct public speeches. Nevertheless, not worrying about what they lacked in skill or their insignificant social status, they used their fishermen lingo and with ineloquent speech they boldly proclaimed the news about the Jesus whom they knew.

The Bible says in Acts 4:13 that this religious council marveled, probably at the fact that some *unlearned* fishermen stood up in opposition and proclaimed the gospel truth. No matter the reason, certainly, their boldness in speech compelled this crowd to realize that Peter and John had been with Jesus.

I do not know about you, but this story encourages me a lot. It is not a question of knowing what to do; we can easily learn that from the Scriptures. It is a question of whether or not we have the courage to do it. For example, we do not have to know how to speak eloquently or perfectly. All we need to do in speaking the gospel is just be ourselves and talk as we know how to talk (of course, without corrupt communications such as swearing [Ephesians 4:29; 5:4]).

For example, do you know how to talk about food? Do you know how to talk about your car, your house, or your favorite hobby? Of course you do! Then you know how to talk about Jesus. Therefore, I encourage you to go out and just be yourself, use your simple everyday lingo, take courage, and tell others about the Jesus of the Bible whom you know. People will take notice that you too have been with Christ, if you muster up the courage to proclaim Him.

It is ordinary men whom God calls to take courage and proclaim His extraordinary gospel. Most eloquent fancy speakers who have high degrees and experience in mastering the art of public speaking are not worth a buck for the kingdom of God. Their efforts and attention are too focused on how they sound, what they are wearing, and the details of their information. God is more interested in the heart of a man than such vanities. This is why God calls ordinary men, women, and children to proclaim His magnificent gospel. It is the ordinary Christians in society who can go to God and acknowledge they do not know how to minister; these who humbly make themselves available to God are the ones God chooses to use in extraordinary ways.

If you are ordinary, be content—God made you that way. Then make yourself available to God, take courage, and proclaim His gospel in the ordinary manner in which you speak every day of your life. You will begin to see that God will use your commonplace self and your courage to win souls for His kingdom. Then Christ will be exalted, God will be glorified, and you will be astonished as much as others, and many will come to know the Savior as a result. What a wonderful recipe that only God can put together!

On the other hand, if you are extraordinary, remember the warning God gives in 1 Corinthians 1:26-29, saying, *"For ye see your calling, brethren, how that not many wise men after the flesh, not many mighty, not many noble, are called: But God hath chosen the foolish things of the world to confound the wise; and God hath chosen the weak things of the world to confound the things which are mighty; And base things of the world, and things which are despised, hath God chosen, yea, and things which are not, to bring to nought things that are: That no flesh should glory in his presence."*

It is God who has chosen to gift few individuals with great capacities, skills, and abilities. He gives few individuals such extraordinary gifts in order to magnify and demonstrate Himself in amazing ways. If you are one of these few individuals, be keen to remember one thing: God does bestow extraordinary gifts upon some people, but very few of the exceptionally gifted individuals choose to humble themselves and allow God to glorify Himself in extraordinary ways.

If God has gifted you with amazing capabilities, skills, or talents, praise be to God; nevertheless, I strongly encourage you to *"be clothed with humility: for God resisteth the proud, and giveth grace unto the humble"* (1 Peter 5:5). Fasting, praying, being still before God for extended periods of time, and again fasting and praying some more, are all needful ways to seek God for humility, so that He might use your God-given extraordinary gifts and abilities for His honor and glory.

The LORD God repeats over and over in the Bible the words, *"Be strong and of good courage...be not afraid nor dismayed...for I the Lord thy God am with thee."* Therefore, let us be determined to allow God to glorify Himself through us. Let us be determined to abide in Christ, *daily*, as well as to go out and courageously proclaim His gospel to a lost and dying world. *"What shall we then say to these things? If God be for us, who can be against us?"* (Romans 8:31)

As best stated by one of the most courageous men in the Bible, may we take heed to the words he was inspired by God to pen: He, the apostle Peter, wrote, *"Ye therefore, beloved, seeing ye know these things before, beware lest ye also, being led away with the error of the wicked, fall from your own stedfastness. But grow in grace, and in the knowledge of our Lord and Saviour Jesus Christ. To him be glory both now and for ever. Amen"* (2 Peter 3:17-18).

Chapter Eighteen

WHAT ARE YOU
HOLDING ONTO?

YOU AND I are largely creatures of habits. By birth, we all start this life with a great deal of selfishness, and by long practice we have lived to please ourselves. We have long been debtors to certain fleshly tendencies, such as self-centeredness.

If you could think back for a moment to your babyhood, you would find that you were selfish. When you and I left our mothers' wombs and became part of this world, we had a natural inclination to be selfish. Every single one of us on this earth shows up self-interested, self-loving, self-caring, and self-serving. It is in our genes.

As much as I love to hold a brand new baby, and although we might say that babies are precious and adorable, in the background of each little delightful one there is a case of selfishness built since day one. Immediately on coming out of the womb, we yelled and cried because of the absence of our mothers' warmth. We wanted to be intimately near within her. We wanted the comfort of her being.

After we realized that we would never be given the opportunity again to be inside our mother, we quit demanding a return to the womb. We settled for the new experience of being held in her arms next to her bosom. This gave way to a new satisfaction, and within moments we were inclined to demand being held at all times. Then, within a few hours, we learned of hunger, and we cried and yelled for feeding. We would not stop until we got what we wanted!

As babies, and even as toddlers, we never once thought about our parents' needs. It was our needs and an alleviation from our discomforts that we screamed and demanded attention for, even in the middle of the night when we felt hungry and demanded milk. All we thought about was our discomfort and irritation and for our need to be satisfied.

As we grow older, hopefully, we learn to embrace discomforts and disregard our selfish desires in order to put the needs of others before our own. But sadly, it seems that selfishness just happens to be ingrained in some people more than others.

For example, I will use food to explain this point. Food is a wonderful necessity from God. It nourishes us, and it can comfort us, and it can even bring us happiness for short periods of time. However, there are greater reasons why God has given us food. One reason is as a learning mechanism to help teach us godly character.

Sadly, some of us never surpass the ache for food. God supplies us with food so that we can use it to learn to deny our selfish wants and mortify our demands and learn to place God and people first, such as through *fasting*. This is why fasting is so good. One of its benefits is to empower us to develop unselfish attitudes and to demand less, as well as to train us to be available servants for God and people, even during times of discomfort and weakness. Just read Isaiah 58, in particular to verse 7.

Beyond a longing for food, there are people, including Christians, who in general mean to get all they can. They have not overcome their selfish thinking; they are self-consumed and go about making choices that benefit themselves before the interests of others or of God. They make decisions based upon personal concerns and pleasures before thinking about how their choices may or may not affect others. They have never learned how to deny what their flesh craves and to embrace want. They always think about themselves instead of others.

We should not be lovers of our own selves nor lovers of pleasures more than lovers of God. That is the custom of the world, especially during these perilous times we live in (2 Timothy 3:1-4). We are to use our communications and our manner of life, along with our personal resources, as means to do good for the edifying of others. We should allow our lives to be available as instruments in God's hands for Him to minister grace unto others in whatever way He desires.

Therefore, we must have the opposite attitude from that of a selfish man. We must seek our own interests last. Moreover, we must place our personal pleasures at the bottom of all lists. We must be determined to disregard self-centered desires and forsake covetousness. We must learn to be content with what we have and not desire what we do not have (Hebrews 13:5). If the LORD is our Shepherd, we shall not want.

How is this possible? Hebrews 13:5 gives the answer. The verse ends by explaining, *"for he* [Christ] *hath said, I will never leave thee, nor forsake thee."* It is only possible to be entirely unselfish when we are content with Christ alone. Jesus promised, *"I will not leave you comfortless"* (John 14:18). Christ has given us the indwelling of His Spirit within our inner being. It is the Christian who is responsive to Christ's Spirit who lives refreshed in the presence of the Lord. He recognizes that he is rich because he walks with God. God is his joy and delight. Because he is happy in God alone, he learns to be content with whatsoever state God calls him to. He knows how to be abased, he knows how to abound, and he knows how to suffer need. Nevertheless, he abides with God.

When a Christian is satisfied *in* God alone and he is not concerned with possessions or the lack of things (in most cases), then he comes to be on a greater plane with God (1 Corinthians 7:24). He has safely moved himself away from selfishness and has come to be content with what God gives him: drink, food, raiment, and most importantly the Holy Bible. The scriptures tell us, *"But godliness with contentment is great gain"* (1 Timothy 6:6).

A determined servant of God who desires to have life more abundantly with Christ must yield his character to one of selflessness; he must be unselfish. A man will never influence this world for eternal good nor win one soul to Christ if he is selfish. James 2:14-17 admonishes us with the words: *"What doth it profit, my brethren, though a man say he hath faith, and have not works? can faith save him? If a brother or sister be naked, and destitute of daily food, And one of you say unto them, Depart in peace, be ye warmed and filled; notwithstanding ye give them not those things which are needful to the body; what doth it profit? Even so faith, if it hath not works, is dead, being alone."*

More appalling than physical nakedness is that there are countless numbers of people, near us, who are spiritually naked without Christ's robe of righteousness, dipped in His blood of forgiveness. These *naked* individuals are on their way to an eternity of Hell separated from God forever.

If a man is selfish, his faith will be dead and he will not be concerned with helping to clothe another soul with the forgiveness and righteousness of Jesus Christ. This poor man will only be focused on himself, and he will never open his lips, his hands, or his life to give Christ to anyone. A man will cease to do good in other people's lives or bring men to Christ as soon as he becomes concerned with self-pity and self-interest. His mind is too busy thinking about himself instead of others.

May we heed the wise instructions God gives in 1 Corinthians 10:24. God says, *"Let no man seek his own, but every man another's wealth."* I like how God uses the word *wealth* in this particular verse. Sadly, watered-down versions of the Holy Bible have changed the word to "welfare" or "good." This may hold some weight; however, in the unadulterated King James Bible, God hits the point right on the spot. By using this word *"wealth"* God touches the intimate depth of our hearts when it comes to what is most important to many people. Just hearing the word wealth in this context incites most individuals to pause an extra moment and reconsider what they are getting themselves into. Many times, it is on the basis of the amount of giving of one's money that a Christian decides how much he will involve himself in ministry. Many simply are uncomfortable with being required to give of their money. This should not be.

We Christians are the most blessed people on the earth, and therefore we most certainly should be liberal in the giving of our substance. But if a Christian is unable to relinquish his wealth regularly to God and people, then he assuredly is a selfish man. Until we are able to get over personal aspirations for gain of *wealth*, such as external happiness, prosperity, things, or money, and learn to put God and people first, we will be useless in making a big impact in people's lives.

I am not condemning people for having wealth or riches. Nor am I against people having an abundance of things. We simply must keep in the forefront of our focus that things must not have us. Some individuals are gifted by God with an affluence of capital. God gives them much for the purpose of funding works of God. To whom much is given, the same requires much responsibility. (Check out some scriptures in the Gospel of Luke to see what God makes known about this extraordinary gift—Luke 14:33; 3:11; 16:9-11; 12:33-34.)

Moreover, wealth comes with great responsibilities and serious accountability before God. Those who covet money and poorly handle the affluence which money offers should learn from the examples of others' errors. Many have erred from the faith and pierced themselves through with many sorrows because of the love of money. Many who seek to be rich fall into temptations and snares, and then find themselves in many foolish and hurtful lusts, which drown men in destruction and perdition (1 Timothy 6:9-10).

We have the example of Sodom and Gomorrah. One particular reason why God brought judgment on these two cities is that they were exploiting

God's blessings for themselves. Ezekiel 16:49-50 tells us their iniquity was, *"pride, fulness of bread* (their economy had God's blessings)*, and abundance of idleness* (laziness)*....neither did* [they] *strengthen the hand of the poor and needy."* Sadly, they were only consuming the riches of God's blessings. They were not allowing the riches to productively flow back out from them to others, in particular the poor and needy.

Whether or not you are given much wealth, it is important to keep in mind the admonition from God in Philippians 2:3-5. God instructs, *"Let nothing be done through strife or vainglory; but in lowliness of mind let each esteem other better than themselves. Look not every man on his own things, but every man also on the things of others. Let this mind be in you, which was also in Christ Jesus."* Likewise, an abundant life does not seek to enlarge one's own life; it seeks to enlarge the lives of others.

One way we can esteem others better than ourselves and look out for the things of others better than our own is to be as Christ. Jesus is our example. So how did Jesus handle Himself? One scripture for the question is Romans 15:3. The verse opens by explaining Christ's approach, saying, *"For even Christ pleased not himself."* Christ, our example, put the needs of others first. We too need to be like Christ and put the needs of others before our needs. Then and only then will we be able to follow the great instruction found two verses before as to how to be like Christ: *"We then that are strong ought to bear the infirmities of the weak, and not to please ourselves. Let every one of us please his neighbour for his good to edification"* (Romans 15:1-2).

We are to walk in this life with a readiness of mind to be available to help bear the needs of other people. We need to be as pallbearers, servants readily available in the *now* who help lift the burdens of people, not after they are dead but right *now* while they are alive, fulfilling the law of Christ by bearing others' burdens (Galatians 6:2). But may we not try to do it alone. We are not designed to bear all burdens alone. God has designed us to depend on Him. God alone is able to bear all burdens.

Neither should we ever try to single-handedly bear others' burdens. Isolation is never good. Consider the ant; she gathers her food with an army of others. She carries small loads alone, but she pairs up with other ants to move bigger loads. Or consider Moses; he was rebuked and counseled in Exodus chapter 18 not to bear all the needs of everyone by himself. Such endeavors will surely wear a person down, for none of us is able to bear and perform many tasks alone. Like Moses, you and I can help bear some of the light afflictions of others by ourselves; however, we must learn to work with other people in ministering to bear others' difficult burdens. Some needs are so heavy that we should not dare to lift them alone. We need the congregation of the body of Christ in times like these. This is why we need to surround ourselves with godly Christians (Hebrews 10:24-25).

Proverbs 11:24 teaches, *"There is that* [a person who] *scattereth, and yet increaseth; and there is that* [a person who] *withholdeth more than is meet, but it tendeth to poverty."* The principle to learn is that we have to open up our hands and allow things to flow into and out of our lives. Sometimes God might give us things to enjoy, for a temporary time, but we must keep our hands open so that they may flow back away from us to those in need. If our hands are always just reaching to have something, then we are being selfish, and that tends to lead to poverty.

When a Christian tries to put the thought of money altogether away from himself, the money will often come back to him abundantly in a variety of ways; but if he seeks to grab and grasp all that he can, he will very likely find that it will not come to him at all. Those who are selfish in the matter of money will be the same in everything else. For instance, selfish individuals do not want people in their sphere of influence to know anyone else who can do something better than themselves; they cannot bear to hear of any good going on anywhere except what is spoken about their own lives.

I remember on one occasion meeting a selfish "minister" of God. He was more concerned about his own gains than the victories of other Christians. It was quite pitiful to witness his demeanor and hear his words. Quite frankly, I was embarrassed to be near him as I was afraid others might think I held the same egoistical attitude. I wanted to openly rebuke the minister, but God had not given me the authority to do so. Hence, I prayed for him.

Another sad example I have witnessed is of some Christians participating in the glorious work of public evangelism. Normally, I would rejoice and be glad to hear someone's testimony of leading another to Christ. This is wonderful news! But sadly, I have met some who only want to talk about the one new convert that God allowed them to reach within the year. Yet they despise talking about any others' success in the work. This should not be!

For who are we? NOTHING. *"So then neither is he that planteth any thing, neither he that watereth; but God that giveth the increase. For we are labourers together with God: ye are God's husbandry"* and God is the husbandman (1 Corinthians 3:7,9; John 15:1).

It must be remembered that God is the One behind the scenes who orchestrates events in life. He is the One who lets us meet another, who allows us to share the gospel with someone. God is the One who allows us to soulwin.

God is the Creator and Sustainer of life. He gives us life, but not for ourselves. God gives us life for others. When you really think about it, God even gives us air to breathe for *others*. So a determined servant of God must have a character that yields to giving and not selfishness. He must be aware that he is alive for the glory of God and a ministry to others.

An unselfish Christian makes it a priority to give his life to the Lord by outreach to others (2 Corinthians 8:5). He makes up his mind to follow his Savior and walk as He walked. Jesus loved the world, so he too must love the people around him. Jesus stated, *"Greater love hath no man than this, that a man lay down his life for his friends"* (John 15:13). His Savior laid down His life, so he too lays down his life for God and people. This does not necessarily mean a physical death. More often, it means that he lays down his life for the needs and benefits of others. Like his Savior, a servant of God makes himself easily accessible and available for people. He makes himself reachable, and even touchable. If someone needs a hand, he is there to help. If someone needs a shoulder to cry on, he is there to listen and embrace. If someone needs an encouragement, he is there to speak and uplift the person in his burdens.

None of us by our own resolve can lay down our lives for others. Our carnal nature simply will not do it. This is why God says, *"Walk in the Spirit, and ye shall not fulfill the lust of the flesh. For the flesh lusteth against the Spirit, and the Spirit against the flesh: and these are contrary the one to the other: so that ye cannot do the things that ye would"* (Galatians 6:16-17). The Spirit dwells within us that He may quicken our mortal bodies and provoke us to live life as a servant to others. When we are led of the Spirit our minds and bodies then are enabled to choose the path of Christ, a path of meekness, humility, and giving of oneself to others. Thus the Spirit inspires us to take Christ's meek nature upon ourselves, so that we may then be bidden to go get involved in others' lives and trust that Christ's servanthood may be manifested through us unto all.

Although our carnal nature is self-loving, the Spirit can enable us to mortify our flesh so that we may live a life of giving. Romans 8:13 says, *"For if ye live after the flesh, ye shall die: but if ye through the Spirit do mortify the deeds of the body, ye shall live."*

Our hearts quite often do not value the things acceptable to God: for burdens, lowliness and sorrow generally come along with the things of God. Jesus, our great example, was a man of sorrow and was acquainted with grief. Why? Because *in* love He bore the griefs of others and carried their sorrows. Likewise, a Christian who chooses to walk as Christ walked must abide in Christ. This is done by picking up one's personal cross *daily* and following Christ's lead. To follow Christ will undoubtedly take one directly into the center of people's heartaches. A disciple of Christ most certainly will come to experience feeling great heaviness and sorrow in his heart while lifting the burdens of others. The soul of a servant of God will travail for the benefit of others in order that people might be made whole.

The Spirit of the Lord is upon a determined servant of God, because God has anointed him to preach the gospel to the poor (*spiritual* poor, that is). God has sent him to heal the brokenhearted and to preach deliverance to those captive to sin. In addition, God has empowered him to help individuals to escape who are in spiritual darkness by enlightening them with the light of Christ. Furthermore, God has gifted him with discernment and understanding so that he may appropriately serve others by compassionate acts of kindness along with God's Word; then those who are bound by sin may be set at liberty.

A servant of God must savor the things of God, or suffer exhaustion by the heaviness of trials that will come upon him. His heart needs renewing so that he may relish the presence of God; then he can have a spirit that waits patiently for God to guide and direct him unto all good works. Then, as he commits his works unto the LORD, his thoughts will be established in peace, and the desires of his regenerated heart shall be given to him (Psalm 37:4-5).

Continual prayer with God is what we need. Selflessness and prayer go hand-in-hand. You cannot be selfless unless your communion with God is right. Thus, a prayer life should be enriched in communion with God; this then moves us beyond the mere bringing of requests about our selfish wants, desires, and needs. Prayer is God's means to get us to reflect on Him and His glory. Then, as we see God in His light, we will be emptied of ourselves and filled with God's understanding to see people as God views them; thus correctly seeing people's real needs. Then we will be moved to offer specific Spirit-led requests for others to God. God does not hearken unto prayers consumed with self-interests, self-pity or self-promotion. May we take heed to what God says in the book of James: "[*Ye*] *desire to have, and cannot obtain...Ye ask, and receive not, because ye ask amiss, that ye may consume it upon your lusts*" (James 4:2-3). What are your prayers most concerned with?

In our solitude with God, we should be more ready to hear than to act as a fool and give God an oblation full of ourselves. We certainly should converse with God, for He is our Father, but we must not be rash with our mouths, and we should not let our hearts be hasty to utter anything before Him. Our Heavenly Father is in Heaven on His holy throne, and we are upon earth: therefore our words should be few (Ecclesiastics 5:1-2).

We should frequently probe our inner thoughts to seek the actual reason why we present our requests before God. A mere quick thought might reveal our lack of searching within our hearts to discover any unknown selfish motives that might be negatively influencing our prayers. This is one reason why the psalmist wrote, *"Search me, O God, and know my heart: try me, and know my thoughts: And see if there be any wicked way in me, and lead me in the way everlasting"* (Psalm 139:23-24).

Quite often, we need to arrest our restless minds before God and sit quiet. A careful pondering in quietness often helps us to search and find selfish intentions. If our probing proves to discover any vain motive rather than to esteem God and others, we must immediately confess the iniquity and cast it down before God's throne of grace. God surely will not answer prayer that comprises of promotion of self, no matter how minor it might seem in our own reasoning.

Prayer must be sincerely approached with a mindset to glorify God and to learn and understand His mind on matters. Many times we view prayer as an opportunity for us to tell God what we think needs to be done. This is an insult to our omniscient God. God designed prayer that we may come to Him and hear what needs to be done and how we should act accordingly. God is not at all obliged to answer any prayer, most certainly not one that is inspired by vain desires.

We can learn from the example of Hannah in the book of First Samuel. In chapter 1 it is written that Hannah was loved by her husband and treated with highest regard above all other family members. But she lived a life consumed with feelings of grief because she could not have children. Each year Hannah would go up to the house of the LORD, only to be bitterly provoked to tears because of her sorrow; and because of this, she did not wholly worship God. Her prayers were amiss before God, because all her time in prayer was consumed selfishly with what she did not posses. For this reason, God did not hearken to her request.

Finally, one year, she came to the house of the LORD still vexed in her soul, but she had a change of heart regarding her request. At last, she had pondered over her desire, and she came to recognize what she must do in order for God to receive the glory that is due to Him amidst her problem. She must have the mind of God and be a giver rather than a receiver.

This time her prayer did not focus on her wants but instead had regard to God. The scripture records, *"And she vowed a vow, and said, O LORD of hosts, if thou wilt indeed look on the affliction of thine handmaid, and remember me, and not forget thine handmaid, but wilt give unto thine handmaid a man child, then I will give him unto the LORD all the days of his life, and there shall no rasor come upon his head"* (vs. 11). Therefore, she was able to arise from the altar and appropriately worship God (vs. 19) without any bitterness or sorrow of heart.

She expelled her selfishness though understandable wants, and vowed to give God the child for His glory. God saw the right attitude of her heart, a willingness to give rather than to receive, and graciously God bestowed favor upon her. Within a year she gave birth to a son; and God did even more than that. God went far beyond her request and called that child to be a servant who would later become one of Israel's most important prophets.

So we too must have the mind of God. This is one reason we are commanded in scripture to *"put ye on the Lord Jesus Christ..."* (Romans 13:14) So that we will make no provision for the flesh. Then and only then will we be able to fulfill God's desires rather than the lusts of our carnal nature. Our flesh is covetous and seeks only to fulfill its own lusts, but the Lord Jesus Christ is a giver and transforms the mind to think as He thinks (1 Corinthians 2:16).

So how can we put on the Lord Jesus Christ? Good question. We must put on the whole armor of God. Ephesians 6:14-18 can be summarized as follows: we must have our loins girt about with truth; we must have on the breastplate of righteousness; our feet must be shod with the preparation of the gospel of peace; we must take the shield of faith, we must take the helmet of salvation and the sword of the Spirit (which is the Word of God) and *"pray always with all prayer and supplication in the Spirit, watching thereunto with all perseverance."*

But what does all that mean? In one brief statement it is a most vivid, beautiful description of our Lord Jesus. The whole armor portrays the Lord Jesus and our great need for Him and how through Him we are to exercise our faith. We as born again believers know that our hearts and minds have been girded (surrounded) by the glorious truth of the gospel when we received Jesus Christ as our Savior. We now have the "Spirit of Christ" (Romans 8:9), which is the "Spirit of truth" (John 16:13), whereby we indeed have "put on Christ" which is "the truth" (John 14:6).

We are now empowered to firmly press forward in our Christian course and to engage in life's warfare because we are *"in Christ Jesus."* We are acceptably united to God and now are empowered to be soldiers who are both stout-hearted and well armed. Christ is our armor and in Him we are able to resist all the fiery darts of the enemy and stand firm against the wiles of the devil, the deceptions of our heart, the lusts of our flesh, the course of this world, and the pride of life.

The armor of God is a perfect picture of Jesus Christ because it is He who both prepares us and is our strength and shield (Psalm 28:7). This armor is ours to have, but we must put it on; that is, we must pray for the grace of the Spirit, and draw them out into acts of benevolence as there is occasion. We must abide in Christ, for as the Bible says, *"the LORD my strength, which teacheth my hands to war, and my fingers to fight:* [He is my] *goodness, and my fortress; my high tower, and my deliverer; my shield, and he in whom I trust; who subdueth my people under me"* (Psalm 144:1-2).

In essence, our whole being must be of Christ. We must conduct ourselves filled with His presence and manifest His gospel before others, even when we feel as though we are walking through a valley of the shadow of death. We must live a life that is right in the sight of God and before people: one that is enriched in prayer, with the love of Christ extending peace toward all men.

Second Corinthians 5:17 explains that *"if any man be in Christ, he is a new creature: old things are passed away; behold, all things are become new."* Therefore, we should put on the new man, so that we may walk in righteousness and true holiness. This is the proof of our salvation. As we have opportunity, we need to make sure that we do good unto all men, especially unto those who are of the body of Christ (Galatians 6:8-10).

In addition, we should not be deceived; for whatsoever a man sows, that shall he also reap. A selfish man who partakes in the lusts of his flesh shall in the same manner reap corruption; but the unselfish man who partakes of the things of God shall reap peace of mind, length of days, and influence extended into the lives of generations. For this reason, we should not be weary in well doing: for in due season we shall see the good results of our unselfish labors if we do not faint.

However, if you struggle with selfishness, your real problem is that you are too consumed with "I." You are not regarding God or others; hence, you should seek to purposefully put yourself last in **all** matters. It would be wise for you to humble yourself, pray and seek God's face, and renounce your selfishness.

It is not until we deny ourselves that we can come to know and experience God on a higher glorious plane. Christ can give us victory over selfishness and wantonness by death to our self. Christ died, and we must die daily (1 Corinthians 15:31b). Christ arose in victory over sin and death and we too can experience a resurrected life. Christ's victory opens the glorious opportunity for us to fellowship with God, and know the fellowship of His sufferings (Philippians 3:10).

The scripture says, *"I am crucified with Christ: nevertheless I live; yet not I, but Christ liveth in me: and the life which I now live in the flesh I live by the faith of the Son of God, who loved me, and gave himself for me"* (Galatians 2:20). When we die to ourselves, then God is able to pour His power through us that His love might be manifested to others by the death of our flesh.

It is not until we are dead to ourselves that we can be liberated from selfishness. Selflessness brings liberty from thoughts of oneself and therefore empowers one to lay down his life in whatever means necessary. Insecurities are dissolved and people are able to come near a selfless individual. Selflessness makes a person amenable to the possibility of people intruding his personal space and entering into the privacy of his life. Selflessness births love, and love dispels discomfort and fills the heart with joy, knowing that people can hear and see Christ in us more clearly. Selflessness assures the heart that people will be helped, relationships will be restored and knit together as they receive the Spirit of Christ through us. A selfless Christian is happily empowered to live willing to spend and be spent for the benefit of others (2 Corinthians 12:15). He views himself as a doormat for people to use for help at anytime.

The critics might complain or call names, but a selfless servant of the Lord concerns himself with thoughts of helping people. He is unequivocally focused on serving people in the best way possible. His stance is to be less than others so that he might give them his life as a help to them (Matthew 20:26-28).

God's work done through us must be accomplished with an attitude of selflessness regarding the use of our money, time, energy, gifts, and abilities. Our actions and reactions to the choices of others must demonstrate selflessness and goodness, whether or not we agree with them. God's work is hindered when we refuse to share God's many resources that we have at our disposal, all because someone fails to say, do, or act as we expect. We must not hinder God's work with selfish actions, words, or ideals.

If our decisions spring from selfish objectives, how can we expect to have life more abundantly with Christ and advance His Kingdom? We surely will not seek God's or people's best interest when we refuse to expend any valued resource beyond the "kingdom of me."

In the Sermon on the Mount, Jesus laid out what God thinks about choosing covetousness over benevolence. It is not a good thing. Jesus said, *"Lay not up for yourselves treasures upon earth, where moth and rust doth corrupt, and where thieves break through and steal: But lay up for yourselves treasures in heaven, where neither moth nor rust doth corrupt, and where thieves do not break through nor steal: For where your treasure is, there will your heart be also. No man can serve two masters: for either he will hate the one, and love the other; or else he will hold to the one, and despise the other. Ye cannot serve God and mammon. Therefore I say unto you, Take no thought for your life, what ye shall eat, or what ye shall drink; nor yet for your body, what ye shall put on. Is not the life more than meat, and the body than raiment? Behold the fowls of the air: for they sow not, neither do they reap, nor gather into barns; yet your heavenly Father feedeth them. Are ye not much better than they? Which of you by taking thought can add one cubit unto his stature? And why take ye thought for raiment? Consider the lilies of the field, how they grow; they toil not, neither do they spin: And yet I say unto you, That even Solomon in all his glory was not arrayed like one of these. Wherefore, if God so clothe the grass of the field, which to day is, and to morrow is cast into the oven, shall he not much more clothe you, O ye of little faith? Therefore take no thought, saying, What shall we eat? or, What shall we drink? or, Wherewithal shall we be clothed? (For after all these things do the Gentiles seek:) for your heavenly Father knoweth that ye have need of all these things. But seek ye first the kingdom of God, and his righteousness; and all these things shall be added unto you"* (Matthew 6:19-21, 24-33).

May we heed the words of Christ and not seek the acquisition of temporary selfish wants, whether they be things of our senses, things of our mind, or things of our emotions. No tangible or intangible thing should come before God and people. There are only two things that have eternal value: God's Word and people. Therefore, our attitude should be to know and understand God and to selflessly minister to people.

Perhaps it can all best be summed up by the words of the well-known martyred missionary James Elliott. He said, "He is no fool who gives what he cannot keep to gain what he cannot lose." His focus was on eternal things. If we do this, surely we will not be selfish, but givers of God unto all men. Are not Jesus and people more important than all the things we could aspire to have?

Chapter Nineteen

WHAT ARE YOU
PASSIONATE ABOUT?

THERE IS A POPULAR OLD ADAGE that says the world is run by earnest men. And it is true, for we daily see that our nation is run by intense leaders—and that wars are won by keen generals—and that peace is secured by devoted diplomats—and that extensive legislation is accomplished by determined legislators. The reason for this is that such leaders are willing to put themselves out there whenever necessary in order to accomplish their noteworthy and heartfelt tasks. They have within themselves an earnest temperament.

The lost and dying world must be ministered to with the same fervor. Christians must understand that we will never do great things for God without willingness and a determination to extend ourselves to others, even if we are bone-tired exhausted. Likewise, another quality that a determined servant of God must possess in his work among people is a deep, earnest fervor for the souls of mankind. This earnestness must be evident and outwardly demonstrated in a Christian's character.

So what is your heart earnest for? Earnestness—meaning a passionate compassion, zeal, and an enthusiasm for souls in a believer's emotions, attitude, actions, and speech. Is your heart for God and the benefit of people, or is it always concerned about your interests and concerns? If your heart is for people then you must not be fake or pretentious before people; you must have a natural predisposition to earnestly seek the betterment of the souls of mankind.

Christ's whole life demonstrated that our hearts must of necessity be earnest, laboring hearts among people. Christ's life teaches how serious we must be about the giving of ourselves to people. No one can be serious about giving of himself unless his heart is filled with an earnest desire to help.

Another example is the apostle Paul and his missionary team. They also demonstrated an earnest heart for souls. In one of his letters, Paul wrote to some believers, saying, *"For ye remember, brethren, our labour and travail* [hardship]: *for labouring night and day, because we would not be chargeable* [a burden] *unto any of you, we preached unto you the gospel of God"* (1 Thessalonians 2:9). Not only did he and his team seek to preach the gospel, but their demeanor to the believers was exceptionally filled with love and care as well. In the same letter he explained, *"But we were gentle among you, even as a nurse cherisheth her children: So being affectionately desirous of you, we were willing to have imparted unto you, not the gospel of God only, but also our own souls, because ye were dear unto us"* (1 Thessalonians 2:7-8).

Paul and his team earnestly served people with gentleness, affection, and willingness so that they might gain more people to know Christ. His earnestness to keep his attitude and actions right was done for the gospel's sake, that he and his team might not be chargeable unto anyone, but that they might be partakers of life more abundantly with Jesus Christ. They viewed people to be so dear that they held people close to their heart, and therefore they were filled with the fervency to treat individuals with tenderness and affection. Because of this, many people were aided with help from God's Word.

Paul and his team did not begrudge meeting new people. They were delighted to see those whom God had given them to serve. Therefore, they endeavored to serve more people, and this gave them satisfaction in their labors. Their work ethic was impeccable. They labored night and day. They travailed through difficulties because they possessed a desire not only to give the Word of God to people, but also to give their whole lives to people. That is how important and dear people were to their hearts.

To another group of believers, in Corinth, he conveyed similar sentiments, saying, *"in weariness and painfulness, in watchings often, in hunger and thirst, in fastings often, in cold and nakedness..."* (2 Corinthians 11:27) This godly work ethic was always embedded in the hearts and minds of Paul and his men. No matter the pain or the troubles that came with the ministry, Paul learned from Christ's example to be steadfast and resolute in his work; likewise, he was able to earnestly give all of himself to people so that others might come to know the Lord.

Any Christian who desires to serve men in a godly sense and make an eternal difference must labor with an earnest heart for people. He must be determined to beg God to give him a fervent heart like fire deep within his bones, or else he will be of no profit.

The Bible instructs us in Jude 1:3 to *"...earnestly contend for the faith."* Keep in mind that this is not a suggestion from God. It is a directive: *"ye should earnestly contend for the faith."* God expects us to have a real zest, and to be whole-heartedly passionate and enthusiastic in representing Christ to people in our manner of service and communications. We are dealing with eternal souls!

We can compare gospel earnestness to that of a football game. Perhaps you have been to a football game or have seen one on television. If so, have you ever noticed a football game where the crowd does not care? Of course not! I know that sounds ridiculous, and it should sound crazy. That is because all the spectators are earnestly contending for what is happening on the playing field. They are filled with passion and fervor, and many of them have given their whole hearts, and have fixated their total thoughts and focus on the game. They are devotedly dedicated to the game.

Just like these earnest spectators, we Christians are to be filled with the same seriousness in our intentions, purpose, and efforts to serve Christ and people. We are also to be devotedly dedicated to people. Jesus several times referred to the command that we are to love people. He instructed, *"Thou shalt love thy neighbour as thyself"* (Matthew 19:19; 22:39). This is only effectually carried out when we do Christ's first command: *"Thou shalt love the Lord thy God with all thy heart, and with all thy soul, and with all thy mind, and with all thy strength"* (Matthew 22:37). That is, we are to love Jesus with all our passions, desires, abilities, and thoughts. In order to have that kind of love, we must be filled with great earnestness for Him and His mission. If a man is to be a servant of God, there must be within him an intensity of emotion as well as sincerity of heart and a focus of thoughts and actions to accomplish the work he purposes to do. A Christian must be serious in his intention to get the gospel out to people and be as their servant.

God has given each of us a heart full of emotion. We get to choose which emotions abide and pour out of our hearts. Either we fill our hearts with unproductive agitations of annoyance, resentment, jealousy, frustration, disappointment, and anger, or we fill our hearts with the excitement of love, joy, peace, longsuffering, gentleness, meekness, and temperance. So, which do you yield your heart to?

We need our hearts to be filled with fervent sentiments established in the grace of faith, hope, and charity. Such grace then will spur us to go out with a determined purpose to win souls and to disciple them.

This is why some babes in Christ are effective in leading others to Christ so rapidly. They know little to no Bible, they lack wisdom, yet many brand-new babes in Christ go out and win souls to Christ. They are filled with an earnestness to tell everyone they can about what the Lord just did for them. They are enamored with their newfound Love—Jesus. Therefore, their thoughts are not concerned about what people think or say about them. They are deeply concerned for others who they know Jesus can help just as much as He helped them. Similarly, do you find your love for Christ growing deeper with each new day, or have you left your first Love?

The power of the gospel is not measured by how we speak. Its authority stands alone. Nonetheless, the intent and manner of how it is spoken many times helps bring an astounding effect because earnestness gets people's attention so that they will listen and seek understanding. This is why earnest babes in Christ can and do win souls. People who normally would not pay attention to hear the gospel, all of the sudden open their ears to listen.

It is not the eloquence or the number of Bible verses you utter. It is the power of the seriousness with which a Christian delivers the gospel that decides what is to come forth. Perhaps, most of the time, this is why we should not give attention to men who criticize us for being too enthusiastic or too devoted for the cause of Christ. Such criticism should encourage us to continue going out with more enthusiasm, serving to win souls for Jesus. How can you be too devoted to the One who shed His blood on a cross for you? How can you be too devoted to the One who delivered your soul from the fiery pit of Hell? You cannot! It is just ludicrous to think so.

So let the critics complain. Nevertheless, pray for them and allow their silliness to provoke you to have an earnest temperament with wisdom for the Lord Jesus and people's souls.

The theme of the gospel deserves an earnest attitude. We Christians are privileged to tell of an earnest Savior, an earnest Heaven, and an earnest Hell. Jesus was earnest when He left His riches to come to be made sin for us (Philippians 2:5-8 and Hebrews 12:2). Heaven and all creation are earnest in patiently waiting for us to be united with the Lord Jesus and God the Father (Romans 8:19). Hell is earnest in its unsatisfied craving for more souls to swallow up in perdition (Habakkuk 2:5; Isaiah 5:14, 14:9).

Therefore, we are to be very earnest in our work. We have to deal with souls that are immortal, with sin that is eternal in its effects, with pardon that is infinite, and with terrors and joys that are to last forever!

A Christian who is not earnest when he has such important work as this may just be stuck in religion and needs to come to the Savior's cross.

Think about this: if a Christian lacks an earnest attitude to promptly tell the gospel to someone, and then finally gets around to telling the lost sinner that he is on his way to Hell and is in need of the Savior, that nonbeliever then might decide not to believe the truth from him. Why? Because he might come back to the Christian with the legitimate rebuttal, "If you really believed I was on my way to Hell, you would have told me long before now. I don't believe your religion of Hell and Heaven. Get away from me, you hypocrite!" Though the lost sinner is in error, he is accurate in his assessment of the Christian's hypocrisy for not proclaiming the gospel to him at a much earlier time. What a tragedy!

May we not be found disloyal in proclaiming the gospel to those whom we are commanded to tell. The truth of the gospel and the consequences of not hearing it demand a sense of earnest urgency. It is always a shame when a Christian spends months trying to gain a lost sinner's respect (friendship evangelism) and then loses that respect the moment the Christian suddenly displays a concern for his soul.

A Christian will not be an effectual servant of God until he has begged God for a fervency in earnest concern for souls. A Christian will not enjoy life more abundantly in being an effectual servant of God until he has adequately sought the Lord and allowed the Lord to squeeze and wring all selfishness out of his heart, and then saturate his heart with tears and anguish for the souls of mankind. When a servant of the Lord is consumed with such an earnest attitude for souls, then the world will see Christ through him.

We would do ourselves a great favor if each morning we would wake up and beg God to fill us with an earnest concern for the glory of God and the souls of men. Might I even add, we would do ourselves and the people around us a great service if we would lay still on the ground before God and not leave the prayer until we become filled with a genuine concern for souls. Oh, that the souls of mankind would become a more intense concern within our hearts than the temporal things we enjoy. Then we might see more souls come to know our wonderful Savior. Therefore, with such an important need, will you seek God to give you an earnest zeal?

Without an earnest temperament, without our hearts being more concerned for people than for self-interests or things, we will never be useful in the winning of many souls for Christ; neither will we ever be useful for the discipling of men. The costs are just too high!

Chapter Twenty

WHAT MOVES YOUR HEART?

IN THE NORTHERN STATES of Minnesota and Wisconsin there are great mines of taconite iron ore. For many decades this iron has been important for construction and building projects throughout many states in America. In the late 1950s a company by the name of Great Lakes Engineering Works built the largest lake freighter of its kind, spanning over two football fields in length: the steamship *Edmund Fitzgerald*. Until the mid-70s, it was used to haul thousands of tons of iron ore across the Great Lakes over to Michigan and Ohio. . Its captain, Ernest M. McSorley, ran the steamship long and hard each year, until the winter months stopped all movement across the Lakes.

In November of 1975, Captain McSorley had a full cargo of iron ore needing to be moved across Lake Superior from Wisconsin to Detroit, Michigan. The National Weather Service predicted an early winter storm was developing out on the lake. Captain McSorley had seen harsh weather before in his 47 years of service, so the weather was not that unusual to him. However, in assessing the waters and the harsh early winter weather, the question still arose: should he and his team sail, or not?

After contemplation, he decided to go for it and try to make one last run before the hiatus of the winter months. He and his crew of 29 men cruised from the shore and joined a second massive freighter, the *Arthur Anderson* with Captain Jesse B. Cooper.

En route to Detroit, Captain McSorley of the *Edmund Fitzgerald* led the way, steering ten to twelve miles ahead of the *Arthur Anderson*. The next day of their voyage together, the two ships were suddenly caught in the midst of the severe winter storm. The storm intensified to a level greater than either captain had ever experienced before in their decades traveling the Great Lakes. The blustery weather pounded their ships with waves up to thirty-five feet high and hurricane-force winds.

Although both ships had five or six radio towers, their radio communications experienced a lot of interference. Suddenly, in the midst of the storm, communication with the *Edmund Fitzgerald* stopped, and they were not heard from any more. The *Edmund Fitzgerald* was in trouble.

Captain Cooper of the *Arthur Anderson* feared that maybe the radio antennas had been knocked down by the storm. Horribly concerned for the *Edmund Fitzgerald*, he and his team slowed down but carried on through the rough seas. The *Arthur Anderson* was soon able to get to a sheltering island. There they put down an anchor to wait for the horrific storm to pass.

While they waited the storm out, distressed about the *Edmund Fitzgerald*, a call came in from the nearby coast guard. The coast guard feared that the ship was in trouble and wanted to know if Captain Cooper had heard from them.

History reports that Captain Cooper answered with worry in his voice, saying, "No we haven't heard anything. We were traveling with them, and we lost radio contact. But we haven't heard anything."

After a moment's pause, the coast guard responded with a daring question. They thought perhaps there might be survivors and wanted to know if the *Arthur Anderson* would be willing to go out into the storm and try to locate and help save the crew.

Captain Cooper was not sure. The storm had given his ship a brutal beating. They had been battered worse than anything they had ever seen. The captain understood that he and his crew were miraculously fortunate that they had even survived the storm. He stated to the coast guard on the radio, "I have no question that the *Edmund Fitzgerald* is in trouble. A storm like this is more than any vessel can handle." Then he paused, and continued, "But we'll go."

The captain had a compassionate, concerned heart for the men on the *Edmund Fitzgerald* stuck in the middle of Lake Superior. His tender heart sank for them. At that point, he turned to his own crew and explained the problem in detail and his desire to help. He told his men, "Here's the problem: there is a chance that if we go out we will not survive." Then the tears from his heart could be heard through his words. Continuing, he said, "But the men out there need us! And if we don't go, who will?" He looked his men in their eyes. Then he said, "If we were out there in trouble, we would want somebody to come out and help us."

His men listened intently and thought about his words. Their captain continued, "But here's the dilemma: I can't run this ship without you. I need each and every one of you to help me captain this ship so that we don't sink. I need a 100% vote that you will go back into the storm and try to save the men that are out there."

In an instant, the men cried out in unison, "Let's push. Let's push." With that, the captain gave orders to pull the anchor and cast off the lines. He yelled, "We're going back into the storm!" Then he sobered up and said to his crew, "You men understand that this might be our last sail?"

Every man cried back, "Let's launch."

So they went back out into the wailing storm and searched for the *Edmund Fitzgerald* and its crew. Sadly, this story ends on a negative note. They never did find the ship. The twenty-nine crewmembers of the *Edmund Fitzgerald* died that day, November 10, 1975. Despite the unhappy ending, the story illustrates the compassion that drove the men of the *Arthur Anderson* to risk their own lives to try to help save the lives of others.

Despite the tragic loss of life that day, great valor and compassion was demonstrated. When it was all settled and done, and the world heard about what Captain Cooper and his crew endeavored to do, great honor was given to these men. They went out into a horrific, deadly storm, despite the potential danger of losing their own lives. That storm tore their ship to pieces. A news reporter asked Captain Cooper, "Why?" He is reported to have answered, "Somebody had to go. Somebody had to care. And we were the somebody."

This crew had hearts full of compassion and tenderness, which moved them to think about others above themselves, putting their lives in peril in order to try to save others' lives. As shown in this story, compassion and tenderheartedness provoke individuals to love and do good works for the benefit of others, even at a great cost.

This captain and his men received all kinds of accolades and honors for their great bravery and valor out on that lake. Even to this day, when stories are told of great seamanship, Captain Jesse Cooper and his crewmen still receive great validation for what they did.

On his deathbed, someone asked Captain Cooper, "What is the greatest memory you have out on the seas?"

He responded without hesitation, "My greatest memory is when my *friends* said, 'Let's go out and sail. Let's go back into the storm.' And not one hesitated. That was my greatest moment. I couldn't do it without them."

How true that is. You and I certainly cannot do any great exploit without the assistance of another. Ecclesiastics 4:9-12 says, *"Two are better than one; because they have a good reward for their labour. For if they fall, the one will lift up his fellow: but woe to him that is alone when he falleth; for he hath not another to help him up...And if one prevail against him, two shall withstand him; and a threefold cord is not quickly broken."*

We need the company of others for encouragement, support, and success in life. Thank God that when we might find ourselves isolated or secluded from others we are still never alone. We have Christ, who shall never leave nor forsake us. He *"is a friend that sticketh closer than a brother"* (Proverbs 18:24). His presence and words provide us with encouragement and strength. He is there to spur us to continue, and He compels us to *"Fight the good fight of faith..."* (1 Timothy 6:12)

In ministry, as well as in life, God's people experience rough seas at times and need the help and support of others. Occasions arise where we suffer greatly. Certainly, suffering comes as a result of our own misdoings. Nonetheless, we are sometimes afflicted because of our labors to bring forth good works. We might be making an effort for a good cause, such as when the compassion within our hearts moves us to do something special and help to bring about good in others' lives. We must remember that good never comes without a fight. Sometimes situations in life or human adversaries will rise up and seek to halt our good work. Critics also might come out of the crevices and reproach us for doing good works. In times like these, we need to keep our minds fixed on Christ and persevere in our efforts to bring about good (Hebrews 12:2-4). May we be reminded of what the scripture says when we suffer for good, *"For it is better, if the will of God be so, that ye suffer for well doing, than for evil doing"* (1 Peter 3:17).

In addition, we can be encouraged by the examples of individuals gone before us. One such example is Captain Cooper and his crew. Yet we also have the perfect example of Christ. *"For Christ also hath once suffered for sins, the just for the unjust, that he might bring us to God, being put to death in the flesh, but quickened by the Spirit"* (1 Peter 3:18). Furthermore, we have other people to learn from in the Bible who toiled to do good and suffered greatly for it: individuals such as Moses, Joshua, Ruth, Nehemiah, and Mary, to name a few.

Moses persevered to help the children of Israel despite their bemoaning. Joshua stayed in the battles to defeat the enemies of Israel. Ruth stayed by the side of Naomi in her distress, even when asked to leave. Nehemiah kept steadfast in God's work until it was finished, although enemies and hecklers harassed and assaulted him. Mary carried on, although some in the community shunned her as a fornicator (John 8:41). These individuals were unmovable in accomplishing the task that God had for them. Their testimonies give us great encouragement and attest that we do not need to *"be weary in well doing, for in due season we shall reap, if we faint not"* (Galatians 6:9).

If evil is spoken against us or if we suffer in seeking to do something wonderful for a good cause, we are to keep our faith in God and continue steadfast in the task. May we remember in times of suffering what the scriptures encourage us to do: "[*Have*] *a good conscience; that, whereas they speak evil of you, as of evildoers, they may be ashamed that falsely accuse your good conversation* [behaviors] *in Christ. For it is better, if the will of God be so, that ye suffer for well doing, than for evil doing"* (1 Peter 3:16-17). More importantly, may we keep our mind fixated on Christ and His example, as Hebrews 12:3-4 tells us, saying, *"For consider* [Christ] *that endured such contradiction of sinners against himself, lest ye be wearied and faint in your minds. Ye have not yet resisted unto blood, striving against sin."*

When our hearts are filled with compassion and tenderness, our spirits are enabled to get us involved in the lives of people. Such attitudes impel us to be like Jesus: whether good or bad arises, we can still endure serving people and not give up. Then God will be glorified. But we simply must not be weary or faint, as though we were a people with no hope.

Consider Christ: Jesus possessed a heart filled with compassion and tenderness. Jesus was humble and meek and sat with sinners. Jesus was lowly in heart and stooped down to receive sinners. Jesus appropriately addressed the errors of religiosity. Jesus confessed that the Son of man has come to seek and to save that which was lost (Luke 19:10).

On many occasions the religious leaders outspokenly complained that He kept company with sinners. In one occurrence the Bible records, *"When Jesus heard it, he saith unto them, They that are whole have no need of the physician, but they that are sick: I came not to call the righteous, but sinners to repentance"* (Mark 2:17). Those who believed they were good and had no need for the great Physician, He did not aid. But to those who knew their need, He showed Himself as their great Comforter.

The compassion and tenderheartedness of Jesus moved Him toward helping people. Jesus saw the great needs of people, and because they were like sheep without a shepherd His heart was moved to help them. The Lord Jesus certainly was a true servant (Mark 10:45). Though Christ's heart was all about redeeming mankind back to God, Christ maintained a heart that was both compassionate and tender (James 5:11). He always exhibited these two important qualities toward people amid His great work of redeeming the lost. Christ always showed mercy and attended to wholly taking care of people's distresses, sufferings, and infirmities while preaching His gospel message.

Likewise, a determined servant of God needs to have a heart that is compassionate and tender. These two attributes are placed together because they are interrelated, though with many people one usually dominates over the other. If the compassionate heart is predominant, you will have a temperament to pity others and suffer with them by helping to bear their burdens. You will be easily inclined to show sorrow and express mercy toward people in distress. You will not necessarily be flamboyant in your move to help, but you will be likely to engage in an act of charity or benevolence aimed toward the lifting up of others in their needs. If the tender heart is predominant, you will show kindness and attend to others' distress. You will have a great sensibility for finding the underlying cause of the real needs of people, and then seek to provide the best help you can give them. Unlike us, Jesus was both all the time. Just like Christ, a determined servant of God needs to have a heart that has pity for people and one that takes action to attend to their needs. If a Christian does not possess these qualities, then he should beg God to fill him with compassion and tenderheartedness for others. It would be wise for a Christian to examine the life of Christ and allow his mind to be flooded with the stories of Jesus attending to the needs of people. This surely should inspire any Christian to lay down his life for his fellow man; then the results will cause him to become a better servant, filled with compassion and tenderness to lift up people in their burdens.

Compassion always gives us a correct perspective of people. It always corrects our own view of people by allowing us to see "into" people and not just "through" them. Then any discomfort we might experience in serving and helping them in unpleasant situations cannot only be tolerated but valued and used to bring them the help desired. If you can see into people without judging them and seek to find out why they are in an unpleasant situation, then you will be able to serve and help them for their betterment.

An example of this is the time Jesus was with a great multitude of people. He stopped what He was doing, looked over the crowd, and the Bible records that He *"was moved with compassion on them"* (Matthew 9:36). The passage explains that when He looked over the multitude and saw they were faint, He noticed the cause of their distress: *"they were as sheep having no shepherd."* Like Jesus, compassion will always enable us to see beyond the effects of sin and help us to discern the deeper reasons for people's problems. Then we can be better servants and appropriately minister to people.

In the biblical usage, the words *"compassion"* and *"tenderhearted"* are very fervent words that interrelate and work together within one's heart. These words in the Bible many times depict a movement of the heart from a focus on oneself to a focus on the other. Therefore, when someone is compassionate and is filled with tenderness, his heart purposefully takes upon itself the suffering of another, enabling the person suffering to share that burden with another.

Proverbs 17:17 says, *"A friend loveth at all times, and a brother is born for adversity."* In essence, you and I were created to help people. A compassionate and tenderhearted individual takes some ownership of another's distress and shares the burden. Compassion works to make you sympathize with the sufferer and moves you to have a tender heart. A tender heart works to relieve the suffering of one person and to share it among others. When we have compassion and tenderheartedness, we stand in the place of the other and serve to lift some of the other's burden.

This is exactly what Jesus did all the time. On many occasions when He looked around and observed individuals, He would be overwhelmed with compassion, and then He would tenderly labor to lift them up.

Another example of Christ's compassion is found in Mark 8:2 when Jesus saw another crowd. He observed over four thousand individuals who were hungry and thirsty. They were drained, irritable, weary, and ready to pass out. They had been following Jesus for three days and had not sufficiently eaten or drank. Amazingly, such a multitude wwas still following Him!

Nevertheless, Jesus intentionally led these people into this predicament. He had a higher aim, to show His compassion by providing a great feast to satisfy their physical appetite. He seized the opportunity to display His compassion in order to supply a text for His subsequent sermon and teach the multitude that, "I, Jesus the Son of God Incarnate, am the bread of life. What this bread is to your bodies, I myself am to your souls." Therefore, compassion opened the door for communications in the feast to reveal to the needy that Jesus is all they need; more than food, water, or raiment.

The feeding of the people was the natural outcome of Christ's compassion. It was not an outcome of magic or trickery. It was the result of the manifestation of the kingdom of God and His righteousness. When you and I are filled with compassion for people, we too will be moved to do extraordinary feats to help the physical needs of people as well as their spiritual needs.

Jesus knew very well that the people who followed Him were not saints or holy men and women. Many times, they did not follow Him solely for spiritual reasons or even with pure motives (John 6:26). Nonetheless, He still allowed them to approach and be near Him. Jesus understood that oftentimes people would follow Him because they had great temporal problems and they were hoping for a quick fix. They were in terrible circumstances because the good things in life were taken away by those who had amassed for themselves economic, political, and cultural supremacy at the expense of others.

Jesus indeed noticed people in pitiful situations who were reaching out to anything or anyone who would help. On many occasions the sight moved Jesus to demonstrate compassion. This is one reason why many kept coming to Jesus; He proved His love for them by compassionate acts of kindness. Christ's compassion always moved Him to serve the people's physical needs, and this proved to the people that He genuinely cared for them. After Jesus would physically serve and meet people's needs, this always opened the opportunity for Him to preach the Word of God; His service got their attention and then they were willing to listen to what He had to teach.

Nothing has changed over the last 2,000 years. People are the same today as back then. People will generally give attention and listen to someone who goes far above expectations to help them in their needs. This is why it is important for us to give our lives to people and help them, teaching the Word of God in the midst of service. Serving gives us an opportunity to arrest people's attention, and the expounding of the Bible gives understanding to the simple. He who knows the truth shall be made free indeed (John 8:32). Jesus came to deliver the captives and set at liberty them that are bruised by this world (Luke 4:18). We simply must make opportunities in service to draw people's attention to hear the Word of God.

A determined servant of God can learn from the Lord's example. If we have compassion and a tender heart then we will rise up to help the physical needs of people around us. Then we will see more people willing to listen to the gospel. However, we must keep our priorities correct. Our primary purpose is always to share the Word of our Lord with people. We must never serve the physical needs of people at the expense of preaching Christ. For we are not called to bring about social reform; our first duty is to bring about spiritual reform, then social reform will naturally transpire. This is biblical balance.

Jude 1:22-23 informs us of two methods we are to use when winning souls to Christ. The verse reads, *"And of some have compassion, making a difference: And others save with fear, pulling them out of the fire."* One way to win some souls to Christ is to be forthright and candid about spiritual matters with people. Straightforwardness is needed sometimes. Nonetheless, verse 22 also informs us of a second important means, that is, to be subtle and compassionate with people.

Indeed, both approaches always need to be communicated in grace. It would be very wise and helpful in communicating the gospel if we would understand when to use a direct boldness of speech and when to use a soft-spoken, compassionate approach. It is true that with some people we definitely need to be outright direct about Hell, judgment, and sin. Nonetheless, unto others we need to deliver the gospel message with delicacy and compassion.

Ephesians 4:32 reminds us that we need to demonstrate kindness and tenderheartedness toward people. We are instructed, *"[Be] ye tenderhearted."* Tenderheartedness only comes about from having compassion within one's heart. Therefore, being tenderhearted helps us to recognize which is the best approach to minister unto someone. It supplies us with an understanding of when to keep silent and serve people, in order to make a difference in their physical lives, before we open our mouths to attempt to make a spiritual difference.

Sometimes keeping quiet is needful because some people will not allow us to speak the Lord's gospel to them. They will talk and have good conversations about anything in this life, but the moment we try to talk about the gospel they will shut us off and not listen. This may be one reason the apostle Paul wrote in 1 Corinthians 9:18 and 22, *"Verily that, when I preach the gospel, I may make the gospel of Christ without charge, that I abuse not my power in the gospel. To the weak became I as weak, that I might gain the weak: I am made all things to all men, that I might by all means save some."*

The great news is that God has entrusted you and me with the liberty to proclaim His gospel, but some people are too disturbed to hear the good news. With these people, we must not abuse our liberty and force the gospel on them. Instead, we need to learn the act of diplomacy by putting the powerful Word edgeways into our conversations. We need to subtly tell them little gospel bits of truth here and there intertwined in the middle of conversations. This is being wise, and becoming *"all things to all men."* Then, and maybe only then, will they finally one day allow us to clearly explain the glorious good news of our Lord Jesus Christ.

People all around us generally are not saints or close to being anything like Jesus. Nonetheless, a Christian needs to be like the Lord (1 John 2:6) and properly represent Him to this blind generation. For example, in the presence of lost sinners, we need to show tenderheartedness toward them even when they are contemptible before us. If we are to be of much use to God, there must be in our hearts a great deal of compassionate tenderness.

A Christian who is filled with tender compassion will become better aware of people and notice that many are wanderers; they are simply wandering around this world, grasping after anything or anyone they think might bring them the hope they are so desperately seeking, even if it is a temporary fix. This is why people go from one sin to another sin to another sin and then to another sin. They are grasping onto temporary hopes until another temporary hope comes their way.

We Christians know that life does not have to be about reaching out to temporary fixes or momentary hopes. We have the Eternal Hope that the world unknowingly desires and needs. Nevertheless, before we can even give people the real Eternal Hope above all hopes we ourselves must be filled with Christ's compassion for them, or else they may not listen or believe us when we try to tell them who the real Hope is.

A very important attribute we need to possess in order to reach difficult people with the message of the gospel is a tender, fervent, genuine, compassionate heart. This kind of heart will compel us to get involved in people's physical problems and serve to bring some type of relief to them. This is what the early church brethren did, as written about in the book of Acts. They sought to care for their neighbors, even when they themselves lacked sufficiency.

For example, Acts 11:28-29 records that there was a global famine. During this dearth, the Christians still gathered themselves together and sent relief to others in need of food. Why? Because they possessed compassionate and tender hearts.

We should not underestimate the power of genuine care and kindness extended toward others. We should run to the aid of people and learn to support them. Often times before some individuals will receive the gospel message from our lips, they first need to see the gospel demonstrated by our deeds, to prove God's love for them by our genuine care.

Like the brethren of the early church, we can get involved in other people's circumstances and serve. Certainly, we can help people in the essentials. For example, we can take someone to the supermarket and purchase a few groceries. Perhaps we can drive someone to an appointment or to do some errands, if he or she does not have a vehicle. Or we could give relief to a married couple by babysitting their children on occasion, or help to rake a neighbor's leaves or mow their lawn. Simply put, it is advantageous for us to do some kind of good deeds, just so others can see that we really do care for them (James 2:14-18).

Some people have more serious needs than others do. For example, there are those without a home. To such, we could give some of our time and help them find a home. This may include opening up our own home and allowing someone to live with us temporarily, or even long-term. It is my personal conviction that *we* Christians should be the first people on this planet to open our homes and invite someone in need to live with us. Not only does it help someone get back on their feet, it also brings about innumerable blessings to the host. (For more on this topic, read my book: *A Practical Approach in Doing the Great Commission.*)

Even more dire is the situation of many individuals who need someone to visit them. Some are feeling abandoned at a nursing home, some are feeling desolate inside a hospital, and some are lonely in a jail cell. May we Christians engage in the weekly practice of reaching out to visit a variety of lonely people. Life is more than an endless pursuit of daily errands and futile busyness. There are so many who are stuck somewhere and need some love poured upon them in a simple visit.

These are a number of reasons why we must adopt the custom of having an awareness of people around us so that we might be a support. All are in need. Perhaps we can be the answer that God wants to transfer

His blessing through to help encourage someone else. We simply must have hearts filled with compassion to care for others, then pay attention and observe the needs of others. Once you notice a need, then go out of your way to serve the individual[s] and see what God will do.

If we genuinely care for people, then there are four things that we must be willing to sacrifice to help others. We first have to be willing to surrender our good name. This means we must be willing to put our reputation on the line to help others. Our worries about our reputations should not matter because a caring character will ultimately be recognized. Second, we have to put in our time. Without a willingness to make time for people and use it for them we will be of no use in the lives of others. Third, we have to give our comforts. Serving people normally demands more out of us than we may initially consider. And lastly, we must be wiling to give up our money and resources. If our wallet is not in it, than our heart is not fully in it for the best of others.

I mention of these four important sacrifices because so many times people half-heartedly want to serve people and do not take into consideration the full import of what that entails. We must keep in mind what the scriptures say: *"What doth it profit, my brethren, though a man say he hath faith, and have not works? can faith save him? If a brother or sister be naked, and destitute of daily food, And one of you say unto them, Depart in peace, be ye warmed and filled; notwithstanding ye give them not those things which are needful to the body; what doth it profit? Even so faith, if it hath not works, is dead, being alone"* (James 2:14-17).

Jesus once taught, *"Which of you shall have a friend, and shall go unto him at midnight, and say unto him, Friend, lend me three loaves; For a friend of mine in his journey is come to me, and I have nothing to set before him? And he from within shall answer and say, Trouble me not: the door is now shut, and my children are with me in bed; I cannot rise and give thee. I say unto you, Though he will not rise and give him, because he is his friend, yet because of his importunity he will rise and give him as many as he needeth"* (Luke 11:5-8).

These words of Christ demonstrate that there will certainly be times when the Lord will place a need directly in our paths. These needs are placed there by the Lord for us to deal with and not for us to pass them along or pray for someone else to address them. Too often, we look at what we have to offer (money, time, etc.) and see that it is too little to really help someone and we think to ourselves that we simply do not have what it takes to meet a need. We fail to look closely at Luke 11 and see that sometimes a need will be placed in front of us so that we must go to the Lord to provide for the needs of others. The Lord does not always want what we have; He looks to test our faith and build our trust in Him so that He may provide what we need to meet the needs of others even though at the present we may not have what is needed.

We certainly cannot meet every need in our church or community, but there are certain needs that will be our responsibility to take on and deal with. How do we know when we are to take on a need? The answer to this may have a series of different answers. First, do we know the person in need? Notice the phrase *"a friend of mine"* in verse 6. Many times the needs we see the most belong to those that we care about the most. Oftentimes, we feel helpless when we see a friend in need. That should not make us feel helpless, but should instead compel us to go to God's throne of grace. We can ask God to give us a specific blessing so that we may turn and give that blessing to those who have needs.

Please do not misinterpret this to mean that we should not care for strangers, for Matthew 25:35 says that we should be careful not to ignore strangers, as they may be sent from the Lord as well, but oftentimes the needs of friends are the needs that we are to deal with.

Another question may be: does the need fall in an area of ministry where we currently serve? The person who has needs may not be our friend, but if a need arises that falls within our service, it would be wise of us to pray about how the Lord would want us to handle the need that is placed in front of us.

Ultimately, knowing when and how to serve people will come down to our walk with God. The Lord does not intend for us to meet every need that is placed in front of us. In Luke 22:32, the Lord recognized that Peter was about to go through a serious trial. The Lord certainly could have intervened and helped Peter to avoid the trial, but the Lord knew that Peter's failure during His crucifixion would be critical in preparing Peter for what was coming later—Pentecost! At times a need is placed in front of us so that we would pray that a believer's *"faith fail not."*

As I just stated, it will come down to our walk with God. The danger is that many times we are simply too quick to dismiss an opportunity without taking the matter to the Lord and asking Him if we are to intervene or simply keep the matter before the Lord in prayer. As we pray the Lord will make it clear which people we are to help and by what means.

The Lord gave us words of caution to consider as we serve people. Jesus stated in Matthew 6:1 and verse 4, *"Take heed that ye do not your alms before men, to be seen of them: otherwise ye have no reward of your Father which is in heaven. That thine alms may be in secret: and thy Father which seeth in secret himself shall reward thee openly.*" When we go out of our way to succor people, we must be sure to help with the right motives. Serving people with the desire to be noticed, thanked, appreciated, acknowledged, or praised by others is self-centered, and in the long run is not beneficial for us or for the individuals we serve.

Ministry should always provoke us to run to God in secret prayer with supplication. Do you privately seek God in prayer to learn how to serve people best? For example, do you privately seek God to increase your discernment, so that you may become better aware of the roots of people's problems and therefore be able to serve them better? Do you regularly take people's burdens to the Lord and not only pray for them but also weep for them before God? In the Bible, we read that God is moved to intervene on behalf of those in need by the prayers of His servants; moreover, God's heart is greatly touched when His servants, out of a tender heart, weep and cry for people before Him. A compassionate and tender heart should move us to fervently seek God to help us serve others for their benefit without any thought of recognition or return. A compassionate and tender heart has no thought of itself, but only of others.

God makes known in 1 Thessalonians 2:4 that we Christians are the created beings He has entrusted with His gospel. Not only have we been given the opportunity to serve and help people with their physical needs; we have been given the extraordinary privilege and the divine obligation to serve people's spiritual needs, speaking truth to them. Though the gospel many times will offend, it is still our firm obligation to be faithful in reaching out to sinners and it is necessary that we sometimes speak unpalatable truths.

When we are given the opportunity to proclaim the gospel, it is true that we ought to have some boldness, but a Christian does not need to have an impudent, brazenfaced demeanor. That would be foolish. In the majority of the times when we speak the gospel, we should speak forthrightly while trying to be very tender about it. If there happens to be an unpleasant thing to be said, then we should make sure that we speak it in the kindest possible manner. The gospel itself, according to Galatians 5:11 and 1 Peter 2:8, is likely to be an offense to people. We do not need to give any additional reasons for people to be offended by our lack of compassion or poor attitudes.

We should compassionately try to deliver the gospel message in such a fashion that they will receive the offense with godly conviction and not dismissive resentment. Nevertheless, if they do take offense, then it is between them and God. However, if a Christian is compassionate and tenderhearted toward sinners, then the probability is that they will not be offended, but that the gospel message will take effect upon their conscience, and the ones reproved will feel positively grateful for us speaking the truth to them.

Once again, we Christians have the truth that can save the lost and make them free. Even though we know without a shadow of doubt that we have the answer, many may not listen to it until we demonstrate compassion. People do not care what we know until they know we care for them. After we have proven our genuine care, then the doors will open wide for us to present the gospel. Compassion and tenderhearted actions arrest the attention of people and make them want to listen to what we have to say. Then God's Word will have liberty without restraint, and they will hear its truths and be given the opportunity to make an important decision.

The work of the Lord should be done by individuals that possess compassionate and tenderhearted temperaments—like Captain Cooper and his crew, Moses, Joshua, Ruth, Nehemiah, Mary, and most assuredly the Lord Jesus Christ. It is wise to get your thoughts, your attitudes, and your spirit filled with compassion and tenderheartedness. Permeate the very atmosphere in which you live and labor with a tender and compassionate spirit. Then you can surely expect the fullest and richest blessings from God. If you do this, you will be filled with great joy in the many experiences that will open for you to speak Christ's gospel, and get involved in the lives of people who will know Christ. This is a life most abundant.

Chapter Twenty-One

HOW GOOD ARE YOU AT GETTING SMALL?

IN THE FIRST CHAPTER OF THE BIBLE, we read the Genesis account of God's magnificent creation. We read about His unfathomable imagination and His awesome ability to take thought and create it into matter and energy teeming with an abundance of perfect creation: light, stars, galaxies, planets, dirt, rocks, plants, grasses, fish, whales, beasts, cattle, winged fowls, creeping things—everything from the minutest atom to the humongous celestial bodies in the universe. The list goes on and on. I imagine the angels must have been filled with wonder as they witnessed God creating the vast cosmos, for they certainly did shout for joy (Job 38:7).

As God began to focus attention on making planets, there was one that stood out above all others. The angels' inquisitiveness must have got the best of them as they desired to look into this very tiny sphere we call Earth. Oh, they were impressed by its abundance of beautiful plants, exotic fish, comely beasts and exquisite animals; this certainly got them thinking about God's magnificence. Surely, God's plan to reveal Himself in a greater way was being outspread right before their very eyes.

Then, God's process in creation veered into a profound new revelation of Himself for the angels to behold. The Genesis narrative tells us that God took a magnificent excursion and created something unlike any other form He had ever fashioned. God's handiwork soon revealed that He had not been merely interested in demonstrating His might through creation. God's intention was a greater one: a way to share His inheritance in love and grace toward a creation undeserving of it. God created man and woman.

Genesis 1:26-28 tells us, *"And God said, Let us make man in our image, after our likeness: and let them have dominion over the fish of the sea, and over the fowl of the air, and over the cattle, and over all the earth, and over every creeping thing that creepeth upon the earth. So God created man in his own image, in the image of God created he him; male and female created he them. And God blessed them, and God said unto them, Be fruitful, and multiply, and replenish the earth, and subdue it: and have dominion over the fish of the sea, and over the fowl of the air, and over every living thing that moveth upon the earth."*

Whenever I read the Genesis account, I am greatly fascinated by God's spectacular involvement concerning the creation of mankind. Here we are given astounding understanding of God's heart in His miraculous work: God desires to intimately share Himself with unworthy man.

The Bible tells us that man and woman were created in the image of God. They were created as a triune being: body and soul and spirit. Our first parents, Adam and Eve, began life in a state of innocence, and they were living glorious reflections of God. They completely yielded to God's way of life. They walked upon this earth flawless, displaying God's attributes in character, action, and speech. God is love, and so they loved. God is truth, and so they never bore false witness. God is good, and so they demonstrated goodness. God is meek, and so they exhibited meekness before all the living. Anything and everything our first parents ever thought, spoke, and did demonstrated *uprightly* God's nature and brought Him honor and glory.

The Bible tells us that when God created man, His very first act upon them was something extraordinary: God blessed mankind (Genesis 1:28). Then God stooped Himself down to man's plane and did another extraordinary act: God walked with man, and gave man the authority to reign. God bequeathed man with responsibilities to carry out on this earth. God gave man the duty to work. And He also bestowed upon man the aptitude to work. *"God said unto them* [Adam and Eve]*, Be fruitful, and multiply, and replenish the earth, and subdue it: and have dominion..."* This was a divine command, confirming from the very beginning that work is a blessing and not a curse. God Himself works and so man should work. Work is made possible by God for the ultimate purpose of extending His Kingdom.

Jesus taught that while it is day we must be working. The night is coming when no man can work (John 9:4). Or in other words, while we still have life in this body, we should be about the Father's will, for death soon shall come knocking at our door. As the scripture says, *"[B]e ye stedfast, unmoveable, always abounding in the work of the Lord, forasmuch as ye know that your labour is not in vain in the Lord"* (1 Corinthians 15:58).

Now God has given each of us a diversity of gifts and abilities to use while here on earth. We learn in both the Old and New Testaments that after the ascension of Christ into Heaven, God has given gifts unto all men (Ephesians 4:8), even to those who usurp their gifts for rebellious acts (Psalm 68:18).

A reason why God graciously endows us with gifts is so the LORD might dwell among the people (Psalm 68:18); meaning, that man might come to the knowledge of Christ and humbly walk with God in an intimate love relationship (Micah 6:8; John 17:3). God's gifts are to be used to help us effectually work together, so that we might, as a unified body, be able to minister to the needs of others, to edify and perfect believers, and to bring knowledge of the Son of God to all people. By doing such good works through the administration of our gifts we serve not only to help people but also to bring honor to the Lord Jesus Christ (Ephesians 4:12-16).

These are honorable reasons to serve, and as we seek to accomplish God's divine purpose for our lives we seriously need to seek God to become like Him. God is humble and therefore we need to seek to embrace humility as well. God our Provider graciously blesses each man with a variety of talents, skills, and abilities. With these gifts, God gives us a choice (Joshua 24:15). We have to decide whether to use his gifts for the honor of Christ or for our self. God confronts each Christian and requests that He be allowed to increase and that the man be decreased (John 3:30). So man must choose. The first—self-interest—if chosen, in due course leads a man down a way to death (Proverbs 16:25); but the second choice—to humble oneself before God—always leads to life more abundantly (Deuteronomy 30).

You and I must daily choose whether we will promote our own advancements and self-ambitions or humble ourselves before Almighty God and reverence Him. All men are confronted with this dividing-line. This is the line that divides believers of Christ from followers of Christ. Any man who decides to follow Christ discovers that this line is found in the service of Jesus Christ. To be a servant and follower of Christ you have to withdraw from the service of self-interest; you must fear the LORD and be in awe of Christ (Joshua 22:5; 2 Samuel 23:3; Zechariah 7:9).

To be a servant and follower of Christ is the most noble and magnificent position among all men. We are given the honor of ambassadorship for the Kingdom of Heaven to Earth (2 Corinthians 5:20). This marvelous vocation sanctions us to deal with men's souls. Hence, it is of utmost importance to determine to be humble, meek, and lowly-minded. There is no room for self-promotion, self-pity, or self-vindication. The Christian who endeavors to bring honor and glory to Christ in the lives of people must happily abandon himself at the foot of the cross, and continually walk in a spirit of humility, serving Christ before man.

Many men will try to tempt a servant of Christ and lavish him with praise and admiration for the gifts that he uses to esteem Christ in the lives of others. However, a servant and follower of Christ must reflect that praise back to God and not take thought or value of himself. A servant of Christ has no identification but in Christ alone.

For example, I once met a very capable artist who painted masterpieces as beautiful as my eyes see this world. She claimed to be a Christian, although she embraced the praise of man. Many men lifted her up and spoke highly of her because of the gift that God had bestowed upon her. She was lifted in pride and conceit. Then one day, alone in the silence of her home, she felt the conviction of God's Spirit. God laid His hand upon her heart and grasped her attention to realize that she is who she is because of God. All the admirations of her talents and works immediately departed from her soul. She suddenly understood her depravity before God. She then humbled herself under the mighty hand of God; she confessed and forsook her sins of pride, conceit, and self-admiration, and begged God for mercy.

God was merciful to her (Proverbs 28:13). He compelled her to stop her vain dealings in her skillful work, and to live life anew, fresh in His presence. She at once obeyed and made drastic changes. For months, she began to study her Bible and read books about service to God. She drew near to God and He drew near to her (James 4:8). Her faith grew, her heart softened, and she became a humble servant and follower of Jesus Christ.

Today, she is living life more abundantly with Christ. God has returned her back to art, but now she is painting for Christ's honor and glory. Now she shuns invitations that promote her, and only accepts work that brings glory to Jesus. It is God who is opening the doors for her service now. She does not seek work; it finds her. Her focus is Christ.

She, like so many others, had to learn a priceless lesson in life. We cannot be Christ's servant and promote ourselves at the same time. Christ said, *"No servant can serve two masters: for either he will hate the one, and love the other; or else he will hold to the one, and despise the other. Ye cannot serve God and mammon"* (Luke 16:13).

A man who tries to serve God and mammon at the same time is surely striving to serve himself, and this is most vexing to the soul. On the contrary, it is most liberating to the soul to value all of one's endowments, talents, and abilities as gifts given by the Lord. It is a most glorious humility to understand that all gifts are freely given to us for the Lord's honor.

In Luke chapter 16 Christ presented us with a good example of a rich man who tried to serve both God and mammon (himself) at the same time. We learn that this man's failure to humble himself in the sight of God led to the ruin of his life, and the eternal ruin of his soul. Based on his conversation with Abraham we learn that during his life on earth he was a man who observed the Law of Moses (he was religious). Thus, he tried in his own efforts to serve God, but he also served mammon: this we learn, too, from the description given to us of his life, from the mention of the gorgeous apparel and the sumptuous feeding. He tried to have the best of both worlds: service to God and service to himself. Nevertheless, the service of the two was incompatible, and we know from the somber sequel of the story which master the rich man really served, and whom—alas for him!—in his heart he truly despised.

When one tries to serve God and mammon (one's own interests), one becomes a friend to one and an enemy to the other. God counsels that any service to yourself makes you an enemy to God.

I too have had to learn that it is impossible to try to serve Christ's mission and my mission at the same time. Thankfully, God has given me correction and whole lot of mercy and abundant grace.

Immediately after high school, God opened a great door for me to go to college. It was an exciting time for my family and me, as no one else in my family had ever had the opportunity to attend college. We simply never had the financial means. So when God gave me the opportunity I took advantage of it with great appreciation.

At the university, I studied business with a concentration in international relations. I had some intriguing professors who really stirred my thinking and challenged my faith. Some of the professors sought to ingrain into our minds popular business philosophies that oppose wholesome biblical principles.

One core belief they taught concerned how to strive for success and attain it in life. Certain instructors and particular business leaders we had the opportunity to meet shared the belief that to substantially move ahead in life one should pursue the American rat race—an endless pursuit of the highest level of happiness possible by placing oneself first, even if this results in having to put the success or needs of others last; simply put, striving to be number one, no matter what. Sure, they offered guidance and information regarding ethics and charity. However, the main message they sought to ingrain in our minds was "Be all you can be, and work for *your* success. It is there to be taken."

Nevertheless, Jesus Christ is my Lord and the Holy Bible is my guidebook, and because of this God has helped me to recognize that these particular business principles are inferior. They are comprehensive concerning self-serving ambitions and purpose. They are of the world's way of thinking, and the world's philosophies and methods are contrary to God's doctrine and methods. Perhaps, these business principles might bring about a sort of success in gains of money, materialism, or recognition, but they diminish human relationships and kill contentment. The world's riches are temporal and cankered; they heap up apprehension, worry, sorrow, isolation, and separation (James 5:3).

God too has a set of guidelines, but His guidelines always bring about success and true riches. When you follow God's principles, there is liberty from anxiety. There is a bountiful supply of contentment, satisfaction, and fulfillment (Psalm 145:15-20). This is true richness. As the Proverb says, *"The blessing of the LORD, it maketh rich, and he addeth no sorrow with it"* (Proverbs 22:10).

Sadly, all too many believers follow the world's way of thinking and strive toward concerns of money, possessions, and social popularity or status. They may attain these desires, but in the end they discover them to be unsatisfactory and empty. They have their understanding darkened and are alienated from an abundant life with God because of the blindness of their own hearts. Their selfish lusts and greed lead them to live by imprudent feelings and therefore they give themselves over to lasciviousness and greed. They have not learned Christ (Ephesians 4:19-20).

In God's economy, a Christian who desires to experience life more abundantly with Christ must henceforth not conduct his affairs as the world does. He cannot walk in the vanity of his mind (Ephesians 4:17). Rather, God must be his first priority—for God knows what is best—then people second. Finally, one's own self must come last.

The world teaches to rank ourselves as first in priorities and then go help others. God's way teaches to position ourselves last and go about helping people first. God's economy is all about *giving*, not receiving. Proverbs 11:24 tells an important principle. It says, *"There is that scattereth, and yet increaseth; and there is that withholdeth more than is meet, but it tendeth to poverty."* In order for us to have success with longevity, we must pour our lives into the lives of others. Hence, the more you give of yourself, the greater your increase.

Or in other words, sometimes the way to expand upward is to grow downward. For example, in 2 Kings 19:30, we find that if you want to bear fruit upward (to be productive and have success), it sometimes comes through taking root downward. Meaning, one must at times decide to take a humble route in order to get to the abundance of God's blessing and increase. This is vividly seen in the life of Elisha.

Before God called the man Elisha to become His great prophet to the nation of Israel, he first had to go through lessons in humility. When God invited Elisha to join the ministry, 1 Kings 19:19-21 tells us that Elisha was already an esteemed, prominent man in his community. He was a farmer who plowed much land, and because of this he had the ability and influence to provide food for many families. Nonetheless, God's calling necessitated that he leave his influential status to become a mere coat-bearer for the prophet Elijah and attend to the latter's needs. Now, this appeared to be a demotion from his elevated position in life to that of a lowly servant (vs. 20); he was unaware that God was preparing him to be anointed as the next prophet. Even so, Elisha surrendered his ambitions and influence and he chose the humble route.

You would think that because Elisha already had an influential role in society that God would choose to use that as a reason to move him into the prominent role of a prophet. However, our ways are not God's ways. Even though Elisha seemingly had something to offer in God's work, God foresaw ahead of time that Elisha, like all of us, must thoroughly understand servanthood and possess immense humility. God is not interested in one bit of what we can offer or do for Him in this needy world. He has been quite content and successful in doing much good in this world before you or I ever came along.

The matter at hand is that we must willingly give of ourselves, but it must be done with a servant's attitude: a mindset of humility and lowliness, taking no credit for any accomplishments.

You and I must get down and stay down at the foot of the cross of Calvary. When you are down at the foot of the cross, you cannot fall. You can grow weary, you can become faint, but you cannot fall, for you are already down, and it is a good place to be down and humble at the foot of the cross. However, if you are standing with your head up, positioned in life by your own strength, you surely can fall, and will eventually fall. Therefore, the blessed certainty that would do us well is to humble ourselves before God and stay lowly before His cross each day.

For the Christian, humility is absolutely indispensable. Without it there can be no self-knowledge, no repentance, no faith and no salvation. The promises of God are made to the humble: the proud man by his pride forfeits every blessing promised to the lowly in heart, and from the hand of God he can expect only justice.

God takes pleasure in using humble men, women, and children. God searches for hearts that are humble and available for Him to show Himself BIG. History records God rejecting many men who once served Him influentially, until pride got a hold of them and God took away His favor. Today, you do not hear about those individuals any longer. But the individuals in history who humbled themselves, we have their testimonies to encourage and stir us to lower ourselves under the mighty hand of God.

One such example was a poor, skinny young man named Evan Roberts, who saw the need for a movement of God in Wales in 1904. Men were drinking themselves to death, the police departments were busy with crimes, and worst of all, the churches were empty. The country unquestionably needed a touch from God.

So one day Evan Roberts and a handful of Christians began to join themselves together in prayer, begging God for divine intervention. For over a decade, in these prayer meetings, Evan Roberts would bend forward on his knees before God, and he would cry, "Oh God! Bend me God! God, bend me, please God! Bend every bit of my will in me. Make my will totally Yours. Bend me!"

God saw Evan's heart and heard his prayers. One morning in a prayer meeting, God surely bent Evan, and bent him toward Christ. After the prayer meeting, Evan was so stirred up that he returned to his childhood hometown and began preaching. The power of God was released through him in a mighty way. Revival came! God opened the doors for him to go about preaching everywhere; and everywhere he preached, hundreds would turn from sin and get saved! Soon, tens of thousands in Wales turned to Christ.

God started to clean up Wales. The bars went out of business, churches became full every day of the week, and some of the police departments even had to close because there was little to no crime in the cities. God surely had poured His power upon this small nation, and all because a young man and a group of other individuals decided to get small and allow God to be the big God He is.

Oh, if just one of us today would humble himself like that, and get so small that God would raise us up for another revival. God knows our land desperately needs a touch of His Spirit. But we need to seek Him and be humble servants as best we can be until God brings about such a restoration on our land. We ought to beg God to bend us to become more lowly than we know how to be. For when we are meek and humble in heart, then we are able to view those around us correctly, and see that we are their servants.

A determined servant understands that his purpose is to attend to the needs of others. He pushes his needs and personal desires toward the background and positions others' needs before himself. Likewise, he can appropriately serve people without the distractions of his personal wants or requests because he keeps his own attitude subservient. A servant is not to be made known. A servant quietly works and fulfills his responsibilities without any notice or detection. The lesser he makes himself the greater the increase for others. Likewise, the more you allow yourself to get smaller before God and people, the bigger God will show Himself in your life. Thus, how good are you at getting small?

Do you find yourself boasting about yourself or things you are involved with before others? How about your thought-life, is it all about your own self? Do you wish people would thank you, show you appreciation, or recognize you? Do you think of yourself as important? Are you engaged in interests merely about yourself and not for God or others? You and I must learn to deplete ourselves of self-gratification, and keep a servant's attitude for the glory of God and the benefit of others.

A very important king in the Old Testament had to learn this important principle at the expense of his kingdom's stability. After the reign of King Solomon, his son Rehoboam was given the kingdom of Israel. Rehoboam started his reign off right; he humbled himself and sought counsel before making decisions. However, one day he rejected good counsel and followed foolish counsel, and because of his arrogance the kingdom split into two: Judah to the south and Israel to the north. He lost jurisdiction over Israel. Soon afterwards, he turned for the worse. Instead of humbling his heart to seek the LORD and be dependent on God, he got to thinking, and he resorted to human reasonings for wealth, strength, and prestige.

The Bible says that he *"strengthened himself"* (2 Chronicles 12:1). How awful a thing it is when an individual turns his back on God's principles and opts to help and strengthen himself by logic and common sense. It surely always brings about the ways of death.

In the natural sense, Rehoboam engaged himself with matters that brought retribution to himself in Judah. He trusted in human rationale to build strong cities for defense; he fortified the nation's strongholds and provided the nation with a great amount of armor. The people of Judah enjoyed an abundance of riches, but this would only be short-lived.

Behind the scenes of all this busyness, the Bible says Rehoboam and the kingdom of Judah forsook the worship of God. Judah sank low and took pleasure in sodomy, and Rehoboam took for himself eighteen wives and sixty concubines. Their depravity and immorality brought about idolatry: Rehoboam exchanged God's priests for priests of devils, and utterly forsook the law of the Lord (2 Chronicles 11:15).

Likewise, whenever someone lifts himself in thinking there is peace and safety without God, then sudden destruction shall come upon him, and he shall not escape. God resists the proud and abases the vanities and self-respect of humans. Sin leaves you vulnerable and alone, for the wages of sin is death. Sin leaves you in the hands of your enemies, such as the devil, to do as they please. As in Rehoboam's case, Judah's prosperity blinded their vigilance. Their self-regard and indulgence of entertainment and pleasures led them to forsake God. They leaned on their own understanding instead of trusting in the LORD Almighty. Then suddenly, without warning their enemies waged war on them. They were quickly overtaken and made captives. Their transgressions brought the judgment of God upon them.

When King Rehoboam and the kingdom of Judah found themselves entrenched in trouble and anguish, they finally turned to do the right thing, they repented of their sin, *pride*. They recalled the law of God and sought for God's grace rather than judgment. The Bible records that the king and the people humbled themselves before God (2 Chronicles 12:6). Because the Lord is plenteous in mercy and slow to anger (Psalm 103:8), God withheld His full wrath and gave them some deliverance when they humbled themselves. He allowed them to live rather than be killed. Rehoboam learned a good lesson, and it would cost him the enjoyment of life the rest of his days. Although the remainder of his reign would be spent in continual battles with King Jeroboam, he learned that God resists the proud and gives grace to the humble.

Likewise, if a Christian is determined to have life more abundantly with Christ and experience God's rest and blessings, then that Christian must possess a spirit of humility. Without humility, it is hopeless for a man to experience rest (such as mental rest) or even think that God is going to use him. God explains in Isaiah 42:8, "*[M]y glory will I not give to another, neither my praise...*" God must increase, but we must decrease (John 3:30).

Now some of us are just better than others at getting small. If you are anything like me, then you may struggle at humbling yourself. What do we do then? To be transparent, I still am seeking God for better understanding; nonetheless, one answer is that we beg God to mercifully intervene and transform our hearts to be humble, gentle, meek, and lowly. God attends to prayer like this, and He will answer. However, do not be surprised or upset when troubles inevitably enter your life to prove and fashion you into that humble servant.

Another response is that we should simply recognize the insignificant state of who we are, and embrace it with gladness. Our frame is weak and we are but dust (Genesis 3:19); that is, we are nothing but insignificant minute living specks of cosmos dust that breathe and move at will (Psalm 103:14). Such an understanding can put you into a proper perspective of good lowliness.

A lowly man who understands who he really is and is satisfied at being insignificant is on the road to true humility. A humble man believes that in his fallen nature dwells no good thing. He acknowledges that apart from God he is nothing, has nothing, knows nothing, and can do nothing. But this knowledge does not discourage him, for he knows also that in Christ he is somebody. He knows that he is so dear to God that he is in the apple of His eye, and that he can do all things through Christ who strengthens him; that is, he can do all that lies within the will of God for him to do.

The truly humble man does not expect to find virtue in himself, and when he finds none he is not disappointed. He knows that any good deed he may do is the result of God's working in him, and if it is his own work he knows that it is not good, however good it may appear to be.

When this belief becomes so much a part of a man that it functions as a kind of unconscious reaction he is liberated from the burden of trying to live up to any opinion of himself. He can rest and count upon the Spirit to fulfill God's law within him (Galatians 5). The emphasis of his life shifts from himself to Christ, where it should have been in the first place, and he is thus set free to serve his generation by God's will without concern of countless hindrances. Thus a man has a humble spirit if his attitude about himself is at par with meekness and lowliness, yet even better if his attitude contains no interest in himself.

In all actuality, humility is not thinking either highly or lowly of yourself; it is the freedom not to have to think of yourself at all. A Christian who is humble has died to himself and now lives a more abundant life in Christ. His thoughts, actions, and life belong to Jesus. Galatians 2:20 explains it, saying, *"I am crucified with Christ: nevertheless I live; yet not I, but Christ liveth in me: and the life which I now live in the flesh I live by the faith of the Son of God, who loved me, and gave himself for me."* This is the true spirit of humility: a personal martyrdom of oneself, *daily*. Martyrs have been *crucified with Christ*, which is past tense. So if the old man no longer lives, who is living in your body today? Jesus Christ! We trust God's Word by faith. A dead man cannot have thoughts for himself. Therefore, humility is having the mind of Christ, casting down imaginations and every high thing that exalts itself against the knowledge of God, and bringing into captivity every thought to the obedience of Christ (2 Corinthians 10:5).

Humility is not having a mean opinion of oneself. Humility is an appropriate perspective of myself that I am nothing, I am weak, and I cannot do it, but God is all, God is strong, and God can do it. Humility is having a correct recognition of who and what one is and who and what one is not with a desire to become who and what God desires and can make one to be. I know that was a tongue-and-mind-twister, so let me repeat and break it down. Humility is having a correct recognition of who and what you are. Humility is having a correct recognition of who and what you are not. A humble individual seeks to become who and what God desires for him to be.

If a man has a low opinion of himself, it is very possible that he is correct in his estimation. He realizes there is nothing in himself that can appease God. A humble spirit understands that God is Sovereign. A humble Christian understands that all the work is solely of the Lord Jesus Christ, and any work that the Christian has the privilege of participating in is solely of the Lord's kindness. God is the One who brings us into contact with the right people so that they may hear the gospel. God is the One who convicts and convinces people of their great need for Christ. God is the One who saves the soul. God is the One who gives us the ability to breathe, speak, and function so that we may do His work. Therefore, humble Christians know there is not one drop of effort or skill that is of their own power, but that all results are of God.

Now I would like to share a story (I apologize, but I cannot remember the preacher who told me this) about a humble individual who knew he had no skill, education, or anything to offer. The world considered this man stupid, useless, and a reject. Though he might have been useless to the world, God raised him up to be a great influence for the kingdom of Christ.

Years ago in the Midwest, a pastor had the privilege of leading an uneducated man to the Lord. Some time had passed and the thought came to the man that he ought to try to win souls for the Lord. However, he had a big dilemma. He could not read or write. In addition, he felt dumb because society had dismissed him as useless. Though he knew Jesus as his Savior, he was not sure if God could or would use him. Nevertheless, he begged God to let him lead someone to Christ.

One afternoon, he approached his pastor and asked if he thought God would want to use him too, and if so, how? The pastor immediately responded that God certainly did want to use him; but in exactly what capacity or way, he did not know. After a few minutes of deep thought, he looked the uneducated man in the eyes and told him, "Brother, I'll tell you what. You see this box of gospel tracts?" He handed them to the man. "You pass these gospel tracts out to every single person you meet. Let's see if God might do something." So the uneducated man took the gospel tracts and went on his way, passing them out to everyone he met.

Though the man considered himself dumb, he faithfully passed out hundreds of tracts to everyone he met all over his city each week. Then one day while he was passing them out, God gave him an idea. He thought that since he did not know how to read or write, perhaps he could ask people if they would be so kind as to read the tract back to him. He was not sure if it was a good idea or not, but he tried it.

He would take the tracts that his pastor had given him and he would approach an individual, and say, "Someone gave this to me, but I can't read or write. Could you read it to me and explain what it says?" Many people would pity the man and halfheartedly agree to read it to him. He would just stand there and listen to them read the gospel tract. Sometimes he would stop them and ask a question or two about what the things they were reading meant, and they would look it over again and explain the gospel in their own words.

As you would imagine, the gospel tracts were filled with Bible verses; and so the Holy Spirit would go to work on many of these people. Ultimately, God would use His scriptures to convict people of their sins and convince them to call on Jesus Christ for salvation; all because a humble, uneducated man had a real desire to lead people to Christ, though he considered himself a nobody. Over the years of him doing this, his church saw an increase in new visitors, hundreds of people saved and baptized, and a growth of God's Word across their city.

Though this man seemingly had nothing to offer what we humans would consider valuable, he kept himself humble and admitted it. He could have been like many foolish Christians and hidden behind pride and portrayed himself as someone he really was not. But he did not. He humbly acknowledged his limitations and dilemmas and solicited God and even man for an opportunity to do something for the Lord. Moreover, it was this humility, not pride, which opened the door for him to discover the way that God could and would use him to win countless individuals to Christ.

Pride shuts doors and humility opens doors. It is then probably safe to say that the majority of people on this earth would most likely not employ a very proud man. No right-minded employer would attempt to hire someone who portrays himself as someone who has no limitations or dilemmas, or someone who thinks he knows it all and that he has it within himself to do everything there is to do without any suggestions, criticisms, or reports. This would be foolish.

If humans are appalled by very proud individuals then how much more is God appalled? I would say, very much so! Certainly, God has a gentle heart for those who are humble. The Bible says in Isaiah 57:15: *"For thus saith the high and lofty One that inhabiteth eternity, whose name is Holy; I dwell in the high and holy place, with him also that is of a contrite and humble spirit, to revive the spirit of the humble, and to revive the heart of the contrite ones."*

Amazing! There is much mentioned in that particular verse, but did you catch the truth I underlined? God says He dwells with the individual who is humble! God considers the inner being of a humble person to be a high and holy place for His habitation. Quite the opposite of what we consider fit for a king. Nonetheless, God deems it right and appropriate for the King above all gods (Psalm 95:3).

Why? Because God takes great pleasure in being close to those who trust Him; and you cannot get any closer than living within someone. He enjoys relationships with people. This is one of the reasons God hates pride so much. Pride destroys our ability to enjoy a relationship with Him. Pride damages both parts of our relationship with God. It keeps us from seeking Him, and when we do try to come into His presence with pride in our hearts, it repulses God. James 4:6 says, *"But he giveth more grace. Wherefore he saith, God resisteth the proud, but giveth grace unto the humble."*

I tell you, God is for the humble! God feels great disgust toward the proud. Whenever He sees individuals with high and mighty attitudes, He passes them by. Whenever God sees individuals with self-absorbed thinking who believe they have the "right stuff" to do His work or think God should use them for whatever reason they come up with, He just passes them by; but whenever God finds a lowly heart in an individual, He takes great pleasure in exalting that one.

Jesus said, *"For whosoever exalteth himself shall be abased; and he that humbleth himself shall be exalted"* (Luke 14:11). God repeats in 1 Peter 5:5 and James 4:6 that He resists the proud and gives grace to the humble. When an individual thinks more highly of himself than he ought to think, that individual has a faulty perspective and disables himself for use. However, when an individual thinks lowly of himself, that individual makes himself available to God. God certainly does abundantly delight in choosing to work with such individuals (Psalm 147:10-11).

God takes no pleasure in working with the prideful or the self-conceited.

They are too confident in their own ideas. They will argue with God when He declines their ideas or when He gives them instruction on His way, for His ways are not our ways. The humble, though, wait for God's instruction. They do as they are told without rebuttal, questions, or buts. They are appreciative and honored that God would even choose and include them as part of His great work.

The scriptures warn in James 4:10 that we are to humble ourselves in the sight of the Lord. Please note, it does not say to humble ourselves in the sight of ourselves. No, if we do that we will get very comfortable humbling ourselves to ourselves because we are good at putting on a religious act and fooling ourselves. Instead, the scripture instructs that we are to humble ourselves in the sight of the Lord. For when we humble ourselves in God's sight then we are enlightened to see our depravity; and then, as God promises in the same verse, He shall lift us up. Not for the purpose of our own honor, but so we can accomplish His perfect will and give Christ the glory that He so rightly deserves.

We need to recognize who we are, and in meekness with grateful hearts, we should thank God that He would even consider us, let alone use us for His glory. In Job 25:6, God equates us to the likes of little worms. Nevertheless, God chooses to use the little humble *"worms"* who correctly think lowly of themselves, because God knows that He can take such little worms and transform them into magnificent living beings who work for His glory and honor. Hallelujah! What a God!

God likes to use little things to illustrate big important truths of His wisdom, nature, power and glory. For example, Proverbs 30:24-28 describes four creatures God created, all small in stature, that God uses to manifest His exceeding wisdom: ants displaying wisdom in preparation, conies displaying wisdom in anticipation, locusts displaying wisdom in organization, and the spider displaying wisdom in determination. As these four creatures are little upon the earth, so are we in the view of God. Likewise, God desires to use us little *worms* to teach great things to this lost world.

One of the most awful things to happen to a Christian is to become proud. There are few things that can give the devil more happiness than this. It delights the devil so much when he finds a Christian who is serving God but ensnares himself in self-trust. Satan watches with great amusement knowing that the preparations for a great fall are underway in that Christian's life. Moreover, that Christian will become of no worry for the devil. The devil knows that such an individual will busy himself more and more about self-centered issues rather than focus on God and people. Therefore, God warns in

Proverbs 18:12, *"Before destruction the heart of man is haughty."* Pride urges a believer to take it easy and relax, when he should be busy in God's harvest field. The devils go about happily watching such a foolish Christian relax arrogantly in the middle of the battle of souls.

Thus, humble men heed to the warning of 1 Corinthians 10:12: *"Wherefore let him that thinketh he standeth take heed lest he fall."* Even a humble man must seek God daily to keep himself a great distance away from self-trust, presumption, pride, arrogance, conceit, vainglory, and a haughty spirit. If he does not, destruction is soon to befall him.

Some examples of vain ways that people show their pride are by their "achievements" in God's kingdom. They become conceited and start boasting about their work, as if they have arrived, and are now a success in God's work. They begin to show despite toward those who have been less successful, or denounce them as deficient in zeal. Little do they realize that God calls their own work *"filthy rags"*! They themselves are fading as a leaf. (Isaiah 64:6). If they do have any good work, they forget that the work is not because of them but is because of God (2 Corinthians 9:8).

Another way that others show their pride is by a focus on quantity rather than quality. They foolishly begin boasting about their perceived "great" and "large" numbers rather than crying for one more soul that still needs Christ. Quickly they have forgotten that God goes to great lengths to seek and search out another one lost soul (Luke 15:1-7). They have forgotten that Christ is interested in loyalty rather than show (John 6:60-68).

Another example of their pride, which by the way they call humility but in reality is only false humility (sugar coated pride) is this: they seek to appear devout and religious before their peers; therefore, they outwardly present themselves humble by wearing a cloak where everyone can see it. They walk around saying benevolent gestures like, "I just want to love everyone", "I just want to serve", or "Let's not be critical, we're all brothers and sisters in the Lord." They often quote self-serving phrases and they would be mortified if they were ever accused of offending anyone. They do not even see that they are blinded by their own pride and have a false sense of humility. Inwardly before God *"they are full of extortion and excess and full of all uncleanness"* (Matthew 23).

A last example of how others show their pride, similar to the previous example, is by exalting themselves. They fall into carnal security respecting their own spiritual state, deeming it impossible that any thing can go wrong with those who are so devoted and used by God. Some do this by presenting elaborate mannerisms of speech, while others manifest their pride in their common talk, in which they continually exaggerate the deficiencies of others and magnify their own perceived "extraordinary" excellences. These have forgotten that Christ has sent them, *"to preach the gospel: not with wisdom of words, lest the cross of Christ should be made of none effect"* (1 Corinthians 1:17). They are ones Paul spoke of, who were *"Having a form of godliness, but denying the power thereof"* (2 Timothy 3:5); therefore, they are foolish to think too highly of themselves as capable individuals.

There are two sorts of proud people, and it is difficult to understand which of the two is the worse. First, there is the kind that is full of vanity that seeks its own glory and preeminence, but is too foolish to know that the glory it seeks is not glory at all (Proverbs 25:27). This proud person prates about himself, and invites other people to talk about him, pat him on the back, compliment him, and rub shoulders with him the right way. He is full of self-trust and promotion, and he goes strutting about, prating, and repeatedly saying, "Admire me. Oh someone praise me, please, I want to be noticed," like a little child who approaches each person in a room, and says, "See my new haircut? Aren't I pretty?"

The other haughty person has a type of pride too big for that sort of obsession. He looks at that sort of pride as chaos. He does not care for it. He despises people so much that he does not condescend to desire the recognition or praise of others. He is so supremely satisfied with himself that he does not stoop to consider what others think of himself. He is all full of himself, and goes wandering aloof from people, not desiring for anyone to speak to or touch him. Two kinds of proud people, each just as appalling as the other.

There are Christians who have been faced with humility and, instead of embracing it, they run from it and refuse to learn a humble attitude. These individuals have been set adrift away from the service of God's work and placed on God's shelf of uselessness for the Lord will not use Christians who will not ascribe all honor entirely unto Jesus Christ. God says in Isaiah 42:8, *"I am the LORD: that is my name: and my glory will I not give to another."* Without a humble attitude, a Christian will try to usurp God's glory, and God will never allow this to happen because we are never to take God's credit from Him.

Humility is one of the most important qualities for usefulness. It is so paramount in God's eyes that He only exalts those individuals who make themselves lowly like a dependent child. Little children seek assistance from their parents and elders. They acknowledge that they are dependent and seek help for people to do things for them. This is what God looks for: individuals who acknowledge and seek the help of God. Jesus said, *"Whosoever therefore shall humble himself as this little child, the same is greatest in the kingdom of heaven"* (Matthew 18:4).

Sadly, many followers of God have fallen prey to their foolish pride. Take, for instance, Samson in the book of Judges. Samson had God's favor on his life. He was strong, had the respect of many, and he was a man who did mighty exploits. But his heart changed, and he turned to rely on his God-given abilities rather than depend on God. His pride got the best of him, and one evening he foolishly expressed to his love Delilah that his strength was found in his hair, and not in God. That next morning he awoke and *"wist not that the Lord was departed from him"* (Judges 16:20). God finally took His favor off of Samson's life, and he found himself hopeless and in grave danger. He was soon taken into bondage by the Philistines, and there in their pagan temple, his life was bowed to death.

Like Samson, many Christians have defected from God's call because they have been lifted up with pride, and so have fallen into an awful snare of the devil and have become of no use for the kingdom of God. This is why a determined servant of God is very content to do God's work without recognition. A servant of God is not preoccupied with having a title or a so-called "prominent" position. God blesses this servant's work and he is content for only God to receive the admiration. His concern is that Christ alone be honored. His humility keeps him low and out of the limelight; so Christ is honored, and this is the evidence that everyone can see, which proves his humility.

The Christian who puts on *"humbleness of mind"* (Colossians 3:12) is greatly blessed when he comes to the place of not thinking of himself. Humility, as I mentioned before, is not having a mean opinion of oneself. Nor is humility having an opinion of oneself that is so low that one thinks so little of his own God-given powers and abilities that he never ventures to attempt to do any good in the world. It is incorrect to be so low that you have no self-reliance. That is slothfulness. And slothfulness is fatal (Proverbs 21:25), because it is sin (Romans 6:23).

Concerning being slothful, there are then the others who consider themselves so "humble" that they have always liked to pick an easy place for themselves. They are so withdrawn from humanity that they refuse to do anything that would bring any blame upon themselves. This might just be a lethargic, sinful love of ease—laziness. Again, slothfulness is sin and God will not have anything to do with it. True humility will lead you to have the right opinion about yourself, and to step out and help others.

In the matter of laboring with God, humility permits you to correctly sense the truth that you are nothing and a nobody, and that, if God gives you success in the work, you will be driven to ascribe all glory to Christ, for none of the credit could properly belong to you in any case. If you do not have success, humility will lead you to blame your own folly and disobedient willfulness, not God's sovereignty. God will not give blessing and then let an individual claim the glory of His success. God lets us know in Isaiah 48:11 that He will not allow anyone to steal His glory: God asserts, *"I will not give my glory unto another."* The glory from doing the Lord's work belongs to Jesus Christ, and to Him alone, no one else.

A humble attitude helps to bring a Christian into the center of God's will. Humility enables a Christian to willingly be obedient and courageously endeavor in the will of the Father regardless of personal costs. Humility gives a Christian opportunities to experience God's abundant power and anointing in his life because humility provides the temperance within oneself to wait on God and then patiently work alongside Him. Micah 6:8 reminds us of our duty. It says, *"He* [God] *hath shewed thee, O man, what is good; and what doth the LORD require of thee, but to do justly, and to love mercy, and to walk humbly with thy God?"*

If we are to walk humbly with God then we are to depend on Him. Humility helps a Christian to learn his insufficiency and the sufficiency of God's grace. Humility helps to clear our distorted perspective allowing us to see that we indeed are frail, weak, and need to depend on God's divine assistance. Humility helps us to embrace and appreciate our weaknesses so that the power of Christ may rest upon us and shine God's glory through us (2 Corinthians 12:8-9).

Humility takes us beyond ourselves so that God may carry out great exploits through us beyond what we can ask or think. A humble Christian gives the Holy Spirit the occasion to strengthen him and enable him to be godly and wise in every type of circumstances he encounters. Humility reveals God's grace in and through us. God's grace is not given to make us feel better, or to be happy, but is given to glorify Christ. Modern Christianity's subtle, underlying agenda for good feelings and hype is a sham and mockery to God. We want pain to go away. We want to feel better in difficult situations, but God wants us to glorify Christ in each and every situation of life. Good feelings may come, or they may not, but that is not the issue. The issue is whether or not we honor God by the way we respond to our circumstances. Humility enables us to respond in a godly fashion.

Humility enables a believer to be satisfied with God's supply toward his necessities for today. Humility frees a believer's mind from covetousness for things he does not have. In place of covetousness and want, humility gives an individual's heart the ability to learn total dependence in God, and it rests his mind in perfect peace to believe God will supply all his need (Philippians 4:19). Then such an individual is readily available for God to use in any way He pleases. For his mind, his heart, and his spirit are all at peace and awaiting God's guidance.

A humble individual is the one who makes himself available to God to bring forth much fruit for Christ's cause. He is dependent on God to manifest the evidence of His power through Him. Such a believer appreciates the truth of the Lord's words, *"for without me ye can do nothing"* (John 15:5).

Sadly, very little work is done today in total dependence upon God. Many Christians are not working along with God, but instead are devising and implementing ideological methods, plans, and techniques in efforts to *do* work *for* God. Nevertheless, embracing and using techniques similar to what the world and its agents use in order to accomplish a work in "Christ's" name can only bring temporal social improvements that lack eternal results. Those involved have a focus on themselves and forget the need for prayer and an inner filling of the Holy Ghost to do the work of Christ. They have busied themselves with many inspiring works, but they *"wist not that the LORD was departed from* [them]", meaning, they are unaware that God is not in their work (Judges 16:20).

As the Lord made known to David (1 Chronicles 28:19), it is my prayer that the Lord would make us understand that we too need His hand upon us. If we will seek God in the pages of His Holy Bible and return to the good old paths discovered within these pages, then we can learn how to enrich our ministry toward people by using the patterns God clearly lays out: Dependence on God and His Word, communion with God through prayer and fastings, and possessing a quiet spirit that rests and waits upon the Lord God.

Jeremiah 6:16 instructs, *"Thus saith the LORD, Stand ye in the ways, and see, and ask for the old paths, where is the good way, and walk therein, and ye shall find rest for your souls. But they said, We will not walk therein."* What a wonderful instruction from God! What a wonderful promise from God too—rest for our souls. But, how grievous the response of these believers. What will your response be?

The Bible is filled with many examples of individuals who understood the need to walk in the *old paths.* Many believers in both the Old and New Testaments had no interest in new philosophical methods developed from rudiments of the world to serve God. Neither did they use or embrace any creative ideals acquired from the world. The old paths had been tried and tested, and proven effective. Therefore, they humbled themselves, prayed to God, and waited upon Him. This is the reason many wise men and women of God were able to courageously accomplish eternal results of a great magnitude, which indirectly promoted social reform too, and have further influenced every generation since.

Sadly, when Christians spend more time in consultation, planning, and committee meetings than in prayer, it is a clear indication the believers have lost touch with the supernatural and have forgotten the Lord Himself. These self-willed individuals have ended up serving alone in place of serving with God.

Nevertheless, there is good news! Only when we humble our hearts and are emptied of self-sufficiency can we enjoy God and see Him mightily use us. Jesus said, *"Herein is my Father glorified, that ye bear much fruit; so shall ye be my disciples. Ye have not chosen me, but I have chosen you, and ordained you, that ye should go and bring forth fruit, and that your fruit should remain..."* It is those individuals who humble themselves and wait on God who will enjoy much fruit that remains.

I hear critics complain that God's way is slow. Whether it is or not, His timing is perfect. The underlying complaint of their murmuring is that their minds are preoccupied with their own will and aspirations; they do not want to wait, and wait on God.

God's ways oftentimes involve waiting. We must learn to sit still and wait. *"It is good that a man should both hope and quietly wait for the salvation of the LORD"* (Lamentations 3:26). God oftentimes gives us periods of waiting so that we should attend to Him. When alone in His presence we can learn to rid ourselves of our dependency on self and discover the strength of Christ. In addition, God gives us times of waiting so that we might learn how to love Christ more and effectually display His love to others; in other words, to conform us to be like Christ.

Periods of waiting can also work for our advantage to produce charity, hope, and faith within our character. More often than not it is a mechanism God uses to still our souls so that we may learn to enjoy Him. Sometimes we get off focus and our thoughts begin to wander and become consumed mainly with the work of God instead of focusing on Christ. This should not be. Therefore, God must remind us of what is most important: our relationship with Him. Our delight is to be found in Christ, not His work (Luke 10:20).

Let us learn from one of the Lord's parables concerning waiting on God. Although Christ's parable (in Luke 12:35-40) concerns future prophecy, there are several important applications that can be understood and implemented for practical living *today.*

Jesus said, *"Let your loins be girded about, and your lights burning; And ye yourselves like unto men that wait for their lord, when he will return from the wedding; that when he cometh and knocketh, they may open unto him immediately. Blessed are those servants, whom the lord when he cometh shall find watching: verily I say unto you, that he shall gird himself, and make them to sit down to meat, and will come forth and serve them. And if he shall come in the second watch, or come in the third watch, and find them so, blessed are those servants. And this know, that if the goodman of the house had known what hour the thief would come, he would have watched, and not have suffered his house to be broken through. Be ye therefore ready also: for the Son of man cometh at an hour when ye think not"* (Luke 12:35-40).

During times of waiting, we need to *let* our *loins be girded about*—that is, during times of waiting we are to carry on normal business, doing what we know to do, and be in a mindset of readiness. We should most assuredly let our light shine before the world, but we need to be about the Father's business in personal development as well: preparing our hearts to always do what is right, pouring ourselves over the scriptures in Bible studies, prayer, and fastings, so that we can prepare ourselves to aptly teach God's Word to those around us.

During seasons of waiting, we can rest assured that God, in His perfect timing, will open an effectual door for the gospel that we may serve with Him in a greater level of glory. However, we must keep a readiness of mind so that when an opportunity arises for us to serve, we may be ready to immediately rise up and walk through the open door.

Additionally, if we keep our spirit right, Christ will use the time of waiting to sup with us and us with Him. Waiting, as I mentioned earlier, is a time to enjoy Christ and His fellowship in the Word and prayer. It can be used as a season for divine silence so that we may rest in His presence and enjoy intimacy with God. Likewise, do you ever pause and sit in silence at the feet of Christ? Do you ever just quietly sit before God only to enjoy Him and His presence? Or simply wait and listen for Christ to speak? I would strongly encourage you to make it a habit.

At the end of Christ's parable in Luke 12:35-40 Jesus said, *"Be ye therefore ready also: for the Son of man cometh at an hour when ye think not."* In other words, we must possess an attitude of contentment when God chooses for us to wait: Contentment in God alone: to rest assured that God is in control, and contentment in enjoying Christ today. Meanwhile, have an expectation that God will invite you to walk in a greater service with Him, at an hour when you don't expect it.

When Joseph was in prison, he waited for the Lord. In the book of Genesis we do not read that Joseph complained, murmured, or questioned God. He did, understandably, on occasion get mentally strained, as detected in the choices of his words found in Genesis 40:14-15. Nevertheless, Joseph for the most part kept His focus correct: on God and reaching out to help people. Joseph saw beyond the physical and understood the spiritual. Joseph did not have his eyes on himself. In prison, Joseph had his eyes on others, so that he might be able to serve them. He used his time of waiting to be profitable for God and of service to others.

Waiting is not wasting time. Waiting is a time of development, preparation, and learning, especially trusting in God alone. It paid off for Joseph. God, later, at a perfect time, got him out of prison and elevated him to a government position where he could extend his helping hand to people of many nations in a time of great famine. Joseph had learned to trust God's sovereignty, and therefore glorified Him. As Egypt's powerful Prime Minister, he humbly declared to his brothers who years before had betrayed him that though they thought evil against him, it was God who meant it all for good, because God foresaw *"to bring to pass, as it is this day, to save much people alive"* (Genesis 50:20).

If you are in a time of waiting, may Psalm 37:9 encourage you: *"But those that wait upon the LORD, they shall inherit the earth."* God has wonderful plans to glorify Himself through you, but sometimes you simply have to wait.

Another example is of the children of Israel in the wilderness. God gave them specific orders of what they were to do and not to do, for their protection. Sadly, the children of Israel did not faithfully obey God in all orders and therefore suffered the consequences. However, there is one order in which He gave them which they obeyed: God directed that they were to follow the cloud when it moved, and they were to rest when it stood still. This they did and so they were preserved in God's providential protection.

May we learn from their example to wait upon the Lord, and then to wait on the LORD some more (Psalm 27:14), even if the cloud stays still for a long time. If you move when God is not moving, then surely you will walk away from His will and get lost and hurt in self-reliance. Before you know it, the enemy will come upon you and destroy you. But stay near God, even in times of waiting, and He shall preserve you.

When God has you waiting, stay put and carry on with what you know you are to do; meanwhile, wait for God to guide you into new adventures in His perfect timing.

Don't get ahead of God. Use your time wisely. Take advantage of the afforded time to present yourself often before the throne of God for extra refining. Seek God to become more as Christ is. Humble yourself and learn of Him to be lowly, meek, and gentle. Develop sensitivity to the Holy Spirit's voice, and cast down at the foot of the cross any pride, conceit, arrogance, or stubborn selfish attitudes that He will often bring to your attention. When the Holy Spirit enlightens you of sin, have a contrite heart and confess it, forsake it, and allow God to purge and purify your heart. These are wondrous practices to get in the habit of with God in times of waiting, so that once your life takes on a busy schedule you will have already developed a custom of meeting with God regularly. It is so important for us to relish the presence of God, and seek to be as He is, holy. It is imperative for us to humbly display practical holiness in the sight of God and before man.

A determined servant of God realizes that the little bit of dwarf pride and the monstrous ogre pride are both abominations in the sight of God. He understands that the moment he permits any pride to remain or become puffed up, he has positioned himself to be useless for God. This is why a determined servant of God never forgets that he is a disciple of Jesus Christ. He, as a disciple, must constantly be stooped before the feet of Jesus and be a student of Christ and His Word so that he may become a better servant of Christ (Luke 10:39).

The Lord Jesus is the One who is directing; we are the ones receiving directions. If you are not, then you are insubordinate and need to yield yourself to God right away (Romans 6:13). Jesus always exemplifies His directions before us. We can do what He orders simply by looking to Him. For example, Jesus best exemplified humility by leaving His riches and honor to come to this cursed sinful world. One evening after supper, Jesus humbled himself before his disciples, laid aside His position as their Master, and took on the position of a lowly feet-washer. In John 13:4-5, Christ did the unthinkable to his disciples: He knelt down before them and washed their feet, Israel's most menial task during their generation.

We would do good to humble ourselves and be as Christ. Not necessary a feet-washer, but a humble servant unto God and men. Philippians 2:5-8 exhorts us to let this mind be in us, which was also in Christ Jesus: *"Who* [Jesus], *being in the form of God, thought it not robbery to be equal with God: But made himself of no reputation, and took upon him the form of a servant, and was made in the likeness of men: And being found in fashion as a man, he humbled himself, and became obedient unto death, even the death of the cross."*

Jesus said, *"Learn of me; for I am meek and lowly in heart"* (Matthew 11:29). Do you truly desire to learn of Christ? Do you desire to be as He is, meek and lowly in heart?

If the King of kings and the Lord of lords is meek and lowly in heart, then shouldn't you and I certainly present ourselves meek and lowly-minded too? It would do us a lot of good to present ourselves as servants unto all, just as *"[Christ] came not to be ministered unto, but to minister, and to give his life a ransom for many"* (Mark 10:45).

But the question is, How determined are you to be as Christ? Will you learn and put into practice, like your Savior, the grace of humility, meekness, and lowliness of heart? If not, what areas of your life are causing you to falter from being humble as Christ? What are you going to do about these matters?

Chapter Twenty-Two

———⯈★⯇———

WHAT ARE YOU
DETERMINED TO HAVE?

AS I HAVE NOTED SEVERAL TIMES, God has gloriously chosen to privilege you and me with the wonderful grace to know Him and work with Him, *right now*, and not just someday in eternity. I have shown you from the Bible many key points about some important qualities we Christians need in order to experience life more abundantly with Jesus Christ. Any Christian who is determined to have life more abundantly and enjoy Christ should prayerfully seek God to have these qualities become real in his or her life.

The Christians who choose to humbly walk with God and labor with Him, such as in evangelism and discipling babes in Christ, discover how much of a delight it is to labor with God. Though the body might often become weary and tired, the spirit is renewed day by day (2 Corinthians 4:16).

The few who do rise up in God's blessed work will always be a minority. Jesus stated it clearly, explaining, *"Because strait is the gate, and narrow is the way, which leadeth unto life, and few there be that find it"* (Matthew 7:14). Most individuals will not experience life more abundantly because they are too enamored by the world's glittery temporal attractions, and cheat themselves out of Christ's blessings. Instead of having their attention on Christ, they are captivated by politics, the arts, science, money, or even ambition, social status, or business power. They let Satan get an advantage over them and keep themselves ignorant of his devices. They forget that, *"There is a way which seemeth right unto a man, but the end thereof are the ways of death"* (Proverbs 14:12).

The scriptures declare that God has set before you this day *"life and good, and death and evil"* (Deuteronomy 30:15). God commands you this day to love the LORD your God, to walk in His ways, and to keep His commandments and His statutes and His judgments. God gives these commands not to restrict you but to ensure a means for you to have security, liberty and enjoyment, so that you may live in freedom from sin and its consequences and experience life more abundantly with Christ. God desires to bless you, and the blessings can only be attained by obedience to His Word. Deuteronomy 30:19 expressly repeats that God has set before you *"life and death, blessing and cursing."* Therefore, choose life, that you may enjoy life most abundantly with Christ and be a blessing to others around you.

You must obey the Spirit's voice, and you must cleave to Christ: for He is your life, and the longevity of your days, just as He was to our fathers, to Abraham, to Isaac, and to Jacob. But the question is, will you hear and lay God's Word to your heart, and obey what the Spirit says? Will you give your life as a demonstration for glory and honor to Jesus Christ? If not, then you will not experience the most blessed life that God desires you to have. However, if you do choose obedience, then Christ will bless you because you have laid His Word to your heart.

God has given His Word; it lays out how we may walk with Christ and have life more abundantly with Him. His Word brings out a right fear of God while showing how we may have peace of mind. The Christian who is determined to experience life more abundantly must have the law of truth in his mouth, and must depart from iniquity. He must seek God to bridle His tongue and keep it under subjection by the power of the Holy Ghost. A Christian must be determined to walk humbly with God in peace and equity. Then the results of his life will be one that bears much fruit that shall remain. An individual of this character is the Christian who helps turn many away from their sins, and what a joy that is!

I am thrilled that you have read this book. However, it is only a means to provoke you to press toward the mark for the prize of the high calling of God in Christ Jesus (Philippians 3:14). God certainly wants to give you life more abundantly, but you must choose and determine to live it. In doing so, you must continue to study the Bible and keep seeking wisdom and learning knowledge. You must apply understanding by doing what you know is biblically right. You must continue to seek God in His Word, so that you may live as an effectual servant of God to a lost and dying world and be an encourager to believing Christians.

Did you know that if you would go out and win just one soul to God in your entire lifetime, you will have a blessing that the average Christian will never know anything about? It is sad, but the majority of Christians have no inkling of the blessings that come along with winning a soul to God. Oh, that all the Lord's people were determined servants of God and that He would fill them with His Spirit. Then maybe all Christians could better understand the richness of God and get a yearning for some of the many promised treasures of God, which come along with guiding people to Christ! Then maybe, just maybe, more Christians would get off their comfortable pews, and determinedly get involved in other people's lives by sharing the gospel with the lost and discipling babes in Christ.

When Jesus walked upon this earth He stated in John 9:4: *"I must work the works of Him that sent me."* Our Lord had a priority and it was to be about His Father's business; He kept focused on the kingdom work. Jesus understood His mission, and therefore He was able to stand up publicly and proclaim it: *"The Spirit of the Lord is upon me, because he hath anointed me to preach the gospel to the poor; he hath sent me to heal the brokenhearted, to preach deliverance to the captives, and recovering of sight to the blind, to set at liberty them that are bruised, To preach the acceptable year of the Lord"* (Luke 4:18-19).

Notice that the Lord's mission included using His mouth to preach the gospel as well as ambitiously laboring to serve brokenhearted people; then preaching some more and serving the blind; then preaching some more and serving individuals needing liberty. Sounds like soulwinning to me!

Jesus was a soulwinner! A determined Christian should carefully observe the Lord's mission and then make it his mission, too. The Christian who is determined to experience life more abundantly with Jesus will understand Christ's mission—*the reconciling of lost people to God.* The work of reconciliation uses both mouth and life. Therefore, a determined servant will implement ways of communicating the gospel while doing good deeds in service toward people.

The gospel of Jesus Christ must have preeminence in everything we do. We should serve and help people. However, we must communicate the gospel as well, or else we are merely acting as social reformers and missing the greatest need—eternal reformation. It would be as if we were covering a deep wound with a band-aid. That just won't work. You need right medical attention for deep wounds. Eternal matters call for more than social reform. They call for the attention of gospel laborers pouring in the love of Christ's healing gospel.

Mark 3:13-15 tells us, *"And he [Jesus] goeth up into a mountain, and calleth unto him whom he would: and they came unto him. And he ordained twelve, that they should be with him, and that he might send them forth to preach, And to have power to heal sicknesses, and to cast out devils."* Jesus spent three and a half years exemplifying before twelve young men the work they were to do. Many times, Jesus would instruct them to go into their communities, preach, and get involved in the problems and turmoil of people's lives. These times of involvement in others' lives would be learning experiences to teach them how to implement God's power through their service and preaching.

Later, after our Lord's death and resurrection, it was time for His disciples to carry on Christ's mission in far greater works. Therefore, before He ascended back to Heaven, He left a mandate for all disciples down the generations to execute, not just the twelve. Christ stated, *"But ye shall receive power, after that the Holy Ghost is come upon you: and ye shall be witnesses unto me both in Jerusalem, and in all Judaea, and in Samaria, and unto the uttermost part of the earth. All power is given unto me in heaven and in earth. Go ye therefore, and teach all nations, baptizing them in the name of the Father, and of the Son, and of the Holy Ghost: Teaching them to observe all things whatsoever I have commanded you: and, lo, I am with you alway, even unto the end of the world. Amen"* (Acts 1:8; Matthew 28:18-20).

Notice that Jesus instructed that we *"shall be witnesses."* This is not a suggestion, but a directive. Jesus ordered us not only to be witnesses in our own communities, but that our efforts should expand beyond ourselves to the whole world. In addition, Christ has supplied us with the means to carry out His orders. Jesus has empowered us with the Holy Ghost to persuade people to come to Christ. He has promised to be with us, even to the remotest places that we might be unfamiliar or uncomfortable to go, like traveling to Africa, or even as close as to our neighbors and to the low-income areas within our own cities.

You would think that since the King has proclaimed the mission for our lives, each one of us would choose to live toward the fulfillment of these orders. Sadly, it is quite the contrary. The obedience of many Christians is absent; not all are choosing to heed Christ's declaration and get involved in people's lives.

Some Christians wonder why God never uses them to guide a person to Christ. I am grieved that the answer for most Christians lies with the fact that they simply do not try to win a soul. The majority of Christians are not winning souls, and even worse, they are not even attempting to win souls. If you do not even attempt something then you certainly will lack any results. Even more disheartening is not making any effort *to learn* how to win souls to Christ either. This is a dire problem that only the King in His longsuffering can address. May the Holy Ghost bring such a conviction upon us that we will fall flat on our faces, and sorrow and weep, and repent of our apathetic indolence.

Besides this, there are several other reasons why so many Christians do not win souls for Christ. Each reason is interconnected with the others. However, all reasons boil down to the reality that there is a dire hindrance. It is a serious obstruction within the Christian's life. This problem is centered on the Christian's relationship with the Lord Jesus Christ. Actually, any hindrance in a Christian's relationship with God will negatively affect all other areas of his life, such as winning souls for God. (For further explanation, read my book: *A Simple Understanding of the Great Commission.*)

A Christian who does not labor to guide souls to Christ is a failure at this present moment in his life. Now I understand that you might be thinking, "Come on, Lawrence. That's a very critical statement." I must disagree. It might seem like a reprimand, but only to those Christians who are capable of laboring with God and are choosing not to do so. It is only a plea to those Christians who are self-centered to please stop thinking about themselves. I plead with them to rise up, involve themselves in someone else's life, and tell another soul the gospel. Make an investment in the life of another by serving someone often, and just see what good things the Lord will do.

Nonetheless, any appeal for change should be followed with a resolution (Judges 4:4-14). There is good news! Any Christian who is a failure today does not have to stay in a useless state. They can choose to be useful! Their self-centered mentality can be realigned so that if they are a failure right now, they may adjust accordingly, and get themselves back on track with God's agenda and become a success for Christ's cause. Because in Christ there is always hope for *transformation!*

The certainty is that every single Christian can and should win souls. Jesus surrounded Himself with a group of knucklehead disciples with bad habits and slow minds for learning. These men could not have been more knuckleheaded than anyone else on the planet. Yet, Christ gave these men a command so clearly that they could understand every word He ordered. If Jesus said it to them, then the same orders certainly apply to any one of us today—no matter what the excuse. Dumb or smart!

The reconciliation of men unto God is the principal concern of God (1 John 3:18). It is so important to God that He left all His riches, glory, and honor and came to this earth to accomplish this objective (Philippians 2:7). Then He exemplified before twelve men for three and half years, how they were to go fruitfully extend His kingdom into the lives of other people around the world. Finally, He allowed Himself to be brutally humiliated and killed by an agonizing, slow death: the reprehensible death on a cross (Philippians 2:8). Lastly, He conquered the grave and gave us hope.

So if it is first on God's priority list then it must be first in our priorities, well before anything else we choose in life (Philippians 2:4-5). For this reason, we should be determined only to look toward God to know what to do. Do not merely look toward men.

If guiding people to Christ is not the first priority with a preacher, the preacher is not right. If guiding people to Christ is not the first priority with a church, the church is not true. If guiding people to Christ is not the first priority for a Sunday school teacher, he or she is not a wise Sunday school teacher. If guiding people to Christ is not the main reason for a Christian school to be in business, it is not a very good Christian educator. If guiding people to Christ is not the main mission for a Christian organization, then the ministry is off-track and is not what it ought to be about. If guiding people to Christ is not the priority in a mother's life, then the mother is not tending to the things of God. If guiding people to Christ is not the priority in a father's life, then the father is not vigilant.

The first and main priority with God is to reconcile souls to Himself. Therefore, the first and main priority for us should be the ministry of reconciling souls in whatsoever we do in life—at church, home, community, business, or school. This ought to be our determination.

The apostle Paul realized and understood God's priority; therefore, he wrote in 1 Timothy 1:15: *"This is a faithful saying, and worthy of all acceptation..."* Let's stop for a moment before we look at the rest of the verse! That sounds like it was a saying often repeated among New Testament Christians. What was the saying? The verse further along explains the faithful saying, *"...that Christ Jesus came into the world to save sinners."* Jesus came to save sinners. That's the point. The reason for Jesus coming into the world was to save sinners. His priority was to save sinners. His concern, passion, zeal, and zest for living was and still is to save sinners. Jesus said in Luke 5:32: *"I came not to call the righteous, but sinners to repentance."* Jesus came to save sinners. Jesus reiterated this in Luke 19:10: *"For the Son of man is come to seek and to save that which was lost."* Jesus came to save sinners. This is what Jesus died and rose from the grave for. That is why the Bible was written (John 20:31), why churches are organized (Acts 2:47), why preachers are called to preach (Romans 10:14), and why Christian disciples are called to serve (Ephesians 4:12). To save sinners!

Christ's Great Commission is of such importance with God that He had it repeated in each of the four gospels, using slightly different wording. The first mention comes about on the day that Jesus rose from the dead, John 20:19. Jesus entered into the room where the disciples were shut up for fear of the Jews, and Jesus breathed on them and said, *"As my Father hath sent me, even so send I you"* (John 20:21).

The second time is mentioned in Luke 24:47-49. Jesus met His disciples on a mountain, and commanded them to preach the gospel. He instructed: *"[R]epentance and remission of sins should be preached in his name among all nations."* Whose name? The name of Jesus Christ, of course!

The third time, mentioned in Mark 16:15, Jesus appeared to the disciples as they were eating and said to them, *"Go ye into all the world, and preach the gospel to every creature."*

The fourth mention of the Great Commission in the Gospels is Matthew 28:18-20. I realize that I have already repeated this passage many times, but it must be emphasized, for it is our Great Commission. Immediately before Jesus ascended into Heaven, He gave orders to His disciples, saying, *"All power is given unto me in heaven and in earth. Go ye therefore, and teach all nations, baptizing them in the name of the Father, and of the Son, and of the Holy Ghost: Teaching them to observe all things whatsoever I have commanded you: and, lo, I am with you alway, even unto the end of the world. Amen."*

However, hold on for a moment. There is yet a fifth time that the Lord's Great Commission is mentioned in the Holy Bible. Though God repeated Christ's command a significant number of times in the Gospels, God also has it written once more for us. It is recorded in the book of Acts by Dr. Luke.

The beginning of Acts chapter 1 is the written record of what took place just minutes before Christ departed unto Heaven. Once again, God allows us to have a look in on this very important occasion. These moments are Christ's last words on earth that He will have spoken to His eleven disciples. This is very significant because when a person is departing, his parting words are likely to be about the things which are most pressing on his heart, the thing that is most important to him. And laboring to guide people to God is the one main subject Jesus talked about right before His departure.

This main objective Christ left for us to do is His passion—His Great Commission. It is so important to Christ that God inspired it to be repeated these five times in the first five books of the New Testament. Acts 1:8, Jesus said, *"But ye shall receive power, after that the Holy Ghost is come upon you: and ye shall be witnesses unto me both in Jerusalem, and in all Judea, and in Samaria, and unto the uttermost part of the earth."*

Although the Bible clearly commissions us at least five times to go win and guide souls to Christ, still many Christians say, "But I don't feel led to win souls." What a ridiculous statement! That thought is filled with apathetic, lackadaisical, emotional self-centeredness. The root of that statement means that the individual is not being led by the Spirit of God, nor understands the heart of God. Because if God were leading such an individual, he would be led to partake in what Christ's passion is all about: to guide people to the Lord Jesus.

In addition, we are not to go about life by feelings. We are to go about it in obedience to God's commands. Jesus Christ did not feel like going to the cross, but He went anyway. It was the right thing to do. We do not always feel like serving people, but we are to go and do it anyway. It is the right thing to do.

God absolutely and always leads people to do what is on His heart and what His Word says. Therefore, a Christian ought to be determined to be in fellowship with God by obedience to His Word. A Christian ought to be determined to make Christ known, win souls and disciple them. He should determine within himself to live a holy life that invests time, energy, resources, and interests into the lives of people. That is a grand important fixation on God's heart. Likewise, the Christian who is not living with this determination to serve and influence others for the kingdom of God has a dire problem.

Thankfully, we do not and should not compare ourselves with one another. Yes, I am laboring with God, and perhaps some of your Christian brethren may be laboring with God too, but it really just boils down to you and God. You will be all alone with God at the Judgment. *"For we must all appear before the judgment seat of Christ; that every one may receive the things done in his body, according to that he hath done, whether it be good or bad"* (2 Corinthians 5:10). I hope that today you will consider your coming judgment, and today endeavor with determination to have life more abundantly with God—for your good and His glory..

Christ has bought the world with His blood. Christ has redeemed all believers and given us an eternal relationship with Him by grace and faith in Him. You and I are the purchased property of God! You are not your own, but *"bought with a price"* (1 Corinthians 6:20). Therefore, here are some questions I would ask you to seriously consider and respond to: In consideration of this marvelous reality, to what extent is this divine truth ruling your life? How far is this fact dominating your daily walk? You are not your own; you belong to Christ! Do you truly realize this within your heart?

How does your walk manifest this truth before your neighbors? Would anybody want what you have with God?

You are not your own—you are the property of Another! Then should you not say, *"For me to live is Christ"* (Galatians 2:20)? Can you truthfully say it? "For me to live is *Christ*"? Is it true that you have only one aim, one desire, and one ambition? Are all your efforts concentrated in obeying, honoring, and magnifying Christ?

Oh my friend, by the grace of God I pray you stoop yourself low before the foot of Christ's cross and stay low until your heart burns with fire for Christ and Christ alone. Then you shall experience life more abundantly.

If you are not yet at such an determination within your heart then I pray you will seek God to change you. For God promises in 2 Chronicles 7:14, *"If my people, which are called by my name, shall humble themselves, and pray, and seek my face, and turn from their wicked ways; then will I hear from heaven, and will forgive their sin, and will heal their land."* Your personal land is your heart!

In hearing such things, a doubter might exclaim that he has time after time put the truths found in this book to the test, and the result has always been sadly disappointing. I once can recall a doubter saying, "it does not seem to help to hear so much about the determined life in Christ. Such a life seems to be too strenuous an effort and the time, trouble, and endless exertion just costs too much."

To such a doubter I respond, "I have never mentioned that exertion and struggle are required, because I am so entirely convinced that our efforts are futile, unless we first learn to abide in Christ by simple faith. No amount of human-level determination will equip us to be an adequate servant of God if we're not an intimate disciple of Jesus Christ. Every single one of us must personally and constantly be communing with God."

Jesus said, *"I am the resurrection, and the life: he that believeth in me, though he were dead, yet shall he live: And whosoever liveth and believeth in me shall never die. **Believest thou this?**"* (John 11:25)

What you and I both need daily is this: That our relationship to our living Savior is what it ought to be. We are to die to ourselves and **live in Christ**'s presence, rejoice in His life, and rest in His resurrection. For when our relationship with the Savior is what it ought to be, it certainly makes it possible for us to attain success in living life more abundantly with Jesus Christ. But we cannot enjoy Christ nor have life more abundantly if we are carnally minded and live in the flesh. Therefore, **we must live in Christ** (John 11:25); it takes life, the life of the cross, to replace the depravity of our flesh.

Yielding to Christ and His cross gives us the power and ability, as well as desire, to *live* and to *commune* with God and to *preach* according to God's blessed will (Philippians 2:13).

Are you determined to seek God in His Word and prayer often, so that you may glory that you understand and know God, *"that* [He] *is the LORD which exercises lovingkindness, judgment, and righteousness in the earth"* (Jeremiah 9:24)? Are you determined to abide in Christ each day so that you *"should go and bring forth fruit, and that your fruit should remain"* (John 15:16)? Are you determined to be faithful and a good steward over your life so that you may give God the pleasure to say unto you, *"Well done, thou good and faithful servant"* (Matthew 25:21)?

Or will you refuse God's best and merely partake in a commonplace "Christian" experience, and then one day stand before God with great remorse because you exercised a life consumed on many interests instead of Christ?

Now that you are finished reading this book, what will your response be? You must decide, and there are at least three possible choices. One is to rise up in shocked indignation and accuse me of irresponsible reporting. Another is to nod in general agreement with what is written here but take comfort that there are exceptions and you are among the exceptions. The other is to bow down in humility before God and confess that you have grieved the Spirit and dishonored the Lord in failing to give Him the place His Father has given Him as Head and Lord of your life.

Either the first or the second will simply confirm the wrong. The third, if carried out to its conclusion, can remove the curse and position you toward living life more abundantly. The decision lies with you.

What are you determined to have?

ENDNOTES

INCASE YOU DESIRE more readings of a specific topic after you have read a chapter, you may view below to learn of the books, websites, literature, and individuals I have consulted to assist me in writing each chapter. Although I have used different authors for various references, I respectfully would like to inform you that I may or may not necessarily agree with all of their biblical viewpoints, opinions, beliefs, and teachings.

I must acknowledge a great error on my behalf, an error which no author should desire to make. While putting together this book, I made the great mistake not to precisely keep tract of *all* my resources. There are additional resources which I have used to compose this book; however, with great sorrow I cannot recall to which chapter they belong for credit. Nonetheless, I have listed each and every resource in the *Bibliography*. I sincerely apologize to any author I fail to properly acknowledge in this *Endnotes* section. I am with great appreciation of all the resources God has brought to my attention in writing this book, and I hope that the *Bibliography* may do somewhat of justice to bring light to those whom honor and credit so rightly deserve.

Chapter 1: Do You Hear God Calling?

Bernall, Misty. *She Said Yes: The Unlikely Martyrdom of Cassie Bernall.* Toronto: HarperCollins, 1999. Print.

Chambers, Oswald. *My Utmost for His Highest.* August 2: The Discipline of Difficulty. Uhrichsville, Ohio, USA: Barbour Publications, 2007. Print.

"Charles Finney : Father of American Revivalism." Charles Finney | Christian History. ChristianityHistory.net, 8 Aug. 2008. Web. 26 Aug. 2013. <http://www.christianitytoday.com/ch/131christians/evangelistsandapologists/finney.html>.

Curington, Steven B. *Tall Law: When "Trying Hard To Do Better" Isn't Good Enough!.* Rockford, Illinois, USA: Reformers Unanimous International Publishing, 2013. Print. Page 33-34, 41.

Hodgin, E. Michael. *1002 Humorous Illustrations For Public Speaking.* Grand Rapids, Michigan, USA.:Zondervan, 2004. Print.

"Jim Elliot." *Wikipedia, the Free Encyclopedia.* 6 August. 2013. Web. 6 August 2013. http://en.wikipedia.org/wiki/Jim_Elliot.

Maxwell, Leslie E. *Born Crucified.* Chicago, Illinois, USA: Moody Press, 1945. Print. Page 78.

Strobel, Lee. *The Case for Christ: A Journalist's Personal Investigation of the Evidence for Jesus.* Grand Rapids, Michigan, USA: Zondervan, 1998. Print. Pages 266-267

"Webster's Dictionary." *Wikipedia, the Free Encyclopedia.* Web. June 4, 2013. <https://en.wikipedia.org/wiki/Webster's_Dictionary>.

Witt, David and El Masih, Mujahid. *Fearless Love : In the Midst of Terror.* Clarkdale, Arizona, USA: Martus Publishing, 2008. Print. Pages 118, 134, 137-139, 144.

Chapter 2: What Is Your Purpose?

Bruce, Alexander.Balmain. *The Training of the Twelve.* Grand Rapids, Michigan, USA: Kregel Publications, 1988. Print. Page 13.

Chapter 3: Who Are You Living For?

Curington, Steven B. *Tall Law: When "Trying Hard To Do Better" Isn't Good Enough!.* Rockford, Illinois, USA: Reformers Unanimous International Publishing, 2013. Print. Page 39.

Chapter 5: What Are You Are You Seeking?

Curington, Steven B. *Tall Law: When "Trying Hard To Do Better" Isn't Good Enough!.* Rockford, Illinois, USA: Reformers Unanimous International Publishing, 2013. Print. Page 58.

Maxwell, Leslie E. *Born Crucified.* Chicago, Illinois, USA: Moody Press, 1945. Print. Page 151-152.

Chapter 6: Is Your Life Bearing Lasting Fruit?

Curington, Steven B. *Tall Law: When "Trying Hard To Do Better" Isn't Good Enough!.* Rockford, Illinois, USA: Reformers Unanimous International Publishing, 2013. Print. Page 56.

Pink, Arthur W., *The Prophetic Parable of Matthew 13.* Memphis, Tennessee, USA.: Bottom of the Hill Publishing, 2011. Print. Pages 11-12, 31, 63-68, 71.

Chapter 8: How Is Your Love Evident Before Others?

Adsit, Christopher B. *Personal Disciplemaking: A Step-by-step Guide for Leading a Christian From New Birth to Maturity.* Orlando, Florida, USA: Campus Crusade for Christ. 1996. Print. Page 80.

Curington, Steven B. *Tall Law: When "Trying Hard To Do Better" Isn't Good Enough!.* Rockford, Illinois, USA: Reformers Unanimous International Publishing, 2013. Print. Page 66-67.

Maxwell, Leslie E. *Born Crucified.* Chicago, Illinois, USA: Moody Press, 1945. Print. Page 109.

Witt, David and El Masih, Mujahid. *Fearless Love: Rediscovering Jesus' Spirit of Martyrdom.* Clarkdale, Arizona, USA.: Martus Publishing, 2008. Print. Pages 212-213.

Chapter 9: Why Do You Pray?

Asbury, Chad. The Lighthouse Baptist Church, San Diego, California, USA: Decembre 5, 2013. Preaching.

Chambers, Oswald. *My Utmost for His Highest.* April 5: His Agony and Our Fellowship. Uhrichsville, Ohio, USA: Barbour Publications, 2007. Print.

Chambers, Oswald. *My Utmost for His Highest.* "August 28: What's the Good of Prayer?" Uhrichsville, Ohio, USA: Barbour Publications, 2007. Print.

Piper, John. *Understanding Scripture.* Parnell, Jonathan. "Communion with God: What, Why, How?" *Desiring God.* N.p. March 31, 2012. Web. March 30, 2015. http://www.desiringgod.org/articles/communion-with-god-what-why-how

Spence, H.D.M. and Excell, Joseph S. *Pulpit Commentary.* "Habakkuk 2:1." SwordSearcher. Computer software. Vers. 6.0.2.5. 1995-2010 StudyLamp Software LLC. Web. December 8, 2013.

Chapter 10: Who Are You Submitting To?

Cozacok, Eric. San Diego, California, USA: August 9, 2013. Phone conversation.

Maxwell, Leslie E. *Born Crucified.* Chicago, Illinois, USA: Moody Press, 1945. Print. Pages 34-35.

Pink, Arthur W. *The Prophetic Parable of Matthew 13.* Memphis, Tennessee, USA.: Bottom of the Hill Publishing, 2011. Print. Pages 11-12, 63-68.

Hetzer, David. The Lighthouse Baptist Church, San Diego, California, USA: August 22, 2013. Preaching.

Chapter 11: Are You Living Under The Control Of God's Spirit?

Curington, Steven B. *Tall Law: When "Trying Hard To Do Better" Isn't Good Enough!.* Rockford, Illinois, USA: Reformers Unanimous International Publishing, 2013. Print. Page 56.

Gray, John. The Lighthouse Baptist Church, San Diego, California, USA: June, 2, 2013. Preaching.

Jones, R.R. and Daus, A. Campbell. *Bob Jones Sermons.* Montgomery, Alabama, USA.: The Paragan Press, 1907. Print. Pages 42-43.

Kosin, Frederick L. *Letters Missionaries Never Write.* Florence, South Carolina, USA.: The Parchment House, 2002. Print. Page 134.

Pirolo, Neal. *Serving as Senders.* Waynesboro, Georgia, USA: Operation Mobilization Literature Ministry. 1991. Print. Page 105.

Strobel, Lee. *The Case for Christ: A Journalist's Personal Investigation of the Evidence for Jesus.* Grand Rapids, Michigan, USA.: Zondervan, 1998. Print. Page 133.

Chapter 12: What Are You Doing With God's Word?

Kosin, Frederick L. *Letters Missionaries Never Write.* Florence, South Carolina, USA.: The Parchment House, 2002. Print. Page 134.

Chapter 14: Do You Aspire To Be As Christ—*Holy*?

Bailey, Faith Coxe. *George Mueller.* Chicago, Illinois, USA: Moody Press, 1958. Print. Page 151.

Gipp, Samuel C. The Lighthouse Baptist Church, San Diego, California, USA: November 12, 2013. Preaching.

Maxwell, Leslie E. *Born Crucified.* Chicago, Illinois, USA: Moody Press, 1945. Print. Page 66.

Witt, David and El Masih, Mujahid. *Fearless Love: Rediscovering Jesus' Spirit of Martyrdom.* Clarkdale, Arizona, USA.: Martus Publishing, 2008. Print. Page 19.

Chapter 15: Where Do You Find Security?

Maxwell, Leslie E. *Born Crucified.* Chicago, Illinois, USA: Moody Press, 1945. Print. Pages 109, 184-185, 189.

Endnotes

Matthew Poole's Commentary on the Holy Bible. "Job 33:14." *SwordSearcher*. Computer software. Vers. 6.0.2.5. 1995-2010 StudyLamp Software LLC. Web. July 26, 2013.

Pink, Arthur W., *The Prophetic Parable of Matthew 13*. Memphis, Tennessee, USA.: Bottom of the Hill Publishing, 2011. Print. Page 31.

Spence, H.D.M. and Excell, Joseph S. *Pulpit Commentary*. "Job 33:14." SwordSearcher. Computer software. Vers. 6.0.2.5. 1995-2010 StudyLamp Software LLC. Web. July 24, 2013.

Torres, Gil. *Be Still*. The Lighthouse Baptist Church, San Diego, California, USA: August 4, 2013. Preaching.

Chapter 16: What Is The Evidence That Your Faith Is Genuine?

Gibbs, David. *Faith*. First Baptist Church of Hammond, Hammond, Indiana, USA: July 20, 2014. Preaching.

Spence, H.D.M. and Excell, Joseph S. *Pulpit Commentary*. "Daniel 1:8." SwordSearcher. Computer software. Vers. 6.0.2.5. 1995-2010 StudyLamp Software LLC. Web. 6 Aug. 2013.

Spence, H.D.M. and Excell, Joseph S. *Pulpit Commentary*. "Jeremiah 15:16." SwordSearcher. Computer software. Vers. 6.0.2.5. 1995-2010 StudyLamp Software LLC. Web. 6 Aug. 2013.

Chapter 17: What Are You Courageous About?

Fernandez, Manny. "Filibuster in Texas Senate Tries to Halt Abortion Bill." *NYTimes.com*. N.p., 25 June 2013. Web. 6 Aug. 2013. <http://www.nytimes.com/2013/06/26/us/politics/senate-democrats-in-texas-try-blocking-abortion-bill-with-filibuster.html?_r=0>.

Pirolo, Neal. *Serving as Senders*. Waynesboro, Georgia, USA: Operation Mobilization Literature Ministry. 1991. Print. Page 177-178.

Chapter 18: What Are You Holding Onto??

Maxwell, Leslie E. *Born Crucified*. Chicago, Illinois, USA: Moody Press, 1945. Print. Page 88.

Chapter 20: What Moves Your Heart?

Arthur, Kay. LORD, *I'm Torn Between Two Masters: A Devotional Study on Genuine Faith from the Sermon on the Mount*. Colorado Springs, Colorado, USA: WaterBrook Press, 2003.

Bruce, Alexander.Balmain. *The Training of the Twelve*. Grand Rapids, Michigan, USA: Kregel Publications, 1988. Print. Page 124.

Gibbs, David. *Going Into the Deep*. The Lighthouse Baptist Church, San Diego, California, USA: June 30, 2013. Preaching.

Kline, Michael. 2013, San Diego, California, USA: March 25, 2014. Email.

"SS Edmund Fitzgerald." Wikipedia. Wikimedia Foundation, 26 Aug. 2013. Web. 26 Aug. 2013. <http://en.wikipedia.org/wiki/SS_Edmund_Fitzgerald>.

Chapter 21: How Good Are You At Getting Small?

Arthur, Kay. LORD, *I'm Torn Between Two Masters: A Devotional Study on Genuine Faith from the Sermon on the Mount*. Colorado Springs, Colorado, USA: WaterBrook Press, 2003.

Asbury, Chad. The Lighthouse Baptist Church, San Diego, California, USA: Decembre 5, 2013. Preaching.

Bridges, Jerry. *Transforming Grace : Living Confidently in God's Unfailing Love.* Colorado Springs, Colorado, USA: NAVPRESS, 1991. Print. Pages 142-145.

Brown, Jason. Santee Baptist Church, Santee, California, USA: January, 2014. Preaching.

Brown, Ken. "Humility." Voice of One Crying. Community Fellowship, 2001. Web. 19 March. 2015. <http://www.voiceofonecrying.com/humility.htm/>.

Bruce, Alexander.Balmain. *The Training of the Twelve.* Grand Rapids, Michigan, USA: Kregel Publications, 1988. Print. Page 108.

Curington, Steven B. *Tall Law: When "Trying Hard To Do Better" Isn't Good Enough!.* Rockford, Illinois, USA: Reformers Unanimous International Publishing, 2013. Print. Page 23, 38, 72.

Fisher, Doug. The Lighthouse Baptist Church, San Diego, California, USA: September 8, 2013, Evening. Preaching.

Guiler, Myron. *2 Chronicles 32:24-33: God Left Him.* Trinity Baptist Church, Rio Grande, Ohio, USA: April 11, 2013. Preaching.

Witt, David and El Masih, Mujahid. *Fearless Love : In the Midst of Terror.* Clarkdale, Arizona, USA: Martus Publishing, 2008. Print. Pages 167.

Shaw, S.B. *The Great Revival in Wales: A Classic Revial Reprint Originally Published in 1905.* Pensacola, Florida, USA: Christian Life Books, 2002. Print. Pages 78-79.

Chapter 22: What Are You Determined To Have?

Pink, Arthur W., *The Prophetic Parable of Matthew 13.* Memphis, Tennessee, USA.: Bottom of the Hill Publishing, 2011. Print. Page 72.

"Evan Roberts." *Wikipedia, the Free Encyclopedia.* 1 October, 2013. Web. 1 October 2013. http://en.wikipedia.org/wiki/Evan_Roberts_(minister).

Maxwell, Leslie E. *Born Crucified.* Chicago, Illinois, USA: Moody Press, 1945. Print. Page 118-119.

Pirolo, Neal. *Serving as Senders.* Waynesboro, Georgia, USA: Operation Mobilization Literature Ministry. 1991. Print. Page 41.

BIBLIOGRAPHY

ALTHOUGH I HAVE USED different authors for various references, I respectfully would like to inform you that I may or may not necessarily agree with all of their biblical viewpoints, opinions, beliefs, and teachings.

In some cases during the reading of this book you might have come across a saying which you have heard before. This is due to the overwhelming familiarity we have become with the writings of some of the leaders in the deeper truths of God's Word in so much that we find ourselves quoting them verbatim. Indulgence is begged, therefore, if there has been any failure of proper acknowledgement, I sincerely apologize, and I appreciate your warmest understanding and prayers.

"27 Years of Preaching Experience." *Soulwinning*. Web. Winter 2009. < http://www.soulwinning.info/sp/lessons/05.htm >.

"A Common Word Between Us and You." available: http://en.wikipedia.org/wiki/A_Common_Word_Between_Us_and_You.

Adsit, Christopher B. *Personal Disciplemaking: A Step-by-step Guide for Leading a Christian From New Birth to Maturity*. Orlando, Florida, USA: Campus Crusade for Christ. 1996. Print.

Anderson, Dale. "The Worthy Lamb – History of Moravian Missions « For All Nations." *For All Nations*. 22 Aug. 2008. Web. 09 July 2010. <http://forallnations.wordpress.com/2008/08/22/the-worthy-lamb-history-of-moravian-missions/>.

Arthur, Kay. LORD, *I'm Torn Between Two Masters: A Devotional Study on Genuine Faith from the Sermon on the Mount*. Colorado Springs, Colorado, USA: WaterBrook Press, 2003.

Asbury, Chad. The Lighthouse Baptist Church, San Diego, California, USA: Decembre 5, 2013. Preaching.

Attridge, Harold W., Miroslav Volf, Joseph Cumming, and Emilie M. Townes. "LOVING AND NEIGHBOR TOGETHER: A Christian Response to 'A Common Word Between Us and You'" Yale Center for Faith and Culture. Yale University. Web. 1 Apr. 2012. http://www.yale.edu/faith/acw/acw.htm>.

Authorized King James Version Bible: Chicago, Illinois, USA: Moody Press, 1994. Print

Bachman, Mark A. *Winning Muslims to Christ*. Roanoke, Indiana, USA: Answer Publications, 2009. Print.

Barnes, Albert. "Albert Barnes' Notes on the Bible: Romans 9:3." *SwordSearcher*. Computer software. Vers. 6.0.2.5. 1995-2010 StudyLamp Software LLC. Web. 28 May 26, 2013.

Bean, Cecil. Letter to David Perry. 1995. MS. Rio Grande, Ohio, USA.

Berry, George Ricker, and George Ricker Berry. *Berry's Interlinear Greek-English New Testament: with a Greek- English Lexicon and New Testament Synonyms*. Grand Rapids, Michigan, USA.: Baker Book House, 1897. Print.

Bible Baptist Church. *The Gospel*. Oak Harbor, Washington: Bible Baptist Church Publications, 2001. Gospel Track. Print.

Bonhoeffer, Dietrich. *The Cost of Discipleship*. New York, New York, USA: Touchstone Simon & Schuster. 1995. Print.

Bridges, Jerry. *Transforming Grace : Living Confidently in God's Unfailing Love*. Colorado Springs, Colorado, USA: NAVPRESS, 1991. Print.

Brown, Jason. Santee Baptist Church, Santee, California, USA: January, 2014. Preaching.

Brown, Ken. "Humility." Voice of One Crying. Community Fellowship, 2001. Web. 19 March. 2015. <http://www.voiceofonecrying.com/humility.htm/>.

Bruce, Alexander.Balmain. *The Training of the Twelve*. Grand Rapids, Michigan, USA: Kregel Publications, 1988. Print. Page 13.

Cahill, Mark. *One Thing You Can't Do In Heaven*. Rockwall, Texas, USA.: Biblical Discipleship Publishers, October, 2011. Print.

Cantor, Tom. "Isaiah 53." Message to the author. Dec. 2009. E-mail.

Chambers, Oswald. *My Utmost for His Highest*. Uhrichsville, Ohio, USA: Barbour Publications, 2007. Print.

Comfort, Ray. *"God Doesn't Believe in Atheists."* Orlando, Florida, USA: Bridge-Logos. Print.

Corle, Dennis. *"The Biblical Philosophy of Soulwinning."* Claysburg, Pennsylvania, USA: Revival Fires! Publishers. Print.

Cozakos, Eric J. 2011 Evangelism Teaching CD, San Diego, California, USA: September, 2012. Recorded CD.

Cozakos, Eric J. "Lighthouse Baptist Church." Lighthouse Baptist Church, 2012. Web. 1 Dec. 2012. <http://www.lighthousebaptist.com/ministries/outreach/street-evangelism/>.

Curington, Steven B. *Reformers Unanimous 10 Principles Videos*. San Diego, California, USA: Winter 2010. DVD Video.

Curington, Steven B. *Tall Law: When "Trying Hard To Do Better" Isn't Good Enough!*. Rockford, Illinois, USA: Reformers Unanimous International Publishing, 2013. Print.

Dawood, N. J. *The Koran With Parallel Arabic Text*. London, England: Penguin Books, 2000. Print

"The Doctrine of Street Preaching." *Soulwinning*. Web. Winter 2009. < http://www.soulwinning.info/sp/lessons/01.htm >.

Drake, Paul. San Diego, California, USA: Spring 2010. Conversation.

Eims, LeRoy. *The Lost Art of Disciple Making*. Grand Rapids, Michigan, USA: Zondervan, 1984. Print

Ellis, William T. *Billy Sunday: His Life and Message*. Greenville, South Carolina, USA: Ambassador, 2001. Print.

"Evan Roberts." *Wikipedia, the Free Encyclopedia*. 1 October, 2013. Web. 1 October 2013. http://en.wikipedia.org/wiki/Evan_Roberts_(minister).

Bibliography

Gibbs Jr., David C., and David C. Gibbs III. *KEEPING CHRIST IN AMERICA'S PUBLIC SCHOOLS*. Seminole, Florida, USA: Christian Law Association, 2008. Print.

Gibbs Law Firm, P.A. *Highways, Hedges, and Hearts*. PDF. Gibbs Law Firm, P.A., 2003. Print.

"Gospel." *Wikipedia, the Free Encyclopedia*. 18 Oct. 2010. Web. 23 Oct. 2010. <http://en.wikipedia.org/wiki/Gospel>.

Guiler, Myron. Trinity Baptist Church, Rio Grande, Ohio, USA: April 6, 2012. Preaching.

Guiler, Myron. *2 Chronicles 32:24-33: God Left Him*. Trinity Baptist Church, Rio Grande, Ohio, USA: April 11, 2013. Preaching.

"A History of Street Preaching." *Soulwinning*. Web. Winter 2009. < http://www.soulwinning.info/sp/lessons/02.htm >.

Hinch, Jim. "Rick Warren builds bridge to Muslims." Orange County Register. February 23, 2012. available: http://www.ocregister.com/articles/muslims-341669-warren-saddleback.html:

Hodgin, E. Michael. *1002 Humorous Illustrations For Public Speaking*. Grand Rapids, Michigan, USA.:Zondervan, 2004. Print.

Hopewell Baptist Church, and Mike Ray. "Step 7 SOULWINNING." *One Step At A Time*. Pasig City, M.M. Philippians: Life Line Philippians Baptist Foundation. Print.

Howard, Harry. *Changed Lives in San Quentin*. Dallas, Texas, USA.: Acclaimed, 1986. Print.

Hughes, R. Kent. *Disciplines of a Godly Man*. Wheaton, Illinois, USA.: Crossway Books, 2006. Print.

Hyles, Jack. *Let's Build An Evangelistic Church*. Murfreesboro, Tennessee, USA.: Sword of the Lord Publishers, 1962. Print.

"Introduction to A Common Word Between Us and You." The Official Website of A Common Word. The Royal Aal Al-Bayt Institute for Islamic Thought, 2009. Web. 1 April 2012. http://www.acommonword.com>.

"Iroquois Theatre Fire." *Wikipedia, the Free Encyclopedia*. Web. Dec.ember 2009. <http://en.wikipedia.org/wiki/Iroquois_Theatre_Fire>.

Jones, R.R. and Daus, A. Campbell. *Bob Jones Sermons*. Montgomery, Alabama, USA.: The Paragan Press, 1907. Print. Pages 42-43.

Jordan, Doug. The Lighthouse Baptist Church, San Diego, California, USA: Spring 2010. Preaching.

Joslin, Brent. *"Discipleship of Prayer." Luke 11:1-4 The Example of our Lord Jesus' prayer life*. San Diego, California, USA: 7 August 2010. Outline. Print.

Joslin, Brent. Reformers Unanimous Program at The Lighthouse Baptist Church, San Diego, California, USA: September 2, 2011. Lecture.

Kalvesmaki, Joel. "Table of Old Testament Quotes in the New Testament, in English Translation." *Table of Old Testament Quotes in the New Testament, in English Translation*. Septuagint Online, Nov. 2011. Web. 18 Mar. 2012. <http://kalvesmaki.com/LXX/NTChart.htm>.

Keller, Matt. "Bible - How Many Chapters and Verses Are in the Bible?" Deaf Missions: Home. Web. November 2009. <http://www.deafmissions.com/tally/bkchptrvrs.html>.

Kizziah, Nic. "King James Bible Statistics." *Welcome to Biblebelievers.com*. Web. 17 January 2010. <http://www.biblebelievers.com/believers-org/kjv-stats.html>.

Kline, Michael. 2013, San Diego, California, USA: December 21, 2013. Phone Conversation.

Kosin, Frederick L. *Letters Missionaries Never Write*. Florence, South Carolina, USA.: The Parchment House, 2002. Print.

Lancaster, Philip. *Family Man, Family Leader*. San Antonio, Texas, USA: The Vision Forum, Inc., 2004. Print.

Leader's Guide for Evangelistic Bible Studies (using the Gospel of John). Colorado Springs, Colorado, USA: Navigators, 1973. Print.

Lockyer, Herbert. "All the Prayers of the Bible. A Devotional and Expositional Classic." *The "All" Series*. Grand Rapids, Michigan, USA: Zondervan Publishing House, 1959. Print

"Loving God and Neighbor Together: A Christian Response to A Common Word Between Us and You." available: http://www.yale.edu/divinity/news/071118_news_nytimes.pdf

MacDonald, William. *Believers' Bible Commentary : New Testament An Exposition of the Sacred Scriptures*. Wichita, Kansas, USA: A & O Press, 1989. Print.

Maxwell, Leslie E. *Born Crucified*. Chicago, Illinois, USA: Moody Press, 1945. Print.

"Matthew." *Zondervan Life Application Study Bible: NIV Bible*. Wheaton, Illinois, USA: Tyndale House Publishers, 1991. Print.

"Messianic Prophesies Fulfilled by Jesus Christ." *Jesus -is-Lord.com: Jesus Christ Is the ONLY Way to God*. Web. 15 Nov. 2010. <http://www.jesus-is-lord.com/messiah.htm>;.

Michael, Larry J. *Spurgeon on Leadership : Key Insights for Christian Leaders from the Prince of Preachers*. Grand Rapids, Michigan, USA: Kregel Publications. 2010. Print

Mom of 9's Place. "Hell Is Real." *Mom of 9's Place Delight Thyself Also in the LORD*. Ed. Chris. Web. Winter 2009. <http://www.momof9splace.com/>.

Moody, Dwight L. "The Qualifications for Soulwinning." *Welcome to Biblebelievers.com*. Web. Winter 2010. <http://www.biblebelievers.com/moody_sermons/m1.html>.

Mount Zion Bible Church. "Unabridged and Unedited, Delivered in the Year 1869, at the METROPOLITAN TABERNACLE, NEWINGTON, Soulwinning CH Spurgeon." *Chapel Library: Mount Zion Baptist Church:*. Mount Zion Baptist Church. Web. Winter 2010.

The Navigators. "The Prayer Hand." *The Prayer Hand - The Navigators*. Nav Press. Web. 18 May 2010. <http://www.navigators.org/us/resources/illustrations/items/prayerhand>.

Nelson's NKJV Study Bible: New King James Version. Nashville, Tennessee, USA: Thomas Nelson Publishers, 1997. Print.

Northcutt, Scott. The Lighthouse Baptist Church, San Diego, California, USA: Winter 2010. Preaching.

Nursing Home Ministry, A Manual, Copyrighted in 1982, Chapter 4. *Faithful Friends Nursing Home Ministry*. Web. Winter 2009. <www.faithfulfriends.org/chapter4.doc>.

"One Verse Evangelism - An Outline." FOCUS. Web. Winter 2010. <http://www.ifesgulf.com>.

Bibliography

"One Verse Evangelism." *One Verse Evangelism.* Boyles Ministry. Web. Winter 2009.
<http://boylesministry.org/OneVsEvangelism.htm>.

Perry, David. The University of Rio Grande, Rio Grande, Ohio, USA: Fall 1998-Spring 2003.
Lecture.

Perry, David. Various messages to the author. 2005-2010. E-mail

Philobes, Rev. David R. *Important Verses on The Fundamental Doctrines of the Bible.* San Diego,
California, USA.: Self Published, 2005. Booklet. Print.

Piper, John. *Understanding Scripture.* Parnell, Jonathan. "Communion with God: What, Why,
How?" *Desiring God.* N.p. March 31, 2012. Web. March 30, 2015.
http://www.desiringgod.org/articles/communion-with-god-what-why-how

Pierce, Bill. Message to the author. April, 2012. Pamphlet.

Pirolo, Neal. *Serving as Senders.* Waynesboro, Georgia, USA: Operation Mobilization Literature
Ministry. 1991. Print.

"Practical Preaching Principles." *Soulwinning.* Web. Winter 2009.
< http://www.soulwinning.info/sp/lessons/04.htm >.

"Preaching Principles." *Soulwinning.* Web. Winter 2009.
< http://www.soulwinning.info/sp/lessons/03.htm >.

Raysbrook, Randy D. "How to Share Christ's Love Visually." *Nav Tools - The Navigators.* The
Navigators. Web. Spring 2010. <www.navigators.org/oneverse>.

Raysbrook, Randy D. *One-Verse Evangelism.* Colordo Springs, Colorado, USA: Dawson Media,
2000. Print.

Rice, John R. *Personal Soulwinning: How to Do It.* Murfreesboro, Tennesee, USA.: *Sword of the
Lord Publishers,* 1961. Print.

Rice, John R. "Sevenfold Sin of Not Winning Souls, by Dr. John R. Rice." *GoToTheBible.com
Bible Study.* Web. Winter 2010. <http://www.gotothebible.com/HTML/Sermons/sevenfold.html>.

Riplinger, Gail. Message to the author. June 21, 2013. E-mail.

Ryrie, Charles C. "The Book of Isaiah: Isaiah 53:7-9 Commentary Notes." *Ryrie Study Bible
Expanded Edition: King James Version.* Chicago, Illinois, USA: Moody Press, 1994. Print.

Ryrie, Charles C. "Introduction: Contents to the Book of Leviticus." *Ryrie Study Bible Expanded
Edition: King James Version.* Chicago, Illinois, USA: Moody Press, 1994. Print.

Ryrie, Charles C. "Introduction: Theme to the Book of Numbers." *Ryrie Study Bible Expanded
Edition: King James Version.* Chicago, Illinois, USA: Moody Press, 1994. Print.

Ryrie, Charles C. "The Gospel According to Luke : Luke 16:23 Commentary Notes." *Ryrie Study
Bible Expanded Edition: King James Version.* Chicago, Illinois, USA: Moody Press, 1994. Print.

Schindler, Fred. "Get Committed! Go Soulwinning! - Dr. Fred Schindler." *The Sword of the Lord
Publishers.* Web. Fall 2009.
<http://www.swordofthelord.com/onlinesermons/CommittedSoulwinning.htm>.

Scofield, Cyrus I. "2 Corinthians 6:17." *SwordSearcher.* Computer software. Vers. 6.0.2.5. 1995-
2010 StudyLamp Software LLC. Web. 11 Oct. 2011.

Shaw, S.B. *The Great Revival in Wales: A Classic Revial Reprint Originally Published in 1905.* Pensacola, Florida, USA: Christian Life Books, 2002. Print.

"Soulwinning." *Old Path Mission.* Web. Fall 2009. <http://www.oldpathmission.org/soulwinning.htm?gclid=CICVj-LPpZ4CFQ4MDQodKVqbmw>.

Spence, H.D.M. and Excell, Joseph S. *Pulpit Commentary.* "Habakkuk 2:1." SwordSearcher. Computer software. Vers. 6.0.2.5. 1995-2010 StudyLamp Software LLC. Web. December 8, 2013.

Spence, H.D.M. and Excell, Joseph S. *Pulpit Commentary.* "Luke 17:5." SwordSearcher. Computer software. Vers. 6.0.2.5. 1995-2010 StudyLamp Software LLC. Web. 14 Dec. 2011.

Spence, H.D.M. and Excell, Joseph S. *Pulpit Commentary.* "Matthew 27:14." SwordSearcher. Computer software. Vers. 6.0.2.5. 1995-2010 StudyLamp Software LLC. Web. 28 June 2012.

The Spurgeon Archive. Web. Winter 2010. <http://www.spurgeon.org>.

Spurgeon, Charles H. *Spurgeon's Morning and Evening Devotions From the Bible.* Grand Rapids, Michigan, USA: Baker Book House, 1964. Print.

Spurgeon, Charles H. *The Soul-winner: How to Lead Sinners to the Saviour.* Grand Rapids, Michigan, USA: Eerdmans Publishing, 1974. Print.

Spurgeon, Charles H., and Tom Carter. *Spurgeon at His Best: Over 2200 Striking Quotations from the World's Most Exhaustive and Widely-read Sermon Series.* Grand Rapids, Michigan, USA: Baker Book House. 1988. Print.

Stewart, David J. "Church of Christ Heresies! : DANGER: Wolves in the Sheep Pen!" *Baptismal Regeneration?.* Web. December 18, 2012. <http://www.jesus-is-savior.com/False%20Religions/Church%20of%20Christ/church_of_christ_heresies.htm>.

Stewart, David J. "How to Win a Soul to Christ." *Soulwinning.* Web. Winter 2009. <http://www.soulwinning.info/articles/how_to.htm>.

Stewart, David J. *Soulwinning.* Web. Winter 2009. <http://www.soulwinning.info>.

Stewart, David J. "Starting a Homeless Ministry." *Soulwinning.* Web. Winter 2009. <http://www.soulwinning.info/hm/starting.htm>.

Strong, James, and James Strong. *The New Strong's Exhaustive Concordance of the Bible: with Main Concordance, Appendix to the Main Concordance, Key Verse Comparison Chart, Dictionary of the Hebrew Bible, Dictionary of the Greek Testament.* Nashville, Tennessee, USA.: Thomas Nelson, 1984. Print.

Thayer, Joseph Henry, Carl Ludwig Wilibald Grimm, and Christian Gottlob Wilke. *Thayer's Greek-English Lexicon of the New Testament: Coded with the Numbering System from Strong's Exhaustive Concordance of the Bible.* Peabody, Massachusetts, USA.: Hendrickson, 1981. Print.

"The Final Hour." : An Evangelical Who's Who Sign A Letter Declaring That Allah Is God. Shattered Paradigm, 8 Sept. 2009. Web. 30 Mar. 2012. http://thefinalhour.blogspot.com/2009/09/evangelical-whos-who-sign-letter.html>.

Thompson, Andrea. "How Many Species Exist on Earth? - LiveScience- Msnbc.com." *Breaking News, Weather, Business, Health, Entertainment, Sports, Politics, Travel, Science, Technology, Local, US & World News- Msnbc.com.* 2009 LiveScience.com Article on MSNBC Website, 11:54 a.m. PT, Fri., 3 Aug. 2007. Web. 26 May 2010. <http://www.msnbc.msn.com/id/20109284/>.

Bibliography

Torrey, Reuben A. *How to Witness to Anyone*. New Kensington, Pennsylvania, USA.: Whitaker House, 1986. Print.

Trotman, Dawson E. *Born to Reproduce*. Colorado Springs, Colorado, USA: Nav Press. Print.

Van Impe, Jack. *Jack Van Impe Presents*. www.jvim.com. 31 Mar. 2010. T.V. Program on Internet.

Webster's Encyclopedic Unabridged Dictionary of the English Language. New York, New York, USA: Gramercy Books 1996. Print.

Webster, Noah, and Rosalie J. Slater. *Noah Webster's First Edition of an American Dictionary of the English Language 1828*. San Francisco, California: Foundation for American Christian Education, 1995. Sixteenth Printing, 2004. C.J. Krehbiel Company, Cincinnati, Ohio, USA. Print.

Webster, Noah, and Rosalie J. Slater. *Noah Webster's First Edition of an American Dictionary of the English Language 1828*. San Francisco, California: Foundation for American Christian Education, 1995. Seventheeth Printing, 2005. Graphic Resource, Incorporated, St. Louis, Missouri, USA. Print.

Welch, Charles H. "RIGHT DIVISION." Http://www.charleswelch.net/books.htm. Web. 21 Feb. 2011. <http://www.bibleunderstanding.com/RIGHT%20DIVISION.PDF>.

Wesley, John. "1 Timothy 1:5." *SwordSearcher*. Computer software. Vers. 6.0.2.5. 1995-2010 StudyLamp Software LLC. Web. 6 Nov. 2011.

Wesley, John. "2 John 1:8." *SwordSearcher*. Computer software. Vers. 6.0.2.5. 1995-2010 StudyLamp Software LLC. Web. 6 Nov. 2011.

"What Is Baptism?" *Clarifying Christianity*. Clarifying Christianity (SM). Web. 17 May 2010. <http://www.clarifyingchristianity.com/get_wet.shtml>.

Wiese, Bill. *23 Minutes in Hell*. Lake Mary, Florida, USA.: Charisma House, 2006. Print.

Williams, Theodore. "Nuturing And Discipling New Converts." *Let the Earth Hear His Voice: the Complete Papers from the International Congress on World Evangelization, Lausanne, 1974*. By J. D. Douglas. London, England: World Wide Pubs, 1974. 574-79. Print.

Yohannan, K.P. *Revolution in World Missions*. Carrollton, Texas, USA: Gospel for Asia. 2004. Print.

Mr. Bowman would love to hear from you. If you have any questions, concerns, if you notice any mistakes inside this book, or if you desire to inquire about other resources by Lawrence Bowman, you are invited to contact him at:

www.GoSoulwinning.com
or
www.LawrenceBowman.com
Thank you.

You could be the answer to a child's prayer. When you sponsor a child you will be providing things like food, shelter, clothing, clean water, education, medicine, and a hope for a brighter future.

Let's Love
One More Child

**Please enjoy reading other books
written by Lawrence Bowman.**

Important Soulwinning Verses of the Holy Bible's Fundamental Doctrines

Practical and Effective Methods for Sharing the Gospel

A Practical Approach in Doing the Great Commission

A Simple Understanding of the Great Commission

Left Alive: inspired from a true story

**Lawrence's books may be purchased at Amazon.com,
Barnes and Noble, or any participating bookstores,
as well as at GoSoulwinning.com, or
Gosoulwinningpublishing.com.**